THE LAST ROLL CALL

The 29th Infantry Division
Victorious, 1945

Joseph Balkoski

STACKPOLE
BOOKS

Published by
STACKPOLE BOOKS
5067 Ritter Road
Mechanicsburg, PA 17055
www.stackpolebooks.com

Printed in the United States of America

10 9 8 7 6 5 4 3 2 1

FIRST EDITION

Library of Congress Cataloging-in-Publication Data

Balkoski, Joseph.
    The last roll call : the 29th Infantry Division victorious, 1945 / Joseph Balkoski. — First edition.
        pages cm
    Includes bibliographical references and index.
    ISBN 978-0-8117-1621-5
    1. United States. Army. Infantry Division, 29th.   2. World War, 1939–1945—Regimental histories—United States.   3. World War, 1939–1945—Campaigns—Germany.   I. Title.   II. Title: 29th Infantry Division victorious, 1945.
    D769.329th .B357
    940.54'1273—dc23
                                        2015010620

For the 29ers Who Fell in the Battle

Contents

List of Maps

Introduction: "29, Let's Go!"

Nearly one-third of a century has passed since I began documenting the World War II history of the 29th Infantry Division. In this, the fifth and final volume of the 29th Division's World War II history, the story picks up where Volume IV, *Our Tortured Souls*, ended, on New Year's Eve 1944, opposite Jülich, Germany, on the banks of the Roer River. Compared to what was transpiring forty miles to the south in the Ardennes during the massive German offensive that came to be known as the Battle of the Bulge—from which the Allied high command had mercifully spared the 29th Division—the Jülich front was tranquil: at worst, the 29ers endured sporadic German barrages; now and then they ran patrols across the icy Roer to snoop on the enemy.

But every 29er realized that sooner or later the Allies would take the offensive again: it was just a question of when and where. The 29th Division had been within rifle-shot range of Jülich since late November 1944, when that historic city with Roman origins was a major Allied steppingstone on the road to the Rhine River and ultimately Berlin. That autumn, the enemy had masterfully held back the American juggernaut on the Roer far short of the Rhine, and when the Germans' Ardennes offensive erupted on December 16, Eisenhower reluctantly abandoned any further ideas of reaching the Rhine by Christmas. But nothing had altered Ike's conviction that the Allies would eventually deliver the *coup de grâce* against the enemy on the northern part of the Western Front in that area of the Rhineland known as the Cologne Plain. When the enemy's Ardennes effort petered out and the weather cleared, the 29th Division stood poised to participate in what Eisenhower hoped would mark the denouement of the European war. This would mark the fourth time since D-Day, only eight months in the past, that the 29th would be at the forefront of a major Anglo-American offensive.

And there our story begins . . .

29TH INFANTRY DIVISION ORGANIZATION

In January 1945, the core of the 14,000-man 29th Infantry Division consisted of its three infantry regiments: 115th (1st Maryland), 116th (Stonewall Brigade), and 175th (5th Maryland). According to a venerable U.S. Army custom, the word "regiment" is considered superfluous when designating units of regimental size, and thus references in this book such as "115th Infantry" always imply regiments.

A regiment was configured into three 870-man battalions, designated 1st, 2nd, and 3rd, typically commanded by a major or lieutenant colonel. Battalions in turn were broken down into companies: A, B, C, and D in the 1st; E, F, G, and H in the 2nd; I, K, L, and M in the 3rd. (U.S. Army regiments never had a J Company.) Companies D, H, and M were "heavy weapons" companies, armed with six 81-millimeter mortars and eight machine guns. All other lettered companies were "rifle" companies. Each battalion also contained a headquarters company of 126 men.

Rifle companies were organized into three forty-one-man rifle platoons and a single thirty-five-man weapons platoon, equipped with three 60-millimeter mortars and two machine guns. In turn, each rifle platoon was broken down into three twelve-man rifle squads and a five-man platoon headquarters. Led by a staff sergeant, a rifle squad was equipped with eleven M-1 Garand rifles and a single Browning Automatic Rifle (BAR).

The 29th Division also included thousands of non-infantry soldiers, among them artillerymen, engineers, cavalrymen, military policemen, signalmen, and musicians, as well as medical, ordnance, and quartermaster personnel.

29TH INFANTRY DIVISION, FEBRUARY 23, 1945

DIVISION HEADQUARTERS

Commanding General	Maj. Gen. Charles Gerhardt, Jr.
Assistant Division Commander	Brig. Gen. Leroy Watson

DIVISION STAFF

Chief of Staff	Lt. Col. Louis Smith
G-1 (Personnel)	Lt. Col. Cooper Rhodes
G-2 (Intelligence)	Lt. Col. Paul Krznarich
G-3 (Operations)	Lt. Col. William Witte
G-4 (Supply)	Lt. Col. Louis Gosorn

DIVISION ARTILLERY

Commanding General	Brig. Gen. William Sands
Executive Officer	Col. H. Ridgely Warfield

110th Field Artillery Battalion	Lt. Col. John P. Cooper
111th Field Artillery Battalion	Lt. Col. David McIntosh
224th Field Artillery Battalion	Lt. Col. Clinton Thurston
227th Field Artillery Battalion	Lt. Col. Neal Harper

DIVISION TROOPS

121st Engineer Combat Battalion	Lt. Col. Raleigh Powell
104th Medical Battalion	Lt. Col. Arthur Eriksen

DIVISION SPECIAL TROOPS

29th Cavalry Reconnaissance Troop	Capt. Edward Jones
29th Military Police Platoon	Maj. Vern Johnson
29th Quartermaster Company	Capt. Frank Hines
729th Ordnance Company	Capt. Harold Price
29th Signal Company	Capt. Arba Williamson

115th INFANTRY

Commanding Officer	Lt. Col. William Blandford
Executive Officer	Lt. Col. Anthony Miller
1st Battalion	Lt. Col. Glover Johns
2nd Battalion	Maj. Albert Warfield
3rd Battalion	Lt. Col. Carleton Fisher

116th INFANTRY

Commanding Officer	Lt. Col. Sidney Bingham
Executive Officer	Lt. Col. Harold Cassell
1st Battalion	Lt. Col. Thomas Dallas
2nd Battalion	Lt. Col. Lawrence Meeks
3rd Battalion	Lt. Col. William Puntenney

175th INFANTRY

Commanding Officer	Col. Harry McHugh
Executive Officer	Lt. Col. Arthur Sheppe
1st Battalion	Maj. John Geiglein
2nd Battalion	Maj. Claude Melancon
3rd Battalion	Lt. Col. James Ballard

ONE

We've Come a Hell of a Way

BITTER DELAYING ACTION

The GIs had to admit that this down-on-his-luck Jerry had guts.

True, he was just one in a seemingly endless stream of shuffling ex-Supermen dragged before their American interrogators in late autumn 1944, sullenly handing over their *Soldbücher*—identification books—while mumbling disjointed responses to pressing questions posed by prying intelligence officers. Nazi Germany at this stage of the war was obviously careening like a runaway train toward a calamitous fate, and since the Normandy breakout zealous Allied generals had been searching futilely for clues that the German Army was finally ready to crack. Would that glorious event occur soon? The latest batch of German prisoners might provide hints that the long-awaited crackup was imminent; the sooner the Americans could interrogate them, the higher the chance German tongues would loosen due to the usual stupefaction brought on by recent combat.

This curious German prisoner brought before a U.S. Ninth Army intelligence team most assuredly spoke with a loose tongue, but he displayed neither disjointedness nor stupefaction. Rather than attempting to ingratiate himself with his interrogators, an approach to which terrified German prisoners commonly resorted, he gamely spoke his mind on the current military situation in Europe. "I am thoroughly convinced Germany is going to win the war," he declared unhesitatingly to his astonished captors. The Americans naturally wanted to know how: would success come from the rumored series of *wunderwaffen*—wonder weapons—under development? With a shrug, the German replied, "Perhaps that is going to come one day . . . [but] what I need as an infantryman, I have." The issue was, at least to him, as simple as that. As he was dismissed for transportation to a prisoner-of-war camp, he growled to his enemies, *"Nicht alle soldaten sind mutlos"*—Not all [German] soldiers are despondent.

Indeed, when on December 16, 1944, Hitler launched his bold offensive in the Ardennes—an assault carried out on such a grand scale that Eisenhower understated the case when he confessed the Allies were "surprised by the strength of his attack"—for a fleeting interval the number of despondent German *soldaten* diminished by a considerable factor. But less than two weeks later, during one of his notorious harangues at a December 28 General Staff conference at the *Adlerhorst* command complex in Hesse, even Hitler had to admit, "The offensive didn't succeed. . . . Unfortunately it didn't lead to the decisive success we might have expected." However, he emphasized: "I want to add right away, gentlemen, that when I say this, don't conclude that I've had even the slightest thought of losing this war. I never in my life learned the meaning of the term 'capitulation,' and I'm one of those men who has worked himself up from nothing."

And back to nothing the Allies were resolved he soon would return, despite his confidence that Nazi Germany would retain the initiative in the new year, 1945: "Offensive operations alone can turn the war in the West in a successful direction," he insisted. On December 31, he strove to prove that point by launching another major assault, *Unternehmen Nordwind*—Operation North Wind—against the U.S. Seventh Army's thinly held lines in Alsace. "I am already preparing a third strike," he boasted. In the air, on New Year's Day, the Luftwaffe undertook one of its largest raids of the war by hurling more than 1,000 aircraft against Allied airfields in Belgium and Holland, an aerial assault known in Germany as *Unternehmen Bodenplatte*—Operation Baseplate—but later christened the "Hangover Raid" by the Americans. None of those Nazi initiatives accomplished anything more than killing and wounding thousands on both sides, capturing limited amounts of inconsequential real estate, and postponing Nazi Germany's inevitable demise by a few weeks at most. Indeed, the aged Field Marshal Gerd von Rundstedt, commander-in-chief of German forces in the West, described the failed Ardennes Offensive as "Stalingrad Number Two"; the legendary Luftwaffe flier, Gen. Adolf Galland, noted that Baseplate was the German Air Force's "death blow."

Still, as the anonymous infantryman brought before Ninth Army interrogators had insisted, not all German soldiers were despondent. On one point Hitler was wholly correct: "There is no doubt that the brief offensives we've already made have led to an immediate easing up of the situation along the whole front," he pronounced. "The enemy has had to give up all his offensive plans. He's been forced to reorganize completely. He has had to redeploy units that were worn out. His operational intentions have been totally thrown out. . . . The psychological moment is against him."

Even Ike would have concurred; the Ardennes struggle had changed everything. On New Year's Day, the Western Front stretched for 530 miles from the North Sea to the Swiss border. Viewed on a map, the front line was anything but tidy, zigging and zagging across Holland, Belgium, Luxembourg, France, and Germany, looking more like a stock exchange graph than an orderly line drawn by a staff officer's grease pencil on a map overlay. Of those many zigs and zags, the most prominent by far were in the Western Front's central zone, the notorious Ardennes, the sector now portrayed daily on stateside newspapers' front-page maps, simply labeled the "Bulge."

As the Bulge contracted perceptibly in the first week of 1945, even a military neophyte could discern that the Germans' best chance for turning the war around had evaporated. Would the Allies now resume their efforts to bring down Nazi Germany from the moment the enemy's Ardennes offensive had interrupted them? Or would Eisenhower's armies—as Hitler had claimed—"reorganize completely" and rethink their "operational intentions"?

Whatever Ike decided, he must set out to do it in the face of oppressive time pressure. The Allies were already far behind schedule: Eisenhower's boss, Gen. George C. Marshall, had directed him in an October 23 cable to "conduct operations with the objective of completing the defeat of Germany by January 1." The Allies' late 1944 offensives on Germany's western frontier had utterly failed to bring about Marshall's goal, encountering not only indomitable enemy resistance but also gloomy weather that had caused thousands of debilitating cases of trench foot, to the shock of Allied generals and medical men alike. Little more German territory was under Allied occupation in early January 1945 than ten weeks before. Further, to no one's surprise, January weather shaped up as far more severe than in late autumn. As for the enemy's defiance, the ongoing Ardennes offensive established beyond doubt that Germany was far from defeated. Joseph Goebbels, Hitler's propaganda minister, had spoken for most Germans when he declared in the autumn: "Germany will go on fighting because there is nothing else to do."

The outlook on the Western Front for the Allies had become so dire that Lt. Gen. Omar Bradley, commander of the U.S. Twelfth Army Group, had blurted to a fellow general just days before the enemy came surging out of the Ardennes forest, "It is entirely possible for the Germans to fight bitter delaying actions until January 1, 1946." Such a pessimistic prognostication on New Year's Day 1945 seemed almost inconceivable: fighting "bitter" battles for another year would not only sap the spirit from front-line GIs, but also strain the resolution of housewives, war workers, politicians, and desk generals on the home front. As Marshall would later remark: "You cannot have such a protracted struggle in a democracy in the face of mounting casualties. . . . Speed was essential."

In the early days of the new year, a distressed Marshall looked in vain for exhibitions of decisive military operations on the part of Ike's generals. Marshall also had to manage an even more distant war, the one in the Pacific; unless the Allies could soon fulfill the "Germany First" strategy that four years ago President Roosevelt and Prime Minister Churchill had resolved would be the rock-solid foundation of Allied military operations in World War II, the Pacific war could develop into an island-by-island bloodbath with accompanying casualty lists longer than anyone in the Pentagon dared to imagine. Could the American people take it? Even the irrepressibly upbeat Roosevelt allowed a rare admission of negativity to creep into his January 6 State of the Union report when he notified Americans: "The year ended with a setback for our arms."

Perhaps that setback was merely the proverbial darkest hour before the dawn. Final victory over Hitler was close, so tantalizingly close, a theme touched on by Roosevelt in his report: "In Europe, we shall resume the attack and—despite temporary setbacks here or there—we shall continue the attack relentlessly until Germany is completely defeated. . . . Further desperate attempts may well be made to break our lines, to slow our progress. We must never make the mistake of assuming that the Germans are beaten until the last Nazi has surrendered." Concluded the president: "The new year of 1945 can be the greatest year of achievement in human history. . . . We Americans of today, together with our allies, are making history—and I hope it will be better history than ever has been made before."

The members of the 29th Infantry Division had ringside seats on New Year's Day for a spectacular aerial show the likes of which they had never seen before. Since landing on the sands of Omaha Beach in the opening minutes of the D-Day invasion, the most they had glimpsed of the German Air Force at any given time was a smattering of warplanes, usually just one or two, generally headed home. Allied dominance of the air was so complete that the 29ers had gotten thoroughly used to making the assumption that any group of planes flying over the front lines had to be their own. But on January 1, 1945, the 29th Division held the line directly underneath the flight path of the "Hangover Raid," the Luftwaffe's last-ditch effort to challenge Allied control of the skies in western Europe. More than 1,000 German aircraft—mostly fighters piloted by officers fresh from New Year's Eve fêtes and still attired in unspoiled formal dress uniforms with white gloves and gleaming shoes—took to the air at dawn and headed for sixteen Allied airfields close behind the front, endeavoring to splatter their bombs across runways and, with luck, catch as many parked Thunderbolts, Typhoons, Spitfires, and Mustangs as possible. If the raid worked as well as it looked on paper, Allied tactical air power on the Western Front could be crippled for weeks.

But it did not work. The Luftwaffe top brass timed the raid to exploit their opponents' presumed lack of vigilance following a night of New Year's Eve revelry. The alert 29ers, however, were hardly fooled; nor were any Allied troops occupying front-line positions athwart the enemy's flight lines, for what passed for revels in spartan, bombed-out command posts anywhere near the front could only barely be categorized as distractions. One 29er who spent the night several miles behind the front noted in a V-mail letter to his wife, "I celebrated New Year's Eve last night by drinking the last of the second Coke you sent me."

Luckily, for the past two months the 29th Division had the services of an attached outfit, the 554th Antiaircraft Artillery Battalion, led by Lt. Col. Lawrence Linderer, which had trained for years to shoot down German planes with 40-millimeter guns, built by Chrysler, and half-track–mounted quadruple .50-caliber machine guns. Never before, however, had Linderer's men fired their weapons with the abandon they displayed on New Year's Day. The 554th perceived that the wily enemy was up to no good just a few minutes after midnight, when a couple of German twin-engine night fighters flew low over American

Quadruple .50-caliber machine guns mounted on a half-track in a U.S. Army antiaircraft unit.

lines, dropping flares and a few bombs behind the front—for what object the GIs had yet to discern. Eventually the men correctly surmised that these were pathfinders, heralds of a rapidly approaching storm. The tempest arrived at 9:00 A.M.; Linderer reported that "all planes entered the area from the east at tree-top level, thereby rendering ineffective the local radar air-warning units. No early warning was possible until the flights had actually entered territory visible from local observation posts and gun pits."

To the 29ers, it seemed as if the irresolute German pilots "just flew around aimlessly . . . seemingly without any grouping or coordination." Many of them simply roared over 29th Division lines and disappeared, but occasionally Messerschmitts and Focke-Wulfs streaked in at remarkably low altitudes to strafe or bomb supposed targets in and around the checkerboard Rhineland villages behind the 29th's lines. Flying that low over highly trained American anti-aircraft gunners, however, guaranteed that the Germans would get hurt. The amazed GIs had never seen such enticing targets, and every weapon—quad .50s, 40-millimeter Bofors, and even M-1 rifles and BARs—blazed away amid a cacophony that could be heard for miles. It was the type of noise—like a rapid-fire jackhammer—that antiaircraft men loved to hear, and when the last of the enemy planes vanished an hour later, six of them remained behind as flaming wrecks on the flat Rhineland farmland. The 116th Infantry's operations officer, Maj. Fred McManaway, reported to the 29th Division war room that one of them was "a Focke-Wulf 190 down at 975585 [a map coordinate, near Dürboslar]. I am sending graves registration people up there with a basket—the pilot is sort of smashed up."

One 29er wrote to his wife: "This morning I saw three Jerry planes shot down by our ack-ack boys all within ten minutes—it was quite thrilling—and it was funny how the tracers of .50 calibers kept going up even after the Kraut pilots were drifting down in their chutes. I guess our gunners have been reading reports of the atrocities the Germans committed down south of us [in the Ardennes]. Those dirty bastards!"

Most of those pilots who managed to pass cleanly over American lines found their targets and inflicted serious damage on Allied airfields, destroying nearly 200 parked planes—one of them Field Marshal Sir Bernard Montgomery's personal C-47. But the enemy paid a high price, losing over 200 hard-to-replace pilots killed or captured. "Again, the Luftwaffe had demonstrated its versatility and aggressiveness," the U.S. Army Air Force's official history noted. "[But] the evidence indicated in fact that January 1, 1945, was one of the worst single days for human and aircraft losses that the Luftwaffe ever experienced, and the military effect on the Allies, save for some embarrassment, was truly negligible."

LEARNING DEFENSIVE STUFF

The American top brass had mercifully spared the 29th Division from deployment to the Ardennes during the enemy's ravaging offensive, and now the 29ers held a lengthy and comparatively tranquil nine-mile front along the Roer River opposite Jülich, Germany, forty miles north of the Bulge's northern shoulder. Just a week before the Ardennes fighting erupted, however, the Roer front was anything but tranquil. On December 9, Ninth Army had shut down a 29th Division offensive that had endured for twenty-four grueling days at a cost of 2,600 combat and another 1,100 non-combat casualties—over one-quarter of the division's personnel as of its November 16 start date. Those staggering losses had bought a paltry terrain gain of little more than six miles, a distance a fit soldier could jog in an hour. During that offensive the 29th Division had lost a man every nine minutes—gaining on average three yards for each man lost.

With the bulk of the U.S. Army's infantry replacements heading into the Ardennes to rejuvenate the battered units fighting there, as of New Year's Day the 29th Division still had a long way to go to regain its lost combat power. Of even greater concern, however, was the spiritual impact of 19,117 battle casualties in the seven-month interval since the 29th had landed in the first wave at Omaha Beach, a stunning figure for an outfit that at full strength amounted to 14,000 men. Virtually no American military unit of comparable size had ever lost men at that lethal rate in such a brief period, an unfortunate distinction the 29ers tried their best to forget. Nevertheless, a piece of pervasive scuttlebutt spread by cynics had taken hold: the 29th Division was in truth not a division, they said, but a three-division corps—with a division in the field, a division in the hospital, and a division in the cemetery.

No one could deny that on January 1 the 29th Division was a badly beat-up outfit. But if that classification had spared it deployment to the Ardennes, then all 29ers agreed there was a silver lining to that dark cloud. Actually, the 29th had been much more severely beaten up in the past—it had lost 9,100 men in forty-six days in Normandy plus another 3,000 in twenty-six days in Brittany—but amazingly had always come back a week or so later ready to absorb more punishment and accomplish the sometimes illogical goals of its leaders. That flexibility, according to the generals, was the beauty of the American military system: a timely infusion of well-trained replacements could rejuvenate a battered division in just a few days. How many times, however, could the 29th Division be rejuvenated and still fight on? Army doctrine claimed the number was limitless. Veteran infantrymen knew it was not: it took much more than fresh bodies to make a first-class fighting unit. So far the number of times the 29th had bounced back and continued to fight with impressive tenacity had given U.S. Army generals the accurate impression that it was indeed a first-class outfit.

The downside of that lofty reputation was that whenever the division completed its rejuvenation, it was certain to be in the thick of the fight again, in all likelihood in the decisive sector of the front where Ike and Bradley always wanted their best units. As the Allies were not even across the Rhine yet, and Berlin was a long way beyond that, the 29ers dreaded when their inevitable reentry into combat would come.

One 29er, division commander Maj. Gen. Charles Hunter Gerhardt, Jr., assuredly did not dread that moment, as he was convinced that the fastest way the GIs could get home was to pummel the enemy into extinction—and if pummeling was required, the 29th Division would be one of the best units to do it. Many 29ers were convinced that "Uncle Charlie" Gerhardt had infused the 29th with the high spirit it needed to bear the many traumas of modern warfare; probably a far greater number believed that spirit merely covered up a casualty list of inconceivable length, and even worse obscured the appalling detail that many of those casualties were suffered in battles that should not have taken place at all. Indeed, as a consequence of those high losses and some unrelated shenanigans beyond the battlefield, Gerhardt's former boss in XIX Corps, Maj. Gen. Raymond McLain, had only recently endeavored to fire him unceremoniously. However, Gerhardt's career—at least temporarily—had been saved by West Point classmates, the most important of whom was Dwight D. Eisenhower. Memories of school-time camaraderie and glorious days on the football gridiron and baseball diamond, some cynics thought, could bail out a troubled West Pointer long after he removed his cadet-gray uniform.

The general gave the 29th Division a New Year's Eve pep talk. "We've come a hell of a way," Gerhardt affirmed. "This division is in no mood to release any ground it has gained. The situation here is well in hand. . . . The division is building up its strength; this is a fortunate situation for us. We're learning some defensive stuff. The team is working together extremely well. In talking to individuals scattered all through the outfit—we're doing all right. . . . If we can get the people who are actually up front comfortable so they can get along, nobody has any squawks."

Gerhardt himself was used to squawking, especially when he spied a 29er improperly dressed or failing to follow military protocol to the letter. But those close to the general perceived, much to their pleasure, that he was softening. A few weeks back he had rescinded his notorious order, in effect since D-Day, that prohibited all 29th Division units from setting up a command post or living quarters indoors. Sometime later, members of the general's entourage witnessed an amazing event. On an inspection circuit near the Roer, Gerhardt spotted a jeep driven by a 29er who was wearing a wool cap rather than a helmet. Normally there would have been hell to pay, but when the general began his customary tirade, the soldier interrupted and declared, "General, what do you care what kind of hat I wear, when next week we are going to cross the river and take that town [Jülich] for you?" A flabbergasted Gerhardt later noted, "There being no answer to this one, I wished him well and told him to go ahead."

Gerhardt would need time to absorb and acclimate a vast number of replacements and, even more important, to obtain the go-ahead from his superiors to concentrate the 29th Division on a much narrower front than nine miles before he could seriously contemplate an assault across the Roer to capture Jülich and subsequently head for the Rhine. In the meantime, he would cover his sector according to his favorite "two up, one back" principle, deploying two of his three infantry regiments, 116th on the left and 175th on the right, to guard the division's front along the Roer, while consigning the 115th to divisional reserve.

One of the first activities undertaken by the 29th Division in the new year was marred by tragedy, one of those regrettable accidents for which no one was to blame but occurred regularly on the deadly fringes of no-man's-land in World War II. The 175th Infantry's Company G, commanded by 1st Lt. Hugh Brady, had been manning outposts along a one-mile stretch of the Roer southwest of Jülich for a week. By now Brady knew the sector intimately, and when he received orders to run a patrol across the river after dark on New Year's Day, he entrusted it to 2nd Lt. St. Clair Walker and a few enlisted men, directing them to move north along the only road in his sector to a point on the Roer opposite Jülich.

A twenty-two-year-old native of Louisville, Kentucky, Walker had joined Company G as a replacement officer on December 6 and had yet to see combat. Brady was concerned that the patrol's route would bring it close to the line dividing his own sector and that of the adjacent unit guarding the Roer opposite Jülich, the 116th Infantry's Company E; in the dark Walker and his men could easily be mistaken for prowling Germans. Brady therefore traveled from his command post at a German estate known as Linzenich *Gut* to warn his counterpart at Company E, Capt. Donald Meabon, that a friendly patrol would be operating in the area along the riverbank. According to a 175th Infantry report called in to the 29th Division war room shortly after midnight on January 2: "While [Brady] was there, the [Company E] outpost nearest the river apparently phoned in and told them they saw someone coming on the road. [The outpost] was told by someone in the 116th that it was the Company G patrol coming. [Meabon] sent S/Sgt. George Shaffer down to the outpost to keep them from firing on the patrol. On the way over Shaffer shot and killed Lieutenant Walker. Shaffer claims he challenged Walker and that he didn't answer. Our people said Walker shouted the password twice before he was shot."

According to the 116th Infantry, however, "The officer in charge of Company G's patrol was challenged by [our] sentry four times. The officer then got down on his knees and started to crawl. The sentry thought it was a Jerry and shot him through the heart." Whatever actually happened, yet another good 29er was gone, buried like so many before him in the U.S. military cemetery at Margraten, Holland. Walker left behind a young wife, Ellen, who nineteen days later would receive a letter at her home in the Louisville suburb of Anchorage from a 175th Infantry chaplain, Capt. John McKenna. Her husband, McKenna wrote, "was killed in action January 1, 1945, in Germany and was buried with a protestant burial service in Holland. The places of burial are being made into permanent memorial cemeteries by our government and are made as beautiful as possible. The heroism displayed by the American soldier in these days continues to amaze the world and surely holds the great promise of a great future for our country. Your husband's sacrifice is helping to build a better world for us all. I share your pride in him."

Mercifully, McKenna said not a word about the circumstances of Walker's death. Walker was so new to the 175th Infantry that the Company G clerk, catching up on his paperwork, noted Walker's arrival ("assigned and joined . . .") and his death ("from duty to killed in action . . .") on the same morning report, separated by just a single line.

Since the 29th Division would remain stationary for an indefinite period, Gerhardt's men needed to prepare defensive positions so strong that if the Germans surged across the Roer on either side of Jülich to repeat the stunning surprise attack they had just carried out in the Ardennes, they would be stopped cold. The 29th Division's top-notch intelligence team under Lt. Col. Paul Krznarich—known universally as "Murphy" because no one could pronounce his name—announced that such a possibility was remote, but no GI could forget that only three weeks ago the highest reaches of U.S. Army intelligence had also drawn that same conclusion.

Finance, civil affairs, adjutant general, judge advocate, ordnance, quartermaster, provost marshal, and other support troops typically bound to desks formed emergency rifle platoons and fought mock battles against phantom German paratroopers. Military policemen established roadblocks and asked probing questions of unfamiliar GIs on the identities of Joe DiMaggio and Veronica Lake. Camouflage netting was refined so that snooping enemy aircraft could not detect gun positions and command posts. Above all, despite the chilly weather, the 29ers broke a sweat with prolonged use of their GI shovels by digging entrenchments—and then digging some more. There was even a rumor—true, as it turned out—that Monty had ordered the British Army's 43rd Infantry Division to dig in six miles behind the 29th just in case the Germans broke through the American lines again.

Monty needn't have worried: the Germans weren't going anywhere, Gerhardt's staff insisted, and—if they did—no help was needed. The busiest men in the 29th Division throughout January were the members of the 121st Engineer Combat Battalion, the 29th's elite sapper outfit and former component of the District of Columbia National Guard, the proud holder of a Distinguished Unit Citation streamer on its colors for heroism on Omaha Beach. "The entire period was devoted to the construction of barrier belts and defensive positions along the main line of resistance and around towns which were integral parts of the division defense plan," the 121st's January action report noted. "The primary tasks consisted of erecting wire entanglements, laying minefields (both anti-tank and anti-personnel), and digging various gun emplacements. . . . A total of 18,254 mines was laid." The 121st's commander, twenty-eight-year-old Lt. Col. Robert Ploger, pointed out to an observer how this work was done: "Each mine installation is carefully plotted on paper so that it can be easily found again. Minefields have to be set down in patterns. The mines are laid out, then the engineers go back and bury them, which in the frozen ground is quite a problem. A certain number of the mines are booby-trapped so they cannot be picked up easily."

On the seemingly endless list of challenges the U.S. Army faced in January 1945, no soldier would have placed snow removal high on the list. But that month snow fell in heavy quantities, including one day, January 8, when a nearby Canadian unit noted in its journal that the "snowfall at times attained the proportions of a good old Canadian blizzard"; and another, January 19, during which an entry in the 29th Division's war room transcript stated, "High winds and a blizzard blowing right now." Like all Allied divisions, the 29th was dependent on trucks and jeeps to move materiel from rear-area depots up to the front. If snow blocked the roads, front-line troops could quickly run short of food and, if the enemy attacked, ammunition. A jack-of-all-trades fixture in the 121st's Headquarters Company, thirty-one-year-old M/Sgt. John Hickman, a former Baltimore and Ohio Railroad brakeman with a Grant Wood–style *American Gothic* face and Virginia farmboy twang, almost single-handedly "designed, constructed, and installed" jeep- and truck-mounted plows that kept the roads clear even in heavy snows.

The 29th Division's defensive posture was hardly passive, a detail the reviled enemy learned each time they dared to show themselves at the front. Recent events had undeniably fueled the 29ers' desire to inflict punishment on the enemy. As one soldier wrote home to his wife: "In the *Yank* [magazine] we got tonight, there was a complete story of the survivors of the massacre at Malmedy, when the Germans shot 150 of the First Army men taken prisoner. [The actual number was 84, but many other American troops and Belgian civilians were murdered nearby.] The details are terrible."

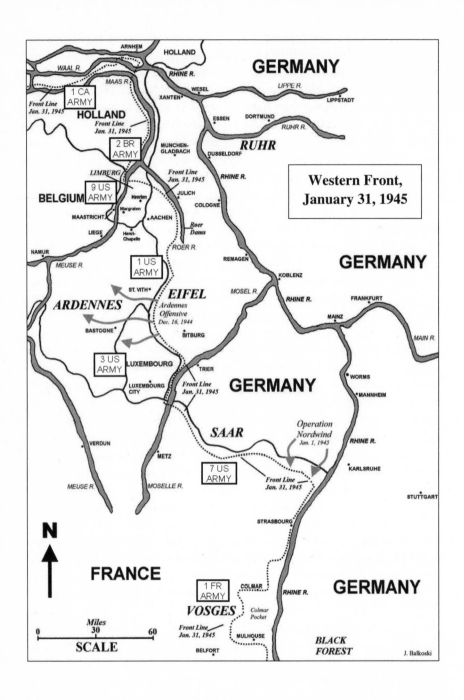

Western Front, January 31, 1945

ARNHEM

HOLLAND

GERMANY

WAAL R.

RHINE R.

MAAS R.

LIPPE R.

1 CA ARMY

Front Line Jan. 31, 1945

HOLLAND

WESEL

XANTEN

LIPPSTADT

Front Line Jan. 31, 1945

ESSEN

DORTMUND

RUHR

2 BR ARMY

MUNCHEN-GLADBACH

DUSSELDORF

RUHR R.

LIMBURG

Front Line Jan. 31, 1945

BELGIUM

9 US ARMY

Heerlen

JULICH

RHINE R.

COLOGNE

MAASTRICHT

Margraten

AACHEN

Roer Dams

LIEGE

Henri-Chapelle

ROER R.

REMAGEN

NAMUR

MEUSE R.

GERMANY

1 US ARMY

ST. VITH

EIFEL

KOBLENZ

ARDENNES

Ardennes Offensive Dec. 16, 1944

MOSEL R.

RHINE R.

FRANKFURT

BASTOGNE

BITBURG

MAINZ

3 US ARMY

LUXEMBOURG

TRIER

MAIN R.

LUXEMBOURG CITY

Front Line Jan. 31, 1945

GERMANY

WORMS

SAAR

MANNHEIM

VERDUN

Operation Nordwind Jan. 1, 1945

METZ

7 US ARMY

RHINE R.

Front Line Jan. 31, 1945

KARLSRUHE

MEUSE R.

MOSELLE R.

STUTTGART

STRASBOURG

N

FRANCE

1 FR ARMY

COLMAR

RHINE R.

GERMANY

VOSGES

Colmar Pocket

Front Line Jan. 31, 1945

MULHOUSE

BLACK FOREST

Miles 30

0   60

SCALE

BELFORT

J. Balkoski

Aside from the normal methods the GIs ordinarily used to mercilessly harass the Germans—sniping, raids, and mortar and artillery barrages—a few novel methods were employed. As related by a story in the division's popular daily newsletter, *29 Let's Go*, Company A of the 175th came up with "a new twist on the David and Goliath yarn by stretching an old inner tube between the trees and loading their improvised slingshot with fragmentation grenades instead of stones." Directed by 1st Lt. Frank Bishop, the men successfully flung several across the river, actions that no doubt startled the Germans as not a sound was audible until the grenades exploded. Nevertheless, the chance of catching a German so close to the Roer outside of entrenchments was virtually nil. Still, it was undeniably ingenious, but the ordnance people would not be mass producing it anytime soon.

Another 175th invention was labeled the "Goslin Grenade" after the 3rd Battalion's S-2, 1st Lt. Arthur Goslin. "The New Hampshire 'looey' [lieutenant] emptied a grenade of its explosive and detonating charges, soldered on improvised grappling hooks, attached 300 yards of heavy telephone cable and proceeded to fire the same [by means of a special propelling cartridge and an M-1 rifle muzzle adapter] at night across the river," wrote Cpl. Jean Lowenthal, editor of *29 Let's Go*. Goslin deduced that the German side of the Roer was so thickly covered with barbed wire that when the 29ers pulled their end of the telephone cable sharply backward, the grenade's grappling hooks were sure to catch on the wire. Plenty of noise would be generated, and in the dark the enemy would assume an American patrol was coming through. A lot of effort—and luck— would be required to fool the enemy, and even then the deception would be momentary. But the 29ers had a lot of time on their hands, and as *29 Let's Go* reported, "Lt. Goslin's chief aim with his new 'weapon' was to get the Jerries to reveal their positions, and they did most obligingly, firing everything from tracers to rockets along their outposts. All of which observers on our side plotted accurately on maps."

An American invention that surpassed all others by a wide margin, however, was a gadget so confidential that U.S. Army chief of staff Gen. George Marshall had withheld it from use in Europe for months for fear that the enemy might figure out the secret before large-scale production took place. The device was so cunning that if it worked the way stateside whiz kids promised, American artillery, both field and antiaircraft varieties, would be able to hit almost any enemy target within range with stunning accuracy. The Germans defending the Roer remained blissfully unaware of it, but they were about to learn its capabilities. As soon as the contraption came into use in Europe on New Year's Day 1945, the GIs promptly changed its inscrutable code name—"Pozit"—to the much more sensible phrase "proximity fuze."

James Phinney Baxter, an American academic whose 1946 book *Scientists Against Time* earned the Pulitzer Prize for history, noted in that work that, aside from the Manhattan Project, the proximity fuze was "the most remarkable scientific achievement of the war." Unlike ordinary field artillery and antiaircraft shells, which detonated either by impacting a solid object or upon the expiration of a preset flight time, proximity shells used miniaturized radio transmitters and receivers, supposedly at a cost of only $20 per fuze, to trigger detonations of shells at consistently lethal distances from targets. Bringing down a Luftwaffe warplane with an antiaircraft gun or spraying deadly shell fragments over a stubborn German machine-gun nest with a howitzer would therefore become infinitely easier.

If proximity fuzes worked as intended, they would make an already mighty Allied artillery arm even mightier. In autumn 1944, impressed U.S. Army cannoneers had been sworn to secrecy when they witnessed Pozit demonstrations for the first time, and they waited eagerly for the chance to employ the new fuze. In the 29th Division, that moment came on January 1, 1945. The *History of the 110th Field Artillery* noted, "When the 110th first fired shells with the new fuze, Lt. Col. [John Purley] Cooper [CO, 110th] demonstrated it from an attic observation post in Koslar to the 115th Infantry's entire regimental staff, including the surgeon and the chaplain." Some kinks needed to be worked out, however, as the history observed: "The cannoneers found that about 20 percent of the bursts were 'prematures,' that is, they exploded high overhead somewhere along the trajectory and long before nearing the target. Such bursts, while terrifically loud, were practically harmless since by the time the fragments neared the ground, they had lost velocity and were falling only with the speed of gravity. Wearing a helmet provided ample protection against the slivers." Since the Pozit's nearly instantaneous bounce-back of the radio transmission to the receiver when a shell neared a solid object set off its detonation, the 29ers learned that tall edifices and trees as well as passing friendly aircraft, heavy rain clouds, and even large birds could set off a premature. Still, assuming sufficient numbers of proximity fuzes would be available once the 29th Division launched its inevitable Roer crossing, enemy resistance could be significantly diminished. Ultimately, American firms produced millions of proximity fuzes, a more than adequate supply for those units in need. As expressed in the Ordnance Department's official World War II history, "The triumph of American research lay in successfully designing a fuze that could be manufactured by assembly-line methods."

The German defenders of the Roer were provided with such a paltry ammunition supply that they could not respond to American provocations in any meaningful way. "The scarcity of artillery ammunition had increased in such a way since the beginning of December that it was unbearable from the point of view of a soldier," wrote *Generalleutnant* (Major General) August Dettling, commander of the 363rd *Volksgrenadier* Division on the Jülich front. "There could be no question of our returning artillery fire! Nor was it often possible for us to deal with other targets in the enemy sector, such as motor vehicle columns, troop movements, concentrations, etc."

One cold winter day, an enemy soldier, no doubt frustrated at his inability to retaliate for the Americans' incessant harassing fire, unwisely attempted to mock the 29th Division's vaunted artillerists. For days, American cannoneers had been vainly striving to score a direct hit on what they assumed was a small, well-camouflaged enemy pillbox near the prominent Broicherhaus manor north of Jülich. The 29th Division's 1948 official history, *29 Let's Go*, related: "As artillery shells fell short or wide of the pillbox, a German soldier would come out and wave a large red flag, as a 'Maggie's Drawers.' [This was Army slang for the distinctive banner waved downrange during target practice to signify a shooter had completely missed the target; the phrase supposedly was drawn from the bawdy song "Those Old Red Flannel Drawers That Maggie Wore."] This clowning on the part of the enemy was not well received on the west bank, where it was considered downright impudent and not at all in accordance with the generally accepted customs of war. . . . A self-propelled 155-millimeter gun [from the 557th Field Artillery Battalion, a XIII Corps unit on loan to the 29th Division], brought up for direct fire, pumped shells into the position [fifty-seven in number, according to one report] and destroyed it."

If the 29ers had to fight a war, they could hardly complain in January 1945 about how the generals had asked them to do it. Certainly the previous seven months, dating back to D-Day, had been infinitely tougher, and the countless number of good doughboys now lying deep in the soil of France, Belgium, and Holland proved it. In January only nine 29ers were killed in action, an agonizing loss to be sure—but compared to Omaha Beach, when GIs had been felled for hours by the enemy's merciless fire like stalks of grain swept up by a John Deere reaper, nine deaths seemed almost trifling to the calloused top brass. St. Lô, Vire, Brest, Würselen, and Bourheim had simply been more of the same under different conditions. In early 1945, however, neither the enemy troops on the far side of the Roer nor German civilians behind the front displayed any of the aggressiveness 29ers had come to expect from Nazis. True, Rhineland weather in midwinter was rough—one day, January 26, reportedly had sub-zero temperatures on the Fahrenheit scale—but thankfully the enemy's passivity allowed 29th Division rifle companies to regularly rotate men from exposed and uncomfortable front-line foxholes along the Roer to the much more habitable confines of an indoor command post in a riverside village. Those smashed-up edifices could hardly match a warm barracks at Fort Meade, but at least the riflemen could thaw their chilled bodies, dry their socks, and sleep in far more comfort than in a cramped slit trench. Even better, to the delight of battalion surgeons, debilitating cases of trench foot and frostbite sharply declined from the alarming numbers of autumn.

Even the bitter cold could not stop the 29ers from concluding that they were more comfortable now than they had been in a long time, a sentiment that had more to do with the total absence of full-scale combat than it did with the weather. The Germans, however, made their usual feeble attempts by means of radio broadcasts and propaganda shells—directed at "the poor devils of the 29th Division"—to convince their opponents that once combat began again in earnest, as it inevitably would, the Americans' fleeting comfort would vanish and many good men would die. "Who is going to launch out into the new battle? Statesmen, politicians, big bankers, munitions manufacturers? No, not one!" a typical Nazi propaganda leaflet blared. "Just you: the men of the 8th, 29th, 102nd, and 104th Divisions, average young Americans with your lives ahead."

So frequently were the leaflets dropped on American lines that they were classified as "The Daily Mail." As the 175th Infantry's 1st Lt. Joe Ewing remarked, "The effect of all this propaganda on American troops was negligible. . . . They listened and laughed." Ewing confessed, however, "Propaganda shells landing in an area were always an occasion of great excitement, and the idea was to 'get hold of some of those Jerry papers.'" The papers were not only preposterous, but also often featured first-class sketches of unclothed women in the arms of male civilians on the homefront—"The Girl You Left Behind . . . Pretty Joan Hopkins, for more than half a year she had not heard from Bob. Poor little Joan! She is still thinking of Bob, yet she is almost hoping that he'll never return."

Ewing fondly remembered listening to a German woman over the radio, a "girl propagandist who used the sweet dreamy approach and sentimental tunes. She had nothing to say about the war, except that it was so terrible. She didn't say that the Americans ought to give up. . . . She didn't even say that Germany was going to win the war. She just kept playing records and announcing their titles with her honest, wholesome, friendly voice." She was hard to resist, and the 29ers admitted her play on homesickness was effective: "And I just know that you'll remember this. This is the song that you and your girl used to hum when you went walking together down along the river road on lovely nights in spring a couple of years ago. Can't you just smell that warm fresh air?" A happy return to the States, however, would have to wait, for how long no one knew. "In the meantime," as the U.S. Army's *Pocket Guide to Germany* recommended, "your very presence on German soil will serve as a constant demonstration to the German people that the master race theory that sent them forth to bathe the world in blood was just so much tragic nonsense."

THE WAY OF ALL FLESH

When pretty Joan Hopkins was still standing behind the ribbon counter of a 5 & 10 cts. store on 3rd Avenue in New York City, she never dreamed of ever seeing the interior of a duplex Park Avenue apartment. Neither did young Bob Harrison, the man she loves. Bob was drafted and sent to the battlefields in Europe thousands of miles away from her. Through Lazare's Employment Agency Joan got a job as private secretary with wily Sam Levy. Sam is piling up big money on war contracts. Should the slaughter end very soon, he would suffer an apoplectic stroke.

Now Joan knows what Bob and his pals are fighting for.

Joan always used to look up to Bob as the guiding star of her life, and she was still a good girl when she started working for Sam Levy. But she often got the blues thinking of Bob, whom she hadn't seen for over two years. Her boss had an understanding heart and was always very kind to her, so kind indeed, that he often invited her up to his place. He had always wanted to show her his "etchings". Besides, Sam wasn't stingy and each time Joan came to see him, he gave her the nicest presents. Now, all women like beautiful and expensive things. But Sam wasn't the man you could play for a sucker. He wanted something. wanted it very definitely.....

Poor little Joan! She is still thinking of Bob, yet she is almost hoping that he'll never return.

Look for the other pictures of this series

A typical German propaganda leaflet.

Now that the 29th Division was in Germany, Gerhardt's superiors expected him to strictly enforce the U.S. Army's controversial "non-fraternization" order, which specified in "absolute" terms that "unless otherwise permitted by higher authority, [U.S. troops] will not visit in German homes or associate with Germans on terms of friendly intimacy, either in public or private." At this stage of the war, however, survival rather than fraternization dominated the 29ers' psyches. On the devastated Rhineland landscape the division had smashed through in November and December, places of human habitation were reduced to dismal heaps of rubble and pervasive dust, populated by pathetic and shoddy inhabitants who not only demonstrated no inclination to fraternize, but whose sullen demeanor hardly encouraged GIs to seek out personal contact.

The recent news of the Malmedy massacre, guaranteed to instigate feelings of hatred in the 29ers' hearts for everything German, would take a long time to dissipate, and with a war still going on and American lives being lost every day, perhaps those feelings would not soothe until after the war ended. American emotions were running high; even German behavior that fell far short of odious Nazi conduct was enough to trigger GI tempers. Decades after the war, Purley Cooper of the 110th Field Artillery—ordinarily one of the 29th's most compassionate field grade officers—still fumed at the recollection of a small group of young German women giggling on the fringes of a crowd staring at a wrecked U.S.

Army jeep and its severely injured occupants who had just driven over and detonated a mine. "We just aren't fighting humans, I guess," an angry 29er wrote to
his wife.

The overworked members of the 29th Division's military government staff—
soon to be elevated in status as Gerhardt's G-5 section—labored to establish order
behind the front line among the rudderless German population. The twenty-six-
year-old head of the military government staff, Lt. Col. Donovan Yeuell—a 1940
West Point graduate—and his able assistants, Majors Robert Walker and Walter
Buttner, long ago had determined that the 29th Division had nothing to fear in
terms of guerrilla war or rear-area sabotage on the part of German citizens. "The
people left behind in this area are human beings with a will to survive," wrote an
observer from Eisenhower's Supreme Headquarters Allied Expeditionary Force
(SHAEF) staff. "Just because we are conquerors, and they know it, they are in
certain ways easier to handle than the liberated Belgians or Frenchmen. They
know they must obey our orders, and if they are allowed to survive and re-
construct their lives by self-help, they do not of themselves cause any trouble. . . .
Minor sabotage would be child's play. It has not happened because the people are
not interested in the war, but looking after themselves."

A key member of Yeuell's team, Sgt. George Curtiss—born in France, a
resident of Hamburg, Germany, in his youth, and once a member of the Hungarian Army—explained military government's mission: "We work with the
regiments and battalions, and if needed the companies, to help the line troops
cope with the civilian population in combat areas," he said. "We gather the Germans together and send them to rear areas. We collect all the livestock in order
to feed the population that has been herded to the rear. We take care of
displaced persons: Poles, Dutch, Russians, French, Belgians, all who have been
brought into Germany as slave labor. We post proclamations of the supreme
commander, which lay down the law to German civilians. Any violations are
handled firmly by military government courts under us. So far we have encountered no major violations." Curtiss himself, however, quietly ventured to a lis-
tener a personal opinion that most 29ers shared: "I still think we are too soft
with the Germans. I say that because I have seen what they have done to the
millions they once conquered."

If any Germans behind the front misbehaved or dared to attempt sabotage,
the 29th Division's minuscule counterintelligence corps (CIC), consisting of only
four officers and ten enlisted men known universally as "G-men in khaki," would
deal with the menace. Fulfillment of the CIC's mission—"to secure our forces
from espionage, sabotage, and subversion, and to destroy all enemy intelligence
services"—seemingly would be a challenge for such a small unit, led by a mere
lieutenant named Ellis Mayfield. Counterintelligence manuals directed Mayfield's

men to interact with local German civilians regularly—sometimes incognito—so fluency in German was a vital skill. As a postwar CIC history noted, however, "The lack of personnel with linguistic ability and a knowledge of the countries where the campaigns were conducted was a serious handicap."

The Army's nearly unknown counterintelligence corps, originating in 1917 as the Corps of Intelligence Police, did not act like a normal Army unit. Stateside, and even occasionally overseas, its members carried out their duties in civilian clothes. Even when they wore U.S. Army uniforms, CIC personnel habitually concealed their rank or wore no rank insignia at all, striving to look more like an Army-accredited war correspondent than a highly trained soldier. Men of the CIC even went so far as to instruct other U.S. Army personnel to address them as "agent" rather than revealing their rank.

Ordinary 29ers could discern no motive for these melodramatic cloak-and-dagger antics, for local Rhineland civilians in January 1945 turned out to be more like sheep than lions. No sabotage here, just a fervent desire among the citizenry for a decent supply of food and heat—and a quick end to the global conflagration that had thoroughly wrecked their homeland. Nevertheless, Mayfield and his little band toiled diligently to keep the 29th Division's rear area safe against threats real and imagined. According to a January 1945 report, his CIC detachment "investigated and appointed or recommended new city officials; recommended the removal of officials who had been ardent Nazis; screened Displaced Persons (DP) who had been working in the area; [investigated] numerous instances of mistreatment of DPs by the Germans; deserters were apprehended and persons guilty of harboring them were arrested; road patrols were established for the purpose of checking the identification of civilians and military personnel."

The longer the 29th Division maintained a static defense in the Rhineland, the less the 29ers perceived all German civilians behind American lines as Nazi thugs. Accordingly, the Army's non-fraternization policy, which only two months in the past had seemed sensible, slowly, imperceptibly, evolved into a decree many GIs would eventually break. As Major Walker of the 29th's military government staff noted, "Without exception, everyone interpreted [non-fraternization] as prohibiting 'intimacy' with German civilians who happened to be cute and friendly." He was right: the most notorious of the Army's non-fraternization imperatives was a $65 fine for "cohabitation" with a German woman, so getting caught breaking that rule would be prohibitive for a GI on a buck private's pay of $60 per month.

Only time would tell if the 29th Division would strictly enforce non-fraternization. According to Walker, those who worked closely with Gerhardt understood that the general was hardly one of the policy's greatest supporters. "Gerhardt eased the confusion somewhat when he let it be known he felt fraternization meant treating someone like a brother," Walker wrote. "And he didn't believe any of our troops were interested in treating any female German civilians like a brother. He added that, in addition, many of our men had German relatives whom they should be allowed to contact." Much of Germany beyond this little corner of the Rhineland, however, still remained under Hitler's control; most 29ers with German relatives would not make contact until much more fighting and dying took place.

At least for now, Walker reported, "The concept of non-fraternization didn't get debated very much."

THE JOES APPRECIATED IT

General Bradley had recently shifted the command to which the 29th Division had been subordinated since its September arrival in Holland, Maj. Gen. Raymond McLain's XIX Corps, southward to take over the Roer sector near Düren, just north of the Bulge. The 29th was then assigned to a new corps, the XIII, commanded by Maj. Gen. Alvan Gillem, one of the Army's eminent advocates of mechanization and a confidant of George Patton. (In 1935, however, a less open-minded Gillem was supposed to have maintained that "tanks were too slow and cumbersome to strike effective blows.") Once more Gerhardt would have to get used to a new boss, his fourth in less than four months, and Gillem, a fifty-six-year-old soldier with a weatherbeaten face and thirty-four years of continuous military service—he had chased Pancho Villa with Pershing in 1916 and served in Siberia during the Great War—was the third of the four who had entered the Army as a private before World War I. No one who knew Charlie Gerhardt would categorize him as a snob, but as a highly popular member of the West Point class of 1917, he was fiercely loyal to his alma mater and its alumni, and rumors abounded that he chafed at working under non–West Pointers, particularly former members of the National Guard like McLain.

By all accounts, however, Gerhardt and Gillem got along famously. In daily phone conversations Gillem invariably asked Gerhardt, "How's everything down there?" Just as predictably, Gerhardt replied, "All quiet," and provided a few trivial details on patrols and enemy activity. In the fall campaign in the Rhineland, Gerhardt had set off McLain's ire more than once, so the affable start between Uncle Charlie and Gillem augured a smooth relationship in the days ahead. The two generals, however, had of course not yet interacted under the overwhelming pressure of full-scale combat, during which continual directives and objectives issued by the high command would filter down through Gillem to the 29th Division. Attempts to fulfill those sometimes irrational orders would inevitably put the jobs of countless men, from mere NCOs to Gerhardt and Gillem themselves, at risk. But that bridge would be crossed later.

The delighted 29ers soon learned that Gillem was a soldier's general, an unsurprising trait given that he himself had started out as a buck private. One 29er related, "General Gillem clearly desired to better the lot of his people in any way in his power, and his interest in individual ingenuity toward that end was a great boost to spirits." Army food impacted those spirits enormously, and according to that same 29er, "The months-long diet of canned goods and powdered eggs, plus the rule that no food could be acquired locally, had taxed the ingenuity of the cooks. Lt. Col. [John P.] Cooper told the

Maj. Gen. Alvan Gillem, commander of XIII Corps.

general that some fresh food would be welcome. Shortly thereafter 'shell' eggs and crates of oranges were issued. . . . As far as the cannoneers were concerned, General Gillem got the credit and the thanks."

Nothing boosted a 29er's spirit more than a substantive break from the front; the farther he distanced himself from the dismal Rhineland, the better. Paris, even on a quick forty-eight-hour pass, could work wonders on a jaded man's soul, but in early January 1945, a few dozen supremely lucky 29ers did even better than that, so much better in fact that when they woke on the morning of January 11, they drew the joyous conclusion that they would never again hear the explosion of a German shell. Most were D-Day veterans, some even prewar members of the Maryland or Virginia National Guard, selected by respectful peers—typically one per company or battery—in honor of their steadiness under fire, to be dispatched home that morning for three months of stateside temporary duty as close to their families as possible. The three-month span did not include round-trip travel time, so by everyone's reckoning they could not possibly return to Europe until mid-May 1945 at the earliest—and by then every 29er expected Adolf Hitler to be in his grave.

They included such veterans as Maj. Eccles Scott, who had landed in the first seconds of the D-Day invasion on Omaha Beach in command of the 116th Infantry's Company G; 1st Sgt. Paul Johnson of the 115th Infantry's Company F, a twenty-seven-year-old native of Cumberland who had enlisted in the Maryland

National Guard in April 1937 and had been wounded three times since June 6; 1st Sgt. Harry Gintling of Company B, 175th Infantry, a resident of a modest east Baltimore neighborhood who had been born in that area of the Rhineland currently occupied by the 29th Division and had emigrated to the United States in his youth; and T/4 Walter Cioffi, a devoted member of the 175th's Cannon Company, a Californian whose voyage to the Presidio in San Francisco for his three months of temporary duty surely was the longest journey of all.

When the men assembled that morning to say goodbye to their comrades, maybe for the last time, a witness noted that "the whole happy crew stood proudly at attention in greeting their commanding general." In his distinctive upper-crust accent, Gerhardt pronounced: "This is one detail everyone is in full accord with. Individuals in ground combat outfits now have something to which they can look forward. The division wishes you *bon voyage*." Not a single one made it back to the Western Front before the war ended.

A much larger number of somewhat less lucky but still overjoyed 29ers received passes to Paris varying in length from forty-eight hours to one week. A GI spent the first couple of hours of his pass with his comrades, sitting on an uncomfortable bench in the bed of a deuce-and-a-half, huddled in a woolen overcoat against the cold and bouncing uncomfortably along roads rutted by the ravages of war. The rough journey, he hoped, would be worth it. It was . . . but the most perceptible image of the legendary *ville de lumière* was how the war had transformed it into a city of startling contrasts, most of which involved the U.S. Army in one form or another. It was a city where perfectly uniformed MPs outside the Communications Zone headquarters on Avenue Kléber admonished passing GIs for failing to salute an officer; but not far away, according to U.S. Army historian Sgt. Forrest Pogue, "soldiers [were] lying drunk on the sidewalks in the Place Vendôme." American GIs with an interest in high culture could take in Molière's hilarious *Le Malade Imaginaire* at the renowned *Comédie-Française* or *Le Jongleur de Notre-Dame* at the historic *L'Opéra*; less than a mile away, in the Pigalle district—home of the famous *Moulin Rouge* cabaret—U.S. soldiers interested in culture of a different kind could track down a *fille de joie* ("woman of joy," or prostitute) in minutes. Above all, Paris was a place where reportedly 10,000 war-weary GIs per day were trucked in from the battlefield to mix with a far greater number of U.S. Army troops who had never been within 100 miles of the front.

This was not the Paris of a prewar Baedeker guide. Now a world-class restaurant could not achieve the culinary standards of a rifle company mess tent, serving, as one irritated GI noted, "a sort of meatloaf surrounded by potatoes" for a main course and applesauce for dessert. Not surprisingly, insufficient energy was available to illuminate Paris with its former intensity; private homes, hotels, and public places remained painfully frigid most of the winter due to a coal shortage. Still, Paris was Paris; even a dingy bistro serving concoctions of God-knows-what and a disreputable flophouse whose rooms changed hands several times per day were a welcome change from K-rations and a bombed-out building on the Roer.

"Paris was OK," wrote Maj. Albert Hoffman of the 29th Division's operations staff after a weeklong visit, "except that they were having the coldest weather in years and there was a shortage of food and fuel. All places of amusement were either closed or underheated, so the prospects of entertainment were none too good. I did take in one show, mainly to hear good French properly enunciated, but got too cold after the second act and went home to bed."

Another 29er, 1st Lt. William Kenney of the "29th Division Air Force," wrote his wife that his time in Paris was "swell," but "it was so cold going there and returning. Snow all the time—and it was cold in Paris too. This was increased by the hotels, clubs, stores, etc. not having any heat. The clubs also close down early—1100 now—because they must conserve the power used for lights." Kenney managed to take in a show at the celebrated *Folies Bergère*, and he noted, "The accent [was] on scantily clad girls. Wowie!"

The town of Heerlen, Holland, was no Paris; for thousands of 29ers out of the line, however, it would have to do. Heerlen turned out to be a delightful place, its affable but war-ravaged citizenry displaying an unadulterated admiration for their American liberators. Every two days, a new group of 300 29ers fresh from the front rotated into town, each a happy holder of a forty-eight-hour pass. They were trucked directly to a nondescript brick building, where they passed through a portal topped by a sign proclaiming "Through these doors pass America's finest fighting men." This was the 29th Division's Recreation Center, run by Maj. Tommy Dukehart, 1st Lt. Bruce Bise, and T/Sgt. Eddie Hauser.

For many, the Rec Center's appeal went no further than its copious supply of plushy cots, made up with clean sheets and arranged with military precision in rooms heated to a delightfully warm temperature. The head mess sergeant, S/Sgt. John Robinson, managed six cooks who worked around the clock to provide three hot meals per day for all. No matter what ingredients went into those repasts, real plates, accompanied by real eating utensils—laid out on real tables around which real conversations with one's buddies could be carried on at a leisurely pace— brought back enjoyment to dining after weeks of cold mess-tin rations served within sight of enemy lines. The Rec Center also featured a spacious game room for those interested in low-key competition at table tennis, chess, checkers, or darts, or perhaps a more competitive round of good old-fashioned Army poker or craps. Nearby buildings housed showers, an indoor pool, a chapel—services were held twice daily, seven days per week—dance halls, and movie theaters. Two

29ers, S/Sgt. Paul Kasinak and T/4 Michael Helenda, rotated as pub managers behind a bona fide bar emblazoned with a handsome "29, Let's Go!" sign and other impressive artwork. The bartenders served beer at a dime per glass from real taps, but even when beer ran out—as it invariably did—the blackboard advertised a glass of wine at "one ration ticket" and a limited supply of cold bottles of Coca-Cola, a drink most 29ers had not tasted for months, even years. As one man recalled, "It was an unbelievable luxury, to be sipped slowly and raved over. . . . Dear Mom: What do you think we had today? Coca-Cola!"

To the GIs, grumbling was a God-given right, and few of the many inequities of Army life provoked more grumbling than the sharp contrast between the austere life of a front-line soldier and the comfort of civilians on the homefront. Happily, however, by the end of January 1945, the number of grumblers in the 29th Division had declined appreciably due to the supreme efforts of U.S. Army Special Services personnel to bring the best of their country's culture, in both low and high forms, as close to the front as possible. The latest Hollywood films had always been a sore point: why did it take so long for the Army to send them overseas? A recent *New York Times* article had explained that the Army's grumblers were dead wrong: "Denying that the Army overseas saw old movies, Brig. Gen. [Joseph] Byron [director of the Special Services Division] said pictures were shown overseas before they were released to civilians. The Army gets 156 pictures a year for overseas distribution, he said." The 29ers soon acknowledged that Byron was right: among the hottest new films playing extended runs in Heerlen that January were *Rhapsody in Blue*, a fanciful depiction of George Gershwin's life starring Al Jolson and Oscar Levant, which did not premiere in New York until June 1945; and *Saratoga Trunk*, an adaptation of an Edna Ferber novel starring Gary Cooper and Ingrid Bergman, which did not open stateside until November. A first-run film, however, did not assure quality; the *Times* would describe *Saratoga Trunk* as "gaudy junk."

"In addition to these first-rate movies, there was more than the usual amount of 'C' and 'D' pictures," the 115th Infantry's regimental history observed, "but good or bad, the makeshift theaters were always well attended and quotas had to be allotted to each company to insure that all had an equal chance to attend." But even more appealing than the films themselves were the stars who played in them, several of whom traveled for performances close enough to the front to gain the 29ers' everlasting gratitude. One of them carried an Army ID card with the name Marie M. Sieber—better known as Marlene Dietrich, the Hollywood bombshell who performed for the 29th Division in a ninety-minute show called "One Night Stand" on Tuesday, February 6, 1945, just a few miles from her native Germany. "Garbed in a clinging, pale rose-colored, nude chiffon gown, adorned with sparkling gold sequins that complimented her svelte figure and golden blond hair, she fairly floated across the stage to the microphone," a spectator reported. Following her seductive trademark greeting, "Hello, boys," she was asked by the host, "What are you going to do for the boys?" Folding her arms alluringly, Dietrich replied after a moment of thought, "Whatever the boys desire"—a response the spectator noted caused the audience to "stir approvingly."

Dietrich brought down the house with a corny off-color mind-reading shtick with a randomly chosen 29er, who, it was said, "was in a cold sweat for five minutes." After a few more acts, she launched, in her incomparable resonant contralto, into her signature tune, "Lili Marlene," which in a second caused the 29ers' boisterous whistles, cheers, and applause to vanish in favor of a reverential silence:

Vor der Kaserne
Vor dem grossen Tor
Stand eine Laterne
Und steht sie noch davor

Underneath the lantern
By the barrack gate
Darling I remember
The way you used to wait . . .

When it came to performances in front of large groups of young American males, it was not advisable to follow "La Dietrich" onstage, even days later. Nevertheless, PFC Mickey Rooney, the pint-sized twenty-four-year-old Brooklynite who had starred in fourteen *Andy Hardy* films, had to try. Not only was he not nearly as nice to look at as Dietrich, he also carried a reputation as "a brash kid"; according to one Army rumor, Rooney had once paid a sucker to fill in for him at menial K.P. tasks. Rooney heatedly denied the gossip—he said a malicious "Topeka typewriter-pounder" had made it up—and proceeded to persuade a 29th Division audience which one witness defined as "frankly hostile" that his concern for the dogface's welfare was genuine. Nearly an hour of captivating "imitations, stories, and songs" convinced the crowd that "Rooney was a regular Joe," and he reinforced that sentiment by signing autographs and posing for photos with anyone who asked.

The Army had recently reconsidered its assumption that front-line troops would not accept high-brow entertainment. Declared a *Times* article in September 1944: "Troops overseas were beginning to demand plays rather than vaudeville." On Wednesday, January 24, the 29th Division proved that the demand was genuine when Katharine Cornell, Brian Aherne, and the cast of *The Barretts of Wimpole Street* played to a Heerlen theater packed with 780 dogfaces and one general,

Charlie Gerhardt. "Miss Kit" Cornell—"The First Lady of the Theater" of whom a *Time* reporter once noted, "There are those who would as soon miss their own wedding as a Katharine Cornell play"—had played the starring role as the poet Elizabeth Barrett to universal acclaim off and on since 1931. *The Barretts*, however, scarcely seemed suitable fare for fighting men: for three hours actors traded lines without a single scene change, and the main character, Elizabeth, spent much of the play lying motionless on a sitting room settee.

Some of the U.S. Army brass scoffed at the very idea of such a play being presented at the front. Even Miss Kit admitted, "We were afraid of the soldiers' reactions at first," and at the opening performance in Italy in August 1944, those fears surfaced when unruly GIs snickered loudly in the first act. An actress noted: "We thought they would go on laughing, and it would never stop and *The Barretts* would go under a tidal wave of derision. But we were wrong." In 150 shows in dilapidated theaters in Italy, France, Belgium, and Holland, Miss Kit's enthralling acting converted even the most sneering cynics into rapturous fans. Before the 29th Division's Heerlen performance, the amazed 29ers had learned that the troupe had cut short its three-week Paris run by two full weeks to bring the play up to the front. "Nothing but brass and neatly pressed uniforms [in Paris] after acting for line soldiers was a let down," declared Miss Kit. A grateful 29er observed that the cast "gave a performance as fresh as though they were playing it for the first time. There was no 'acting down' to what performers sometimes conceive as the GI level. And the Joes appreciated it." They appreciated it so much, in fact, that dozens stayed on after the play to request her autograph on their programs. The classy Miss Kit exchanged banter with them all and remarked, much to their amusement, "Our only regret is that you lads haven't left a theater standing in Germany so we could get further up."

"The rear echelon was always warm and cheerful," remarked Lieutenant Ewing. "The supply sergeant was here with piles of dry socks and clean ODs [olive-drab uniforms]. Here were the mess sergeant and the cooks, grinning in appreciation when the men marveled over the 'swell setup,' while hot meals cooked on the stoves. The mail clerk was here with his card files and packages from home." But all those pleasant diversions, even when a 29er got lucky and was drawn away from the front to see a play or a film, drink a Coca-Cola, take a hot shower, or even play a round of ping-pong, only fleetingly broke what Ewing referred to as "the dull, daily sameness of his Army detail." For a 29er covering the Roer front in January and early February 1945, according to Ewing, "It was a drab, monotonous life he led. In his heavy, clumsy overshoes he splattered the oozing, chocolate-colored roads that ran through an expanse of tiresomely flat snow-covered land, and through a dreary succession of hamlets and villages whose red brick houses stood ragged with the marks of battle.

Every day was the same. . . . On the line he stood guard for two hours, slept for four, and ate K-rations at noon every single day."

MINUTES SEEMED LIKE HOURS

The incessant wind blustered across the Roer on those icy January nights, chilling to the bone those tiny handfuls of men guarding the front for their 13,000 comrades of the 29th Division. In truth, most of the time boredom and the cold were of more concern than the enemy, but still, a 29er let his vigilance slip at his peril. The nights were usually dead quiet, but an inexplicable noise—possibly a Jerry slipping over the river, perhaps a rabbit disturbing a ration can draped on the wire, or maybe even a friendly patrol—could instigate momentary terror and a frantic effort to recall the daily password and countersign in case the generator of that noise had to be challenged. Generally there was no sign of the enemy except for an occasional brightly colored flare that lit up the sky on the far side of the Roer. On those rare nights with no cloud cover, the wondrous heavens gradually rematerialized as the flare faded, revealing such an array of sparkling stars that even an apathetic soldier would wonder how it was that fate had brought him to this spot, so far from home, in the midst of the greatest cataclysm in world history. It had to end soon, without much more bloodshed—God willing.

Now and then the searchlights of XIX Corps's Battery A, 226th Antiaircraft Artillery Searchlight Battalion, each 60 inches in circumference and 800 million candlepower, lit up the heavens above the Roer with a luminosity equal to a dozen full moons. The 226th's personnel, ordinarily trained to track enemy aircraft at night, had recently become experts in the Allies' innovative "artificial moonlight" technique by bouncing their powerful beams off low-lying clouds. "Perhaps no single soldier impression of the division's campaign in Germany will be remembered more clearly than the strong, friendly searchlight beams which pierced the night sky throughout the long months on the river line," declared the 29th's official history.

The 29th Division might not be going anywhere soon, but Gerhardt had no intention of letting his opposite number on the far side of the Roer figure that out. The perplexed Germans would be kept on their toes, the general insisted, by a nonstop series of raids, patrols, whirlwind artillery barrages, and crafty deceptions. On January 5, Gerhardt concocted one of the most unusual schemes in 29th Division history, labeled "Operation *Devil*." Unlike the general's standard technique, which normally called for the application of unmitigated violence, *Devil* was based, at least at first, on an unprecedented display of passivity. A divisional action report noted that for more than twenty-four hours, from 7:00 A.M. on the fifth to 7:15 A.M. on the sixth, "No weapons were fired, radio silence was in effect, and vehicular movement was cut to a minimum."

If the Germans found their opponents' behavior unusual, as they surely would given the Americans' predilection for expending ammunition liberally, they would be in for a much greater shock at 7:15, when every weapon in the 29th Division, from rifles to 155-millimeter howitzers, opened up and maintained their fire steadily for fifteen minutes. Then, at 7:30, a smoke-generating outfit would lay a thick two-mile-long smokescreen along the Roer, aiming to give the enemy the idea that the 29ers were about to mount a major attack.

If the idea was to gauge the Germans' response to a 29th Division offensive, Gerhardt must have been pleasantly surprised that their reaction amounted to— nothing. Obviously these were not the fanatical paratroopers who had made the 29ers' lives hell in Normandy and Brittany. Rather, they must be uninspired and overage *Volksgrenadier*, lacking the materiel and the will to resist. It wouldn't be long now . . .

In a postwar interview, however, *Generalleutnant* Dettling of the 363rd *Volksgrenadier* Division, the commander of German forces defending the Roer opposite the 29th, disagreed. "In view of the dispersal of enemy forces because of the Ardennes offensive, we hardly needed to reckon with an attack at that time," he wrote. As soon as possible, however, Dettling needed to figure out precisely what he would do in the not-too-distant future when he must indeed reckon with a real 29th Division attack. That would be the challenge of his life.

If there were ever a time in war for Gerhardt to adopt a laissez-faire stance against the quiescent Germans, some hopeful 29ers surmised, this was it. But the general's actions in the new year dispelled that fantasy long before it took root. Gerhardt was always an immovable advocate of "aggressive patrolling," even on a comparatively tranquil front, and he regularly extolled the significance of prisoner snatches, disruption of enemy routines, up-to-date intelligence of German defenses, and the overall sense that Dettling must never be allowed to forget that he was up against one of the most hard-hitting divisions in the U.S. Army. Indeed, if history would eventually categorize the 29th Division as an elite outfit, as Gerhardt fervently hoped, its aggressiveness would be one of the reasons why; he once even went so far as to boast that had Hitler launched his December offensive across the Roer instead of in the Ardennes, "There would have been no surprise, as we maintained continual offensive patrols across the river." As always, however, 29th Division infantrymen instructed to fulfill the general's whims displayed little enthusiasm—it would have been far easier and less costly, they thought, to limit harassment of the Germans to artillery fire—but the U.S. Army was not a democracy, and orders were orders.

More than two months of Gerhardt's "aggressive patrols," carried out on a daily basis as frequently as three or four times per night, provided reluctant 29th Division infantrymen a chance to sharpen their soldierly skills, but even the veterans had to admit that the nocturnal setting was hair-raising. "While it is comparatively simple to sum up these patrol activities in a few sentences," a 29er remarked, "it would be a grave injustice to the men who crossed the icy river to prowl around in the dark on strange ground, not knowing when a trip-wire or booby trap would explode or when dreaded mines might go off, bringing down a barrage of enemy fire. It would be a grave injustice indeed to say that this work was routine."

The 29th Division repertoire included two types of patrols: the simple "reconnaissance patrol," consisting of only a handful of men, including one officer whose job was to gain intelligence and nothing more; and the much more ambitious "combat patrol," which did not shy away from contact with the enemy and characteristically attempted to capture a German prisoner. Occasionally, Gerhardt would elevate a combat patrol into a full-fledged raid of up to company strength, which would strive to seize a piece of enemy-held real estate temporarily while inflicting as much carnage as possible, followed by prompt withdrawal to the American side of the Roer.

By far the most common of the 29th Division's winter patrols were of the reconnaissance variety. The point was not to fight; indeed, if gunfire erupted, the patrol leader invariably ordered his men to withdraw posthaste. Rather, the patrollers sought the kind of rock-solid intelligence that prisoner interrogations and air photos rarely provided: the depth and current of the Roer; the sites of enemy foxholes, machine-gun nests, command posts, and minefields; the nature of the ground; the location of gaps—if any—through enemy wire. In addition, as a 175th report observed, "The information gathered served also to select targets for our supporting artillery, which was frequently called upon to fire on designated targets and areas."

Shortly after midnight on January 7, one typical patrol was carried out by three men from the 175th's Company B—1st Lt. Carl Geer, Sgt. Floyd Gross, and Sgt. Philip LeClair—plus a fourth man from Company C, Pvt. Leonard Roseler. All four 29ers were hardened combat veterans: Roseler and Gross had landed on Omaha Beach on D+1, June 7; Geer had joined the regiment shortly after the fall of St. Lô and had gained two Purple Hearts since; and LeClair had fought in every 29th Division campaign since the fall of Brest in September. The 29ers departed the forward command post at Linzenich *Gut* and stealthily crept toward the 175th's forwardmost outpost along the Roer. There, they picked up a four-man inflatable boat and moved down to the riverbank, interrupted twice by German flares, causing them to assume prone positions hastily and remain immobile until the flares expired. Each flare triggered a delay of only a few minutes, but it seemed like hours.

Company G's 1st Lt. Joe Ewing, who occupied Linzenich *Gut* that night, observed, "A light snow had fallen, and the temperature was below freezing." He also noted that the patrol members wore their field jackets inside out, a common 29th Division practice since the jacket's outer shell reflected light. "We waded into the water, and Sgt. LeClair, Sgt. Gross, PFC Roseler, and I got in the boat," Geer wrote. "The river here was about fifty yards wide and five feet deep." That information alone was valuable, but it was not enough; Uncle Charlie certainly would expect more.

On the far side of the river, Geer's men disembarked and tiptoed onward to see what additional information they could gather. Their well-being depended entirely, as *Baltimore Sun* reporter Holbrook Bradley noted, on "the element of surprise. . . . The men in the group were cautioned again and again before they set out against talking or making any noise that might be picked up by enemy listening posts. . . . This night patrol job is one of the most nerve-racking that any front-line troops must undertake. Usually it means creeping or crawling over muddy, rain-soaked, or snow-covered ground. Sometimes it means crossing waist-high or shoulder-high streams of icy water, often through an enemy field of fire."

The slightest sound could lead to disaster. "Then one of the men coughed," Geer recalled. "He covered his face as he began to cough, but it made some noise, and in the silence it seemed louder. We remained motionless for some time and

A U.S. Army patrol moves through the woods. U.S. ARMY SIGNAL CORPS

heard noises in houses twenty-five yards ahead of us. It sounded like a door being opened. . . . We worked over to our left and saw a light in another house." When the same 29er erupted in another coughing fit, Geer wisely decided to go back, re-cross the Roer, and return to his command post. He carried out the withdrawal without further incident and, following hot coffee for all, made his report. A mission that had lasted for hours had to be summarized in just a few sentences, an entirely inadequate number to reflect the moments of agonizing strain the men had just endured. No one had gotten hurt, fortunately, and even though Geer had not learned much that Gerhardt did not already know, the general would gain at least some satisfaction from the knowledge that his men had plodded deep into enemy territory, right under the Germans' noses really, and had not been detected. That was the way the 29th Division should do things.

A January 13 recon patrol run by the 116th Infantry's Company G, led by 2nd Lt. William Arendt, learned the hard lesson that once the Germans detected a patrol, continuation of the mission made little sense. Arendt, who had suffered a serious wound to his right hand on September 5 at Brest, defined his mission as a "listening" and "capture-if-you-can" job. The patrol moved out silently on either side of a narrow lane leading down to the Roer near the village of Barmen. A few hundred yards shy of the riverbank, an abrupt pop—the unmistakable sound of a German flare—broke the silence, followed by a sharper pop as it ignited. The flare, descending back to earth with a distinctive hiss, had caught the 29ers in the open. "I held up both arms, our signal to freeze in place, crouched if we had time," Arendt remembered. "Hopefully the Krauts would miss us—but they didn't. Within seconds, in came the mortars. . . . The flare's light was dying, but it was too late now. After the first shells exploded, I hollered 'Hit it!' and I expect everyone dove for the ditches—I know I did. I got up after the first few rounds had blasted the road and surrounding fields, knowing that we had to get out of that zone. I started running down the road toward the river, shouting 'Let's move it!'"

The men reassembled on the riverbank; the only casualty was Arendt himself, the victim of a knee wound. "My concern mainly involved the snow-dunking all of us took in the road ditches," he noted. "It was terribly cold, and we were all at least partially wet. . . . I figured we could take it only for another twenty to thirty minutes if we could stay reasonably quiet for that time." They did, but when they set out for home, they were a cold and dispirited group of men. Declared Arendt: "Everybody just fell out when we reached the company area, eager to get something warm." Uncle Charlie, if he learned of this patrol, would not be pleased. The next day, the 2nd Battalion surgeon, Capt. Jorge Hereter, evacuated Arendt as a "non-battle casualty"—Arendt noted, "If there ever was such a problem as combat fatigue, I had it in my last twenty-four hours with George Company." Back at a rear-echelon hospital, alarmed doctors noted that his wounded right hand had failed to recover, and he was restricted to non-combat duty. Arendt never returned to the 29th Division.

The much more challenging mission known as a "combat patrol" was a type all 29th Division infantrymen dreaded because they knew the chance of violent contact with the enemy would be high. Indeed, a combat patrol's standard objective—the capture of a German prisoner—virtually assured that fighting would erupt. Even worse, as the 115th Infantry's history asserted, "The men assigned to these combat [patrols] knew that the odds favored their engaging the Germans in hand-to-hand combat if they were to accomplish their mission." That history further asserted that patrols typically were "instructed to remain on the east bank of the Roer until one [prisoner] had been taken or until the patrol engaged the enemy in a fire fight and was forced to withdraw."

One of the 29th Division's most successful combat patrols was carried out on the night of January 16 by twelve men from the 116th Infantry's Company K, led by 2nd Lt. Arthur Dempsey. A thirty-year-old New Yorker who had studied for a year at Columbia University, Dempsey had been in uniform for more than three years, but his only "combat" experience had occurred as an enlisted man in an antiaircraft outfit that opened fire in defense of Los Angeles against a phantom

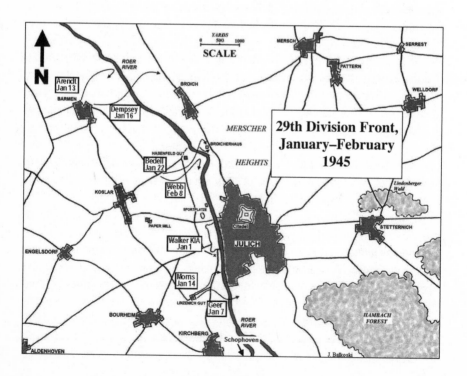

Japanese air attack on the night of February 24, 1942. Eventually he gained a commission and on December 9, 1944, was assigned as a platoon leader in the 116th Infantry. Although his tenure in Company K thus far had been short, Dempsey's platoon members recognized him as a bona fide character due to his skill as a flute player and his practice of wearing a fur hat made from rabbit and fox pelts—a habit that promptly earned him the nickname "Daniel Boone." He had previously carried out several patrols across the Roer, reportedly alone, and on the morning of his January 16 adventure, he had taken the back seat in a diminutive L-4 Cub observation plane to get an aerial view of the ground his men would soon explore.

Dempsey and his eleven followers, clad in white camouflage suits to blend in with the snow, moved out at 9:00 P.M. and headed for a sharp bend in the Roer two-thirds of a mile east of Barmen. Another Company K platoon leader who had recently crossed that same ground, 1st Lt. Robert Easton, recalled in a letter to his wife: "Sometimes the blackness is so thick you can't see more than three or four yards. . . . Progress consists of a few steps, followed by long minutes of looking and listening, usually crouched, sometimes prone. A high degree of alertness is essential. The slightest sound carries long distances in the still, cold air. A careless footstep on ice-encrusted snow can sound like an explosion. A cough or sneeze can be disastrous. The hardest part is sorting out imaginary images of danger from real ones."

On one of his earlier patrols, Dempsey had crossed that same bend in the river, using a huge tree that had toppled across the Roer as an ad hoc bridge. With a wide interval between men and moving as quietly as possible—Dempsey remarked a few steps on the ice sounded like "walking on crackers"—the 29ers tiptoed across the fallen tree into enemy territory, led by "Boone." Each man carried extra grenades, but neither the Thompson submachine guns hauled by some nor the M3 "grease gun" carried by Dempsey's second-in-command, S/Sgt. Joseph Keating, were authorized weapons in a U.S. Army rifle platoon. As for Dempsey, he left behind the officers' standard M-1 carbine in favor of two .45 Colts: "I'm accustomed to pistols," he said. "They don't encumber me."

Dempsey was unencumbered enough to lead his men through a gap in the German wire, followed by Keating, PFC Joe Rigdon, and the other eight patrol members. They turned north; a further advance of 200 yards brought into view what was described as something looking "like an Eskimo igloo," with a sled and a hay bale lying nearby. It was an earthen German bunker, covered with snow and expertly camouflaged—but where were the Germans?

Dempsey learned within a few seconds that they were close. As he pondered his next move, two Germans came plodding down a narrow trail toward the bunker, obviously unaware they were about to come face-to-face with the

Americans. Would those two become Dempsey's coveted prisoners? They would not; as they neared the bunker, a GI inadvertently made a noise, divulging the patrol's presence. "They went down on their bellies and started crawling away," Dempsey reported. Another account noted, "Dempsey moved toward them, and they took off on the run." The two Germans made a clean escape into the nearby woods, and even worse, Dempsey realized that within a few minutes they would warn their comrades of the American incursion and all hell would break loose.

Dempsey had to work fast. He had not yet inspected the enemy bunker, so there was still a chance the patrol could report something positive when it returned to American lines: some captured papers or maps, perhaps; maybe even trophies, such as a Luger or an MG42 machine gun. He warily approached the entrance; a report noted: "What he had thought to be a glimmer of light from some sort of reflector in the doorway turned out to be a five-inch square ventilation tube leading into an [earthen] hut. Looking into the tube, he saw a man's head directly in front of the hole. He asked Sgt. Keating to come up and have a peak." Dempsey declared: "I had the impression I was looking through some kind of periscope to a faraway room. . . . Sgt. Keating stepped up to the hole and said, 'Man, that's a Jerry! . . . Hell, he's right in front of you!'"

Here was the reason the 29ers had crossed the Roer. "Boone Dempsey pulled one of his .45s out and shoved it through the hole almost to arm's length," reported Lowenthal in a *29 Let's Go* article after interviewing Dempsey three days later. "Then he spoke into the opening, in German—*Kamerad!* The Kraut's head jerked toward the hole within six inches of the muzzle, and his hands went straight up to the ceiling as if they had been pulled up by strings. He came out dressed in an overcoat and cap and carrying biscuits in each hand. Keating and Boone Dempsey each had a go inside the hut—they tore down a field telephone and carried away some arms."

The captive was a Leipzig native named "Willie," described by another Company K member as "a rather pathetic-looking middle-aged member of Hitler's 'master race' . . . [who] declares himself only too glad to be done with war and to have a cup of hot coffee in a warm cellar." On their hasty return to American lines, Willie fell into the river while following his captors over the Roer log bridge. "He was a sorry-looking sack when Boone Dempsey and his men led him into their CP," wrote Lowenthal. The patrol was back home by ten minutes after midnight on January 17, so the whole affair took only three hours. A hasty interrogation by the 3rd Battalion's intelligence officer revealed that Willie had been snatched from a Luftwaffe unit in October and attached to the *Fusilier* (Reconnaissance) Battalion of the 59th *Volksgrenadier* Division. The interrogator concluded: "He was in the 'rest' bunker, forty meters behind the outpost line. Two men manned the outpost [with a machine gun and rifle], and one rested in the bunker. . . . Up until three days ago, his battalion had been back about five kilometers digging trenches. . . . His company has fifty to sixty men. Food is brought up around midnight to the platoon CP, which is at Broich. They have a cold breakfast and cold lunch—only one hot meal."

When Gerhardt heard the news, he phoned Gillem at XIII Corps headquarters and declared, "We caught one in [Lt. Col. Sidney] Bingham's outfit [116th Infantry] last night!" He also contacted Bingham and announced: "Nice going! And congratulate that fellow [Dempsey]!"

A less successful but much more violent combat patrol took place on January 29, carried out by members of the 115th Infantry's Company F. Led by 2nd Lt. William Salem, a neophyte who had joined the 29th Division less than three weeks in the past, the eight-man patrol was scheduled to move out from the company command post in the village of Schophoven at 1:30 A.M. with the goal of crossing the Roer and capturing one or more German prisoners. As the moon was nearly full and unusually bright due to a lack of cloud cover, Salem delayed departure, but at 3:00 A.M., as the regimental history observed, "the visibility gave no signs of diminishing," so Salem's band moved out. They had planned to cross the river by means of a hefty tree limb that had fallen near the riverbank, but it turned out to be far too short to span the thirty-foot river. The night was so piercingly cold that when the 29ers reached the Roer, they saw it was frozen: would the ice support their weight? A volunteer, twenty-one-year-old T/Sgt. Robert Aubin, would find out. Aubin, a veteran platoon sergeant from Rhode Island, had the job of covering the patrol's crossing with a BAR, but he simply rose and walked upright across the river. It worked; the rest of the patrol followed and made it to the far side without getting wet.

The patrol divided into two groups and stealthily advanced according to the age-old leapfrog method. At one point a 29er spotted a low tripwire to his front; whether it was set to detonate a mine if triggered or simply warn the Germans of their opponents' approach, no one knew since the vigilant soldier promptly snipped it. In the bright moonlight the GIs perceived a high embankment 250 yards ahead, which Salem knew from his 1:25,000 map marked the course of a canal, probably an old millrace carrying the Roer's waters to a nearby paper mill. Could this be the spot where the 29ers could snatch an unwary German soldier on outpost duty?

"As one of the men covered him, Lt. Salem began crawling forward to investigate the canal," noted a 115th Infantry account. "He inched his way up to within a few feet of the protecting embankment when a German sentry suddenly popped his head over the embrasure. Sighting the white-clad lieutenant, the sentry began to scream wildly in alarm and fright and began running down the bank of the canal. He was felled by a bullet from Salem's carbine. Another sentry nearby also jumped up and began running off. He was shot in the back as he ran." But a captive was of no value if dead: "Salem ran up to [the first German], hoping that he might take him prisoner and get back at once. Hasty examination revealed that the man had been shot through the head and was close to death. The lieutenant had scarcely made this discovery when a grenade was thrown into the canal, and the Germans began opening up with their automatic weapons." The ensuing cacophony could be heard on the American side of the Roer, and a concerned 115th Infantry clerk promptly made a 3:30 A.M. entry in the 2nd Battalion journal: "Believe Company F patrol across river involved in a fire fight."

Proper patrol principles indicated that the 29ers should immediately withdraw, and this they did in haste, despite "a great deal of small arms fire whizzing around them." American mortars and artillery opened up to prevent the Germans from pursuing, and within just a few minutes Salem's men, all uninjured, had returned to the Roer's west bank—without a prisoner. "When questioned later as to why he hadn't stopped to search the wounded man for identification papers," the report noted, "Lt. Salem replied, 'Hell, when they start throwing grenades at you and firing burp guns, you don't stop to think of things like that!'"

The journal looked on the bright side by noting that the patrol had "killed two enemy" and "located an eight-man Jerry strongpoint." How Gerhardt would react to that news would depend on his mood. Happily for Salem, that mood was good: at 7:42 A.M., the general phoned Lt. Col. William Blandford, the 115th's commander, and declared: "Got the report on your patrol, and evidently it inflicted some casualties on the enemy." A nervous Blandford rejoined, "We didn't get any prisoners," a response that caused Gerhardt to reassure him: "You did all right."

The Germans, too, dispatched small patrols across the Roer, but they undertook them much less frequently than the 29th Division and never dared to attempt anything as audacious as the company-size raid that Col. William Purnell, the 175th's commander, planned for the early hours of January 14. Purnell intended to test the enemy's resolve by sending half of his Company B, amounting to eighty-four men, across the Roer straight into the linchpin of the Germans' Roer defenses, the city of Jülich. "The plan of the raid," as an action report later noted, "called for the company to cross the Roer at a point just south of the Aldenhoven-Jülich bridge [now destroyed], destroy two fortified houses on the eastern side of the river, and bring back prisoners." As of that date, it was the 29th's boldest incursion into enemy territory, and all participants, from Company B commander, Capt. Charles Morris, down to his rawest private, suspected the Germans would be no pushovers. Jülich had been the 29th Division's prized objective for over two months, and by now the enemy's retention of its ancient and hallowed city had taken on a symbolic meaning far outweighing its military importance.

For days, Morris studied maps and air photos; consulted with members of supporting artillery, chemical mortar, machine-gun, and searchlight outfits; and went over the plan again and again in meetings and rehearsals with his platoon leaders and senior NCOs. At the appointed hour, 2:00 A.M. on the fourteenth, Morris's men would quietly move forward to the riverbank, board fourteen inflatable rubber boats—six men per boat—and paddle to the opposite shore, a task that under perfect conditions would only take a minute or two as the Roer's width at that point was only about thirty yards. Each man knew by heart the location of the two riverside buildings in Jülich and his role in their destruction. As in all 29th Division raids, the men understood that they must move fast, do their dirty work efficiently, and get out as quickly as possible before the enemy's inevitable reaction.

Those who knew Bill Purnell understood that he was not a dugout-bound colonel, and they were hardly surprised when the 175th's commander announced to Gerhardt the night before the raid, "I'm going down to the river" so he could observe the raid first-hand. When the general cautioned him, "You watch yourself now," Purnell replied: "Yes, sir. Everything has been gone over in the most elaborate detail, and I think it should be a success." That same night, Gerhardt did something highly unusual when he directly phoned a company commander, Captain Morris, and said, "I just want to wish you luck. It looks like everything ought to go all right."

Despite Morris's meticulous preparations, things did not go all right. Two elements of the godforsaken Rhineland weather threw his plans into disarray, one of which ultimately worked to the Americans' advantage while the other most assuredly did not. "About midnight," the 175th's report of the raid noted, "a fog began to set in, and by 0200 hours the entire area was covered [and] visibility was limited to about fifty yards. Otherwise the night was quite light [due to artificial light provided by American searchlights, as January 14, 1945, marked the first day of a new moon] and had been clear until midnight."

Furthermore, after a short thaw, the temperature on January 13 had dropped precipitously, so much so that a nearby Allied outfit reported that "roads and paths are in a very icy condition." When Morris's men reached the river a little after 2:00 A.M., "the principal obstacle to the success of the raid and which had been unforeseen was encountered. Ice extending from the shore for about eight to ten yards into the river was thick enough to support the weight of a man for part of the distance, but broke through further out. This condition effectively prevented getting the boats launched and resulted in considerable noise."

Noise was the only signal the alert enemy needed to respond. They immediately popped some flares, which did little good on such a foggy night, and started firing every weapon at their disposal—rifles, machine pistols, machine guns, mortars, artillery—at the general area from where the noise emanated. Morris promptly used his radio to call for his own supporting mortar and artillery fire—some of which used the new Pozit shells—and for a short time the continuous whistle of incoming and outgoing ordnance, mixed with the thunderous reverberation of their explosions, made it almost impossible for a man to think. Although the enemy fired its fusillade blindly, in just a few minutes it inflicted five Company B casualties, two of whom were officers: 1st Lt. Erwin Prasse and 2nd Lt. Richard Swain. A Chicago native, Prasse had been an All-American end on the 1939 University of Iowa football team, nicknamed the "Ironmen" because many of its players, Prasse included, were on the field the entire game—for offense as well as defense. Swain had joined Company B as a platoon leader just two weeks after D-Day and had suffered a severe wound at Vire in August. He had only just returned to the company following his recovery when he was hit again during the January 14 raid.

Surely the surprise element was lost, and not one of Morris's men had set foot on the enemy side of the river. At 3:35 A.M., however, Gerhardt's war room received a radio message from Maj. Henry Reed, the 175th's operations officer, that Company B was "reorganizing and preparing to go again." But then something inexplicable happened. "Three whistle blasts were blown, three times in succession, on the enemy side of the river," the action report noted. "This was the [American] signal planned for withdrawal of the company from the objective at the conclusion of the raid, and when it was heard, the men, in good faith, returned to their original assembly area in good order." Not everyone agreed with that recap: a liaison officer on the scene reported to the war room at 3:37 A.M. "that things were getting out of control." Had the Germans, by remarkable coincidence, also been using a whistle to signal their troops? Or had they somehow figured out the Americans' withdrawal signal and hoodwinked them? Perhaps the oppressive fog and numbing battle noise had played tricks on the 29ers' ears, triggering a false rumor that the withdrawal order had been issued.

No one ever figured it out. Purnell wisely cancelled the raid: more casualties would certainly have occurred for no useful purpose if Morris's men had pressed ahead over the river. Purnell returned to his command post, and at 7:24 that morning Gerhardt phoned to inquire how such a carefully planned raid had gone awry. An astonished Purnell must have thought Gerhardt had turned a new leaf, for the general had no reaction whatsoever to Purnell's four-sentence raid summary, which included the lament, "We thought we had covered every possibility." Purnell helped pacify the general when he concluded that the withdrawal, despite the rumors Gerhardt may have heard, "wasn't particularly disorganized."

If the general measured a raid's success not by its prisoner count or haul of fresh intelligence, but by the hurt inflicted upon the enemy, the fifty-four-man mission carried out shortly after midnight on January 22 by the 116th Infantry's

Company C must have been viewed enthusiastically by Gerhardt. The raid's target was a large edifice labeled "Broicherhaus" on U.S. Army maps, just 150 yards deep in enemy territory. Described as "a large mansion" and "the lone white house," and already the victim of a two-month deluge of American shells and bombs, the battered and highly conspicuous Broicherhaus sat halfway between Jülich and Broich and was rumored to be the site of an enemy observation post. Wreaking more damage on the structure would obviously do no further good, but snatching or killing any German occupants would in the future discourage the enemy from using that building and surely boost Gerhardt's spirits.

An earlier mission against Broicherhaus had to be cancelled when the raiders made too much noise launching their rubber boats on the ice-encrusted Roer. But the 29ers, led by their company commander, Capt. Robert Bedell, did not repeat that mistake when they moved out from their forward positions at Hasenfeld *Gut* at 2:03 A.M. on January 22 and reached the Roer a few minutes later. Launching their inflatables into the frigid water, the raiders traversed the river in less than a minute, disembarked, and moved as silently as possible across the river flats through fresh snow several inches deep. Not many 29th Division soldiers had more combat experience than Bedell, a bona fide D-Day hero who led one of the first American penetrations through the German defenses by climbing the Omaha Beach bluffs alongside the legendary "Dutch" Cota. Wounded twice in Normandy, first on June 17 and again on August 5, he had only recently returned to Company C as its leader after serving a spell as a 1st Battalion staff officer. For the raid, Bedell later reported that "75 percent of the patrol was armed with automatic weapons [Thompson submachine guns, "grease guns," and BARs]. This fact gave the men a lot of confidence."

Several rehearsals and even flyovers in observation aircraft had demonstrated to the raiders that the 150-yard procession from the river to Broicherhaus would be significantly slowed by German barbed wire, mines, and above all the need for stealth. Those lessons proved valid when the raid's point man, twenty-two-year-old Sgt. Roy Nichols, a D-Day veteran and former Arkansas farmhand, stumbled on a wire. "Nothing happened," an account noted. "No mine and no flare. Sergeant Nichols got down and examined it closely and cautiously, and on finding it looked like a telephone wire, he cut it."

Bedell's plan called for the raiders to surround the house, set up BAR teams to provide covering fire, and send forward a dozen men to seize the target. Overcast obscured the meager first-quarter moonlight, but still the 29ers had no trouble perceiving the looming house through the gloom as they plodded eastward from the river. The GIs were within a stone's throw of the house. . . . Still no Germans; no flares; no wire; no mines; not even footprints in the snow. Were any Germans present?

They were. A twenty-five-year-old Indian from Nevada, Pvt. Carl Dick, noted: "I had wire cutters and had gone around the south side of the house to prepare a place for a BAR team. I heard a noise behind the house and dropped on my stomach. My snow suit blended in with the snow. A German soldier, wearing a wool cap and white poncho and holding a machine pistol walked around the southeast corner of the house. He came within ten feet of where I was lying, saw some of our men west of the house, turned his head, and called in a low voice. Four Germans similarly dressed and armed came around the house. One of them saw me and yelled. I had my M3 submachine ["grease"] gun in front of my shoulder, and I started firing. All of them fell to the ground. Sergeant Nichols ran up. The Germans were thrashing around in the snow, so we threw grenades at them."

A report for Gerhardt written that same night by Maj. Asbury Jackson, the 116th's intelligence officer, observed, "It is [the raiders'] opinion that only five of the enemy were present, and all of them were killed." But the short firefight had already drawn an enemy response in the form of scattered machine-gun and mortar fire, so Bedell promptly signaled for his men to withdraw. Just to make sure no Germans lingered in Broicherhaus, the 29ers blasted the already wrecked building with three captured German rocket launchers. When Bedell had nearly reached the river, he realized that the group was missing a three-man BAR team that apparently had not received the withdrawal order, so he dispatched a man to fetch them and lead them back. Later, Bedell would note regretfully, "The withdrawal should have been started on a [flare] signal instead of on [voice] command."

This would have been an opportune moment for American mortars and howitzers on the opposite bank of the Roer to open fire and suppress the enemy's increasingly violent reaction, but according to Bedell's plan the American gunners would not initiate that supporting fire until they perceived the launch of a flare of a prearranged color. But the only man among the raiders carrying that flare, Bronx native PFC Arthur Valdevento, met a tragic end on the retreat to the river when he stepped on a mine and was killed instantly. Valdevento, who had joined Company C at St. Lô and suffered a severe wound at Brest, had celebrated his twentieth birthday just four days before his death. The mine blast also wounded thirty-year-old Sgt. John Sirmeyer of Michigan, who was standing a few yards away from Valdevento.

Minus Valdevento, Bedell's men re-crossed the Roer at 4:45 A.M. By the standards of the pitiless methods by which generals measured success in war, Bedell had succeeded: his men had killed five Germans; the 29ers had lost only Valdevento, plus two men wounded. The benefits to Jackson's intelligence staff, however, were meager. In fact, the only conclusion reached by Jackson's report stated "that the [German] group at the house consisted of part of the outpost line, or was a resting place for men of the outpost line." Whether that information was worth Valdevento's life, or for that matter whether one American life was worth the lives of five Germans, would surely stir passionate debate among the 29ers.

Little more than two weeks later, in that same sector, mines yet again wreaked havoc on a 29th Division patrol. Whether those mines were German or American, no one knew—but by the time they had done their dirty work, it was too late to ask. The 115th Infantry's Company K ran the five-man recon patrol early on February 8 with the usual objective of learning what the enemy was up to on the far side of the Roer. Lt. Jack Kussman, who had only recently returned to the division following an August wound suffered in Normandy, was selected by Capt. Robert Armstrong to lead the patrol, but just as Kussman was preparing to depart the front to report back to the company command post in Koslar for a briefing, Armstrong called back and told Kussman to stay put; 1st Lt. Jackson Webb would lead the patrol instead.

Webb and his four men—S/Sgt. Warren Owenby, a D-Day veteran who had been seriously wounded in Normandy; and PFCs Clarence Ruth, Robert Kribs, and Willie Edens—set out from Hasenfeld *Gut* to the Roer at 3:00 A.M. on the eighth. "We got to the riverbank OK, and there we left Edens to cover us with his BAR," reported the twenty-year-old Ruth, a Normandy veteran from Louisville. "The other four of us got into boats and started to paddle across. About halfway across, the current got so swift that we had to return. . . . Then [we] started back toward the bunker which we were using as the 2nd Platoon CP. Halfway back, Owenby stumbled on a mine, and before I knew it, Webb hit one too. The other three of us managed to get them back to safety without a shot being fired. The lieutenant lost his left foot and Owenby his right. Kribs was hit by some small fragments of the mine, and Edens received a concussion. I was the only one who didn't go to the hospital."

Kussman recalled: "Webb and the sergeant stayed in my CP until stretcher bearers came down from Koslar to get them. I remember telling Webb that I was sorry he got hurt on a mission to which I was originally assigned, and he told me that he was the lucky one since he was getting out, and that I had to stay and take my chances. At the time I think I agreed with him."

Individually, the 29th Division's missions across the Roer had not yielded much beneficial intelligence on the Germans and their defenses; collectively, however, the hundreds of cross-river patrols and raids conducted from New Year's Day through mid-February 1945 had painted a picture of the enemy that cheered Gerhardt mightily. The Roer, even following heavy rains and snow melt-offs, was not much of an obstacle; even better, German defenses on the river's east bank—barbed wire, minefields, trenches, pillboxes—were surprisingly feeble and could be penetrated by just a handful of men. Had those defenses been more formidable, the 29th Division's January casualty count of ninety-seven would have been much higher. Finally, the number of German troops guarding the Roer line seemed astonishingly low; the defenders' skill and morale were evidently even lower. Once the 29th Division unleashed its full power, backed by the might of the Ninth Army and Ninth Air Force, Gerhardt surmised that the job ahead should not be too difficult.

THE FIRST PARADE

Few details of Army life struck combat soldiers as more absurd than close-order drill in a war zone; when that endeavor was elevated one step into a full-fledged formal parade, it was more ludicrous still. On the other hand, one had to admit that participation in a military review was a lot more enjoyable and safe than sitting in a front-line foxhole in the depths of a freezing Rhineland winter.

One morning, comfortably situated in Aldenhoven for several days in that glorious status known as "division reserve," the men of Lt. Col. Claude Melancon's 2nd Battalion, 175th Infantry, were astonished by their growling non-coms' inflexible orders to fall in in full kit—including their GI overcoats—with as much soldierly bearing as they could muster. That day, Sunday, February 4, 1945— exactly four years plus one day after President Roosevelt had called the 29th Division into active service for a period that supposedly would not exceed one year—the 2nd Battalion would participate in that venerable Army ritual known as a pass in review. Hardly any of the veterans of the 1941 call-up remained, but the hundreds of draftees who had arrived since would make up for the lost men.

Melancon, a Louisiana Cajun, was not used to such frigid weather. Assembled in the gateway of a drab Aldenhoven train depot, he and his executive, plus the S-1, S-2, S-3, and S-4, huddled together to break the icy wind, collars turned up for warmth, stamping their feet to preserve circulation, some even with their hands in their pockets—an action that was strictly taboo within the 29th Division. When the 29th's expert band broke into a rousing march, the six officers snapped to attention, Melancon in front, ready to receive his beloved battalion. One could hardly believe that such an activity was in progress within easy range of German artillery—someone claimed it was "the first parade of any U.S. Army unit within the German border during the war"—but the sight of hundreds of fighting men, about to bestow and receive age-old military honors between soldiers and their leaders, could not fail to move even a hardened warfighter.

Presently each of the battalion's five companies came swinging up the street, the band's first-class music contributing immeasurably to the 29ers' perfect cadence. The 175th even had its own regimental march, "The Dandy Fifth of Maryland," although by now hardly a man knew the words. A color party with the national and regimental colors led the column, the colorbearers clutching their staffs with all their strength to control the flags in the incessant tailwind. To

The 175th Infantry's 2nd Battalion conducts a pass in review in Aldenhoven, Germany, on February 4, 1945.

those colors and each of the follow-on company guidons lowered in salute, Melancon and his staff returned snappy salutes, offered in response to each company's "eyes right."

One of the many distinctive features of the 175th Infantry, known as the 5th Maryland only four years in the past, was its unique regimental flag, adopted in 1899 and in continuous use since. So popular was the regimental color that in 1904 the design was adopted by Maryland as its state flag. Unlike the standard dark blue flag emblazoned with an eagle in use with most U.S. Army regiments, the 175th's color featured four quadrants of equal size: two identical quadrants in upper and lower corners displayed the black-and-gold coat of arms of the Calvert family, the 1634 founders of Maryland; the other two quadrants, also identical and in opposite corners, displayed red and white bottony crosses, the symbol of a Calvert ancestral line. The ensign's bright colors contrasted sharply with the dreary winter weather and the decrepit German community.

Just one thing went wrong: the regimental color was attached to its staff upside down. No one, not even Melancon, noticed. The regimental history blamed it on "replacement personnel" who were "unfamiliar with regimental customs."

TWO

Hurry Up and Wait

LOCALITIS

The pinprick war of patrols and raids along the Roer had to end soon. By early January 1945, the Allies had stopped the Nazis cold in the Ardennes, and every 29er, from the greenest replacement to General Gerhardt, had begun to steel himself for the moment when his outfit would launch an all-out assault across the river that would make the recent spell of positional warfare look like child's play. Precisely when that moment would come was up to generals far above Gerhardt's station, but the wait would be longer than anyone had imagined.

American generalship on the Western Front had been dominated by the Bulge ever since the enemy had stormed out of the mists in the Ardennes on the morning of December 16, 1944. Until the drama in the Ardennes played out to its denouement, Allied plans for the Rhine crossing and the advance on Berlin had to be put on hold indefinitely. "My present estimate is that the enemy's attack had delayed our offensive operations by at least six weeks," Eisenhower declared. Of greater concern was that indefinable military benefit known as momentum: the Allies had definitely lost it; when they would reseize it was anybody's guess. On January 18—nearly five weeks after the enemy's offensive had begun—Ike told Bradley and Montgomery, "My intention is to regain the strategical initiative."

Surprisingly, the place Eisenhower sought to regain it was the same location he had lost it in the first place: the Ardennes. In response to the enemy offensive, vast numbers of Allied troops had deployed to the Bulge, but rather than promptly sending them whence they had come once the Germans were contained and then recommencing offensives both north and south of the Ardennes, Ike resolved to "meet this all-out German effort [in the Ardennes] by an all-out effort of our own." The U.S. Army would therefore concentrate on shrinking the infamous Bulge and ultimately pushing it in the opposite direction by driving the enemy out of Belgium and Luxembourg into the hilly Eifel region of Germany. Before the enemy's offensive had erupted, any Allied general who had chosen the Ardennes and Eifel as suitable places for a set-piece offensive into Germany would have been considered foolhardy. Since the Germans had thrown down the gauntlet and cast everything on a final, desperate gamble, however, Ike would accept their challenge on the same rough ground and attempt to reverse the enemy's effort into a decisive Allied victory.

Many of Ike's generals harbored doubts about the sensibility of such a strategy, but as long as it was in effect, Gerhardt's 29th Division would not be attacking over the Roer any time soon. But Eisenhower added the significant provision that the American counteroffensive in the Ardennes "will be pressed with all possible vigor so long as there is a reasonable chance of securing a decisive success. However, as an alternative, we must be prepared to pass quickly to the defensive in the Ardennes and to attack in the sector of the Northern Group of Armies"— that is, Montgomery's Twenty-First Army Group, which included the U.S. Ninth Army and the 29th Division. Belatedly, Ike added, "Some regrouping will be necessary before offensive operations can be resumed."

Not unexpectedly, the Ardennes counteroffensive achieved no "decisive success." Save for a multi-division assault aimed at capturing a set of pivotal dams at the headwaters of the Roer, an operation that would profoundly influence the 29th Division's upcoming mission, Eisenhower shut down the counteroffensive in early February. Ike's subsequent "regrouping" of American troops, however, proved to be a much tougher proposition than he had imagined, not so much because of the logistical and administrative challenge of large-scale troop movements, which by this stage of the war had become second nature to the U.S. Army, but because the reshuffling of troops involved taking units away from one commander and giving them to another. Unhappily, that procedure was anything but second nature to some prickly American commanders who were infected by what General Marshall termed "localitis," an unshakeable conviction held by many generals that whatever front they currently occupied was the one that offered the most promising attack route into Germany. General Bradley's case of localitis was particularly acute: when on January 24 SHAEF began to shift American divisions out of the Ardennes to sectors beyond the reach of his Twelfth Army Group, he howled to a senior SHAEF general: "As far as I am concerned you can take any goddamned division or corps in the Twelfth Army Group, do with them as you see fit, and those of us that you leave behind will sit on our ass until hell freezes over. . . . I want to impress on you that I am goddamn well incensed."

Ike had to cure the affected generals of localitis straight away, whether the patients were willing or not, because the grand offensive he and the entire free world hoped would bring an end to Nazism forever would take place in the Rhineland in February, as soon the requisite regrouping of Allied forces was complete. "Without exception all of us have agreed from the beginning that the main invasion into Germany, when it becomes possible, should be by the north flank," Eisenhower expounded to Marshall. "Terrain, length of our own lines of communication, and location of important geographical objectives in Germany, all confirm the necessity of making the principal invasion along the northern line. Long before D-Day this general concept of operations was outlined by my staff and approved by me." Regrouping, however, would be slow, and the process could be even more prolonged if the current frigid temperatures, described by the local Dutch citizenry as "freak weather," did not improve.

The 29th Division had been serving under the able leadership of Lt. Gen. William Simpson, Ninth Army's commander, for most of the previous five months. At a January 15 conference at Ninth Army's Maastricht command post, Montgomery, in the words of an American staff officer, "tossed a bombshell" by ordering Simpson "to prepare plans for the Ninth Army, [to consist of] four corps and sixteen divisions, to advance on Cologne and the Rhine River at the earliest practicable date." That was indeed a bombshell, especially when Simpson considered that as of January 15, his army contained only five divisions. Where would the extra eleven divisions come from, and when would they arrive?

That problem could be solved later. Meantime, the anonymous staff officer crowed, "This would mean that the Ninth was to carry the ball for the Western Front drive—the Main Effort, while the First Army [commanded by Lt. Gen. Courtney Hodges] would assume a holding mission to our south and, after the breakthrough, protect the Ninth's southern flank. . . . [That] would be the greatest and most satisfying crack at the Grand Old [First] Army possible! How all would love to see that in print!"

Simpson spoke personally to the 29th Division staff, and eventually to all divisional staffs under his command, declaring "that this push was the main effort of the Twenty-First Army Group and SHAEF as well, and probably would be one of the most important battles in the war—if not the most decisive." The general concluded that the 29th and all other Ninth Army divisions must advance "as fast as God would let them, regardless of the relative progress of the friendly units on their flanks."

On February 4, Simpson traveled from Maastricht to nearby Zonhoven, Belgium, to confer with his immediate boss, Montgomery, about the upcoming offensive. There, in Monty's legendary command trailer replete with chirping canaries and other assorted pets, Simpson learned details of the operation he had anticipated for months. Code-named Operation *Grenade*, instead of the four corps and sixteen divisions promised in January, Simpson would instead command three corps and eleven divisions in the advance to the Rhine. Whether that diminution was due to weather or localitis—or both—Simpson declined to ask. Concurrently, Gen. Harry Crerar's Canadian First Army would launch Operation *Veritable* "on a narrow sector from the Maas River to the Rhine River, hitting at every known [German] gun, field, and foxhole emplacement. . . . Everything in the British [and Canadian] forces will be thrown into this move, carrying out the field marshal's principle of 'mass' and 'concentration.'" Crerar would advance southward, although Monty observed that "progress is expected to be slow because of the extremely low nature of the ground and the mud conditions"; Simpson, after assaulting across the formidable Roer barrier, would subsequently turn northeast to meet his allies between the Rhine and the Maas, thereby pocketing any Germans

**Lt. Gen. William Simpson of U.S. Ninth Army (at left) helps
Lt. Gen. Miles Dempsey of the British Second Army with his jacket.**
U.S. ARMY SIGNAL CORPS

who had refrained from retreating eastward over the Rhine. A Ninth Army diarist concluded: "The field marshal is cocky in his confidence of success."

So cocky was Monty that one of Simpson's toughest challenges would be to follow the orders of a man whose reputation in the eyes of most Americans had recently plunged to rock-bottom level. During the Battle of the Bulge, the field marshal had taken Hodges's First Army under his command and, in the aftermath of the titanic struggle, had commented to the press that his primary goal was "to tidy up the battlefield," followed by the exaggerated claim that to turn back the Germans, "I employed the whole available power of the British group of armies." Bradley observed acidly that in the British press, "Montgomery was depicted as St. George come to save the American command from disaster."

The quiet and modest Simpson was about as opposite from Monty as a man could be, and not surprisingly the Ninth Army staff's loyalty to its British boss was hardly enthusiastic. An unidentified staff officer injudiciously allowed a highly disparaging tone to creep into the Ninth Army's daily journal: "Any future moves of the Ninth in the light of present British publicity policy," he wrote, "will be to the greater glory of the FM [field marshal] himself, since he sees fit to assume all the glory and scarcely permits the mention of an army commander's name. Bitterness and real resentment is creeping in because of both the FM's and the British press's attitude in presenting British military accomplishments won with American blood, broadcast throughout Europe by the BBC."

THE SHOE PINCHED EVERYWHERE

Had anyone other than Adolf Hitler been in charge of German military policy on the Western Front, Operation *Grenade* would never have occurred at all. The failure of the Ardennes offensive and the decimation of the units that had carried it out presented the German high command with a stark choice: withdraw the battered remnants of the German Army behind the Rhine or fight in place, holding on to Germany's western frontier far forward of that majestic waterway. The Führer's opinion was the only one that counted, of course, and he had not budged an inch from his notorious directive, first circulated in autumn 1944, that every foot of the Fatherland must be defended tenaciously; any withdrawals yielding ground to the enemy save for those of a purely tactical nature must be sanctioned by him. "A strategic withdrawal would merely mean moving the catastrophe from one place to another," Hitler proclaimed. Knowledgeable military men disagreed but kept silent for fear the Gestapo would notice their pessimism.

Perhaps it made no difference what strategy Hitler chose, as most generals in the West concurred that Germany could no longer avoid defeat. A February 1945 high-level Allied intelligence report starkly delineated Germany's current predicament in words no German general dared to speak openly. "The enemy's

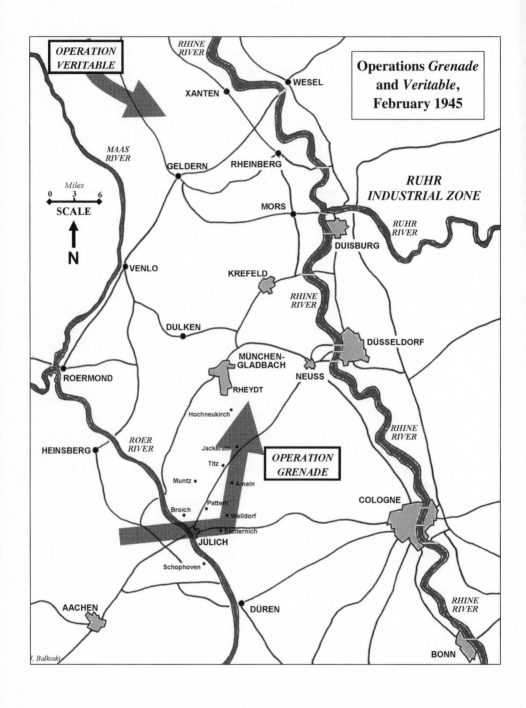

capabilities grow fewer," the summary began. "Today, Hitler's only real ones are the measures he can take to stave off the day of unconditional surrender. By a flat refusal to admit defeat, and by concentrating what remains of his resources on one front or the other, Hitler may be able to prolong the struggle, but he cannot overcome the irrefutable fact that each day Germany's position deteriorates in relation to the power of the Allies. . . . Defeated in December and January in the west, torn asunder in the east and now again in the west, Hitler's juggling of divisions has been lamentable. His timings, which at first may have appeared to be sound, now show themselves to be entirely faulty: time and the Allies wait for no man—not even Hitler." According to a thoroughly browbeaten attendee at a Führer conference in Berlin on January 24, Hitler bellowed: "In the future, anyone who tells anyone else that the war is lost will be treated as a traitor, with all the consequences for him and his family. I will take action without regard to rank and prestige!"

Although yielding any part of the *Heimat* (homeland) to the enemy was regrettable, German generals reasoned that a retreat behind the Rhine, one of the most formidable military barriers in western Europe, offered Hitler the most sensible means of staving off defeat. The general facing the nearly impossible challenge of holding back the Americans on the Roer, Gustav von Zangen of Fifteenth Army, noted mournfully in a postwar interrogation: "The German supreme command did not act according to military points of view. Judging by the state of defense, could the decision still be doubtful as to the point where the decisive battle should be accepted? At the Roer, with its very limited possibilities as an obstacle, with its unoccupied rear, with its ideal territory for armor operations on a large scale? Or at the Rhine, which as a massive obstacle, would have required a new [Allied] campaign for which there was still time to prepare an extraordinary defensive position—an obstacle that could have offset many of the weaknesses of the [German] troops and would have offered the possibility for real rehabilitation? Despite all protests, [Hitler's] decision remained: 'battle for the Roer until the last!'"

To von Zangen, the imminent fight was hardly fair. "The shoe pinched everywhere," he grumbled. "All divisions had gone through the 'Third Battle of Aachen' [in November 1944]. They had lost their best fighters in these severe battles and also experienced great losses in materiel. . . . The morale of the troops had, as expected, again suffered. The outward discipline of the exhausted soldier remained perfect. But the disappointment over the failure to succeed in combat, the non-appearance of new weapons, the non-fulfillment of other promises—air power, protection of the home territory, etc.—began to show its effects. Contrary to the brave efforts in former battles, it soon became evident that the old unified combat spirit no longer prevailed." The Allies did not fail to notice this dramatic deterioration in their opponents' competence: the very first sentence in Montgomery's January 21 field order to Simpson declared, "The enemy is in a bad way."

So bad, in fact, that a quick glance at Ninth Army's daily situation map on the eve of *Grenade* revealed only two understrength *Volksgrenadier* divisions, the 59th and 363rd, holding the line of the Roer at the point where Simpson intended to strike with virtually his entire army, which outnumbered the defenders by ten to one and by a much greater ratio in terms of artillery and air power. The 363rd's commander, *Generalleutnant* Dettling, reported that his division held a sixteen-mile front, which with his "meager strength" was far too lengthy to defend resolutely; the best he could do was to maintain "a line of security, or even a line of observation" on the Roer. That would hardly be sufficient to stop the imminent American onslaught, a situation Simpson well understood based on analysis of reports like the one filed in early February by the 29th Division's 116th Infantry: "Our combat patrols, while looking for opposition, found little or nothing in the way of resistance from the enemy in making their excursions into enemy lines." Dozens of similar reports triggered unusual optimism within Ninth Army. "It is considered that a quick breakthrough of the enemy's Roer River line, followed by the vigorous exploitation of every enemy weakness, could enable Ninth U.S. Army to accomplish its mission with rapidity," stated one field order. Even the enemy echoed that sentiment: "The corps operating on the Roer was certainly in no position to prevent the American advance to the Rhine," a German general later admitted.

In *Grenade* plans, Simpson cautioned his men to prepare for "the sudden appearance" of German panzer divisions that intelligence reports had hinted were positioned on the Cologne Plain in reserve. A German corps commander on the Roer front, however, noted that "counterthrusts require the best-trained and equipped troops, which were not available. Besides, the absence of our own air support made it doubtful that such a counterattack would have any chance of success altogether." Another German lamented that the few panzer units in reserve "had been split up so that they fought separately with several divisions," and therefore "the containment of an enemy penetration by a combined operation on division or corps level could not be undertaken."

General von Zangen's admission in January that "the time of the enemy attack can no longer be in the too distant future" prompted the distressing realization among every soldier in his army that they were about to be struck by an American tempest of unprecedented force. "The population near the front lines demonstrated their weariness and dwindling confidence in the German command more openly than the troops," von Zangen observed. "The flare-up of hope for a more favorable conclusion of the war that began with the commencement of the Ardennes operation had now yielded to a feeling of hopelessness."

Apparently von Zangen stood no chance against the mighty American host. Yet as of early February, one vital factor outweighed all of von Zangen's disadvantages, and that was the Roer River itself—more specifically the headwater dams thirty miles south of Jülich that in more peaceful times had generated power for the downriver settlements of the Roer valley. Coveted by the Americans since October but still under the Germans' undisputed control, the immense Urft and the even larger Schwammenauel dams represented a power far greater than any weapon in the Nazis' arsenal. Should the Germans use explosives to demolish both dams, a wall of water would gush downstream with a destructive force that would make the notorious 1889 Johnstown flood seem puny in comparison. For a distance of fifty miles north of the dams, the torrent would sweep away everything across a wide swath of the valley: trees, houses, bridges, animals, and people.

The Germans could of course only play that trump card once; if they did, the deluge would end some eight hours later, leaving behind immeasurable amounts of debris and a swollen river fifteen feet higher than normal and more than a mile wide in most places. But by the next day the river's current would return to its normal velocity, and several days after that the inundated fields beyond the Roer's natural banks would for the most part be drained, assuming heavy rains did not set in. If the Americans had not already crossed the Roer, or were not in the process of crossing, they could avoid the most destructive effects of the flash flood by following the advice of a top secret engineer report: "It is recommended that large bodies of troops and heavy equipment be kept above the 10-meter line." If the Americans' patience could hold for just a week, they would be able to launch a large-scale assault across the river confident in the knowledge that the enemy could no longer manipulate the dams. If the Americans had already crossed the Roer when the Germans destroyed the dams, however, those units occupying the far side of the river would face an acute crisis since their lines of supply would be severed. Indeed, those units close to or actually crossing the river would be directly caught in the flood wave with calamitous results.

The Germans had pondered a much more subtle means of manipulating the dams, a method they hoped would paralyze American offensive action across the river for weeks. According to that novel scheme, the Germans would leave the dams themselves alone, but would open their discharge valves while destroying the mechanisms for closing them. Water would thereby be expelled downriver at a steady rate for a period, some engineers estimated, of seventeen days, although the flow would not come close to matching the deluge of a flash flood. The Germans could also heighten that mighty discharge by demolishing a mountainside sluice gate controlling the water flow through a tunnel from the Urft reservoir into the Roer at a point just downriver from the Schwammenauel. As Ninth Army's official historian noted, "The water stored by the two reservoirs, reinforced by the substantial run-off of abnormal rain and snow, was a weapon of great value and [would be] extremely well employed by the German command." So well, in fact, that Operation *Grenade* would get nowhere unless Ninth Army's plan to assault across the Roer meticulously spelled out the Americans' optimal courses of action for every conceivable contingency associated with the upriver dams.

General Simpson would not have had to plan for any contingencies at all had the Royal Air Force's Bomber Command succeeded in destroying both the Schwammenauel and Urft dams by aerial attack in early December 1944, just as the squadron of Lancaster "Dambusters" had done in May 1943 to comparable dams in the Ruhr valley. Success would have triggered a flash flood down the Roer, but by February 1945 its effects would long since have dissipated and the Germans could no longer have wielded the dams as strategic trump cards. But Bomber Command's leader, Air Chief Marshal Sir Arthur Harris, did not have his heart in the endeavor: according to the U.S. official history of the campaign, Harris "objected to the project on the theory that irreplaceable personnel were being wasted in an effort foredoomed to failure." Eisenhower nevertheless insisted that the RAF make the attempt, but several tries failed to achieve results. As a U.S. First Army diarist recorded, the effort was a "dud," and no further bombing raids were made against the dams after December 11.

The scenario Eisenhower coveted most envisioned that First Army would seize control of the dams by a *coup de main* prior to *Grenade*'s jump-off date—before the enemy managed to destroy the dams or their discharge valves. By early February 1, 1945, however, the impracticability of that outcome was becoming more evident to Simpson by the day. Montgomery had originally directed Ninth Army to launch *Grenade* "at the earliest possible date after February 15," but to better support Monty's February 8 initiation of Operation *Veritable*, *Grenade*'s target date was moved up to February 10. The long-awaited attack by First Army's 78th Division to seize the Schwammenauel dam, however, did not even begin until February 5, only five days before Simpson's jump-off date. Even worse, although the dam was just over five miles distant from the 78th Division's front line, progress would certainly be slow not only due to severe weather and extraordinarily rough terrain, but also because the division must punch through the enemy's formidable *Westwall* fortifications to reach its objective.

Despite a U.S. Army historian's assertion that "until the [Schwammenauel] dam was in hand, the Ninth Army dared not cross the Roer," Simpson, an astute reader of military history and an apparent believer in Stonewall Jackson's pronouncement that generals should never take counsel of their fears, fully intended to launch his army across the Roer even if on *Grenade*'s start date the Germans controlled the dams. A Ninth Army directive in early February declared: "The probability that the Roer River dams may be in enemy hands at the time of crossing the Roer requires strong initial build-up east of the Roer River to insure self-sufficiency of the bridgehead during the possible flood period. Flooding can be expected to inundate all of the Roer River valley and to interrupt traffic for five or six days." If that self-sufficiency was strained by German counterattacks or particularly persistent floodwaters, food and ammunition could be provided by air drops and amphibious vehicles until the waters finally receded.

On February 6, the second day of the 78th Division's offensive to capture Schwammenauel dam, the man the Ninth Army headquarters diary referred to as "General Ike," accompanied by his West Point classmate, Omar Bradley, met with Simpson for a tour of the Roer front. The 78th had made impressive progress toward the dam on the fifth, but gained virtually no ground the next day: could it capture Schwammenauel before Simpson gave the go-ahead for *Grenade* on February 10? That and many other vital issues would be the discussion topics at a luncheon attended by Ike, Bradley, and Simpson at General Gillem's XIII Corps headquarters at Kerkrade, Holland. After lunch the three generals headed to another of Simpson's corps headquarters at nearby Sittard by following what a staff officer described as "a muddy detour road." The result was memorable. As related by that officer, "The sedan carrying Generals Eisenhower, Bradley, and Simpson became bogged down in the rutted, muddy road. A collection of stars was invoked to hoist it out, with Bradley and Simpson pushing like beavers, and Ike standing by directing the project."

The 78th Division's race to capture Schwammenauel before Simpson gave the word to commence *Grenade* was, as the Duke of Wellington said of Waterloo, "a near-run thing." As dawn broke on the fifth day of its offensive, February 9—less than twenty-fours before the 29th Division and other outfits were scheduled to assault across the Roer—the 78th was still separated from the dam by more than a mile of some of the toughest terrain in western Germany. And when they finally arrived at the dam, would the GIs all be swept away by a colossal wall of water if the enemy set off demolition charges inside the dam's gloomy tunnels? No one knew, but Hodges considered the mission so critical that he threw elements of the 82nd Airborne and 9th Infantry Divisions into the fight that morning.

Meanwhile, "Texas Bill" Simpson received some disquieting news at his Ninth Army command post at Maastricht just before he was unexpectedly obliged to host a visit and lunch with his immediate boss, Montgomery. Forward American outposts on the Roer were reporting that the river's depth had increased dramatically since dawn; on the 29th Division front the Roer was nearly seven feet deep—considerably deeper than in January, when 29ers had routinely patrolled to the enemy's side of the river simply by walking across waist- or chest-deep water. Moreover, the river flow had increased to more than nine feet per second, a sharp rise from the previous day. Finally, as Simpson observed to a subordinate, "I understand there is 80–100 feet extra width [of the river] in front of Charlie [Gerhardt]." Simpson knew the 78th Division was close to capturing Schwammenauel: had the enemy destroyed the dam, or just its discharge valves? Or perhaps the change had simply been triggered by the recent thaw and incessant rain. Whatever the cause, *Grenade* was set to go in twelve hours. If Simpson had to postpone the offensive, he must make that decision by nightfall on February 9.

At 3:00 P.M., Simpson polled his two chief underlings, Gillem of XIII Corps and McLain of XIX Corps, both of whom held the weighty responsibility of rupturing the German defenses starting at dawn on the tenth. Neither Gillem nor McLain could have attained his general's stars without displaying traits that were unwaveringly aggressive, and when Simpson phoned that day, they both exhibited those traits to their boss. "It is not too favorable, but we can make it," said Gillem; "I think we ought to go," declared McLain. Since at that moment the enemy still controlled Schwammenauel dam and could within a few hours send a mountain of water down the Roer, their confidence seemed misplaced. Happily, Simpson, who would shoulder the blame if *Grenade* got off to a calamitous start, maintained a much more rational view. He remarked to Gillem: "You know, that [at] nine feet per second—no patrols could operate. . . . We are right on the danger line, with the possibility of it getting worse. . . . We are going to postpone it twenty-four hours. Get the word around as fast as you can. . . . That is the decision." He later remarked that it "was a hard one to make," but by the next morning every soldier in Ninth Army knew it was the right thing to do, as the Roer's depth, width, and current surged to much more severe levels over the next twenty-four hours.

The reason for those changes in the river crystallized early on February 10, when engineers from the 78th Division finally drove the enemy from Schwammenauel and began their inspection of the dam. As the U.S. Army's official history of the campaign noted, "They expected at any moment to be blown to kingdom come" in a catastrophic explosion that brought down the entire dam, an event Hitler had ordered, but the German Fifth Panzer Army commander, General Hasso von Manteuffel, defiantly had disobeyed. Rather than triggering an immense flash flood, von Manteuffel had resolved to instigate a more persistent although much less severe gradual flood by ordering his men to open the discharge valves at both the Schwammenauel and Urft dams and then wreck the closing mechanisms.

Water gushes from a damaged outlet on one of the Roer River dams in February 1945. U.S. ARMY SIGNAL CORPS

So the Germans had finally done it, and by the following morning, February 10, even the aggressive McLain had to admit that a crossing was "impossible." A report from the Schwammenauel front shortly after midnight on the tenth indicated a "tremendous torrent rushing through spillway at F086274 [a map coordinate] at foot of the dam. . . . Surface of the river indicates a very rapid flow. . . . Dam remains intact." On the 29th Division front, the 115th Infantry's intelligence officer, Maj. William Bruning, observed: "I ordered the 3rd Battalion to send out some people to check on the river, which they did at 2300 hours [February 9] and couldn't even get to their [measuring] stake. They installed a new stake and returned at 2348 and found it had risen two inches. They went back again at 0013 [February 10] and found it had risen eleven inches, making a total rise of thirteen inches [in four hours]." So turbulent was the Roer, in fact, that the initial postponement of twenty-four hours envisioned by Simpson would obviously have to be extended.

Meanwhile, the GIs who had to carry out the cross-river assault remained in their spartan and waterlogged front-line dugouts, staring across the raging Roer, steeling themselves each morning for the order to get moving. That order must eventually come—but when?

Hurry up and wait . . .

NO SOAP ON THE PARTY

When the peculiar message, "No soap on the party," was received by a mystified clerk at the 29th Division war room at 4:50 P.M. on February 9, 1945, Gerhardt promptly ordered the word passed down the chain of command to every 29er: Operation *Grenade*, the momentous offensive that would carry the 29th Division to the Rhine River, was postponed. Fretful infantrymen who wondered whether they would survive the brass hats' latest idea would in all likelihood live to see a few more sunrises. Saturday, February 10, the day Gerhardt had imagined would long be remembered in World War II history books, was abruptly transformed into just another humdrum day on the Roer, little different from any of the others over the past two months except for the vital detail that the raging river separating the GIs from the enemy was two feet deeper and noticeably wider than it had been the night before. Crossing the river in either direction would be impossible for the foreseeable future, a point the relieved 29ers in the first assault waves could not fail to notice.

The 29th Division was about to play an entirely familiar role, one it had performed several times since the D-Day invasion, smack in the middle of an army-level offensive involving hundreds of thousands of GIs whose actions over the next few days would be detailed on countless front-page stories in stateside newspapers. Operation *Grenade*, however, would be different because if the brass's confidence was credible, it could be the 29th Division's last act of World War II. According to *Grenade*'s exhaustive plan book, the 29th—along with three other Ninth Army infantry divisions and two others from First Army shielding the Ninth's right flank—would spearhead the assault across the Roer, assisted by more than 2,000 artillery pieces, described by a staff officer as "the greatest barrage that the Army has yet put over a small area." On the 29th Division front, riflemen with modest skill in mathematics calculated gleefully that for every ten yards of front, they would be backed up by a single cannon, totaling more than 350 in support of the 29th alone. That would be a prop the 29ers had never experienced: even the pre-assault naval bombardment on D-Day would look puny in comparison.

After smashing through the Germans' Roer defenses, *Grenade* plans called for the 29th Division and most of the rest of Ninth Army, including three highly mobile armored divisions, to swing 90 degrees to the left and advance in a north-easterly direction toward the Rhine near Düsseldorf, aiming to join Monty's Twenty-First Army Group as Operation *Veritable* progressed southward. The First Army divisions supporting Simpson's right flank would simultaneously drive relentlessly eastward, striving to seize the historic Rhine city of Cologne. If the Americans pressed ahead rapidly, and if the enemy failed to organize a coherent defense short of the Rhine, Simpson might get lucky and seize intact one or more of the ten Rhine bridges in Ninth Army's sector. In that event, the end of the war could be even closer than Ike's optimists dared to dream.

The plan was undeniably bold; should it succeed, the Americans would achieve a breakthrough, followed by a breakout, on a more impressive scale than last summer's Operation *Cobra* in Normandy. Even better, the flat Rhineland landscape, with its notable network of modern roadways, would be a much more suitable place than the constrictive Norman *bocage* for the Americans' highly mechanized army to practice blitzkrieg on a level that would even impress its German inventors. To enhance its chance of success, the 29th Division and all other outfits involved in *Grenade*'s initial punch must master that cardinal principle of military science—concentration of force. On February 4, Simpson had reassigned the 29th from Gillem's XIII Corps back to the organization to which the division had belonged in all the major battles it had fought since September, McLain's XIX Corps. (Gerhardt did not view that development favorably, as he and McLain maintained a much frostier relationship than the warm rapport he had with Gillem.) On February 10, Gillem's and McLain's two corps, consisting of nearly 200,000 men, were jammed into a frontage of only fifteen miles, little more than the 29th Division alone had covered for most of December and all of January. By that same date, Gerhardt's sector had been narrowed to under four miles, with the equally compressed 102nd Division on his left and his longtime battle partner dating back to Normandy, the 30th Division, on his right.

Simpson studied military history keenly and modeled his generalship not only on the notable warrior he had learned of in his West Point history classes, Robert E. Lee, but also on Edmund Allenby, the dynamic British cavalryman who had carried out a highly successful campaign in the Middle East against the Turks in the closing months of World War I. According to Simpson, Allenby "didn't devil his staff to death. He laid down the general policy he wanted to follow and gave them all the instructions they needed, and then let them go ahead and do it without sitting on top of them and trying to do it all himself like a lot of commanders do or have done. Lee also did that. . . . He only intervened when it was necessary. I suppose there are lots of times when some commanders look over a fellow's shoulder too damn much."

Simpson rarely deviated from that policy; in *Grenade* he never interfered with his two corps and eleven division commanders, including Gerhardt, in the planning process for the Roer crossing and the subsequent exploitation to the Rhine. Although pep talks were not a strong component of Simpson's repertoire, he visited the 115th Infantry's command post in Aldenhoven on February 8 to meet with Gerhardt and his regimental commanders and emphasize the significance of the upcoming offensive. Gerhardt's minions, a Simpson aide related, "showed themselves thoroughly prepared for the operation, confident and sure of success. . . . Captured prisoners seemed to confirm the fact that only light opposition might be expected at the initial crossings. The extensive entrenchments overlooking the east river bank were still an unknown factor. Heavy fighting was to be expected when [German] counterattacking reserves were thrown in." Simpson emerged from this meeting the recipient of a beneficial reverse pep talk courtesy of Charlie Gerhardt: "I was impressed with his cheerful and confident manner and attitude, so much so that later on, whenever I myself felt blue or downcast or doubtful, I made it a point to visit General Gerhardt knowing that his cheerful, confident air and determined outlook would cheer me up tremendously, with the result that I always left him refreshed."

One of those highly competent subordinates whom Simpson knew would carry out his orders faithfully was Col. Richard Nicholas, Ninth Army's chief engineer. The fifty-four-year-old Nicholas, who graduated fourth in the West Point class of 1913, was the first member of Simpson's staff to discern that the enemy would rely on manipulation of the Roer dams' discharge valves rather than outright demolition to impede the Americans' inevitable assault across the river. In the aftermath of the 78th Division's capture of Schwammenauel dam on February 9, Simpson and Nicholas conferred to review the data on the depth, width, and current of the Roer, and although the general harbored some hope that he could initiate *Grenade* within the week, Nicholas calculated that the river's status would change little until the upstream dams emptied nearly all the vast amounts of water stored in their reservoirs. If Nicholas's estimate was correct, the river would return to its normal placid status no earlier than February 24, and the saturated ground on either side of the Roer would not dry out until long after that. Later events proved, as Simpson asserted, "He hit it right on the nail."

The men of the 29th Division must stand down, in all probability for more than two weeks. "Morale was at a high peak," a member of the 115th Infantry commented, "and the officers and men, thoroughly briefed as to their job, were ready to go ahead and complete it. . . . The men felt that they could accomplish almost anything. The postponement caused a lowering of that spirit, and any coming attack was an anticlimax." Nevertheless, if practice makes perfect, the postponement provided the 29th Division the opportunity to come as close to perfection as a U.S. Army outfit possibly could. Gerhardt's infantrymen got even more used to lugging their 410-pound flat-bottomed assault boats across the sodden terrain, clambering in—a twelve-man rifle squad and three engineers per boat—and paddling furiously across a diminutive waterway or pond somewhere behind the front before clambering out again. Gerhardt even trucked as many of his infantry battalions as he could over thirty miles of rutted roads back to Visé, Belgium, where the nearby Meuse River's width and swift current closely matched the existing conditions of the Roer.

Once more, 29th Division artillerymen pored over fire plans, the most comprehensive they had compiled so far in the war. To stockpile ammunition for the big push, Brig. Gen. William Sands, Gerhardt's top artillerist, ordered his gunners "to shoot only necessary registrations." The 110th Field Artillery's historian observed: "For the first time in the war, the batteries had practically no firing assignments, and each was maintained only by a small stand-by crew at the guns. One by one the cannoneers took the howitzers out of action for a complete overhaul and repainting." Uncle Charlie always insisted that his men and vehicles must look their best, even in battle, a practice that the 110th adhered to during the postponement: "To insure spic and span condition for all vehicles making the historic river crossing, Sgt. Leroy A. Morris set up his high-pressure washing service at the bridge over the tiny Merz River in front of Merzenhausen." Holbrook Bradley noted in a *Baltimore Sun* article that the artillerymen "have taken advantage of everything available to make living conditions the best possible under the circumstances. Most of the crews by now have dugouts that are fairly comfortable. Sunk shoulder-deep or more in the ground, they are either straw- or wood-lined, roofed over with heavy timbers, boards, and thick layers of dirt or sod. . . . Some of the more industrious members of the sections have taken furniture from the nearby houses and now boast innerspring mattresses, lighting, and even radios. Coal from the cellars of the surrounding villages insures adequate heat and keeps the dugouts dry. . . . [Howitzers] poke their barrels skyward from tightly stretched camouflage nets scattered through the muddy battle-littered fields. There is little sound of combat other than the constant roar of Allied fighter-bombers overhead and the distant roll of cannonading to the north."

No 29th Division unit had more diverse and complex responsibilities for the upcoming offensive than the 121st Engineer Combat Battalion, and the unexpected two-week delay proved a blessing for those overworked sappers on whom the infantrymen wholly depended once Simpson uttered the word "go." The 121st had undergone a change of command on January 25, but its veteran sappers wondered how the new man, Lt. Col. Raleigh Powell, could possibly fill the shoes of the esteemed Lt. Col. Robert Ploger, who had taken over the battalion in the fall of 1943 and quickly transformed it into one of Gerhardt's most efficient outfits. Now Ploger was on his way to the Pentagon to serve at a desk job under General Marshall, and Powell—who just three years in the past had entered active service as a lowly lieutenant—would be tested by a situation just as challenging as Omaha Beach and poles apart from conventional schoolbook solutions at the U.S. Army engineer course at Fort Belvoir. Described by a reporter as "aggressive and genial," Powell would meet those challenges with the consummate skill of a veteran.

In addition to enhancing the infantrymen's skill with assault boats, the engineers' principal challenge, as the 121st's February action report noted, was "maintenance of roads in the division area necessitated by the early heavy thaw. Where formerly had been hard dirt roads there now existed mucky morasses, which required the full employment of all companies of this unit. . . . Company B furnished a detail to demolish buildings and brick walls in the partially destroyed town of Aldenhoven. The purpose was the supply of rubble for road maintenance."

Powell also had to gather vast amounts of equipment near preselected bridge sites, where his men must hastily begin to erect footbridges and much more complex pontoon bridges over the Roer within minutes of *Grenade*'s jump-off. That preparation involved the hazardous job of clearing hundreds of enemy mines still lingering on the American side of the Roer, as well as the thoroughly depressing task of removing newly discovered American and German corpses still scattered in the fields after the heavy fighting in December. "All of this clearance had to be done during darkness because of the close proximity of the enemy," the 121st's report observed. "Discontinuance of work at times was caused by enemy harassing fire."

The danger of that sort of work was proved just after dark on February 18 when twenty-three-year-old Sgt. Salvatore Pisani, a New Yorker, was helping to remove a body near the bridge site at Hasenfeld *Gut* when he set off a mine. "We lost [Pisani] on a *Schu* mine at the *Gut*," a sapper reported to the war room. "The mine went off in his face. It looked as though the Germans had put more mines around the bodies after they were hit." Pisani survived but never returned to the outfit. (The *Schu* mine reference was probably in error; the enemy's much more devious *Schrapnellmine*, known to the 29ers as a "Bouncing Betty" because it popped five feet out of the ground before detonating, was the more likely culprit.) Two days later, the 29th Division lost another GI when 1st Lt. Roy Parkinson, who in August had joined the 175th Infantry's 3rd Battalion Headquarters Company in Normandy, wandered into an uncleared patch of ground near the Roer and was killed by stepping on a mine—the first battle casualty in the company in fifty-four days. When Gerhardt learned of Parkinson's death, he phoned the 175th's command post and pronounced, "Let's get some accurate daylight reconnaissance and get that [area] taped off."

Throughout the 29th Division's late-autumn offensive, which had brought the division to its current stance on the Roer, the 29ers' customary search for high ground on the battlefield had been stymied for the obvious reason that the Rhineland terrain over which much of the battle was fought was as flat as a pool table. Accordingly, both sides' artillery observers struggled mightily to gain dominant observation of their opponents; on the rare occasions when they succeeded in doing so, they gained it not by seizing elevated terrain but by utilizing battered church steeples and scattered coal-slag piles. That situation changed, however, when the 29th reached the Roer, and this time the advantage was entirely with the enemy. In the zone where the 29th intended to cross the river, between Jülich and Broich, the German-held terrain on the far side of the Roer rose sharply, forming a two-mile-long ridge 800 yards east of the river. In daylight and good weather, enemy troops atop that ridge, 120 feet higher than their opponents, could observe American movements with clarity on the Roer's west side. Indeed, a road junction near Koslar through which processions of American GIs and vehicles regularly traveled on their way to or from the riverfront was such a tempting target for German mortars and artillery that 29ers came to dread passing through that intersection anytime between dawn and dusk.

Powell came up with a remarkably innovative solution to the problem. He suggested that during the hours of darkness his sappers could construct a massive canopy of camouflage netting over the vulnerable junction and all its adjoining roads, thereby depriving enemy observers of their formerly clear sightline and alleviating the lethality of German mortar and artillery fire. Gerhardt enthusiastically supported the scheme, and in four consecutive nights of strenuous work, Company A sappers completed it. According to the 121st's February 1945 action report, "A total of 750 yards of screening was erected, and proved its worth by reducing enemy observed fire to simple interdictory fire."

On February 12—Abraham Lincoln's birthday—Montgomery, Simpson, and McLain traveled in a long caravan of U.S. Army jeeps from Ninth Army headquarters in Maastricht to the 29th Division's command post at Siersdorf Castle. A "drenching downpour" forced the drivers to raise the jeeps' olive-drab canvas rain hoods—a practice strictly forbidden in the 29th Division—and caused the road to turn into "a quagmire." In a courtyard facing the castle, a group of about one hundred stalwart 29ers, impeccably dressed in their below-the-knee GI woolen overcoats and deployed in a neat three-sided formation, greeted the brass as the jeep caravan roared up shortly before noon. All eyes were on Monty as the diminutive field marshal, "attired in his familiar jaunty black beret [and] a camouflaged parachutist's jacket," leaped nimbly out of the jeep to accept and return Gerhardt's salute.

Gerhardt had timed a 175th Infantry awards ceremony for the VIPs' arrival, and presently eyes shifted from Monty to a solitary 29er standing at attention in the center of the square, a twenty-year-old Georgian named 2nd Lt. Paul Musick from Company C. Musick, described as "a Georgia cracker if you ever saw one," had recently gained a battlefield commission and was about to be recognized for his November 26 heroics at Bourheim, Germany, by receiving only the thirtieth Distinguished Service Cross awarded within the 29th Division since its initiation to combat on D-Day. Simpson pinned the medal on Musick as Gerhardt beamed.

Second Lt. Paul Musick of the 175th Infantry wearing the Distinguished Service Cross presented to him at Siersdorf Castle on February 12, 1945.

Monty had only recently launched *Veritable*, but four days of hard fighting in the Reichswald forest and the flooded lowlands adjacent to the Rhine and Waal Rivers had failed to crack the enemy defenses and had resulted in what Ike would label "a bitter slugging match." Even worse, Montgomery had envisioned *Veritable* and *Grenade* as a devastating one-two knockout punch, but *Grenade*'s postponement had changed everything, allowing the enemy to concentrate mobile reserves against the narrow zone where British and Canadian troops were attacking. If those events troubled Monty, however, he did not show it. After the medal ceremony, the legendary field marshal conversed with the young second lieutenant for a minute or two despite the pouring rain. Monty, along with his flock of American general officers, soon repaired to the basement of Siersdorf Castle for an elaborate meal courtesy of the 29th Division, served, as a Ninth Army officer noted, "in the luxury of white linen table cloths, sparkling silver service, and fine china. In an excellent mood and talkative, the field marshal apparently enjoyed the fine luncheon greatly."

That night, the startling onset of an intense German bombardment, which dropped more than fifty deafening artillery shells in just a few minutes, profoundly shocked the 29ers occupying positions in and around Aldenhoven, just a few miles east of Siersdorf Castle. Ewing's Company G had occupied a reserve position just outside that village for more than two weeks and had grown complacent: since New Year's Day, only one company member had been wounded, Pvt. Cecil McGriff on January 9. (Another, 2nd Lt. St. Clair Walker, had been killed in the unfortunate friendly-fire incident on January 1.) True, a few miscreants had gone AWOL, and one had been arrested due to a self-inflicted wound, but overall Company G had been impacted only marginally by enemy action for nearly two months. Happily, the enemy's abrupt bombardment of Aldenhoven caused no casualties, but it did shake the 29ers' nerves. Company G's lighthearted newsletter, *The Chin Strap* ("The Only Newspaper Published on the Front Lines"), noted with alarm that the enemy shelling "seriously threatened George Company's recently opened five-hole, roof-covered streamlined latrine . . . the most elegant in the regiment." However, the anonymous writer commented with relief that the "modern frame crapper" remained intact "only because of the excellence of the material and workmanship. . . . Early morning visitors at the five-holer, apprehensive as to its fate in the night's shelling, saw it standing proudly in the murky dawn—all five holes still there, ready to serve our fighting men another day."

For the tense 29ers at the front, the overriding question remained: when would Simpson initiate *Grenade*? At 6:11 P.M. on February 17, McLain informed Gerhardt, "It won't be long." He was wrong: Ninth Army's chief of staff, Brig. Gen. James Moore, noted that Colonel Nicholas "was the key," adding, "I used to have him in the office about five times a day. He had observers all along the river checking the flow of the water, to determine when we could make a crossing." Every day, harried Ninth Army planners pored over Nicholas's latest reports from the riverfront so they could advise the army commander on the optimal day to launch the attack. Not until a staff conference at 2:00 P.M. on February 21 did Ninth Army's journal report, "Predictions look very promising." Thirty minutes later Montgomery arrived at the command post by air and conferred alone with Simpson. The two agreed that *Grenade* would commence "at 0330 on the twenty-third of February." That was one day prior to Nicholas's prophecy that the Roer would finally subside, but as Moore related, "We deliberately decided we'd take a few losses on the crossing if we could get surprise—which we did. I think we saved quite a lot of lives by doing it that way. . . . [The Germans] knew we were going to come, but thought the following day [February 24]. We did get across and surprise them."

As Ninth Army's diary noted, however, "The river banks themselves, where the approaches to the bridges must be constructed, appear to be the worst problem still confronting the army, as they are soft and wet after being weeks under water, and they will require a great amount of engineer work to make them useable."

NERVOUS EXCITEMENT

No 29er would ever think of his long wait for Operation *Grenade* as uneventful. That the Germans still had much life left in them became evident on the morning of February 15, when a stream of enemy V-1 rockets—six or seven, by Gerhardt's count—passed low over the 29th Division's lines to unknown targets behind the Allies' front, emitting the distinctive reverberation—a sound like intense radio static—to which the 29ers had grown accustomed since autumn. The GIs, however, had never before seen the doodlebugs come over the lines at such a rapid-fire clip; it was not a cheery thought to contemplate that in a matter

of minutes, a lot of people would be killed or injured by the V-1s' 2,000-pound
warheads. That morning Gerhardt somewhat insensitively remarked to Colonel
Bingham, "Just as long as they keep on going, it will be all right." Where they
were going in all likelihood was Antwerp, 100 miles to the northwest, the Belgian
port city on which the Allies' massive logistical effort on the Western Front thoroughly depended, so heavily that Hitler's primary goal in the recent Ardennes
offensive had been to capture it. Antwerp, a place *Time* magazine would soon
label "The City of Sudden Death," was currently undergoing its worst pounding
of the war: more than one-third of the 628 V-1s that impacted in the city fell during the month of February 1945.

When calamity struck the 175th Infantry on February 19, Gerhardt surely
speculated on the validity of the old adage that no one in a military outfit should
be irreplaceable. Col. Bill Purnell had been a member of the regiment since 1924
and had commanded it proficiently for the last six months; the general recognized
that despite Purnell's field grade rank and prewar career as a Harvard–trained
lawyer, he was anything but a desk solider. Indeed, no one in the 29th Division
had gained more medals than the forty-one-year-old Purnell: two Silver Stars and
six Bronze Stars in eight months. On the afternoon of the nineteenth, Purnell traveled down to the outpost line on the Roer with his driver, T/4 Paul Powell, to
adjust mortar fire against some pesky German targets on the river's far side.
Army policy did not recommend that colonels in command of 3,100-man regiments carry out that sort of work, but 175th soldiers had grown used to seeing
Purnell at the front, chatting amicably with the enlisted men—particularly the
old-timers of the prewar Maryland National Guard—and peering intently with
binoculars at the enemy lines. Purnell's luck, however, ran out that day. "Just one
[German] round came in and killed his driver and wounded him in the ankle, but-
tocks, and cheek," Gerhardt reported to McLain. "Nothing serious, but they estimate at the clearing station that he will be out for about two months." The
twenty-five-year-old Powell was a dyed-in-the-wool Baltimorean; in March 1939
he had walked just a few blocks from his home in a working-class neighborhood
to the majestic Fifth Regiment Armory, signing up with the proud Maryland
Guard outfit in which he would serve for six years until his death in a dismal corner of Germany, loyally serving his commander to the last.

Purnell was as close to irreplaceable as any man in the 29th Division. In a
conversation with McLain on the nineteenth, Gerhardt recommended a West
Point comrade and fellow cavalryman, Lt. Col. Alexander George, for the job.
George was currently in the replacement pipeline and had just recuperated from
a serious eye wound he had suffered on June 17, 1944, during his two-day spell
as the 175th's commander in the regiment's epic struggle on Hill 108—"Purple
Heart Hill"—in Normandy. George had also led a battalion of the 132nd Infantry

on Guadalcanal, but according to a credible story known to only a few, had been relieved on February 7, 1943, due to a self-inflicted wound. George would clearly not do; for the moment, Lt. Col. Arthur Sheppe, the 175th's executive, filled Purnell's slot. Replacing the irreplaceable would be a challenge, but Simpson had to try; the next day he decided on an outsider, forty-two-year-old Col. Harry McHugh, who had recently recovered from a September 1944 wound suffered in Lorraine when commanding the 318th Infantry, a component of the 80th Infantry Division of Patton's Third Army. Gerhardt ordinarily would have frowned upon a replacement drawn from outside the 29th Division family, but in this instance the pinch-hitter was a fellow West Pointer, class of 1924, with plenty of combat experience.

Powell's death and Purnell's wound from a seemingly random German shell highlighted the fatalistic attitude currently shared by many 29ers. That impalpable attribute known as luck determined your fate, they said; there was no way to tell who had it and who didn't, so why worry? How many times had jinxed GIs died from a direct hit on an ostensibly safe foxhole, while others standing in the open during enemy bombardments were untouched? A tragedy suffered by the 29th Division after dark on February 21 did not help to dispel that irrational notion. A platoon of the 115th Infantry's Antitank Company, bivouacked well over a mile behind the front, was resting amid the relatively luxurious comfort of a decrepit Koslar row house cellar when a Luftwaffe bomber came over and dropped two 500-pound bombs on the village. One scored a direct hit on the edifice occupied by the platoon, instantly killing four members and wounding eleven more— roughly 10 percent of the company. The four unlucky ones were T/5 Glenn Bridges, PFC Robert Arrington, PFC Dayton Davis, and PFC Irving De Shong. Their numbers had come up, and they would be sorely missed—but as every 29er well understood, the Army would hold no wakes for those poor unfortunate souls.

The 29ers continued to monitor the Roer like a doctor gauging the recovery of a patient. Front-line troops armed with upright measuring sticks crept down to the riverbank hourly to check the water level, while comrades heaved empty ration cans into the gushing stream to judge its current. One detail was certain, as Bradley noted to his *Baltimore Sun* readers: "There is a touch of spring in the air." Bradley went on to observe on a visit to the front that 29ers "took a moment out for the first time to relax in the warm sunlight and air their bedding or dry their clothing in the mild breezes. A couple of the more hearty GIs even tried sunbathing in a protected lea. . . . The ground has begun to dry up again, and the mud is disappearing from the streets." Bradley, never one to flinch from visiting the front, made it as far as the forwardmost observation post east of Barmen, occupied by the 29th Cavalry Reconnaissance Troop, and wrote: "From the sandbagged CP, where Pvt. Raye Almond of Chicago stood guard, we could survey the ground to the river and see the water spreading back more than a quarter of a mile at a spot normally yards, or slightly more, in width. There was no visible sign of the enemy."

Indeed, in the imminent offensive, Gerhardt feared the Roer River more than he did the German Army. Two months' worth of patrol reports indicated that enemy troops and defenses on the far side of the Roer did not amount to much. The most challenging part of the operation would be getting large bodies of GIs, their heavy equipment, and vehicles over the swollen river, and given Simpson's decision to attack on February 23—one day before the Roer's supposed subsidence to normal levels—the 29th Division must choreograph its movements as meticulously as Red Blaik's renowned West Point football team. In addition, Gerhardt could display no subtlety in his attack; planners understood that the coming offensive was a frontal assault, pure and simple, a major part of which would be made directly against Jülich, a stout fortress-city since Roman and Frankish times.

Overwhelming firepower, concentration of force, and swift maneuver, Gerhardt correctly surmised, would be the keys to victory. On February 23 the 29th Division would attack on a constricted front of only 2,100 yards—little more than a mile—which in the not-too-distant past had been covered by only a single 800-man infantry battalion. The 175th Infantry, on the right, would carry the division's main effort by assaulting across the Roer on slender footbridges directly into Jülich. The 115th Infantry, on the left, would cross the Roer in diminutive twelve-man plywood assault boats, aiming to capture the village of Broich and seize the dominating ridge beyond. The 116th Infantry would be held in reserve, but would commit a single battalion to follow the 175th into Jülich and capture the ancient Citadel in the heart of the devastated city. The offensive would be preceded by a barrage only forty-five minutes in duration, but one the divisional history would later define as "the most intense of the entire war" in 29th Division annals, provided by hundreds of artillery pieces, tank and tank destroyer cannon, mortars, and even .50-caliber machine guns, all tightly packed into the 29th's front.

Gerhardt would not repeat the grievous miscalculation he had made on November 16, 1944, when he initiated the 29th Division's role in Ninth Army's massive late-fall Rhineland offensive by committing only two infantry battalions to the assault while holding seven in reserve. That blunder had triggered McLain's wrath and, much worse, utterly failed to crack the German defenses. In sharp contrast, Gerhardt intended to reverse the ratio in the February 23 attack by committing seven battalions to the initial push over the Roer and holding two in reserve. Never again would Gerhardt be accused of underutilizing his division's massive combat power.

That power, according to Gerhardt's intelligence officers, should greatly overmatch the enemy. "At Jülich, the Germans had an outpost line along the river edge, a main line of resistance along the ridge line north of the city, and a secondary defense line of trenches behind the town extending in depth to the east," wrote Maj. Bob Minor of the 29th's G-2 section in his February 1945 monthly report. "The line at Jülich was held by the 5th Company of the 1036th Grenadier Regiment, 59th Infantry Division, north of Broich; and by the 1st and 2nd Battalions of the 959th Regiment, 363rd *Volksgrenadier* Division—one battalion in Broich and along the riverbank to the northern outskirts of Jülich; the other in Jülich proper." The enemy units were known to be shells of their former selves; still, the 29ers had learned in the past that even understrength German infantry outfits could hold up the Americans for days. However, the 363rd *Volksgrenadier* Division's *Generalleutnant* Dettling expressed the opinion that his grenadiers could not be expected to hold for long. "The division was occupying a sector that was still too broad compared to its fighting strength for it to be able to repel a large-scale attack with certainty," he wrote. "The troops, particularly the infantry, were now under strain after being steadily engaged for weeks in bad weather, in an inadequately built position, disappointed as they were by the failure of the Ardennes offensive. The ammunition supply of the artillery in no way corresponded with the requirements of a large-scale engagement."

Last-minute changes to plans as ambitious as *Grenade*'s could be expected to throw a proverbial monkey wrench in the 29th Division's well-oiled machine. But less than thirty-six hours before the division was to launch its assault, Gerhardt initiated two significant modifications that all 29ers welcomed wholeheartedly. First, the general attached a platoon of Sherman flamethrower tanks to the 175th Infantry; these were drawn from the 739th Tank Battalion, a special outfit equipped with not only flamethrowers but also innovative mine-clearing tanks and tank dozers, all considered so valuable in the upcoming operation that Simpson had split the battalion and attached its companies to each of Ninth Army's three component corps. The 29ers had witnessed the high value of flamethrowing tanks at the siege of Brest, when British Crocodiles had spurted their deadly flame-jets against the walls of Fort Montbarey, held by obstinate enemy paratroopers. Gerhardt suspected that Jülich's Citadel would be defended equally stubbornly.

Even more important additions to the 29th Division's repertoire were seven LVT-4 (Landing Vehicle, Tracked) "Alligators"—also known as "Buffalos"—operated by the 234th Engineer Combat Battalion, which Gerhardt had snatched the moment McLain noted their availability. Although these impressive amphibious landing vehicles had been in use in the Pacific since Guadalcanal, the 29ers had never before seen them in action. A nearly nine-ton LVT made twenty-five miles per hour on land, seven on water, and carried up to forty troops under the protection of steel armor. An Alligator could cross the Roer loaded with its occupants much more efficiently than a twelve-man plywood boat powered by oars, and in the coming operation the 115th Infantry intended to employ those cutting-edge contraptions to the greatest extent possible.

So it had come at last. For the first time in seventy-seven days, the 29th Division would attack—not an ordinary attack, like the countless ones the 29th had carried out since D-Day, but a supreme effort by the entire Ninth Army, dwarfing anything in the division's history except for the Omaha Beach invasion and carried out by a well-rested outfit whose efficiency and morale had climbed immeasurably since the dark days of November.

On the eve of battle, an aide noted that Simpson "was too restless to remain long in his office and took off for the front to escape his own thoughts by talking to the corps commanders." When Simpson returned to his command post at Maastricht, the aide observed, "[He] seemed greatly quieted, admittedly by the confidence radiated by the corps and division commanders who will actually make the assault operation." That night Simpson and his aides relaxed, watching Hollywood's biggest 1944 blockbuster, *Going My Way* with Bing Crosby, a film that three weeks later would win an Academy Award for best motion picture. The headquarters diary concluded: "A nightcap, toasting luck on the next day, and the general was off to bed."

No man in the 29th Division would get a good sleep that night. Assault infantrymen, freshly satiated by the hot meal the Army habitually served prior to a big push, donned their cumbersome woolen overcoats and, as a participant remarked, "carried combat packs, one-day K-rations, three D-bars [a dense emergency chocolate ration], four extra pairs of socks, full ammunition belts, and primacord for blowing paths in minefields and barbed wire." Then they plodded down to assembly points, as close as fifty yards from the Roer, and took refuge in cellars or the subterranean tunnels—known as "The Catacombs" to the 29ers—of the old Napoleonic–era fort on the river's west bank opposite Jülich. "The soft tread and shuffle of this slow approach were silent. The night was still—a rifle shot, a flare, a burp gun, or a BAR firing at sounds or shadows on the outpost line," a 175th soldier remembered. "That was all. No artillery. No mortars. No killing machine gun fire. Nothing. The Germans were apparently deaf to the approach and showed no reaction at all until men began stumbling over garbage cans and tripping over chicken wire in the wet backyards of houses on the west riverbank." Then the 29ers waited: "In their nervous excitement, they talked volubly at first, but then dozed and fell asleep in a tangle of arms and legs, rifles and ammunition boxes. Flickering candlelight shook shadows across these sleeping forms—a weird scene of soldiers waiting for battle."

Thousands of engineers were busy too, hauling their immense piles of bridging equipment down to the river in lengthy truck columns, which barely squeezed through the narrow roads heading toward the Roer. "The large number of troops involved and the necessary movement of engineer vehicles made a certain amount of noise unavoidable," the 29th Division February 1945 summary of operations observed, "but the enemy, from his position on the east bank, showed no reaction at all." An engineer action report noted: "The bridge trains started to roll at 1900 hours on February 22 into their respective assembly areas. Advantage was taken of every possible concealment of these trains. Sixty-yard interval was strictly adhered to, but the size of the trains precluded the possibility of complete concealment. At 10:00 P.M. on February 22, all bridge trains were in their respective assembly areas, ready for the operation. Anxious moments were spent in anticipation that enemy air strikes of the previous night might be repeated, and an enemy plane might drop a flare at a point which would disclose the entire plan and later subject the bridge trains to heavy bombing attacks." Much to the sappers' relief, the Luftwaffe did not make an appearance. Meanwhile, the members of the 83rd Chemical Smoke Generating Company stood ready on the banks of the Roer for the word to fire up their machines and begin spewing a massive vaporous haze along the river to conceal their infantry and engineer brethren from enemy fire once dawn broke.

No German response at all. Still, the enemy could not fail to perceive what was about to occur. On no previous night in recent memory could the sounds of their opponents' growling truck engines, their squealing tank bogie wheels, and even clanging mess tins and human voices be picked up so plainly. The Americans were up to something, for sure—yet the Germans could do nothing to stop it.

The shoe indeed pinched everywhere.

SORRY IT IS SO MESSED UP

In his postwar memoir, *Crusade in Europe*, Ike recalled the electrifying portent of the moment, noting that "the mounting difficulties of the German war machine" hinted "that one more great campaign" would finally bring victory to the Allies. Every 29er suspected he was right, and for Gerhardt and the 29th Division, the final act would begin shortly after midnight on February 23, 1945, a night the divisional action report described as "clear with a bright moon." At precisely 2:45 A.M. an audiovisual display the likes of which the 29ers had never before experienced abruptly transformed a tranquil darkness into an infernal maelstrom, the kind of overpowering warfare the U.S. Army had trained for years to inflict upon the hapless enemy but had almost never put into practice at such an immense level.

The concussive drumbeat of cannon fire from behind the front was accompanied by the dancing light of nonstop muzzle flashes, a remarkable spectacle of
firepower that reassured 29th Division infantrymen, waiting fretfully to advance
across the Roer, far more effectively than pep talks by company top kicks or even
Uncle Charlie or Texas Bill Simpson. American shells were bursting on the far
side of the river with the rapidity of machine-gun fire, and the dull reverberations
of those distant blasts drifted back over American lines like peals of thunder in a
summer tempest rolling over the Kansas prairie. Front-line dogfaces could hardly
imagine how anyone could live under such a hail of steel. "The whole riverbank
and land east of the river was a sheet of fire," noted the commander of the 115th
Infantry's Company I, 1st Lt. Mark Hogan, who had joined the 29th Division in
Normandy and suffered two wounds since. "The noise was deafening. We were
within 100 yards of the edge of the impact area for ten minutes. . . . There were a
few short rounds, and one of our men was injured by a shell fragment. There was
no fire coming from the German side. A platoon of American medium tanks was
drawn up along the river south of us, firing machine guns into the east bank."
According to Ninth Army's postwar history, the massive bombardment
smothered the enemy "with an average of nearly two and a half projectiles per
yard of front." Assuming they survived to see another sunset, all 29ers knew that
the images of this night would be seared into their psyches forever.

The skilled artillerymen of the 29th Division had never before been able to
practice their craft with such prodigious quantities of ammunition, which for the
first time in a major offensive included a copious supply of cutting-edge Pozit
proximity fuzes. The U.S. Army's highly scientific gunnery manual had been written for scenarios like this, and the fervent gunners proceeded to carry out their mission with the methodical procedures prescribed by the book. "Against buildings
and strongpoints the cannoneers used delay and percussion fuzes, and to force the
Germans to keep down while the infantry advanced, they fired time and Pozit air
burst fuzes over open entrenchments," wrote Purley Cooper, the 110th Field
Artillery's CO. Cooper added that his men sometimes fired howitzer volleys with
a fuze mixture, "in which a first volley of shells with Pozit fuzes burst in the air to
obtain maximum surprise and effect against troops caught in the open, a second
volley fitted with percussion or contact fuzes caught the enemy on the ground as
he crawled for cover, and a third volley with delay fuzes allowed the shells to dig
in and destroy the cover—all concentrated in fifteen seconds or less on the same
area." Cooper concluded: "The shoot was by far the biggest in which the 110th
participated during the war. . . . The enemy response was practically nil."

Would German resistance remain feeble when the 29ers commenced the
Roer crossing? The 175th Infantry would be the first of Gerhardt's units to ascer-
tain the answer to that question when its leading wave traversed the river opposite

Jülich. The assault plan specified that the 175th would cross the swollen waterway on three flimsy floating footbridges built by XIX Corps's 246th Engineer Combat Battalion, whose members would proceed down to the river to initiate their arduous work in darkness, even before the furious American artillery barrage of the far bank lifted. The job required the sappers at each bridge site to extend a flexible steel wire across the Roer—about 300 feet—and anchor those cables not only on the American riverbank, but also on the enemy side. To safeguard the engineers, the 175th must therefore send a few boatloads of troops across the Roer at 3:00 A.M., a half hour before *Grenade*'s scheduled jump-off time of 3:30, to establish footholds on the river's far side. They would have to paddle across the surging river in pitch darkness, fighting a current of six miles per hour, and disembark on enemy turf known to be heavily mined; should the enemy detect their maneuver, they would face withering machine-gun, mortar, and artillery fire. If any task in World War II was the equivalent of the "forlorn hope" in bygone days of siege warfare, in which a small body of volunteers would lead a charge into the breach of a fortress, this was it.

The one-mile stretch of the Roer opposite Jülich covered by the 175th Infantry was the only portion of the river in the 29th Division's sector over which the Americans could hope to build one or more bridges on *Grenade*'s thunderous opening day. Both upstream and downstream from the 175th's zone, flooding had inundated vast areas of the Roer valley, and as of February 23— nearly two weeks after the Germans had blown the Roer dams' discharge valves—the river in those places was still roughly 1,500 feet in width. In the 175th's sector, however, the Roer's width averaged only a small fraction of that distance because of the Jülich natives' centuries-long effort to avert devastating floods by canalizing the river and building sturdy levees. The Germans had also inadvertently lessened their opponents' river-crossing burden when in November they had demolished a major bridge at Jülich as the 29th Division shoved them back across the Roer. The immense wreckage from that bridge partially obstructed the river's water flow, slowing the current in the area upstream from the 175th's bridge sites by a considerable factor. "The fact that this [unplanned] dam existed played a great part in site selection for the [29th Division's] bridges," an engineer report concluded.

A forlorn hope comprised of twenty-seven men led by 1st Lt. Warren Snyder, drawn from the 175th Infantry's Company A, set out for the far bank at 3:00 A.M. in three fragile plywood boats. Unreeling telephone wire behind them and fighting the strong current, the 29ers reached the opposite side and scrambled out of the boats in the darkness to establish a hasty skirmish line on the riverbank. According to Company A's commander, 1st Lt. Frank Bishop, "While the covering force was crossing the river, Germans on the east bank fired automatic weapons at them. The men fired tracer ammunition at the Germans, marking their positions, and the supporting tanks [on the Roer's west side] opened up with machine guns and 76-millimeter guns. The Germans ceased firing, and when [Snyder's] party landed, ten Germans crawled out of a narrow communication trench and surrendered. The Germans were trembling and seemed unnerved by the artillery and tank fire." Teams from the 246th Engineers followed Snyder's boats across, unwinding the steel cables that would fix their footbridges in place. They anchored the cables on the German side of the river and promptly began their backbreaking work on the three vital footbridges that were supposed to carry the bulk of the 175th Infantry across the Roer. Operation *Grenade* had begun.

Seven hundred yards downstream, the 246th Engineers commenced an even tougher assignment, the construction of a much larger floating bridge that would

The 175th Infantry crossed the Roer on February 23, 1945, over footbridges (not yet built when this photo was taken) in the lower-right portion of the picture. The Citadel is visible at left; the towers of the *Hexenturm*, a fourteenth-century city gate, can be seen in the center.

be capable of bearing the weight of jeeps and trucks. This bridge would be a vital supply lifeline once the men of the 175th crossed the Roer, allowing heavy materiel to be brought forward and, more importantly, wounded to be conveyed back to rear-area hospitals for critical care. So pivotal was this bridge in *Grenade* plans that the sappers intended to begin construction in the dark at H-Hour, 3:30 A.M., and have it completed shortly after first light.

They were overly optimistic. To support the engineers' effort to anchor a steel cable on the far side of the river, at 3:00 A.M. the 175th sent over another forlorn hope, this time two boatloads comprising twenty-eight men drawn from Company F. That outfit was in disarray; just hours before the mission, anxious Company F officers had witnessed their leader, Capt. Reginald Bushnell, being evacuated from the front as a non-battle casualty, forcing 1st Lt. James Lightfoot to assume command of a rifle company for the first time in his military career, on the eve of one of its most important battles of the war. To lead the team over the river, Lightfoot selected 2nd Lt. Ralph Howland, a highly admired fighter and Normandy veteran who less than two weeks ago had accepted one of the finest accolades his Army could offer, a battlefield commission, resulting in his promotion from technical sergeant to lieutenant. Ordinarily, men elevated from enlisted to officer rank were transferred to different companies, but Howland stayed on in Company F as a platoon leader.

Company F's top NCO since the close of the Normandy campaign, 1st Sgt. Charles Hankinson, watched Howland's men shove off. "The boats were crowded," he recalled. "It was before daylight. We had radio contact with them by SCR-536 [handie-talkie radio]. One boat capsized in the river. The other boat was caught by the current and washed downstream about 350 yards. . . . The men landed [on the enemy side] and tried to work their way south along the riverbank."

It was the last thing many of them ever did. One boat team member, Pvt. Joseph Panus, noted, "It was so pitch dark, you could not even see your hand in front of you, never mind men." Bewildered and lost, the horrified 29ers realized they had plunged into an enemy minefield. "All I could see was flashes from mine explosions," Panus related. "Screams and outlines of men being blown up. It seemed like forever before some daylight started to come in. Then I saw bodies of GIs spread out all around me. Close to me was Sgt. George Flamik, whose leg was blown off right to his hip, and many others whom I do not recall by name." For days, Flamik's status in company records was listed as "missing in action," but his corpse was recovered later and buried in the American military cemetery at Margraten, Holland.

"One fellow near me was one of our men named PFC Joe Zhanel, a blond, husky kid," Panus continued. A Texas native, Zhanel, like Flamik, had been with the company since D-Day and had been wounded twice. Recalled Panus: "I looked at him, and he was alive, but he had both legs blown off to where the combat boot ended. I tried to comfort him and keep him quiet, using his belt and my own as tourniquets. He kept groaning that he couldn't feel his legs and calling out for his mother. I saw medics across the river and waved my arm that we needed help. All I got back from them was a wave back." As Panus tended to Zhanel, a concealed German tossed a potato masher grenade, and when it detonated nearby, the concussion left Panus "numb and shaking like hell." A nearby 29er, PFC Robert Leibiger, spotted the German and according to Panus, "He opened up his BAR and emptied the whole clip at the Kraut; the result was he got him, and I credit Bob for saving my life."

Leibiger crawled over to Panus. "When he saw Zhanel, Bob's expression was, 'What the hell happened to you?' I told him to keep his mouth shut, as Zhanel was delirious and did not know his legs were blown off. . . . A young GI joined us; I understand he was just released from a military prison in England. Zhanel was still alive and suffering, and we decided we had to go for help." Leibiger, Panus, and the unnamed 29er crawled through the minefield, "among the dead, to the edge of the river," Panus remembered. "We almost had it made, but the young fellow must have set off a mine with his foot, and it was blown off. All this time artillery was going off from both sides. Leibiger and I decided to take a dip in the Roer—if one doesn't make it, the other will. We both squeezed the capsules in our lifebelts and went for a swim. [It was] cold and swift. . . . On the other side medics picked us up. We told them there were men on the other side who needed help immediately. The response was: 'We will take care of it.'"

A member of the 121st Engineer Battalion, PFC William Marcinko, jumped into the Roer on the west bank, despite a comrade's claim that "he couldn't swim," and dog-paddled across the river to aid the wounded men. Marcinko and others eventually recovered several Company F members, including Howland and Zhanel, but Zhanel died two days later.

PFC Joe Zhanel of Company F, 175th Infantry, killed in action in the 29th Division's attack across the Roer River on February 23, 1945.

Company F also lost one of its most steady and experienced soldiers in that same minefield. A fixture in the unit since stateside training at Fort Meade and the grueling speed marches on

Bodmin Moor, twenty-five-year-old T/Sgt. Don Miller, from Franklin, Pennsylvania, had landed on Omaha Beach on D+1 as a platoon sergeant and had only just returned to Company F following a five-month hospital stay in England as a result of a July 30 wound in Normandy. "A fellow would do anything for his buddies," Miller recalled, "and remember that we had been together—some of us— since 1941. I went back [to Company F] because I wanted to see if any of my friends were still alive. There were a few."

Striving to help his beleaguered men caught in the lethal minefield, Miller himself detonated a mine, shattering his left foot. "I wasn't bleeding, really, but I couldn't walk," he remarked. Miller made an agonizing crawl to the riverbank, popped the capsules on his lifebelt—only half of it inflated—and swam the Roer to the American side. Said Miller: "Boy, that water was cold!" Miller applied a tourniquet above his left ankle and took refuge in an abandoned building. Two GIs who had come back across the river with him departed and never returned. It was an isolated part of the front, and for nearly a day Miller stayed put, warmed by a discarded German overcoat, before an American antiaircraft battery deployed nearby. He crawled toward the GIs, who promptly conveyed him to the rear. "I had pork chops and potatoes when I got back to the aid station," Miller recollected, but eventually surgeons cut his left leg off below the knee.

The vehicle bridge would not be finished anytime soon. For more than twenty-four hours, members of the 246th Engineers strove to anchor their cable

T/Sgt. Don Miller (at left) of Company F, 175th Infantry, during a route march in England in 1943.

on the river's far bank, but according to an action report, "in each attempt the swift current either overturned the boat trying to cross or swept it downstream. . . . In one case, the assault boat overturned, throwing all the occupants into the water; one engineer officer was actually swept downstream approximately one quarter of a mile before he was able to make his way out on the far bank."

Far more lethal than the river, however, was the enemy. As related by the engineer's account, "This site was subjected to intense small arms, mortar, and artillery fire all during D-Day and D+1, and each time working crews would appear on the riverbank, they were subjected to withering fire from the far shore and houses thereon." Still worse, "The approach road [to the site] had previously been demined by the division engineers, but it was later found that non-metallic 'Topf' mines [undetectable by American mine detectors] had been used on the road and shoulders. When construction of the bridge first started, the bridge train proceeded to the site and casualties to equipment due to these non-metallic mines were two tractors, one 10-ton wrecker, and two dump trucks. The road was again demined by probing the approaches, which took approximately six hours to accomplish."

Upstream, the 246th's sappers achieved much greater success in their effort to construct the three footbridges for the 175th Infantry, despite German "rifle, machine pistol, and machine gun fire from the shell-torn houses on the far shore." To suppress such enemy resistance, the 175th's Company A reinforced its advance party on the opposite bank by dispatching the rest of the company across the river in boats. The engineers completed their first footbridge at 4:24 A.M., less than an hour after they had commenced work. It was a simple structure, nothing more than a series of rectangular floating metal pontoons, roughly six feet long and two feet wide, upon which the sappers laid a narrow wooden-plank walkway and set loose rope handrails on both sides. The steel cable, anchored on both sides of the river, held the structure in place.

All was going well, but in the dark a boat carrying a team of Company A men across the Roer capsized. The swift current swept the boat downstream into the bridge, smashing a gap through the pontoons and breaking up the walkway. "The equipment in the boat, including satchel charges for demolition, was lost," a 175th report noted. "One man [S/Sgt. Charles Zink from California] was lost in the river, and the remaining twelve men were fished out and evacuated, to be treated for shock." Zink was dragged downstream and disappeared. Company morning reports listed him as missing in action, but his buddies presumed he had drowned. Only in April 1945 did the Company A clerk list him as killed in action.

The rest of Company A pressed ahead into Jülich: not a sign of the enemy. "The town was in utter ruin," remarked Lieutenant Bishop. "The stone walls of some houses were still standing—burned out shells—but the streets were piled with rubble and spotted by shell craters full of water." The 246th Engineers repaired the wrecked footbridge by 6:00 A.M., and as soon as they did so, the first two men to use it were German, not American. "These German soldiers came out of an emplacement on the far side and surrendered to the engineers," a 246th report noted. Shortly thereafter, the leading 29ers of Company G, 175th Infantry, commanded by 1st Lt. Hugh Brady, started out across the span. It was an inspiring sight: as the first hint of dawn broke in the eastern sky, the men pounded onto the bridge at well-spaced intervals, sprinting with their heads down, rifles and BARs at trail arms, praying that an enemy shell would not catch them midway across. Nearly three months after the 29th Division had reached the Roer, it was finally traversing it in force.

Would this be the 29th's first step on the road to Berlin? One of the first 29ers to cross the footbridge was thirty-five-year-old 1st Lt. Joe Ewing, the leader of Company G's 1st Platoon and the future author of the 29th Division's history, *29 Let's Go*. "[Germans] began firing when our platoon point was fifty yards from the bridge," Ewing remembered. "We placed rifle and BAR fire on the pillbox. A white cloth was thrown out, and ten Germans came out and surrendered. The Germans seemed dazed and unnerved and offered little fight. There was one dead man near the bridge. He had been hit by artillery and was so badly mangled that it was impossible to be certain, but he seemed to be a German."

Meantime, the 246th Engineers began work on two more footbridges, and both were completed by sunrise. As noted by Brady, the work was hazardous: "The engineers were working busily to get in other footbridges, and were getting shelled by the Germans. I saw two engineers cross the river in a boat, land near the Aldenhoven road bridge, and start up the bank. The second man stepped on a mine and was blown backward into the river. The first man, also caught in the explosion, turned halfway around, collapsed, and tumbled into the river."

The last footbridge completed by the engineers, the southernmost, evidently had no value for the moment because, as a report observed, "until about H-plus-four hours [7:30 A.M.] the near shore approach to the footbridge was covered by machine gun fire from a strongpoint in a house on the far bank." The commander of the 175th's 1st Battalion, Maj. John Geiglein, challenged that assertion, noting, "This bridge received long-range fire from German machine guns and snipers located in south Jülich a considerable distance from the bridgehead. These guns [and snipers] were too far east to be neutralized by the covering party [from Company A]. . . . The more northern footbridge sites were well selected. Houses along the east bank shielded them from long-range small-arms fire." Even so, by sunrise the two northern bridges drew heavy shelling from German artillery and mortars and even scattered machine-gun bursts and sniper fire. Large groups of 29ers from the 175th's 1st and 2nd Battalions still waited anxiously in the riverfront houses on the west bank to cross the Roer, and they well understood that passage over those two serviceable footbridges could be fatal; NCOs advised that the risk could be minimized by making the crossing at a dead run, or at least as fast as one could move burdened by a weapon, a full load of ammunition, and a heavy knapsack.

The 29ers of Company C, led by Capt. Alex Pouska and 1st Sgt. Al Harris—both veteran soldiers who had joined the service long before America's entry into World War II—began their dash over a wobbly footbridge at about 7:30 A.M. The unit maintained textbook intervals between men to minimize casualties if an enemy machine gun opened up or a shell burst overhead; it consumed a quarter of an hour crossing 150 of its members. All of them made it across safely except one, twenty-year-old PFC Henry Harrell—known to family and friends by his middle name of Slade—who became an unlucky victim to the inscrutable fortunes of war. Just before he made it to the far bank, something struck Harrell—whether it was a shell fragment or a bullet, no one knew—and he abruptly crumpled on his knees and fell facedown on the bridge's narrow foot-boards, losing his helmet and M-1 in the process. He remained on his knees, completely motionless, almost as if he were in a pose of supplication. Veterans who had seen men killed in combat immediately knew Harrell was dead; nothing could be done for him any longer save for litter-bearers to pick up the unfortunate GI and return him to American lines once Company C cleared the bridge. A squad leader coming up behind Harrell, S/Sgt. Steven Melnikoff, fired off an entire eight-round clip from his rifle at the spot upstream on the far shore from where he suspected the enemy fire had originated. Running ahead over the slender walkway, the distraught Melnikoff had to step over Harrell's body, an act he remembered seventy years later by noting, "It was tough to walk over the corpse of a guy in your own company."

A native of the rustic village of Sunflower in Alabama's coastal plain, Slade Harrell's Army career lasted exactly one year, from his February 23, 1944, enlist-ment to his death on February 23, 1945. But if it had been up to his father, Claude Eugene Harrell, nicknamed "Bargie," Slade would never have entered military service at all. Bargie ran a farm of more than 100 acres; as he noted in a June 1943 letter to his congressman requesting intervention with the local draft board to classify Slade as II-C—"men necessary for farm labor"—his business had "cat-tle, hogs, and miles of fence, with no one to help keep the farm, the cattle business, or the hog business except [my] son. . . . Over one-fourth of [the farm] has to be cultivated yet."

Slade, a red-haired standout in high school academics and football, had grad-uated in June 1942 fully expecting to follow his older brother Buddy (Claude, Jr.) into military service. But Bargie opposed his son's inclination, even bringing up

Slade's minor asthma affliction to his congressman, Frank Boykin. "I know everything you say
in your good letter is true," Boykin replied. "I see
no earthly reason why they do not let you keep
your boy to help you keep your property that you
have spent seventy years accumulating and
paying taxes on." Later, in a telegram from Washington to his local congressional office in Alabama, Boykin urged an aide: "Please see all
members of the draft board and see if he can be
deferred. I am advised by parties here if the rules
were properly followed, Henry [Slade] could be
deferred and help his folks not only plant, but cul-
tivate and gather the crops which we are going to
need not only there, but all over this nation."

The appeal worked for a few months, but on
December 7, 1943, Slade received a postcard "to
appear for physical examination" at Chatom,
Alabama. Asthma or not, a Dr. W. E. Kimbrough

**Pvt. Henry Slade Harrell
shortly after his entry into
the U.S. Army in 1944.**

considered Slade fit for Army service, and a few weeks later Local Draft Board
Number 1 of Washington County classified him not as II-C, as Bargie had hoped,
but as I-A—"available; fit for general military service." Bargie would have to
care for his cows, hogs, and crops without the help of Henry Slade Harrell.

Private Harrell, Army Serial Number 34971046, received basic military
training as an infantryman, specializing in light machine-gun operations. The
Army shipped him to England shortly after D-Day, and on November 26, 1944,
he joined the 29th Division as a member of the weapons platoon of the 175th
Infantry's Company C in Aldenhoven, Germany. Slade had plenty of time to
acclimate to the front, as the 175th Infantry would not engage in major combat
for nearly three more months. On Christmas Eve, Harrell gained a promotion to
PFC, but in a Christmas card to his Aunt Pearl, he revealed, "I am just fine, but I
sure would like to spend Christmas somewhere besides here in Germany."

On the night before the 175th's jump-off across the Roer—less than twenty-
four hours before his death—Slade wrote home to his younger brother, Sidney. "I
hope that you, mother, and Bargie are well. I am fine as usual," he noted. "I got a
very nice package from La-La [his Aunt Louella]. The candy and pecans she sent
me were very good. A guy never really appreciates mail until he leaves the States.
. . . I wonder if you get out with the weaker sex? I hope you get out often. I hope
that you will have some good times for me, but I am sure going to make up for
lost time when I get back."

A daredevil New Zealand photographer, George Silk, joined the 175th for the Roer crossing and came across the footbridge near the rear of the Company C column. Silk had already produced iconic images of war in North Africa and the Pacific—he had contracted malaria and dengue fever in New Guinea—and was about to produce one more, his most renowned World War II image. Silk remembered that when he came to Harrell's corpse on the bridge, "I jumped over him and then turned around and took one shot of him lying there with the others still coming across." He proceeded to the far bank, and shortly thereafter, while snapping pictures of American troops herding German prisoners to the rear, he was slightly wounded when a German captive "pulled [a] grenade and blew apart the

The photo by George Silk in *LIFE* magazine, March 12, 1945, showing the footbridge used by the 175th Infantry to enter Jülich and the body of PFC Henry Slade Harrell of Company C. GETTY IMAGES

GI in front of me." Silk re-crossed the river. "I made off to the nearest airport," he said, "took the film to London, and it was in New York the next day." Just seventeen days later, Silk's photo of Harrell's body appeared in the March 12, 1945, edition of *LIFE*, a shocking full-page image that jolted homefront civilians who had only rarely viewed a snapshot of dead American troops. However, Harrell was not named in the caption: neither Silk nor anyone at *LIFE* ever learned the unfortunate GI's name. As the image spread like wildfire across the homefront, no one—not even Harrell's parents back in Sunflower, who subscribed to *LIFE*—knew the identity of the anonymous GI on the bridge.

As time passed Company C members, glancing at the famous photo, vaguely remembered only the "red-haired kid from Alabama," a recent replacement whose corpse they had stepped over on the bridge and whose name, unfortunately, none could recall. On the dedication page of his 1948 29th Division history, *29 Let's Go*, Joe Ewing—a fellow member of the 175th—displayed the sobering photo of the unidentified body lying on the bridge accompanied by the simple inscription: "To the soldiers of the 29th who fell in the battle." Seven decades after the war, when data from Company C morning reports and enlistment records at the National Archives were scrutinized in depth and clues emerged from veterans and Harrell's family—still living in Sunflower—the "red-haired kid" in Silk's famous photograph was identified as PFC Henry Slade Harrell.

A February 23, 1945, photo of George Silk, the *LIFE* photographer who snapped the famous image of PFC Slade Harrell lying dead on a Roer River footbridge.

Litter-bearers eventually removed Harrell from the bridge, and graves registration personnel transported the body to Ninth Army's Margraten cemetery in
Holland. Items removed from Harrell's pockets included a Bible, seven dollars
and forty cents in bills and coins, his driver's license, an identification bracelet, a
watch, a cigarette lighter, a pencil, and twenty-one photos. He was buried at 3:30
P.M. on February 26 in Row 4, Grave 90, next to two 175th Infantry comrades,
Pvts. George Anderson and Charles Brownstead. Harrell was disinterred on July
28, 1948; three months later, his body arrived home in Sunflower and he was
buried at the nearby Hooks Cemetery.

The 175th's new commander, Col. Harry McHugh, had been in charge of the
regiment for just four days and did not yet grasp its people nor its methods, but
even ninety-six hours with the 29th Division was long enough to know that if his
men did not hold Jülich by dusk, as *Grenade* plans stipulated, he would receive a
phone call that evening from Gerhardt demanding the reason for that lapse. If
McHugh dared to provide a reason, the general would certainly reject it. This
time McHugh needed no reason; indeed, at 7:35 PM Gerhardt phoned the 175th's
command post and announced to McHugh: "You have done a fine job—nice
going!" The general's contentment derived from the consistently positive reports
that had filtered back from Jülich to the 29th Division's war room during daylight
hours of the twenty-third. As expected, German resistance along the riverbank
had not been resolute; those dazed enemy troops who had survived the lethal

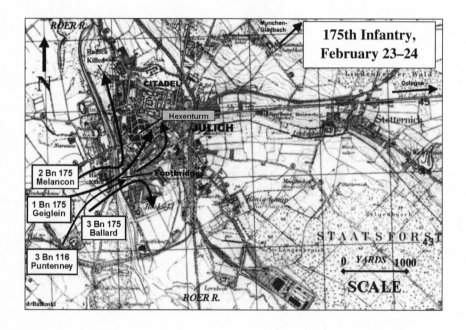

American barrage did not need much inducement to give up or take off for the rear. As each of McHugh's companies tramped across the footbridges, they pushed ahead straight away toward what remained of Jülich's city center: the 1st Battalion headed east; the 2nd Battalion, north; and finally the 3rd Battalion, which started over the Roer at 7:15 A.M., moved south, directly into the tangle of smashed warehouses and factories of Jülich's once-thriving industrial area.

The Germans could not rouse enough defenders to contain the Americans' spirited assault and had no choice but to yield the city they had held so stubbornly for months. Most enemy survivors sought refuge in the northern part of town, inside the massive sixteenth-century walls of the historic Citadel—now used as a German Army noncommissioned officer school—and fled through the arched stone gate leading into its spacious central courtyard, slamming the giant metal doors shut behind them. The archway was topped by a martial eagle and a swastika: so scarred by American shells were those ubiquitous Nazi symbols that most of the downtrodden defenders surely wondered whether Nazism was finished.

"We encountered no resistance in town," noted Company A's CO, Lieutenant Bishop, "but when we reached the Citadel, scattered small-arms fire came from its walls. The Citadel was a large, square stone structure, enclosed by a heavy wall surrounded by a moat. There was one bridge across the moat, and the gate in the wall behind it was closed. We had lost the satchel charges that were to be used to blow the gate, so we surrounded the Citadel, neutralized fire from its walls by firing on it with machine guns and rifles, and sent back for tanks. . . . The tanks were delayed until a treadway bridge could be built across the Roer."

That bridge, and every other bridge under construction in the 175th Infantry's zone, was in trouble. Despite the Americans' easy penetration of the enemy's forward defenses, German gunners had expertly zeroed their howitzers in on the river sites where they knew their opponents must strive to build bridges; although most German artillery units had not survived the Americans' overwhelming pre-assault bombardment, those that did kept up an unremitting and devastating barrage on the bridge sites for as long as they dared. So effective was that fire that the American bridge-builders learned they were in far greater danger of losing their lives than riflemen at the point of the 29th Division's advance.

As soon as possible after the 175th began its attack, General McLain had ordered the 3,000-man 1104th Engineer Group, led by Col. Hugh Colton and consisting of four engineer battalions and six specialized independent companies, to construct three bridges over the Roer that could carry vehicles, from lightweight jeeps to ponderous tanks and tank destroyers. Two more spans capable of carrying vehicles, including a sturdy Bailey bridge, would be built after Jülich had been secured. McHugh could accomplish little without those bridges; riflemen needed tanks to eradicate the German strongpoint at the Citadel, trucks to replenish depleted ammunition, and jeeps to bring back wounded.

Presently, disaster struck the 247th Engineer Combat Battalion at the treadway bridge site. "Construction proceeded at an excellent rate, and approximately 132 feet of bridge was constructed when probably the most unfortunate incident in the operation occurred," Colton's report stated. "At 9:30 A.M. it was estimated that seven rounds of heavy artillery came in on this bridge site, and all rounds landed on the bridge itself, sinking the floats and severely damaging the treadway. The bridge was destroyed with high casualties to the construction unit. . . . It was decided that the center line of the bridge should be shifted upstream due to the fact that the enemy, without question, had this point zeroed in, and that since artillery fire was still coming in, very likely a repetition of the catastrophe might occur." The treadway bridge was not completed until 11:00 A.M. on February 24, but as Colton noted, even the new site "was subjected to observed artillery fire until its completion." A 29th Division infantryman who witnessed the carnage remembered, "There were engineers lying everywhere—I felt so sorry for them."

Dusk was fast approaching on the twenty-third when Colton's men finally completed their first heavy pontoon bridge, but despite the lack of vehicular support during daylight hours, the members of the 175th managed to achieve virtually all their goals by sunset. The regimental monthly action report proudly declared: "By nightfall, although the Citadel had not yet been stormed, the town was in our hands, and the troops were disposed to hold it securely." To aid them in that endeavor, Gerhardt loaned McHugh the 116th Infantry's 3rd Battalion, led by Lt. Col. William Puntenney, who had just returned from a delightful three-day furlough spent at the Cumberland Hotel, adjacent to Hyde Park in London. At dawn on February 23, Puntenney's men departed Schleiden and marched three miles over a muddy quagmire of a road to Aldenhoven, where they made final preparations for the imminent battle; as they marched another four miles to the Roer, the ominous cacophony of combat grew much louder. In late afternoon, after they had trudged over the still-shaky footbridges into Jülich, Company K, commanded by Capt. Elmer Reagor, relieved Bishop's Company A at the Citadel and prepared to assault that redoubtable fortress into which the last of the city's defenders had fled.

That act, Gerhardt hoped, would be the denouement of the Jülich battle, but the general would have to wait just a little longer for the final curtain. "By 6:00 P.M. we were across [the Roer]," Puntenney noted, "but didn't have our flame-throwing tanks [from the 739th Tank Battalion] needed for the assault on the Citadel. We spent the night in the rubble of Jülich and were under constant enemy artillery fire directed at the bridge sites. . . . It wasn't until about midnight that the bridges were completed [the first vehicular bridge was actually finished at 4:00 P.M. on the twenty-third], and our tanks got across, but by then we had to postpone our attack until first light the next day. Three times during the night, German night bombers came in and randomly dropped their bombs in an effort to knock out the bridges. We suffered a number of casualties from these and also the long-range enemy artillery being fired into us from about ten miles to the east."

On the south side of Jülich, as the men of the 175th pushed into the city's industrial wasteland, the commander of the 3rd Battalion, Lt. Col. James Ballard, was wounded and evacuated. The twenty-five-year-old Ballard, a 1940 ROTC graduate of Davidson College in North Carolina and a D-Day veteran, had led the 800-man outfit capably for three months and had gained rare praise from the commanding general, who referred to him as "a good kid." Indeed, the "kid" was younger than many of his riflemen. Capt. Paul Freund, who had enlisted in the Maryland National Guard as a private in 1936 after gaining a law degree, replaced Ballard.

The 175th held Jülich: would it promptly be able to push beyond the city into open ground? The 2nd Battalion's initial attempt to do just that was met, as a report noted, by "heavy automatic weapons fire" emanating from a pillbox on the dominating ridge north of town. Company E, commanded by 1st Lt. John Hartley, lost several members to that fire as it cautiously moved out into an open field from behind the cover provided by buildings. An audacious twenty-four-year-old private named Srecko Radich, who had only been in uniform nine months, dashed into that field to retrieve a wounded comrade. As related by a citation for valor, "Private Radich ran to the wounded soldier, and as he stooped to pick him up, was hit by tracer fire. Even though mortally wounded, Radich carried his comrade to a covered position and fell dead." That astounding episode transpired in just a minute, and when it was over Hartley's weary 29ers had to admit that they had just witnessed an amazing act of selfless heroism.

In a life far too short, Radich had seen a lot of the world. Born in 1920 in that volatile region of Europe known as Slovenia—split in the chaotic aftermath of the Great War between Italy and the new Kingdom of Yugoslavia—Radich emigrated at the age of seven with his parents to the United States. He grew up on the east side of Manhattan, married, and moved to a gritty neighborhood near the banks of the Delaware River in Camden, New Jersey, where he worked as a cook. On May 12, 1944, a date when several of the 29ers with whom Radich served on the Roer were billeted in Cornwall preparing for the D-Day invasion three weeks hence, the U.S. Army drafted Radich into military service and ordered him to report to Fort Dix for training as a rifleman. At the close of the 29th Division's bloody November offensive, Gerhardt was in dire need of exactly that kind of soldier, and Radich was assigned to Company E, 175th Infantry, on November 30 as one of dozens of fresh replacements. By Ninth Army General Order 117, signed on April 20, 1945, PFC Radich was awarded the Distinguished Service Cross for valor, although by then he had been lying for months deep in the soil of the U.S. military cemetery at Margraten. Radich thus became one of only forty 29ers in World War II to gain the exalted award, second in Army precedence to the Medal of Honor, and one of only thirteen to be awarded it after D-Day.

In what remained of Jülich's city center, the 29ers came across a curious stone structure consisting of two medieval round towers connected by a forty-foot wall with a central arched gateway. Maps listed it as the *Hexenturm*, or "Witches Tower," a city gate dating to the fourteenth century that had held up surprisingly well against the American bombardment, except for the towers' caved-in conical roofs. It was the perfect place, a mischievous 175th soldier thought, to demonstrate to the homefront folks that the 29th Division was on the move again. Snatching a white bedsheet from a wrecked house, and somehow managing to locate some paint and a brush, the artistic GI fashioned a crude banner he knew would attract the attention of newspaper reporters and photographers. On the banner's right side, he painted a perfect blue-and-gray 29th Division yin-yang symbol. Then he came up with just the right words: "THIS IS JÜLICH GERMANY. Sorry it is so messed up. But we were in a *HURRY*! 29th (Blue & Grey) Div." Two smiling Company C members, PFC Thomas Snyder of New York City and Pvt. Paul Mattox of Washington, D.C., held up the banner and posed for a photo before hanging the sheet over the *Hexenturm* gate. Within ten days that photo was in newspapers all over the country.

Two members of Company C, 175th Infantry, PFC Thomas Snyder (left) and Pvt. Paul Mattox (right), pose with a banner in front of Jülich's *Hexenturm*.

SUPERMEN, HELL

The 115th Infantry, too, was in a hurry. The 115th's dynamic commander, Lt. Col. William Blandford, had expressed that sentiment forcefully at a pre–*Grenade* conference of field grade and general officers, including Simpson and Gerhardt. "There are two possible ways of making this attack," he asserted. "Either slow or fast. To do it slowly will result in more casualties. To do it quickly, before the enemy has a chance to react, is the best way. [German] fire along the river will be very heavy. Jerry will try to stop reinforcements from coming in. Come out of the boats running, and the same goes for bridges. It is imperative that every man and vehicle driver knows where he is to go after he gets off the bridge. . . . If a vehicle gets hit, make sure you get it off the road. No vehicle will stop for anything."

The 115th held the Roer front on the 29th Division's left, or north flank, and Blandford's supreme confidence that his men could crack the enemy's line was bolstered by the overwhelming firepower at his disposal. As a senior artillery officer remarked at that conference, "We'll have more firepower in this operation than we have ever had before." But the thirty-five-year-old Blandford, a member of the West Point class of 1933, would need more than firepower and confidence to accomplish his *Grenade* mission. When the enemy changed everything on the Roer front on February 9 by smashing the discharge valves on the Roer dams, the 115th's success would ultimately depend on Blandford's adaptability, a trait that only rarely surfaced among U.S. Army field grade officers. For Blandford, however, adaptability was a major asset. Before the torrent descended down the Roer valley, the river in the 115th's sector was easily bridgeable, and Blandford's assault plan mirrored that of the 175th Infantry on his right, relying on engineers to build several bridges immediately after H-Hour. But after the deluge, the river in Blandford's zone looked more like the Rhine than the Roer—much wider than in the 175th's sector, with a faster current—and as an engineer study observed glumly, the 115th must wait for the "recession of flood waters to permit bridging operations."

Blandford proceeded to alter his entire assault plan. Now that parts of the Roer were one-third of a mile wide on the 115th's front, instead of depending on bridges to convey most of his 29ers across the river, Blandford would employ hulking Alligator LVT-4s and plywood assault boats. The regiment would attack at 3:30 A.M., in darkness, but under the modest illumination provided by a moon just a few days short of full. Leading the charge would be the 3rd Battalion, led by thirty-two-year-old Lt. Col. Carleton Fisher, a veteran soldier who in 1935 had enlisted in the 103rd Infantry of the Maine National Guard as a private and after the war would rise to general officer rank, help establish the U.S. Army Special Forces branch, and write several notable books on the American Revolution. The

2nd Battalion, commanded by Maj. Albert Warfield, and the 1st Battalion, under Lt. Col. Glover Johns, would follow Fisher across the river in that order. The 115th had a dual mission: seize the village of Broich, although in truth not much of it was left to seize; and push the German defenders away from the lofty two-mile-long ridge between Broich and Jülich known locally as *Merscher Höhen* (Merscher Heights). Should any unforeseen event hold up Fisher's cross-river assault, Warfield's and Johns's outfits had orders to move south posthaste and cross the Roer on the 175th's footbridges.

Blandford could apply no subtlety to the attack; as a post-battle report noted, the Roer crossing "could only be done by blunt force." Whatever blunt force the 115th could apply, however, was diminished before the assault even started by a series of unfortunate events on the road from Koslar leading down to the river at the regiment's main crossing point near Hasenfeld *Gut*, labeled "Site 5" in *Grenade* plans. For weeks, the 29th Division's 121st Engineer Battalion had swept this road for enemy mines, but it was so close to the front that heavy American vehicles had yet to drive on it. At 3:00 A.M. on February 23, as the massive American bombardment of German lines smashed onto the far side of the Roer, the astonished members of the 747th Tank Battalion's Company C learned that the cunning enemy had expertly placed dozens of mines in the road weeks before, which according to a 747th action report "were plastic and therefore not detected by mine detectors." The lead tank detonated one of those mines, blowing a track off—an event, as Blandford's report observed, that "not only immobilized one of the supporting tanks, but also resulted in a roadblock on the approach over which the Alligators were to travel to reach Site 5."

The commander of the 234th Engineer Battalion's Company C, 1st Lt. Norman Cusick, had orders to move seven Alligators down that road to Site 5 and embark two of Fisher's rifle companies for the river crossing. "Moving halfway down the road, we met a tank backing up," Cusick wrote. "The tank commander said that his lead vehicle had been blown up on a mine, and he was withdrawing the remaining four—and with them went our direct fire support." Cusick's Alligators, led by a Sherman tank with an attached bulldozer blade, proceeded down the road to the disabled tank, which the tank-dozer shoved off the road "without too much trouble."

But Cusick's troubles had only just begun. Near the wrecked tank, Cusick spotted a deuce-and-a-half truck that minutes before had set off another mine, blasting it into an adjacent ditch. The explosion tossed ten small boats carried in an accompanying trailer into the road, and before GIs had a chance to recover them, most of the boats were crushed by the 747th's tanks as they backed up toward Koslar. Lacking the boats, the infantry would need the Alligators more than ever, and Cusick's column plunged ahead. "The lead Alligator started forward and just as it passed the destroyed two-and-a-half-ton truck, the Alligator hit a mine, blowing the track and bogies off the right side," recalled Cusick. "We backed the dozer up to pull the Alligator off the road and hit another mine, disabling the dozer."

On a vital road that supposedly had been cleared of German mines, four U.S. Army vehicles had been wrecked in minutes, just when the fretful infantrymen needed them most. Cusick reported to Fisher "that the road was impassable, and did he have any suggestions? [Fisher] said there was no other way to get his men across the river, so we would have to figure out how to get the Alligators to the stream. He said the fields on both sides of the road were supposed to be *Schu* minefields [antipersonnel mines in small wooden boxes] and asked me if I thought the Alligators would go through there without blowing tracks. I said I didn't know, but we would try, so he gave us a guide to show us the [path] that was supposed to be cleared through the field. The guide led us to the edge of the minefield, said 'That's the way,' and took off. By this time the smoke was so thick that you couldn't see two feet in front of you, so we went straight ahead until we thought we had cleared the minefield. . . . In progressing through the minefield, the [lead] Alligator set off four *Schu* mines, none of which had any apparent effect on the tracks."

The delays triggered by the enemy's nefarious mines convinced Fisher to start his 29ers across the river using just the flat-bottom assault boats rather than waiting for the Alligators to reach the river through the minefield. Fortunately, the 121st Engineers had assembled so many of those craft at the riverbank in the dark that the loss of the ten that had been crushed by tanks in the Koslar road did not crimp the 3rd Battalion's assault. Company I, led by 1st Lt. Mark Hogan, who had joined the 115th in Normandy just after the fall of St. Lô, would lead the attack at 3:50 A.M.—twenty minutes late—by crossing the Roer in boats at "Site 4," half a mile upstream from Hasenfeld.

The 115th's action report proclaimed: "The battle was on!" The members of Company I, engulfed in clouds of smoke that Hogan described as "very dense and nauseating," made the crossing in two waves against enemy resistance that amounted to almost nothing. At 4:25, a happy clerk at Fisher's command post typed in the 3rd Battalion journal: "Company I is across river." However, the 115th's official history noted, "The men of Company I found that their troubles were only beginning." Less than 100 yards from the river, Hogan's astounded 29ers encountered a millrace, twenty feet wide and too deep to wade across. Dozens of patrols and air photos over the past two months had failed to trigger sufficient warnings in the 29th Division that the millrace would be an obstacle; for the moment it had stopped Company I cold. "A nearby tree was felled and thrown across the water," the regimental history reported, "but it was discovered that the branches only stretched about halfway across. PFC Stanley Dombroski

and S/Sgt. Edward Lancione [actually Edo Lancioni] crawled out to the edge of
the tree, swam the balance of the distance, and managed to reach the other side."
The two 29ers located a lengthy piece of wood, which in conjunction with the
felled tree created a makeshift bridge, enabling Hogan's men to tiptoe across the
millrace one at a time. Hogan remembered that "considerable equipment—
ammunition, machine gun tripods, etc.—was lost in the canal."

On the far side of the millrace, the members of Company I's 3rd Platoon, led
by 1st Lt. Ralph Harris, drew the sickening conclusion that they had plunged
unknowingly into a minefield when one detonation after another seriously
wounded more than a dozen GIs, including Harris himself. The rest of the company proceeded into a complex of German zig-zag trenches, although
surprisingly, according to Hogan, "We saw no dead Germans." But his men did
encounter some live ones: as S/Sgt. Henry Lund probed down a trench, he "overheard the sound of voices that seemed unlike those of his buddies. Calling the
assistant squad leader, Sgt. Kenneth Carvell, the two men investigated further and
came upon a German machine gun crew babbling incoherently. While the two
Americans tried to find out why the men hadn't opened fire, the Germans continued their rambling talk, and the dazed expression on their faces soon convinced

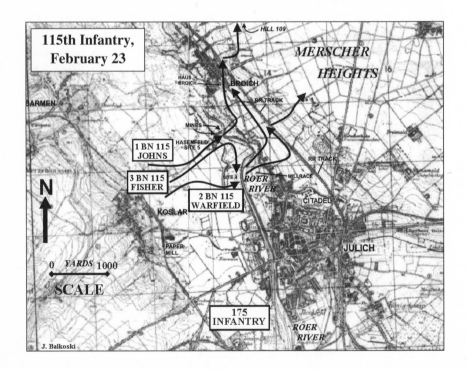

their interrogators that the Germans had been shell-shocked by the terrific barrage." Hogan categorized a dozen more prisoners as "unnerved."

Meantime, on the American side of the Roer, Capt. Robert Armstrong's Company K readied to follow in Company I's wake. Earlier that morning mess personnel had sent a hot breakfast up to the company's bivouac area at Koslar; when it arrived, 2nd Lt. Jack Kussman recalled: "I looked into one of the marmite food containers, in which were stacks of fried eggs in well-congealed grease. With my stomach already in knots in anticipation of the attack over the river, I immediately decided to pass on the hot breakfast. Breakfast has always been my favorite meal, but not that day."

Armstrong was supposed to have moved his troops over the Roer at Hasenfeld, but the mine difficulties on the approach road from Koslar had caused Fisher to order Company K to march by foot to Site 4 instead and cross there. It began its move across the river at 6:00 A.M., just as dawn broke in the eastern sky. "The engineers had three assault boats at this crossing site, into which we loaded and began the crossing," Kussman reported. "The current was strong, and it was somewhat difficult to control the boats. The Germans were shelling the river and its approaches . . . [but] fortunately for us, during our crossing, most of the German shelling was directed at targets beyond the river, and we had only one man slightly wounded in the actual crossing."

Downstream at Hasenfeld, Cusick's Alligators, now down to five in number, loaded up Capt. Arthur Lawson's Company L, which the battalion journal noted at 6:20 A.M. had become "rather disorganized" as a consequence of the freshly discovered mines on the Koslar road and the loss of seven men in a single platoon from accurate German artillery fire. "[We] located a path for the Alligators to enter the water," Cusick wrote. "This path was bordered with Teller [antitank] mines approximately two feet from the track where the Alligators had to pass, so T/4 [John] Kunysz directed each Alligator into and out of the water by use of a flashlight and hand signals. The first Alligator hit the water, and when it came to the middle channel floated downstream about thirty yards before it hit the far bank. The stream was flowing at approximately seven miles per hour. . . . The five Alligators entered the water about twenty-five yards apart, and each managed to work their way out on the far shore—one making five attempts before being successful. They crawled through the swamp-like terrain in back of the riverbank, over an irregular canal [the millrace], and up onto dry land where the assault troops dismounted. The Alligators came back as soon as they were unloaded." As the Alligators emerged from the Roer on the American side to embark 1st Lt. David Woodhouse's Company M, yet another struck a mine, "which completely overturned the vehicle, and it lay upside down, the driver suffering a broken arm and the other man pretty badly shaken up."

**Three U.S. Army
LVT-4 Alligators
prepare for a river-
crossing operation.**

The effort had been more difficult than anticipated, but by 7:30 A.M. Fisher's battalion had gained the far shore, for the most part intact, and now his three rifle companies headed straight for "Objective A," the shattered village of Broich. Company L moved in from the south and on the outskirts of town promptly came across a complex of historic buildings labeled in 115th plans as "The Castle," but known locally as *Haus Broich.* Surrounded by a lofty garden wall and consisting of several sturdy brick buildings, had the Germans possessed sufficient manpower and the will to fight, they might have held *Haus Broich* for days. But they had neither; ultimately a twelve-man Company L rifle squad, led by Sgt. Lawrence Liberty, captured it against opposition that could not even be categorized as half-hearted. Much older than his fellow riflemen, the thirty-four-year-old Liberty, a native of Essex County in northeastern Massachusetts, moved single-handedly across a moat and into the baroque mansion house, forcing the surrender of a team of German soldiers the regimental history described as a "command group." As 29ers with a taste for history would soon learn, the house dated to the seventeenth century, and according to local lore, in 1672 the young French king Louis XIV—*Le Roi-Soleil*, The Sun King—had once stayed overnight.

Even older than Liberty was Company L's top noncommissioned officer, thirty-six-year-old 1st Sgt. Neale Gilson. Ordinarily rifle company "top kicks" stayed behind the front, helping the commander and handling administrative matters. But Gilson, also a Massachusetts native, was a bona fide hero among the dogfaces due to his penchant for staying close to the battle line and routinely volunteering for patrol missions. As Company L methodically worked its way past *Haus Broich* into the luckless village, Gilson grabbed a single man, PFC James Ward of Oklahoma—nineteen years his junior—and approached a dilapidated brick schoolhouse. The Americans' approach caused twenty-five demoralized Germans to exit the main door with their hands over their heads and glumly plod down the front steps as prisoners even though they greatly outnumbered their captors. One German, however, apparently was not so demoralized, and as an account stated, he "tried to make a getaway, but was shot dead by Gilson." Soon the company would have to replace the irreplaceable Gilson, as the intrepid first sergeant was seriously wounded later that day and evacuated, never to return to the 29th Division.

Meanwhile, Companies I and K swung around Broich and entered the village from the east. "There was some scattered opposition," Kussman recalled, "but most of the Germans had the good sense to surrender. One of my squads encountered a machine gun crew that wanted to fight. My men soon took care of the situation and came back with a pistol they had taken from one of the Germans who chose to die rather than surrender." Company K lost six men wounded that day; one of those, twenty-year-old PFC Ralph Roybal from Colorado, died of his wounds the next day.

At a bunker on the town's outskirts, a medic attached to Company K, PFC Gaylord Patterson, asked permission from the executive officer, 1st Lt. Ray Mullhollan, to convince the German occupants to give up without a fight. "After trying to dissuade the medic from going ahead, the lieutenant finally agreed and Patterson picked up a medic's [red cross] flag and went forward to talk to the Jerries," the regimental history noted. "In short order five of the enemy who were manning a machine gun were persuaded by Patterson's eloquence and gave up without further ado. The riflemen were amazed, and Patterson's fellow medics were quite proud of him that day."

With Fisher's 3rd Battalion firmly established on the Roer's east bank, Blandford's tactical flexibility again emerged as he shoved the rest of his regiment across the river as expeditiously as possible. According to *Grenade*'s scrupulously prepared orders, Warfield's 2nd Battalion was supposed to move to Hasenfeld before dawn and cross the river at Site 5 in Cusick's Alligators, but the enemy's unforeseen mines in the Koslar road threatened to delay the crossing and, even worse, throw the assault into chaos. Blandford therefore shifted Warfield's 29ers to the upstream loading point at Site 4 with new orders to cross in the 121st Engineers' assault boats. The sappers at that location made the riflemen's task easier by stretching a sturdy wire across the river just above water level, allowing the boats' occupants to stay on course despite the rapid current by clinging to the wire and pulling hand-over-hand like an old-fashioned cable ferry. It worked: by 10:00 A.M., most of Warfield's battalion was across the Roer, moving toward "Objective C," the high ridge between Jülich and Broich known as Merscher Heights that towered over the low ground adjacent to the river.

When the 29ers reached a north–south railroad track near the base of the ridge, they had a sickening feeling that their day was about to get much tougher.

"Unfortunately the haze and smoke began to clear by mid-morning," an account noted, "and the advancing troops soon found themselves in full view of the enemy who were strongly dug in on the high ground. The entire crest of the hill was covered by grazing automatic-weapons fire from bunkers and emplacements on the reverse slope, making a frontal attack almost suicidal." So suicidal, in fact, that Warfield promptly ordered Capt. Earl Palmer and 1st Lt. Roderick Parsch, the commanders of Companies E and G at the forefront of the 2nd Battalion's advance, "to abandon the plan of a frontal attack and maneuver the entire battalion to the left in an effort to swing around the opposition." Movement of any kind in the face of such heavy fire, however, was lethal. "I saw two men hit by snipers as we crossed the field," declared a Company E man, S/Sgt. Guy Belt. Parsch, a respected D-Day veteran and recipient of a Silver Star, was hit by a shell fragment over an eye and immediately evacuated. His replacement, 1st Lt. Stanley Turowski, who had only been with Company G since January 9, lasted just a few hours in command before he, too, was hit, leaving 2nd Lt. James Larson in charge.

One rifleman who stood out in Company E due to his advanced age of thirty-seven, PFC Robert Boche of Philadelphia, "made a dash for the railroad embankment, but [a] Jerry gunner opened up on him," the 115th's history observed. "Bullets kicked up dirt all around him and about twenty yards from the tracks he was hit four times. [PFC John] Haines went to the rescue, and with the assistance of Cpl. Richard ("Blimp") Newman, Company E's 2nd Platoon medic, and PFC Cleve Murphy, bazookaman, managed to carry Boche up to the embankment, where they gave him first aid." Their aid, however, did no good; Boche died that afternoon.

Haines, a rebellious soldier who twice before had gone AWOL—once for a few days in Paris in September, later for six weeks as the 29th Division slogged across the Rhineland—would die four days later under mysterious circumstances. On February 27, a day in which Haines's Company G was not engaged with the enemy, he died, as a morning report noted, "in the line of duty, pending investigation . . . Injury: upper half of head blown off by M-1 .30 caliber rifle." Whether his death was due to suicide, an accident, or something much more nefarious is not known. Haines is not listed among the names of those 3,720 29ers who died in combat during World War II.

For five terrible hours the enemy atop Merscher Heights subjected Warfield's men, pinned behind the railroad embankment, to murderous fire. In late afternoon the 29ers managed to move to their left and surge up the ridge, but even then the stubborn defenders refused to yield and engaged a Company E platoon led by 2nd Lt. Ira Sliger in a vicious close-range struggle beyond the crest. "Hand grenades were flying back and forth almost like stones," noted one account.

"No-man's-land was only about thirty yards wide. Capt. Earl Palmer, Company E commander, had gone forward to check the situation when he came face to face with a German. Both fired instinctively but wildly at each other and then ducked down out of each other's sight. . . . Meanwhile the battle of the hand grenades continued. Sliger, occupying a hole a short distance from the German positions, quickly vacated the shelter as a grenade landed inside. Moving to another hole, he was again forced to make a hasty exit as a second grenade was lobbed in. When the same thing occurred in the third hole, Sliger decided to hit the ground outside the holes, and in this position he was able to avoid injury."

Palmer directed another platoon under 2nd Lt. William Wimmer to move to Sliger's aid. "As the group moved up," the 115th history recorded, "PFC [Melvin] Walker, who was trying to observe the enemy, was shot squarely between the eyes and died instantly." Walker, a twenty-three-year-old resident of Butte County, California, had been a member of the U.S. Army for only ten months. The regimental history continued: "Throughout the afternoon and early evening, the battle raged back and forth, the Jerries making numerous local counterattacks to drive the Americans back down the hill and the Americans attacking behind artillery concentrations to drive the Germans from their positions. . . . In the midst of the grim fighting a light touch was injected when a white phosphorus shell exploded near the Company E positions. A tiny piece of the phosphorus attached itself to the rear portion of PFC Ray Gavoni's trousers, and the gyrations he went through in trying to rid himself of the burning fragment brought some amusement to the rest of the men."

The Germans on Merscher Heights finally conceded when Company E commenced a close-range attack against an enemy bunker, so neatly camouflaged that air photos had failed to detect it and so sturdy that it had withstood American bombs and shells for nearly three months. "A German lieutenant waving a white towel appeared and, in perfect English, asked if his surrender would be accepted," asserted one account. "The answer was an eager 'Yes,' and the lieutenant and ten of his men stepped from a second pillbox and moved into American lines. When Lieutenant Wimmer attempted to find out how many Germans still remained in the positions, the German officer smiled and replied, 'Lieutenant, I am a soldier. You don't expect me to tell you that!'" Soon after that enemy resistance atop *Merscher Höhen* evaporated; those defenders fortunate enough to have survived pulled back more than a mile to nearby villages.

While the 2nd Battalion was tied up on Merscher Heights, Lt. Col. Glover Johns's 1st Battalion crossed the Roer at Hasenfeld *Gut*. The 234th Engineers, however, were down to only four functional Alligators, so the passage, which did not start until 10:00 A.M., consumed more than two hours. "On one of these trips," the engineer Cusick reported, "an Alligator was hit by a shell, evidently of a small caliber, as it only chipped off a piece of the Alligator's side, [and] a sliver of shrapnel tore the .50-caliber [machine] gun apart." Johns aimed to seize "Objective B" by sunset, a dominating hill, 109 meters high, 1,000 yards northeast of Broich. To reach it, however, the 1st Battalion had to ascend Merscher Heights, execute a tricky 90-degree turn to the north, and advance a mile through open country in full view of the enemy.

It was impossible. Johns's leading unit, Company A, lost its commander, 1st Lt. Albert Pierce, just before dawn when the all-pervasive smoke generated by the 83rd Chemical Smoke Company incapacitated him. ("Whose side are those chemical warfare jerks on?" grumbled some Company A men.) Pierce was replaced by his executive, 1st Lt. James Wellman, who was warned by Johns, "You can expect to run into minefields." Wellman and his men did just that. According to the 115th's action report, "Having cleared a passage through the first minefield by means of primacord rope [a thin, flexible cord filled with explosives], it was again held up almost immediately thereafter by a second minefield, which had the additional hazard of being covered by small-arms fire from the 2nd Battalion area." Caught in the minefield for several hours while taking fire from unseen enemy positions, Wellman reported to Johns in midafternoon, "Losses are painful and growing."

The cacophony of gunfire on Johns's right suggested that Warfield's unfortunate 2nd Battalion was struggling mightily to overcome the enemy on Merscher Heights, but Johns wisely decided that he did not even want to try that route to reach Hill 109. Instead, he radioed Wellman: "Listen carefully; change in plans. At twilight we will pull you out and send you through Broich [occupied by Fisher's 3rd Battalion] to your objective." The maneuver worked perfectly: "Light opposition was met in the form of small-arms fire and the 'screaming meemies' of the German [*Nebelwerfer*] multi-barreled rocket guns," a report observed, "but by 1830, Hill 109 was secured and the men dug in around it." An hour later, Gerhardt phoned Blandford and remarked, "I got the report that you were on Objective B. . . . That's very well done, under hard conditions. Nice going!" The general rarely offered praise to subordinates; Blandford surely savored it because next time Uncle Charlie phoned, he probably would not be in such a good mood.

Wellman had achieved a notable success, but Company A had suffered around twenty casualties, including two dead; twenty-nine-year-old S/Sgt. Glenn Eyler had been one of his finest and most experienced NCOs. On November 16, 1940, Eyler, known as "Pappy" to his family, had walked into the Frederick Armory on Bentz Street to join the Maryland National Guard's Company A, 1st Infantry, later redesignated the 115th. A barber in civilian life, Eyler stood only five feet four inches, but stuck out in Company A as a top-notch soldier. He had served with the outfit at Fort Meade in 1941, at Camps A.P. Hill and Blanding in 1942, in Cornwall in 1943, and of course at Omaha Beach on June 6, 1944. He had defied the law of averages

by fighting through Normandy, Brittany, and the
Rhineland without a scratch until December 8,
1944, the 115th's last day of full-scale combat before Operation *Grenade*, when he was
wounded at Jülich's *Sportplätze* swimming
pool. He had only recently come home to the
29th Division following a two-month recuperation at a hospital in England, a return that,
unluckily for Pappy Eyler, occurred just in time
for him to participate in the 29th's offensive
across the Roer. He did not even last a single
day in that operation, and with his death on February 23 from a mortar fragment, the number of
Company A GIs who could reminisce about
weekly drill nights at the Bentz Street Armory
dwindled by yet another man. By now that number was close to zero.

**S/Sgt. Glenn "Pappy" Eyler
of Company A, 115th
Infantry, killed on February
23, 1945, at Broich, Germany.**

Soldiers more fortunate than Eyler who
survived grim wounds would presently face an
acute crisis: the most seriously wounded of
them could die unless they soon received medical attention beyond the basic care
offered by front-line medics. At the deepest points of the 115th's penetration into
German lines on the far side of the Roer, litter-bearers were in short supply;
moving a grievously injured man to a battalion aid station on the river's opposite
bank with no bridges yet in place in the 115th Infantry's zone could take hours. A
nineteen-year-old medic attached to Company C, PFC Jack Cantrell of Charleston,
West Virginia, dealt with the crisis by making a decisive judgment when treating
a wounded comrade with a hand badly mangled by a shell fragment. His decision
was not part of an aid man's repertoire, but he went ahead anyway: "Taking scissors from his aid pouch," an account reported, "Cantrell cut through the torn bone
and flesh and amputated the man's hand. He then applied a tourniquet and dressed
the wound in a manner which won praise for him when the wounded man eventually reached the aid station."

As the regimental history observed, February 23 "gave the medics one of
their toughest days." Ordinarily, battalion surgeons performed their grisly duties
at aid stations situated well behind the front, but when reports filtered back to the
west side of the river that 115th medical personnel could not convey wounded
men back for hours, Capts. Warren Kirk and Rafael Dufficy, the 2nd and 3rd Battalions' surgeons, moved across the Roer in Alligators to provide immediate care
for the wounded. Only recently abandoned by the enemy, the ramshackle edifices

selected as ad hoc aid stations hardly seemed suitable for the cutting-edge medical practices provided by U.S. Army doctors to save the lives of wounded men. But Kirk, Dufficy, and many others understood that if there was one detail that enhanced an infantryman's morale, it was the likelihood of prompt medical attention by a doctor in the event of a serious wound.

Gerhardt's habitual evening reading of the daily war room journal transcript yielded the irrefutable conclusion that the 29th Division had gained one of its most notable victories of World War II. By nightfall on February 23, the 29th had seized every one of its *Grenade* objectives, save for the massive Citadel, which was surrounded and could not hold out much longer. Even greater results could be expected the next day. Nine Sherman tanks, including four flamethrowing "Crocodile" variants from the 739th Tank Battalion, had already crossed the Roer on a heavy pontoon bridge, although Jülich's omnipresent rubble for the moment thwarted their movement toward the Citadel. Engineers working through the night with bulldozers expected to solve that problem by morning, after which Gerhardt planned to commit his reserve regiment, the 116th Infantry, to finish the job.

Further evidence of the 29th Division's stunning success emerged from the war room's intelligence section, which calculated the February 23 haul of German prisoners as 310. In a February 25 letter to his parents, PFC Glenn Dickerson of Company C, 121st Engineer Battalion, noted that "the infantry usually had a mess of Kraut prisoners for us to march back. That was an interesting experience. We had one [German] major, so we tore off his rank and busted him. He didn't dare bat an eyelash. They are all scared stiff and don't look much like soldiers. All shapes, sizes, and ages, and uniforms not alike. Supermen hell!"

February 23, 1945, as the 115th's official history noted, "was one of the most physically miserable that had been experienced, including the D-Day landings. Many of the doughboys who had come ashore on June 6 remarked afterward that the experiences of the Roer crossing left them feeling more exhausted than had the activities around St. Laurent-sur-Mer [on Omaha Beach]. . . . Many of the men had gotten soaked to the skin in wading through the waist- and neck-deep waters of the canals and trenches along the banks of the flooded river. A few of the shorter men had gone over their heads as they stepped into holes they could not see. Equipment and supplies had become soaked and heavy, and in many cases useless. . . . Movement was limited during the day because of enemy visibility, and the men had no way to dry themselves: they were forced to huddle together in the mud-and-water-filled trenches, shivering, shaking, and praying."

By this phase of World War II, praying was an act that many 29th Division riflemen had gotten thoroughly used to.

THREE

A Fast-moving War

THE BIG PUSH BEGINS

The 29th Division, and the entire Ninth Army for that matter, was on its way to the Rhine. Its first step over the Roer—more of a leap than a step, really—had been the hard part: in the words of Ninth Army's historian, "It had not been done easily, but it had been done." It had been done, in fact, with a consummate skill and power that would have been unachievable in the U.S. Army in the not-too-distant past, and the troops who did it, according to a February 24 front-page *New York Times* article, "went into battle with what one high-ranking officer described as 'the best spirit and morale I have ever seen.'" One engineer colonel asserted, "If a year ago, anyone had said that this Roer crossing was possible, I'd have considered him mad."

Even the Marines' epic battle on Iwo Jima—Joe Rosenthal snapped his flag-raising photo on Mount Suribachi the same day the 29th Division crossed the Roer—took second place in the blaring *Times* headline announcing Operation *Grenade*'s opening act: "EISENHOWER OPENS WIDE ROER OFFENSIVE, 1ST AND 9TH ARMIES DRIVE TOWARD RHINE." Both the stateside readers perusing countless similar headlines and the GIs who executed the massive attack sensed with mounting certainty that, at long last, the end of the European war was in sight. The wretched collection of demoralized soldiers comprising the German Army, with their paltry supplies and worn-out equipment, no longer stood a chance against the mighty Allied host, with its overwhelming superiority in numbers and materiel. Accompanied by a map featuring dramatic arrows punching into the Rhineland, the *Times'* front-page sub-headline hinted at the imminent German collapse: "The Big Push Toward Cologne is Begun."

Nothing could stop it. "The great hammerblow of *Grenade* when viewed as a whole had effectively crushed the enemy," wrote Charles MacDonald in the U.S. Army's official campaign history. "The Germans simply had nothing to counterattack with." As a *Times* reporter noted, "Most of the German soldiers on the west front, as well as most of the civilians, believe that Germany should quit the war, since it is beyond winning." In that February 24 article, the scribe noted that hundreds of Germans "gave themselves up willingly, having decided two or three days ago that there was no point to further resistance." According to one captive *soldat*, "The Nazi party is forcing the people to fight on, and there is no one to stop them."

Ninth Army's stunning success, Simpson later wrote, could be ascribed to catching the enemy by surprise with "the early crossing of the still-flooded Roer." At the army's daily morning briefing on February 24, a staff officer announced that "twenty-eight battalions of infantry were across the river [seven of which were from the 29th Division]; resistance was light to moderate . . . POWs [as of midnight]: 1,239." An hour later Simpson phoned XIX Corps headquarters and declared, "I was delighted with the results of yesterday. Tell General McLain, Leland [Hobbs, commander of the 30th Division], and Charlie [Gerhardt] how pleased I am." So pleased, in fact, that he skipped his normal simple luncheon fare of Army rations and instead enjoyed a sumptuous meal at 1:00 P.M. with his staff at Maastricht's Hotel Du Casque.

The lunch was consumed within ninety minutes because at 2:45 P.M. Field Marshal Montgomery arrived at Maastricht by airplane to discuss future operations with Simpson. Monty's British and Canadian troops had slogged forward in Operation *Veritable* for seventeen days, with "ground conditions," as the official Canadian history stated, "[that] could scarcely have been worse." The Germans had so far resisted Monty's thrust fanatically; indeed, their steady transfer of troops from the Roer northward to contain *Veritable* had greatly enhanced Simpson's ability to crack the German line. Ninth Army's daily chronicle reported that Monty "was well pleased with [Simpson's] progress, and departed at 1545." Pressed by the Americans in one sector and the British and Canadians in another, Monty knew the enemy must crack soon, and his Twenty-First Army Group could be closed up on the Rhine in days. In that event, if the Allies moved with dispatch, they could shorten the war by weeks by seizing one or more of the intact bridges over the Rhine.

Grenade plans stipulated a post-February 23 maneuver that would challenge Ninth Army nearly as much as its Roer River assault. As soon as possible after crossing the river, Simpson must wheel his entire command almost 90 degrees to the left and, rather than heading due east toward Cologne, it must attack northward, aiming to eventually meet the Canadian First Army coming from the opposite direction. Only an expert staff could shift its focus so abruptly from a set-piece offensive to a war of dynamic movement, but before that shift could occur the units of Ninth Army would have to consolidate their slender bridgeheads on the Roer's east side, construct new and sturdier bridges, and continue the steady movement of troops, vehicles, and supplies across the still-swollen river.

In the 29th Division's sector, Gerhardt could not commence his north-eastward movement toward the Rhine until his men secured Jülich, and that meant the massive Citadel—surrounded by the 29ers but still occupied by the enemy—must be captured posthaste. Resolute German troops could have held on to that sturdy fortress for days, even weeks; a reporter observed that it "is sur-rounded by a wall about 2,000 yards long [forming a square with triangular bas-tions at each corner], fourteen feet thick, and forty-five feet high. Outside the wall is a moat twenty feet deep [with only a few inches of water] and seventy to one hundred feet wide—broader than the Roer normally is." The 29th Division's monthly report for February understated the case when it described the Citadel as a "sore spot. . . . Light small arms and machine gun fire had emanated from there and had caused some degree of annoyance."

American bombs and shells could accomplish little more than slingshots against those massive walls and bastions; a February 21 XIX Corps intelligence report noted that "the stout old walls have held up under bombing and 8-inch and 240-millimeter artillery fire. . . . The most recent air strike took place on February 20 when 1,000-pound bombs were dropped. Eight hits were observed on the southwest corner and one hit on the northwest corner—the extent of damage is not yet available." The 29ers therefore would probably not be able to root the enemy out of the Citadel by any means other than an old-fashioned direct assault over one of the narrow bridges traversing the moat, passing into the interior through an arched gateway blocked by immense metallic doors. The battle plan involved no finesse; the attack must be made where the enemy most expected it, against fortifications engineers had labored on for centuries to prevent opponents from accomplishing just what the 29ers were now resolved to do. The XIX Corps report concluded that "complete reduction of this ancient stronghold might be a bitter and costly mission."

Every American attacker knew he would either get inside the Citadel quickly, or he would not get in at all. The unenviable task fell to the 116th Infantry's 3rd Battalion, led by Lt. Col. William Puntenney, specifically Capt. Elmer Reagor's Company K, which would be supported by four Sherman Croco-dile flamethrower tanks from the 739th Tank Battalion and other conventional

Air photo of Jülich's Citadel several weeks prior to the 29th Division's February 23, 1945, attack.

armored vehicles. "We spent the night in a musty cellar close under the Citadel's walls," wrote one of Reagor's platoon leaders, 1st Lt. Robert Easton. "Jerry had slept in it the night before, leaving his distinctive body odor, unpleasantly sour, and we were constantly on the alert lest he counterattack. All night long we listened to our bulldozers clearing rubble. . . . In a doorway not far from ours a dead SS captain lay on his back in a ruin of bricks and dust, his face that strange waxy pallor of death, a potato masher grenade near his outstretched right hand."

In the early afternoon on the twenty-fourth, Reagor ordered the tanks to circle the Citadel as his riflemen inched forward toward the moat. Two Crocodiles broke down, leaving only two to support Reagor. "The leading troops were met by machine gun and rifle fire," observed the 116th's monthly report. Meanwhile, the tanks sprayed "the top of the walls with searing bursts of flame and machine gun fire. [This was the only occasion the Sherman Crocodiles would use their flamethrowers in World War II.] The tanks also fired their 75-millimeter guns into the massive steel door at one end of the doughty old fortress, but these projectiles failed to shatter the entrance." According to Easton, "bullets—ours and Jerry's—whizzed everywhere."

For a few minutes a roaring cacophony and the all-too-familiar odor of cordite overwhelmed the attackers' senses. The 116th's report stated, "The *coup de grâce* was administered by a 155-millimeter self-propelled gun [Puntenney identified it as a Sherman tank from the 747th Tank Battalion armed with a 105-millimeter assault gun], which, with a few rounds, crushed the huge steel door like an eggshell." The *Baltimore Sun*'s Holbrook Bradley witnessed the dramatic episode and wrote: "Almost as the fire ceased, the order came over the radio for the assault platoon [led by 2nd Lt. Clay Purvis of Charlottesville, Virginia] to take off. [Purvis] yelled 'follow me,' and took off through the smoke and dirt toward the bridge over the moat. At the same time other doughboys moved in from the holes on our right, with bayonets fixed and running close to the ground. Even as the first men hit the bridge, another artillery barrage landed inside the fort, and a couple of snipers' bullets kicked up dirt at our feet. Then we hit the main gate and were inside the tunnel."

Easton and his men participated in the charge, "yelling at the top of our lungs with excitement (and fright), and charged through [the] dark smoke-and-dust-filled passageway, expecting to meet Jerry hand-to-hand, but instead emerged into the bright daylight of a huge courtyard and met no one." Bradley added: "Ahead a Yank fired a tommy gun into a gunslit, someone dropped a grenade down the cellar stairs, while rifle fire echoed and reechoed in the courtyard beyond. Inside the fort we found the buildings—once a part of the [NCO] school—almost complete piles of rubble, broken bricks, and masonry. Three German staff cars stood at one side—blown to bits. One was still burning. Over on the other side of the Citadel the Yanks hugged the wall and kept out of the way of snipers as they searched through the buildings and walls."

No Germans remained, other than "a few dead bodies," according to Easton. "Three of them lay around a machine gun on a parapet overlooking the town, from where they'd been firing on us. It is strange, eerie, how commonplace, how matter-of-fact death becomes, when you are in the business of dealing in it. In peacetime the sight of dead bodies would horrify and dismay you. Here they become just part of the debris." Puntenney recalled: "It was later found that an ancient underground tunnel led to *Merscherhöhe* on the high ground to the north and east. [This probably connected the NCO school with a nearby barracks complex.] It was through this tunnel that the bulk of the enemy troops had escaped during the night. We were grateful for this because we feared it might take days to reduce this fort if the Germans chose to stay and fight."

To the long list of invading armies that had besieged and conquered Jülich's formidable Citadel, the 29th Division was now added. The Americans' siege, consuming less than a day, had surely been the quickest in Jülich's history, but the victory was attributable more to the enemy's demoralization than to the 29th Division's skill. Hitler could never have admitted such an outcome was possible, but the Stars and Stripes now flew over the Citadel; Ike and Simpson would soon pass through its gateway as conquering heroes.

To his corps commanders, Simpson had delineated his firm desire to prevent the Germans from regrouping and establishing a strong defensive line east of Jülich. McLain passed the army commander's directive down to Gerhardt on February 24, not in the form of an order, but with the avowal, "I wish you would push to the east as fast as you can." For the moment, however, Gerhardt could not fulfill that wish because his engineers still labored to complete the Roer bridges

A Crocodile Sherman tank from the 739th Tank Battalion. Its flamethrower is visible at left, just above the "739" designation stenciled on the tank.

that were essential to the movement of vehicles, supplies, and troops over the bloated river. Early on the twenty-fourth, Gerhardt's operations officer, Lt. Col. William Witte, phoned the 121st Engineer Battalion's Lt. Col. Raleigh Powell and implored, "The general feels that the whole thing is waiting on this engineer stuff." A harried Powell agreed, "Yes. It is." In response to Witte's question about when some semblance of normal traffic could proceed over the Roer and into and beyond Jülich, Powell affirmed, "Sometime in the middle of the morning."

The 29th Division also needed to regroup before it fulfilled McLain's directive to push east. Although the 115th Infantry had accomplished all its February 23 missions, it was in no position on the twenty-fourth to take the offensive north of Jülich save for a few afternoon patrols toward the twin villages of Mersch and Pattern. The 115th's Roer assault had cost the regiment more than 100 casualties, triggering some disorganization among the rifle companies; all the 115th's heavy equipment, as well as the twelve supporting howitzers of the 110th Field Artillery, could not cross the Roer until engineers completed a heavy treadway bridge in the regimental sector, a job that was not finished until February 25. For most of the twenty-fourth, the 115th's riflemen stayed put in Broich cellars or in foxholes atop Merscher Heights, waiting patiently for someone to tell them what to do. "Positions were improved," noted one account, "areas were checked again, and the men began to warm up and clean up after a harrowing night. . . . About noon a bright sun came out, warming the air and the spirits of the men. It was hard to believe that less than twenty-four hours before the same ground that looked so calm and peaceful now was one of the most miserable and roughest battlefields that the men of the 115th Infantry had ever known."

McLain had temporarily attached Col. Robert Foster's 330th Infantry of the 83rd Division to Gerhardt to help maintain the momentum of the 29th Division's offensive; at sunset on February 24, the men of the 330th filed across the 175th's bridges spanning the Roer and, in the face of "sporadic artillery and mortar fire," pressed ahead into Jülich. Gerhardt promptly decided to shove Foster's outfit into the line to relieve the weary 115th Infantry in its hard-won positions in and around Broich and the nearby heights. At 10:00 P.M. the two regiments completed the relief without a hitch—the dazed enemy thankfully took no notice—and the men of the 115th trudged southward down the river road to seek the bivouac areas in Jülich their leaders had promised would be set aside for them. "Unfortunately there had been some confusion and disagreement as to which areas had been assigned to which battalions, with the result that the men of the 2nd and 3rd Battalions particularly milled around the moonlit streets of the town for over an hour until a temporary arrangement was worked out," remarked PFC Arthur Plaut of the 2nd Battalion. "Most of the 2nd Battalion moved in with the 3rd Battalion for the night, with the exception of Company F, which took a chance on the dark tunnels of the Citadel. Hot chow was served before the men turned in, and the men secured their blanket rolls, which had been brought up and deposited near the billet areas." Those "billet areas" amounted to nothing more than dismal heaps of rubble and freezing, fetid cellars that would have to do for sleeping.

The 115th's so-called rest area, however, was hardly safe. Indeed, any place in and around Jülich was deadly due to the enemy's supreme effort to destroy the Roer bridges by artillery fire and air attack. On February 25, a Sunday, shortly after the 115th held an impromptu church service in a wrecked Jülich edifice, a German warplane streaked overhead at rooftop altitude, strafing and dropping a few bombs before disappearing to the east. The bombs killed a thirty-two-year-old Company L private named Mike Hobartig, a popular member of the outfit since D-Day who had suffered a knee wound in August in Normandy. A married Ukrainian-American from Queens, New York, Hobartig's Army classification as a rifleman was, according to his former platoon leader 2nd Lt. Jack Kussman, "a colossal mistake." A library clerk in civilian life, Hobartig, according to Kussman, was "too old to be an infantry private . . . [and] his physical characteristics made him somewhat less than agile. Just to crawl over a Normandy hedgerow was hard for him to do, and he always had a lot of aches and pains." When Hobartig had returned to the front upon recovery from his wound, Company L assigned him to a much safer position as a runner at 3rd Battalion headquarters. That post, however, proved no more secure than a front-line job. Kussman remembered that in the aftermath of the February 25 air attack, "There were several dead and wounded in the street, and the first body we came to just at the end of the walkway leading to the building we were in was Mike Hobartig. If he had been a little faster, he might have gotten out of the line of fire from the plane, but he didn't make it and was killed instantly." A forlorn Kussman concluded, "I lost a good friend."

The 175th Infantry had spent most of the morning of February 24 mopping up Jülich, although the act of securing an objective that had virtually ceased to exist surely struck many cynical 29ers as ironic. In areas of the city beyond the Citadel, the enemy offered no organized resistance, but Jülich's all-pervading rubble still hid plenty of Germans caught up by the American onslaught, most of whom, as the members of the 175th soon learned, would much rather surrender than attempt to flee a place swarming with heavily armed opponents or, if they lingered too long in cellars, risk being buried alive by debris courtesy of a U.S. Army bulldozer. Many of the enemy soldiers who surrendered, the 175th's chief intelligence officer deduced, were "men from labor battalions who were brought in to dig ditches for the 363rd *Volksgrenadier* Division. These men were unarmed and were digging the night before the [February 23] attack, which showed the enemy had no knowledge of the coming operation." Unluckier German soldiers would be dealt with later by graves registration personnel. "On the east bank of the river, six dead Krauts still lay where they fell during the fighting yesterday," reporter Bradley wrote. "They seemed almost unnoticed by the men busy at the job of a fast-moving war."

As Maj. John Geiglein's 1st Battalion pushed toward Jülich's eastern periphery, a 29er made a curious discovery in the ruins of a building. Bradley described it as a "massive steel key of ancient design, which rests in an ornate silk-cushioned, red-leather box." An infantryman brought the key to Geiglein, who promptly ordered a clerk to type a memo and forward it to Uncle Charlie's war room. "Subject: Key to the City of Jülich," declared the memo. "To: Commanding General of the 29th Division. With the compliments of the 1st Battalion, 175th Infantry." No one ever figured out which door the key unlocked; by the looks of the key, the door was surely medieval, but in all likelihood it had already been smashed to bits by American bombs and shells, like the rest of Jülich. Gerhardt prized the key as one of the 29th Division's most impressive war trophies, and it is displayed today in the 29th Division Museum in the 175th's ancestral home, Baltimore's Fifth Regiment Armory.

Geiglein could not savor the moment, for by 3:00 P.M. on February 24 his battalion was poised to execute the 29th Division's opening "push to the east," as stipulated by McLain to Gerhardt that morning. The 1st Battalion's orders demanded the capture of Stetternich, an inconsequential village separated from Jülich by a

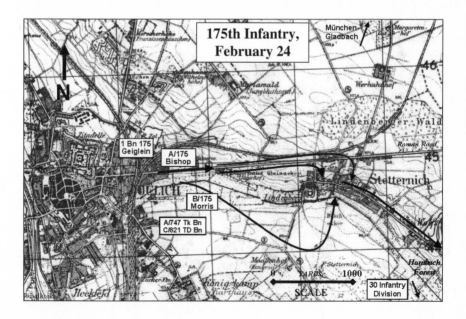

mile and a quarter of the wide-open Rhineland terrain the 29ers had come to loathe in the dreadful offensive that had brought the 29th Division as far as the Roer in November. Jülich and Stetternich were connected by an ancient Roman road known locally as *Römerstrasse*, dating to the first century AD and running twenty-five miles eastward to the Rhine at Cologne, as straight as a yardstick as far as the eye could see and lined by countless poplar trees, most of them shattered. As the *Römerstrasse* represented the Americans' most direct route to the Rhine, a 175th action report noted bluntly: "It was expected the Germans would defend it."

They did. The massive woodlands of the *Staatsforst Hambach* and the *Lindenberger Wald* hemmed Stetternich in on three sides, and Geiglein assumed correctly that German defenders would use the nearly impenetrable cover of those woods to set up positions from which deadly flanking fire could be placed on the attacking Americans. Geiglein's challenge was acute; the mission could only succeed against an irresolute or unprepared enemy. "The plan of attack was for Company B [Capt. Charles Morris, CO] to swing south of the highway [*Römerstrasse*] and enter Stetternich from the south," Geiglein recalled. "Company A [1st Lt. Frank Bishop, CO] was to guide on the highway and attack the town from the north." It all began at 3:55 P.M. when the wary 29ers moved out into the open fields east of Jülich in textbook style, widely dispersed, jogging forward with rifles at port arms and occasionally flopping down on sodden sugar beet fields to throw off the enemy's aim. Company A, 747th Tank Battalion, and Company C, 821st Tank Destroyer Battalion—newly equipped with M-10 self-propelled 3-inch guns, a vast improvement over the towed guns employed by the unit since D-Day—provided indispensable fire support, using both high-explosive and smoke shells to suppress and blind suspected enemy strongpoints. "The tanks [and tank destroyers] were to give the infantry a ten-minute start, firing from Jülich into Stetternich as the infantry advanced," said Geiglein. "[This] kept the tanks away from the infantry so that enemy artillery drawn by the tanks would not fall on the infantry."

Morris related to a U.S. Army historical officer a week later that his "1st Platoon, led by 2nd Lt. Frank Holt, went first, followed by the 3rd Platoon, eighteen enlisted men under T/Sgt. Raymond Welch [a full-strength rifle platoon normally had forty enlisted men]. . . . As we came within 500 yards of Stetternich, the leading elements received rifle and machine gun fire from Stetternich and mortar fire from the town and woods north, south, and east. [American] artillery and tank fire was placed on the Germans, and the men made rapid progress into town. The riflemen used 'marching fire'—[they] fired their weapons from the hip at the target as they charged. . . . Company B went through the town from west to east and advanced down the Hambach road [to the southeast] to the crossroads at F068588 [a map coordinate, a few hundred yards beyond the town], where they were stopped by mortar fire and direct fire from an '88' located in the west edge of Hambach Forest."

Lieutenant Holt, in his first major combat action, ascertained the enemy's passivity when his platoon came across a functional German 88-millimeter gun emplaced in a strongpoint. Ordinarily, the lethal 88s struck fear in the hearts of all 29ers, but this time Holt noted that its eleven crewmen "were in foxholes under the gun. We prodded them out, and they surrendered." Apparently, these pathetic *soldaten* were not the equivalent of the fearsome German paratroopers who often had gotten the better of the 29ers in Normandy and Brittany.

Meantime, Bishop's Company A had approached Stetternich from the opposite direction in what amounted to a clever pincer movement, stretching the beleaguered German garrison to the breaking point. "Company A advanced toward Stetternich with one platoon north of the highway [*Römerstrasse*] and the remainder of the company south of the highway," Bishop informed the historical officer. "We guided on the highway, but our troops were dispersed and not on the road itself. The tanks fired high explosive shells into Stetternich and placed smoke west of town and west of *Lindenberger Wald*. As Company A approached the town, the 1st Platoon received machine gun, mortar, and artillery fire from *Lindenberger Wald*. There was an 88 dug in, commanding the Cologne highway. The 1st Platoon was pinned down by this fire. The remainder of the company encountered only scattered fire and sideslipped right, entering the north part of Stetternich. Our tanks came to the edge of town, turned left, and fired into *Lindenberger Wald*. [At that point, a German *Panzerfaust* antitank rocket knocked out one of the 747th's tanks, but Sgt. Robert Ackerman retaliated by destroying a German self-propelled 88 with a well-aimed round from his Sherman.] The 1st Platoon, under cover of this fire, crossed the highway and got into town. It was getting dark, so the company went into defensive positions for the night in Stetternich."

As darkness fell, Geiglein dispatched patrols into the foreboding *Staatsforst Hambach* to make contact with the neighboring 30th Division, "with instructions to fire green parachute flares" as a precaution against friendly-fire incidents. The patrols soon returned with the comforting news that the 30th Division's 117th Infantry was securely anchored on the 175th's right flank and had already driven the enemy from the woods. Geiglein claimed that on February 24 his outfit "took more than 150 prisoners, four bunkers, six pillboxes, four 88-millimeter guns and four 76-millimeter guns." The 1st Battalion, however, paid a high price for that accomplishment, suffering about two dozen casualties, including four dead: thirty-two-year-old PFC Richard Conklin from Long Island, New York; twenty-three-year-old Pvt. Harlan Schafer from Minnesota; twenty-one-year-old Sgt. John Strum from West Virginia; and thirty-four-year-old Sgt. Joseph Valousky from Pennsylvania.

EVERYONE HAS GONE AWAY

Along the Roer front in Ninth Army's sector, Simpson's industrious engineers put the finishing touches on the bridges that were the keys to Operation *Grenade* and would soon allow the U.S. Army to unleash its unique brand of blitzkrieg on the progenitors of that renowned military theory. The 29th Division's capture of Stetternich on February 24, and other German towns like it by neighboring divisions, provoked the eager Simpson to loosen the reins on February 25 and allow his jubilant troops to push on toward the Rhine as speedily as they could, with little concern for enemy activity on their flanks.

Never before in World War II did Allied generals profess such a high level of buoyancy. At an hour-long press conference given by Eisenhower at the Scribe Hotel in Paris on February 24—his first conference in more than three months— a confident Ike asserted, "Given a continuation of the conditions as we see them now and a reasonable break in the weather—and I am not asking for July in Kansas—the attacks we are now seeing should mark the beginning of the destruction of the German forces west of the Rhine." Stephen Early, President Roosevelt's press secretary, was present at the conference and noted: "It was the most magnificent performance of any man at a press conference I have ever seen. [Ike] knows his facts, he speaks freely and frankly, and he has a sense of humor, he has poise, and he has command."

Ike did not base his opinion on mere whims, but on solid evidence from reliable sources that the German Army was in the midst of disintegration. A *New York Times* reporter highlighted for his readers Eisenhower's belief that "Marshal von Rundstedt's armies opposing the offensive are known to be at their lowest strength since the Allies' invasion of France, and there does not exist a German mobile counterattacking reserve in the sense that it is known to the Allies." Given signals of that kind, stateside civilians at last dared to presume, as a February 25 *Times* editorial remarked, that the "final chapter" of the European war had begun.

If any U.S. Army outfit deserved to be in on the kill, it was the 29th Infantry Division, which had been fighting the Germans almost continuously since the opening of the Second Front and had 20,000 casualties in nine months of combat to prove it. Through it all the 29ers had never felt the exhilaration of a genuine blitzkrieg; perhaps that chance had at last come.

For weeks Gerhardt had known that the 29th and all other units involved in Operation *Grenade* would swing to the north after crossing the Roer; the only issue was—when? At 8:12 P.M. on February 24, McLain phoned Gerhardt with the answer. "[I'll] head you to the north," McLain announced. "[We're] going ahead with the attack in the morning. Keep that attachment [330th Infantry] until you get someone to take over from them on the left." Gerhardt promptly summoned his senior commanders for a hasty meeting in the war room to work out the complex details on how the division would abruptly shift the axis of its assault 90 degrees to its left. Filmed by a U.S. Army cameraman, the dapper general, clothed in a neatly-pressed uniform with glossy black belt, tie tucked into his shirtfront, sprang up to the large 1:25,000 map of the 29th's sector, covered in clear, shiny acetate and propped up on easels, and got straight to the point. "Gentleman, the division bridgehead over the Roer River is now fully secured," Gerhardt pronounced in his clipped, rapid-fire style of speech, as he pointed to the map. "Jülich and the high ground, which dominated our bridge sites, are fully in our hands. We have vehicular bridges in, and everything is rolling now. We just got a directive from corps that changes our plan considerably. Instead of moving due east [toward Cologne] . . . the corps commander has decided to change his effort and move due north with divisions abreast. Our division will be on the left [with the 30th Division on the right]. We'll move early tomorrow morning [February 25] with two regiments abreast."

One question pervaded every attendee's mind: would the Germans offer the kind of fanatical resistance the 29ers had run into so often in the past? Gerhardt called on his chief intelligence officer, Lt. Col. Paul Krznarich, to answer that question, although to no one's surprise the general badly mangled the pronunciation of Krznarich's name: "Cris-nick," Gerhardt sputtered. By this stage of the war, the cerebral Krznarich knew that the general expected him to be brief. "All in all," Krznarich said, "enemy resistance seems to be very light and will continue to be so probably until we reach the Rhine."

"That sounds fine," the general exclaimed. "And of course the only thing we have to worry about now is scattered resistance straight ahead?"

Krznarich replied: "Yes, sir. In the towns . . . I think they'll center all their resistance in the small towns to the north."

"And then our right flank ought to be pretty well secure?" Gerhardt demanded.

"Yes, sir," Krznarich replied with a faint smile. "The first time I haven't said something could hit us on the flanks since we began this war, general."

Gerhardt closed the meeting with an electrifying conclusion: "Well, that's certainly a break for us because ordinarily we have to worry about not only our front, but our flanks too, so this will be a very fine situation."

The men who had to carry out the high command's orders, however, could not at first fathom how the military situation on the 29th Division's front could be categorized as "very fine." The two-regiment attack specified by Gerhardt for February 25 would involve Lt. Col. Sidney Bingham's 116th Infantry on the right and Foster's 330th Infantry, on loan from the 83rd Division, on the left. Bingham's men had blessedly missed the first two days of the fight, aside from the 3rd Battalion's battle at the Citadel on February 24, and when Gerhardt finally ordered them forward from their assembly areas west of the Roer, they fervently hoped that before their two-day grace period was up, the enemy's will to resist would evaporate.

It did not. The 2nd Battalion, commanded by Lt. Col. Lawrence Meeks, learned that regrettable detail just minutes after it traversed the Roer on a foot-bridge into Jülich at 2:30 A.M. on the twenty-fifth. Meeks remembered: "A concentration [of German artillery] fell on the road intersection at 031588 [a map coordinate, near Jülich's *Hexenturm*]. About ten rounds of heavy long-range artillery came in. The men ducked into the cellars of houses, taking whatever cover they could find." The unfortunate Company F, led by Capt. Riley King, thereupon underwent one of its worst episodes since D-Day as the enemy shell bursts wounded more than a dozen men in minutes. Thankfully, none of the wounded died.

For days, enemy warplanes and cannon attempting to destroy the fragile Roer bridges in the 29th Division's zone inflicted heavy casualties on the Americans in Jülich and its environs. "At one intersection," Bradley noted as he crossed the Roer on February 25, "four dead Yanks lay in the road where they had been killed a few minutes before by the blast of a bomb. Nearby, more lay on stretchers or beside the road while medics bent over to administer what first-aid they could on the scene." Nevertheless, Bradley added, "Engineers, working tirelessly since the first crossing of the Roer, had cleared a number of streets and changed the complexion of the city from one massive pile of rubble to a slight semblance of order."

As the 116th's February 1945 monthly report noted, overcoming the "scattered resistance" Gerhardt had expected "proved to be no easy matter." Bingham's orders mandated that by nightfall the 116th control the twin villages of Welldorf and Güsten, three miles northeast of Jülich; to reach them, his 29ers had to pass through the 175th's lines and advance nearly 4,000 yards across "pool-table flatlands," in which "every yard of advance beyond such cover as was available was hazardous in the extreme." The men of the 116th had attacked over the same kind of terrain in November and had lost hundreds of men; this time, the dogfaces hoped, the supposedly demoralized enemy would not stand and fight. On February 25, however, those hopes vanished in an instant. The 29ers encountered, according to the report, "a stubborn enemy, who had a super-abundance of firepower emanating from concealed and dug-in antitank guns, mortars, artillery, and small arms."

Bingham placed Lt. Col. Tom Dallas's 1st Battalion in the forefront of the attack and used the 2nd Battalion—his old command on Omaha Beach, now led by Meeks—as a follow-up force, ready to exploit any seams Dallas discovered in the enemy's defenses. For the first few hundred yards out of Jülich, the movement was easy enough: the leading riflemen, in their usual dispersed formation, trudged up the steep slope of Merscher Heights and without incident reached Neuhaus, an

ancient German *Gut*, or farm manor, atop *Wilhelmshöhe*, the highest point of land
in the Jülich area. They pushed on another half-mile due east to Mariarvald,
another walled-in *Gut*—still no enemy fire. But when the leading units, Capt.
William Williams's Company B and Capt. Robert Bedell's Company C, moved
out into the flatlands toward their next steppingstone, Werhahnhof *Gut*, one mile
distant, all hell broke loose. A report noted "a blanket of grazing fire" emanating
from hidden Germans in the Lindenberger forest, still not cleared by the 175th
Infantry, stopped the Americans cold.

So much for "scattered resistance"; the tragic events of the next two hours
forced shocked 116th veterans to conclude that hardly any day since Omaha
Beach had been blacker than this one. Company B lost 33 of its 143 men on duty
that morning, including three of its four officers—all D-Day veterans. Williams,
the fearless leader known to all as "Wild Bill," who had led the company through
too many scrapes to remember in Normandy, Brittany, and Germany, suffered a

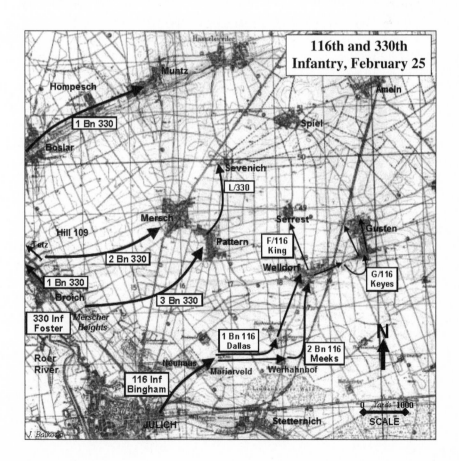

serious wound and would never return to the 29th Division. The addition to the casualty list of 1st Lt. Norvin Nathan and 1st Lt. Albert Blankenbaker—who, with Williams, represented a total of twenty-seven months of combat experience—was a blow from which Company B would take weeks to recover.

The 116th's monthly report cast the episode in a positive light by affirming that against such an intense German fusillade, "Troops other than seasoned, rested, and properly conditioned veterans might easily have come to an impasse. However, the 1st and 2nd Battalions of the battle-tried 116th Infantry bogged down only temporarily." At 1:32 P.M., Gerhardt phoned Bingham and declared, "The 30th [Division] on the right reports good progress. We've got to get to [Objective] 'W' [Welldorf]. . . . Get up there and push it!"

Bingham proceeded to push it. "At approximately 1500 hours," a report stated, "a coordinated attack supported by Company B, 747th Tank Battalion, and strongly motivated by the coldly vengeful fury of the men who had been denied an earlier success, was launched." To obscure the enemy's fields of fire, Bingham ordered his mortars and howitzers to lay down a smokescreen. That tactic worked beautifully, and as the report noted, "The 1st Battalion advanced steadily in the face of stiff resistance and after some brisk fighting was able to secure its objective, Welldorf, with the assistance of the 2nd Battalion." Meeks's operations officer, Capt. Bob Garcia, noted that the 2nd Battalion's "machine-gun fire support of the Welldorf fight was outstanding. It was impossible for the Germans to fight from the trenches outside of Welldorf because of this fire superiority." Meeks added that the supporting machine guns provided "a sheet of fire, which could be [adjusted] ahead of the advancing infantry."

Shortly before dark Meeks's men passed through the 1st Battalion in Welldorf and commenced a two-pronged attack: one company headed for the diminutive farm complex of Serrest, 1,000 yards to the north; the rest of the battalion jumped off toward Güsten, 600 yards northeast, tied to Welldorf by a single-track railroad. Captain King's Company F, still reeling from the losses it had suffered that morning from enemy artillery as it passed Jülich's *Hexenturm*, seized Serrest against little resistance by 8:00 P.M., but Güsten posed a much more difficult trial for the rest of the battalion. "We placed a preparatory barrage on Güsten before we attacked," Meeks told an Army historian. "We walked the barrage northeast as our men advanced, keeping the point of impact 200 yards ahead of the infantry." The historian's summary of the attack stated: "The attack began at 1800. Company G [Capt. Daniel Keyes, CO] led in squad columns, abreast of the road [connecting Welldorf and Güsten]. The tanks moved out with the riflemen. Daylight was fading, but there still was some light."

For a few minutes, the assault looked like a textbook training maneuver at Fort Meade; then the Germans woke up. An enemy antitank gun, cleverly concealed in a Güsten alley, fired two perfect flank shots, disabling the two leading Shermans. "The projectile went straight through the turret of [one] tank, making a clean, round hole about 3.5 inches in radius," a witness observed. Meeks added, "We saw the flash when the Germans knocked out the American tanks and called artillery on the places where the flash was seen." The fire was too hot for Keyes's men to progress any farther, and they retreated back to the safety of Welldorf.

At 7:30 P.M., Meeks tried again, this time maneuvering Company G around the south side of Güsten to look for a soft spot in the German defenses. "The tankers said it was too dark for them to fire effectively," Meeks said, "so the night attack was an infantry job. The men got into town in the darkness and began working north through the village. The southern part of Güsten was clear by 2200. . . . [Later] Companies E [Capt. Donald Meabon, CO] and G worked their way north through the town, E on the left of the main street and G on the right. The men worked slowly in the darkness. The town was clear by 0445 on February 26. At 0500 the tanks and tank destroyers came into Güsten. Perimeter defense was established around the town. . . . The 2nd Battalion took 142 prisoners and accounted for five dead Germans." At 7:44 A.M. on the twenty-sixth, a proud Gerhardt reported to McLain: "We have made the grade." When Meeks inspected Güsten at daylight, he reported, "We found tracks of a tank or SP [self-propelled] gun leading to the place from where the gun fired, empty 88-millimeter shell cases where the tracks ended, shell craters near the tracks, and more tracks where the thing backed up and turned around. . . . We found a wounded German. His right arm was blown off just below the shoulder—the arm was hanging by shreds of skin. He was also cut in the face and mouth by shrapnel, and there were shrapnel holes in his jacket. He was still alive when evacuated."

Holbrook Bradley witnessed the February 25 battle and informed his *Sun* readers that there had been "little glamor" in the fighting. "Unlike Hollywood versions of some war novels, there was no blood-tingling bayonet charge, no flag-waving, and no cheering. Rather, it turned out to be just a routine rush from one broken-up house to another." Despite high casualties and enemy resistance that obviously was still spirited, Bingham's 116th Infantry had gained an important victory. Garcia reflected that "the high morale of the troops" had gained that triumph. "They were on the move constantly from before 0100 Sunday [February 25] until 0500 Monday [February 26], yet showed no signs of reduced efficiency."

Gerhardt's February 25 plan directed Col. Robert Foster's 330th Infantry of the 83rd Division to capture another set of twin towns, Mersch and Pattern, three miles north of Jülich. Working with the temperamental Gerhardt could be a shock for an outsider like Foster, but Gerhardt was impressed by Foster's regiment, which shared with the 29th a long combat history dating to the summer of 1944 in Normandy and Brittany. Unlike the 29th Division, however, the 83rd had been committed to the Ardennes in December to help stem the Germans' massive offensive, and the 330th fought there for three terrible weeks in the Battle of the Bulge. Afterward, in reserve status, a 330th veteran noted, "Billeted in private homes, we enjoyed all the comforts of home (well, not quite all). Warmth, the pleasure of sleeping between white sheets and on soft beds, showers, clean clothes, and movies twice nightly. . . . Quite a change from the Bulge." The 330th's attachment to the 29th Division in *Grenade*, however, caused the same soldier to lament, "Gone were the soft beds, and once again we slept in foxholes."

Foster's men accomplished all that Gerhardt asked of them and more. By the end of February 25, the 330th had seized three key villages, one *Gut*, and advanced nearly four miles, a meteoric pace given the recent history of warfare in the Rhineland. The 2nd Battalion's effort to take Mersch began before dawn, at 5:15 A.M. As the 330th's monthly report stated, however, "They were held up by fire from bunkers and entrenched infantry." The men of the 2nd Battalion maneuvered adroitly around the resistance, and "by 0730 Company G was well into Mersch and was working up the main road running through the town."

The 330th's 3rd Battalion jumped off at the same hour in its attack against Pattern "and by 0810 had occupied all of the town and was engaged in mopping-up operations." The assault, an action report observed, was not easy: "Three light tanks [from Company D, 736th Tank Battalion, equipped with cutting-edge M24 light tanks armed with a 75-millimeter gun] were lost to enemy antitank fire moving into Pattern to support Company L. The enemy hid in holes as the infantry passed and returned to fire on tanks as they came forward."

At 8:43 A.M., Gerhardt phoned Foster and offered him a comment that most 29th Division field grade officers had only rarely received: "Nice going!" Gerhardt added, "Get yourself consolidated and start moving on in the zone to your left. . . . Keep going." Foster proudly reported, "One company has taken three officers and sixty enlisted men prisoner."

Foster indeed kept going. In late afternoon, Company L captured Sevenich, an isolated manor house a mile north of Pattern. At 2:00 P.M., Foster committed his 1st Battalion to a shrewd maneuver against Müntz, two miles north of Mersch. If Müntz could be captured, it would represent Ninth Army's deepest penetration into German lines so far in *Grenade*. The 1st Battalion men marched north from Broich, up the river road for two miles to Tetz, then turned right (east) and pressed ahead against no opposition to Boslar. That movement completely fooled the German garrison in Müntz, leaving the 1st Battalion in perfect position to launch a surprise flank attack. Meantime, Foster ordered the 453rd Antiaircraft Artillery Battalion to dispatch a single 40-millimeter gun and four trailers, each equipped with a quadruple .50-caliber machine-gun mount, to Hill 109, two miles southwest of Müntz. The disorganized Germans had been driven from that commanding elevation on February 23 by the 115th Infantry, and when the men of the 453rd unlimbered their weapons—lethal against enemy aircraft, but just as lethal against ground troops—the concentrated fire they would be able to direct against Müntz could be devastating.

Devastating it was. At 4:15 P.M., with the German garrison of Müntz pinned down by the 453rd's fire, Company C slipped into the town from the southwest. "The 1st Battalion continued the attack during the night," a report noted, "and at 1:30 A.M. on February 26, Companies A and C had cleared and secured the town." That stunning success pleased Gerhardt, but it delighted Foster even more because of the wonderful news that the 330th Infantry did not lose a single man killed in action throughout February 25. A 330th pamphlet published later that year proclaimed: "Pattern [and] Mersch . . . are some of the places we remember. Small stuff as far as the big picture goes, but to the man with the rifle who had to take them—well, to him the whole war is seen over the sights of a rifle."

The 29th Division now possessed a secure bridgehead over the Roer, so solid that Gerhardt ordered his rear-echelon units and four artillery battalions—totaling forty-eight 105- and 155-millimeter howitzers—to shift to the east side of the river. "Nothing emphasized the rapidity of the advance more than this sudden transformation, in which the front line of yesterday became today's 'rear area,'" wrote Ewing in *29 Let's Go.* "It was a heartening spectacle that lifted the confidence of the infantrymen—everything running so smoothly, every piece of the division works operating like a well-lubricated machine."

Firepower was the American Army's hallmark, now more than ever, and with stockpiles of ammunition at their highest levels since D-Day, supply officers took steps to ensure the Ninth Army's imminent blitzkrieg to the Rhine would not outrun its cache of artillery shells. Simpson therefore attached to the 29th Division the 3695th Quartermaster Truck Company, an African-American outfit whose "personnel and equipment," as directed by a quartermaster field manual, "must be ready to haul any kind of cargo, any time of day or night, to and from any place that higher authority may direct." The 3695th allocated fifteen deuce-and-a-half trucks to each of the 29th's three 105-millimeter howitzer battalions, doubling the amount of ammunition available to each firing battery. That policy would prove prudent, as on *Grenade*'s opening day, 29th Division artillery, including attached units, fired more than 20,000 rounds, amounting to one shell every four seconds—its highest rate of fire so far in World War II.

The 3695th deeply impressed the 110th Artillery's commander, Lt. Col. Purley Cooper, who was swamped with requests by its members to get up to the front and see some real fighting. "Tired of the relative inactivity of merely following along with ammunition," Cooper wrote, "they joined in the fight, first by opening ammunition crates and delivering shells to the guns, then by relieving gun crew members. . . . One group, which included a platoon sergeant, voluntarily went forward to reinforce an observer party. . . . Later, [I] sent their commander a letter of commendation for their fine work."

As February 25 closed, the commander of the 29th Division's right-hand neighbor, Maj. Gen. Leland Hobbs of the 30th Division, remarked, "It looks like things are beginning to break a bit." As the U.S. Army's campaign history declared, "To the [XIX] Corps commander, General McLain, it was clear that the way to the Rhine was opening. Only antitank fire remained effective; the German infantry appeared confused and drained of all enthusiasm for the fight." Even the enemy agreed with that assessment: the commander of First *Fallschirmjäger* [Parachute] Army, Lt. Gen. Alfred Schlemm, later observed that the Germans "no longer [held] a coherent defensive front" in the Jülich area, which "created a very dangerous situation. . . . If [the Americans] acted quickly and hurled their powerful armored forces boldly and unhesitatingly along the Rhine to Wesel, the left bank of the river would be lost and [First *Fallschirmjäger*] Army would be cut off from a retreat over the Rhine. There would have been no time to destroy completely the nine large bridges over the Rhine. It would have been impossible to form a new defensive front on the east bank of the river." Apparently the army that had invented blitzkrieg could neither execute it nor defend against it any longer, as another senior German commander, Lt. Gen. Erich Brandenberger, bemoaned: "The mobility of [German] units was generally completely insufficient to be in keeping with the rapidly moving enemy units."

On *Grenade*'s fourth day, February 26, the 330th Infantry continued to impress Gerhardt. The cunning one-two punch technique employed by Foster on the twenty-fifth—a combination of a frontal attack with a wide flanking maneuver—worked even better on the twenty-sixth due to the enemy's mounting breakdown. So confident were the men of the 330th's Company B in the enemy's impotence, in fact, that they dared to cross the open ground between their jump-off line at Hasselsweiler and their objective, Gevelsdorf, while seated atop the M24 tanks of Company D, 736th Tank Battalion, rather than plodding through muddy beet fields on foot. Bolstered by the 29th Division's elite Recon Troop, commanded by Capt. Ed Jones, Company B moved into Gevelsdorf from the south while the 330th's 2nd Battalion pushed in from the west against German resistance Jones later categorized as "light."

By early afternoon, the exultant Americans held Gevelsdorf. Indeed, the enemy offered such a puny defense that Gerhardt ordered Foster and Jones to keep going. Foster thereupon shoved the 330th's 1st Battalion northeastward to capture Isenkroidt *Gut* and the prominent Hill 107 close by. At 1:39 P.M., Witte directed Jones to "reconnoiter at once in the direction of Holzweiler and Katzem. Employ entire troop on this mission. Seize and secure Objective D [Holzweiler]

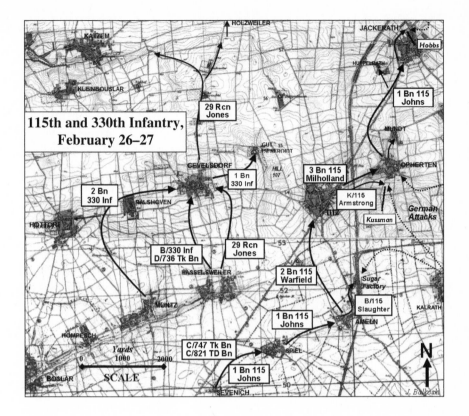

115th and 330th Infantry, February 26–27

if enemy situation warrants." At 5:35 P.M., McLain phoned Gerhardt and implored, "I want you to put all you've got in it." If the Recon Troop advanced the three miles to Holzweiler before sunset, evidence of the Germans' collapse would be irrefutable, and the Americans could be on the Rhine in a few days.

Not quite. Jones's leading troopers, mounted in speedy M8 armored cars, reported to the war room in late afternoon that enemy mines had halted their advance, but "patrols (on foot) continuing on from there." They failed to get far before dark, but Gerhardt hastily arranged for McHugh's 175th Infantry, currently in reserve, to pass through the Recon Troop and resume the attack the next morning, February 27.

At 7:30 P.M., Gerhardt contacted Foster and praised him with another "Nice going!" But the 29th Division, as the general told Foster, would soon lose the 330th Infantry. "You're all finished; get yourself together. You are released from us as of tonight, and we will give you word when you report to your outfit [the 83rd Division]." Foster was glad to accept the acclaim; still, he would be much more comfortable working within his own military family.

Gerhardt's sensible policy of leapfrogging reserves through active front-line units had effectively sustained the 29th Division's momentum. Following a two-day rest after its successful February 23 Roer assault, the 115th Infantry's turn came on the twenty-sixth when Gerhardt directed the regiment to move up from Jülich and launch an attack to seize Spiel; the northeastern axis of that maneuver would squeeze the 116th Infantry out of the line and cast it into division reserve. Orders stipulated that Lt. Col. William Blandford, the 115th's commander, should push his outfit northward beyond Spiel as rapidly as possible following the axis of the Jülich–Düsseldorf railroad. If the German defenders were nearly played out, as Gerhardt hoped, Blandford's mission should not be too difficult.

The 115th's February 26 attack began before dawn, led by Johns's 1st Battalion. As Johns's men trudged forward through the gloomy darkness from Jülich to their jump-off position at Sevenich, five field artillery battalions, including super-heavy 8-inch and 240-millimeter howitzers, fired their sixty field pieces nonstop for three hours against the unfortunate village of Spiel. Separated from Sevenich by a mile of flat farmland, Johns's men had a ringside seat for that impressive bombardment. Capt. Chester Slaughter, commander of Johns's leading unit, Company B, nonchalantly understated the value of that barrage, noting, "It was good."

Two weeks later Johns told an Army historian: "It was an overcast morning with showers and poor visibility. There was no air support. . . . The battalions also had twelve medium tanks [from Company C, 747th Tank Battalion, Capt. George Wagoner, CO]; nine tank destroyers [from Company C, 821st Tank Destroyer Battalion, 1st Lt. Dale Nafziger, CO]; and two assault guns [from the 747th]." Slaughter, a twenty-six-year-old native of Mexia, Texas, who had enlisted as a private in the 143rd Infantry of the Texas National Guard after high school, noted that his men "advanced at a fast walk, in extended formation with several yards interval between men, guiding on the Spiel road. The light artillery barrage was lifted as the leading elements came within 100 yards of Spiel [the heavy 8-inch and 240-millimeter howitzers had to cease fire earlier to avoid friendly-fire casualties], and the leading elements rushed into town at a run. The riflemen entered the town at 0630 and went through the houses. The Germans did little shooting. They came out of the cellars and surrendered."

Less than an hour later, Slaughter's men pressed ahead over the same featureless landscape toward Ameln, a mile beyond Spiel, but that place would be a much tougher objective due to the unexpected appearance of the enemy's 11th Panzer Division, recently rushed to the sector at Hitler's order from the Saarland, where it had been fighting a hopeless battle against Patton's Third Army. For the 11th, a mere shell of its former self, another hopeless battle would ensue; still, it brought about a dozen tanks into the fight, including Mark V Panthers and reportedly even a few more fearsome Mark VI Tigers, vehicles that were guaranteed to instill fear in American troops because of the U.S. Army's failure to produce anti-tank weapons that had a decent chance of penetrating the enemy's armor.

German panzer crews cleverly camouflaged their tanks on the peripheries of Ameln and did not announce their presence until American vehicles and infantry had approached the town at point-blank range. "It was getting light," Johns recalled. "An artillery barrage was called upon Ameln, but the fire was scattered, intermittent, and not so heavy as that on Spiel." The Americans' overconfidence was palpable; they had taken Spiel with no difficulty, and for a while they thought Ameln would be no different. They were wrong: "The advancing infantry encountered only scattered artillery and rifle fire," Johns remarked, "but as the tanks came within 200 yards of town, [German] tanks and antitank guns fired upon them from inside the town, and three American tanks were knocked out in quick succession." The enemy's pinpoint shooting killed four tankers and wounded several more, one of whom was a bona fide hero within the 747th Tank Battalion, Captain Wagoner. Decorated with the prestigious Distinguished Service Cross for heroism in Normandy, Wagoner was described by a fellow armor officer as "the only man I have ever known who was absolutely fearless." Despite wounds to both legs, Wagoner remained at the front long enough to supervise the evacuation of the wounded and come up with a plan to overcome the enemy's defenders.

Insufficient numbers of those defenders were present to hold back the Americans. Slaughter's Company B easily maneuvered around the Germans' scattered strongpoints, and as Johns proudly reported, when the 29ers dashed into the village, "Germans ran out with their hands in the air." The Americans even managed to capture the Panther tank that had wreaked havoc on Wagoner's Shermans. The German panzer commander, according to Johns, "told us he had hidden behind a building and tree to wait for the American tanks. When he knocked out our lead tank, the second American tank fired at him, missed, but hit the tree above his tank. Part of the tree fell across his gun, jamming the traversing mechanism. His crew climbed out and surrendered."

Searching for more concealed Germans—forty-five were eventually captured—Slaughter's resolute band swarmed through Ameln and even 500 yards beyond to a complex of industrial buildings labeled "*Zucker-Fabrik*" (sugar factory) on maps. The 29ers' watches read only 8:30 A.M., so plenty of daylight remained for the 115th to keep pressure on the reeling enemy by pressing northward as Gerhardt's orders stipulated. The follow-on 2nd Battalion was soon expected to pass through Ameln and advance two more miles to capture the key crossroads town of Titz; in the meantime, satisfied with their notable accomplishments so far on February 26, the men of the 1st Battalion in Ameln would take a breather and await orders, which no one hoped would arrive soon.

As an anonymous writer noted sardonically in the 115th's monthly report, "The Germans, however, weren't convinced that [Ameln] could be held by our unit. They spent the rest of the morning indulging in enthusiastic activities against the 1st Battalion." That enthusiasm, according to Slaughter, consisted of "considerable German artillery," which increased markedly at 10:30 A.M. The 11th Panzer Division brought up several antitank guns to Kalrath, a mile east of Ameln, and every minute or so one of those lethal weapons roared, sending a shell screeching over the intervening flatland toward an unfortunate American target in less than two seconds—faster than an M-1 rifle bullet. The 747th's Sherman tanks returned fire in what Slaughter depicted as "a brisk firefight."

But the Germans were not interested in a mere long-range gun duel. They wanted to recapture Ameln and sent forward about one hundred infantrymen and eight tanks—Slaughter avowed two were Tigers—to drive the Americans out. "The German tanks and infantry started south down a long depression, which ran east of the railroad into Ameln," Slaughter related. "We tried to call artillery on them, but our forward observer's SCR-300 radio failed. [The radio did not fail; rather the 110th Field Artillery's liaison officer at Johns's 1st Battalion command post, Capt. Kenneth James, was wounded and therefore could not relay Slaughter's request back to the 110th's howitzers.] The draw protected the Germans from our armor inside and northwest of town." The members of Company B opened fire with everything they had, but the enemy kept coming. "We ran out of antitank rockets for the bazookas," Slaughter noted. "German tanks got into the [sugar] factory area. The tanks began shooting up the factory buildings. They blew holes in the walls with armor-piercing shells and then fired high explosive shells through the holes. The German infantry followed the tanks in and began going through the factory buildings."

The 110th Field Artillery's Capt. William Beehler hastily assumed James's role at the 1st Battalion command post and arranged for a devastating barrage of 105-millimeter howitzer shells on the *Zucker-Fabrik*. Slaughter observed the fire and remarked that "two German tanks withdrew north, both smoking and apparently damaged, [and] a German assault gun was struck by artillery fire and burned. As the Germans began withdrawing north through the draw, we adjusted a heavy artillery barrage on them, placed a barrage on the crossroads at 088672 [a map coordinate, 600 yards north of the factory], and a time-on-target barrage on Kalrath. . . . Company B went back to the sugar factory and dug in there for the night. [From there] we could see thirty-five dead Germans scattered along the draw east of the railroad."

The fracas at the Ameln sugar factory threw the 115th's February 26 plans into disarray. Gerhardt expected Maj. Albert Warfield's 2nd Battalion to be on its way to Titz by early afternoon, but the dire situation in Ameln forced Warfield to detach 1st Lt. Sanford Reamey's Company G to help the beleaguered 1st Battalion. The presence of enemy armored vehicles in large numbers also caused a worried Blandford to request help from the 821st Tank Destroyer Battalion, whose M10 armored vehicles, equipped with deadly 3-inch guns, could counter almost anything in the enemy's repertoire. At 4:11 P.M., an impatient Gerhardt phoned Blandford and demanded, "What time do you think they [the 2nd Battalion] will go?" Blandford's reply—"I don't know, sir"—ordinarily would have vexed the general, but Blandford's prompt follow-up that he was "going up there now to find out what it's all about" soothed Gerhardt.

The delay actually worked to the Americans' advantage. By the time Warfield's men jumped off at 7:00 P.M., darkness had set in; after the heavy fighting at Ameln, the German defenders of Titz did not expect their opponents to resume their advance until the morning of February 27. But resume it they did, with the hope that the enemy was neither ready nor willing to fight. "The night sky was filled with the glare from scores of fires burning in almost every direction," the regimental history observed, "but there were few sounds of battle."

Prior to the attack, a Company G platoon led by 2nd Lt. Don Van Roosen, a D-Day veteran who had recently jumped from enlisted man to officer as a result of a battlefield commission, killed some time in a relatively intact Ameln building. Van Roosen stumbled on a beaten-up piano and, "for my own enjoyment," stepped away from the war for a few relaxing moments by pounding out a few tunes. But the war's harsh reality abruptly reemerged when one of Van Roosen's senior noncommissioned officers announced "he couldn't go on" and professed the intention of holding back from the imminent attack. "I spent some time reasoning with him, giving him the benefit of the doubt, but the longer I talked and the more he weaseled, the more put out I became," Van Roosen remembered. "I laid down an ultimatum: if he shirked his duty, I would see him busted. Eventually, I sent him to the 2nd Battalion command post with a squad leader and instructions that I did not want to see him again, ever."

Minus one NCO, Reamey's Company G moved out toward Titz with 1st Lt. John Baker's Company F on its right. The 29ers would have achieved total surprise had not one of the 821st's M10s hit a mine 200 yards short of the town, an event Van Roosen recalled "sent up a large ball of fire. It lit up the entire area and, even worse, outlined the muzzle of a [German] Mark IV tank about fifteen yards away. It had sheaves of hay draped around it, and we would have walked right by it except for the explosion."

Did Germans occupy the tank? Van Roosen assumed they did; he approached it and could hear its engine idling. "I climbed up on the track," he said, "and reached to turn the handle on the turret door. I confess my heart was beginning to beat faster when I reached inside only to find another door. I opened

that door and reached inside, but this time I touched the shoulder of the tank commander, who was very much awake and waiting for me." Luckily for Van
Roosen, neither the tank commander nor any of his crew had any stomach for
more fighting. Van Roosen continued: "I talked to him in a low voice in German
and told him to bring his crew out and surrender. He did this without comment. . . .
I asked him if he had any weapons, at which point he produced a Luger from a
holster and a small .25-caliber Mauser [pistol], both of which I brought home
with me." The next day, Van Roosen recalled he almost had a "heart attack"
when he saw "our German tank being driven by two GIs. The whole 2nd
Armored Division was going by on the road, and it must have taken very good
luck and control to keep the Mark IV from being blasted into oblivion!"

As Van Roosen's platoon had already discovered, 2nd Battalion men "were
happy to learn that the bulk of the German troops were in no mood to continue
the fight," the regimental history reported. Another Company G soldier, T/Sgt.
John Love, gathered as much when his platoon detected an enemy machine-gun
nest on the outskirts of Titz. A twenty-four-year-old veteran of Company G since
his November 1939 enlistment at the Maryland National Guard's Cumberland
armory, Love—who in a few weeks would also gain a battlefield commission—
had witnessed obstinate behavior on the part of German troops since he had
landed on Omaha Beach on D-Day. Not this time: his cheerful underlings ascertained that "the Germans [were] eager to surrender without firing a shot."

A few intractable German panzers continued to resist, "running around the
northeastern section of the village, firing spasmodically at the main road running
into and through the town." The *Sun*'s Bradley described the phenomenon when
those tanks and assault guns "threw a couple of flat-trajectory rounds down the
main street. There was the unmistakable sound of a shell leaving a gun, a few seconds later a *whiz*, and then the immediate, shattering explosion almost on top of
us. A foot or so of water in the ditches on either side of the road was no deterrent,
and we splashed in and almost held our faces under water."

Regrettably, one of those "shattering explosions" killed twenty-one-year-
old 2nd Lt. Robert Hohenstein III. A native of Westfield, New Jersey, who had
joined Company G little more than a month ago, Hohenstein was a stellar high
school football player and had attended Rutgers University for one year before
gaining an Army commission in the antiaircraft artillery in 1943. By late 1944,
however, the U.S. Army needed fresh infantrymen most of all; Hohenstein
helped meet that demand by requesting a transfer from an all-black antiaircraft
battalion to the much more dangerous infantry branch and soon found himself a
member of the storied 29th Division. Recalled Van Roosen: "He would have
made a very fine officer in my opinion, and his death was a real loss." Hohenstein carried a Colt .45 pistol his father had used in World War I; after his

February 26 death, his comrades tried to retrieve and return it to his father, but the pistol vanished.

Grenade had established beyond doubt that the 29th Division—not known in previous campaigns for its proficiency in nighttime operations—had matured by a considerable factor since D-Day. The 29th no longer routinely "shut down for the night," as Gerhardt used to pronounce most evenings; as the delighted 29ers learned, nocturnal operations saved lives in attacks across wide-open ground, even during nights featuring a near-full moon like the one on February 26. The Americans savored their newfound expertise, although nighttime maneuvers could be just as perplexing for the attacker as the defender. "It was difficult to distinguish any of our troops in the shadows of the buildings," Bradley wrote, "but as we moved in, groups of doughboys could be seen standing guard and searching buildings up the street. On the west and north edges of town, the sounds of firing told us that our men were still cleaning up. Along the main highway one lone self-propelled Jerry gun continued to throw shells in, uncomfortably close."

The crew of one German armored vehicle, probably the same one noted by Bradley, unwisely probed too close to an American foxhole on Titz's outskirts. In the dark, lacking supporting infantry, that action was imprudent; thanks to an odd pair of Company G 29ers sharing that foxhole, it was the last act the German crewmen ever took. Standing up to a dreaded enemy panzer demanded nerves of steel, but PFCs Melvin Ayres and Daniel Mixon (mistakenly identified in *29 Let's Go* as Ayers and Nixon) accepted the challenge. The two men had at first assumed the tank was American; only after they heard the crew speaking German did they make "a collective grab for their bazooka, already loaded and sitting atop their foxhole." Thirty-five years old and married, Ayres, a Virginian, was fifteen years senior to his foxhole buddy, Mixon, from Georgia. However, Mixon, who had just celebrated his twentieth birthday and had recently returned to Company G upon recovery from a serious wound suffered at St. Lô in July, was a seasoned combat veteran compared to Ayres, a recent replacement and participant in his first major battle.

"I picked up the bazooka, and we fired at the turret of the tank," Mixon wrote of the first time he had ever fired the weapon in combat. "The first shot hit the turret, and the Jerries fell back into the tank screaming. The tank driver tried to escape, and we fired another round at him. One Jerry charged out and started for Sgt. Frank Kunclrs [a thirty-year-old Pittsburgh native], our platoon sergeant, in a foxhole nearby. In the fight, Kunclrs killed the Kraut. We tried to get the remaining occupants out by commanding them in German. However, they apparently thought they could get away, for the tank started up. It was foolish. . . . As [the tank] started to go, S/Sgt. Thurman Jones [a twenty-two-year-old Alabamian] crept up and dropped a hand grenade down the hatch. [Actually, he dropped two grenades: first, a white phosphorous version; next, a standard fragmentation grenade.] This knocked the crew out completely." Kunclrs gained a Silver Star for his close-range fight with the frenzied German.

In response to Gerhardt's urgent plea to "push it," Blandford intended to continue his winning leapfrog technique on Tuesday, February 27, with two more leaps forward: at 3:00 A.M., the 3rd Battalion, led by Lt. Col. Randolph Millholland (Lieutenant Colonel Fisher had been wounded and evacuated Sunday evening when his jeep ran over a mine), would move out from Titz to seize Opherten, a mile to the northeast; eight hours later, Johns's 1st Battalion would follow in the 3rd's wake and push on another two miles beyond Opherten to capture Jackerath. Should Johns reach his goal, the 115th's terrain gain in the first four days of *Grenade* would be over ten miles, a rate of advance the regiment had never achieved so far in World War II.

Millholland's leading outfit, Capt. Robert Armstrong's Company K, began the advance toward Opherten with one of its rifle platoons mounted atop the accompanying Shermans of the 747th Tank Battalion. That platoon, led by 2nd Lt. Jack Kussman, could have suffered heavy casualties if the enemy had zeroed in an accurate salvo of howitzers or, even worse, hit the column with a machine-gun fusillade, but Opherten's defenders—assuming there were any—did not open fire. In case the enemy was indeed present, Bradley noted, "The [American] artillery was already plastering the new objective with concentrations zeroed in to cover the [forward] entrenchments and the town, from one end to the other. All around the horizon ahead we could see flashes of artillery and the doughboys of our division moving steadily forward to the right and left of us."

Kussman accompanied the squad led by S/Sgt. Hoyn Woodside, a twenty year old from the foothills of the Blue Ridge in North Carolina, who had joined the 115th Infantry as a replacement on June 22, 1944. Kussman described Woodside as "a great soldier—a very quiet guy who had the complete respect of his men. He was calm under fire and had the ability to

Lt. Jack Kussman of Company K, 115th Infantry, led the attack into Opherten.

hide his fears." The Sherman carrying Woodside's squad, however, broke down halfway to Opherten, so Kussman directed the men to disembark and proceed to the objective on foot. "A short time later," Kussman recalled, "Sergeant Woodside and I observed a column of troops moving toward us at an angle from the lower ground to our right." Who were they? Dawn was still a few hours away, and in the dark it was hard to tell; some thought they were from the neighboring Company M, but Kussman thought otherwise. "We got to within fifteen to twenty yards of the column before the lead man saw Woodside and me," wrote Kussman. "In a questioning manner, he said '*Deutscher*?' . . . Instinctively we took off to get back and warn our column. The Germans, however, were very quick to react and were already firing. . . . I hate to say it, but I saw some [Americans] run away. . . . Sergeant Woodside and his assistant squad leader [thirty-year-old PFC Crystal Green from Kansas] began firing their grenade launchers. The grenades were on target, and this caused the Germans to momentarily stop firing. You could hear screams and cries for help from the Germans. This short pause seemed to wake up our troops, and soon our superior firepower began to take a toll on the Germans."

Meantime the rest of Millholland's 3rd Battalion advanced into Opherten from several directions and began the protracted chore of securing it. Bradley moved into town with a follow-up company and wrote: "Off to the right, a haypile burned brightly in the middle of a field, and once or twice we could see a brilliant spray of machine-gun bullets sweeping the ground from the town ahead [Jackerath]. . . . The lead tanks sent a number of rounds into a farmhouse where [German] fire seemed to be coming from, and the column moved on." Accompanied by his aide and driver, the 29th Division's assistant commander, Brig. Gen. Leroy Watson, roamed the 115th Infantry's sector in his jeep *Task Force*, and at 5:42 A.M. on February 27 he reported to Maj. Lucien Laborde in the 29th Division's war room that Millholland was "having a hell of a fight. We have quite a number of German tanks roving in the town and around it. We got some of them, but there are still some more roaming around. [German] infantry got between some of Millholland's people, but he's working that out." An hour later, Capt. Thomas Neal, the 115th's operations officer, reported to Laborde, "We got it [Opherten], [but] it isn't secure yet."

Millholland's people indeed "worked it out." Reporter Bradley recorded that "buildings over to the left of us blazed up in a shower of sparks. . . . Then it was a rough-and-tumble fight to clear the town, with the doughboys crashing into each house, taking a quick look around upstairs, and diving into the basements where the Krauts usually holed up. . . . Once, as we headed around a corner, there was a slightly tense moment. The street was empty except for a figure standing in a doorway a couple of houses up the street. We yelled, and the man came running—only when he was a couple of yards from us did we recognize that he was a German armed with a Schmeisser [MP40 submachine gun]. The shots and confusion that followed were too much for him, and another prisoner was added to the rapidly increasing haul." At 9:38 A.M., Neal proudly reported to the war room: "AA [code for Opherten] is officially cleared. Seventy prisoners. Our own casualties very light. The 1st Battalion is going into AA now, preparing to go on to BB [code for Jackerath]." The 115th's monthly action report noted: "The [German] troops we encountered had very little enthusiasm toward continuing the war."

Johns professed that same sentiment ten days later when he spoke with a U.S. Army historian, 1st Lt. Herschel Jones, about the 1st Battalion's attack on Jackerath. "The Germans were showing signs of disorganization," Johns asserted. "Everything was moving fast, the men were winning and were in very high spirits." Also in high spirits was Gerhardt, who traveled up to the front in his jeep *Vixen Tor* to watch Johns's men jump off from the start line at Opherten. The attack moved out at 10:45 A.M. as howitzers from the 110th Field Artillery hammered Jackerath and 4.2-inch mortars from Company B, 92nd Chemical Mortar Battalion, laid down a perfect smokescreen to blind the Germans. Ordinarily, an assault over wide-open ground in daylight—the division journal reported "broken overcast with scattered clouds; visibility good"—would have triggered profound misgivings among the riflemen, but this time the men were so confident that Johns's leading unit, 1st Lt. Julian Stoen's Company C, mounted ninety men aboard nine Shermans provided by Company C, 747th Tank Battalion, for the risky journey across no-man's-land.

A twenty-six-year-old Minnesotan, Stoen was a born soldier whose military career would eventually include overseas service in three wars. Since his participation in the Omaha Beach invasion as executive officer of Company B, he had suffered two wounds; the most recent, on October 8 in Germany, had required a three-month recovery. Depicted by Johns as "a fine company commander," Stoen by now was used to the burden of command, but never before had his men been so certain of success. "The tanks formed behind a hill that runs northwest from Opherten," Stoen told Jones. "Riflemen, BAR men, and Tommy gunners led by 1st Lt. [Joseph] Blalock [also from Company B] climbed on them. The tanks started in column northwest, behind the ridge, crossed the Jackerath road, and roared across the fields, their turrets open, firing their machine guns into the town. Ten riflemen were on each tank, standing on the bustle and deck, crowded around the turret. The tanks ran into soft ground at 095705 [a map coordinate, just south of a farm labeled Huppelrath on U.S. Army maps] and were forced back [east] parallel to the road."

Johns noted, "German morale was crumbling." That unmistakable detail emerged when the tanks, still with infantrymen aboard, passed through an orchard just to the east of Huppelrath. Blalock reported: "There were trenches in the orchard, and Germans were huddled in those trenches. As we passed the trenches, the riflemen fired into them and the Germans climbed out and surrendered. The tanks stopped seventy-five yards from the village, and the infantrymen jumped off and charged into town. The riflemen stayed close to the tanks and worked with them. If fire came from a house, the tank would fire into it with its 76-millimeter gun, and the men would rush into the house. The tanks operated with their turrets open, and coordination between the tanks and infantry was excellent."

At 11:12 A.M., Neal conveyed more happy news to the war room: "All finished with BB [Jackerath]. Krauts coming out with their hands up." Johns told Jones that the 1st Battalion "sent [the POWs] south along the road in groups of thirty to forty, guarded by one or two headquarters personnel." He added that "German civilians milled about, getting in the way, begging the soldiers to stop the artillery." As recent experience indicated, however, capturing the town was much easier than holding it against the inevitable German counterattack. That enemy "enthusiasm" materialized in early afternoon when six Mark IV tanks from the 11th Panzer Division—one account reported eight—abruptly clanked over a ridge north of Jackerath and commenced a desperate full-speed charge toward the village.

A twenty-two-year-old Roanoke, Virginia, native named S/Sgt. Mills Hobbs had just deployed the four other members of his squad at a road junction north of town when the panzers roared over the ridge. Hobbs had seen plenty of combat, including on Omaha Beach, and had been wounded twice, the first time in July outside St. Lô and the second in September at Brest, but the current predicament shaped up as his most taxing trial of the war. In a tumultuous scrap that Johns recalled "lasted only a few minutes," Hobbs and his squad members—PFCs Tom Cook from Alabama, Sheldon Flewellen from Wisconsin (curiously, his enlistment records list him as a "negro"), Lewis Haselwood from Missouri, and James Hayhurst from West Virginia—"allowed the tanks to get in close," as a *29 Let's Go* article related. "The tanks were close enough to spit on; ferociously [the Americans] let loose with bazookas [Hobbs actually had only one bazooka—with a single round of ammunition], rifle grenades, and small arms." Johns remarked: "The grenades did not penetrate the [lead] German tank. A bazookaman . . . fired a rocket into the rear of the German tank, and the tank caught fire. The crew climbed out of the burning tank and ran toward the other German tanks." (The next day, Johns inspected the shattered enemy vehicle and thrust his swagger stick through the small hole in the steel armor made by the bazooka rocket. Afterward he awarded Bronze Stars to Hobbs and the other four squad members.)

Some enemy tanks withdrew, but two pressed on and managed to penetrate into the constricted confines of the village. "One followed the street until it was south of Company C," Johns said. "An American [M10] tank destroyer [from Company A, 821st Tank Destroyer Battalion] was in the north of town. Its crew saw the Mark IV south of it, turned around, and fired at it. The shell, a high explosive round that evidently had been in the chamber when the destroyer entered town because it had no time to reload [an "armor-piercing" round would have been more effective against tanks], struck the Mark IV on the left sprocket. The track jammed, and the tank spun around as its crew tried to move it out of the fight. The instant the [American] destroyer fired, a second Mark IV fired at the destroyer from behind and set it on fire. The [American] crew got out."

Company C's second-in-command, 1st Lt. Warren Hecker, along with a private named Jack Jones, loaded and fired a bazooka at the second tank and scored a hit on its 75-millimeter gun. "Realizing that if he remained in the town he would be captured," the regimental history observed, "the German tank commander climbed up through the turret and began directing the driver in backing the vehicle out of the narrow street. Unfortunately for the German tanker, he came into the sights of PFC Robert Chandler's gun and was killed." Still, the nearly cornered panzer managed to get away. Others were not so lucky: "When the crews of the crippled tanks tried to escape, the Yanks mowed them down and forced the others to surrender," noted a *29 Let's Go* article.

Holbrook Bradley concluded, "The 29th had knocked off another town on its way through the Reich." Johns affirmed that his 1st Battalion's assault on Jackerath "was successful because of carefully made plans, which were thoroughly understood and smoothly applied, and because of coordination and cooperation by the artillery and the infantry. Preparation of the fire plans for the attack required . . . intense and precise study of terrain and enemy positions from maps, aerial photos, intelligence reports, and artillery aerial observation. . . . This time we have the stuff we need—tanks, tank destroyers, artillery—and we have them in the quantity we need. . . . The [Germans'] fanatical willingness to fight on, even against long odds, is no longer present. East of the Roer they have put up token resistance, then quit when confronted with a hopeless situation."

The 29ers could smell blood now, and they prepared to go in for the kill of a nearly subjugated enemy. They had never before gained ground against the enemy at their current rate. The remorseless Johns remarked to the historian Jones that his men had learned to follow a simple code: "Make [the Germans] understand, by concrete example as well as by inference, that they can either fight or surrender. They cannot do both. If they fire on us, the game is for keeps. If they surrender without a fight, they know they will be evacuated to safe rear areas within the hour. They seem to understand this. It will not do to let them believe they can hold out, snipe a few more men, and then surrender with guarantee of good treatment."

This was the moment for which Gerhardt had been born. The 29th Division had the Germans on the run; only American lethargy would allow the enemy a chance to restore its defenses. To prevent that lethargy from developing, the general directed Bingham to reinsert his 116th Infantry into the line on February 27. Ordered to initiate his regiment's seven-mile march to the front from its staging area around Güsten and Welldorf as early as possible that Tuesday morning, Gerhardt alerted Bingham that the 116th would attack northward as soon as the 115th had secured Jackerath. Bingham's initial objective would be Immerath, one and a half miles beyond Jackerath; afterward, by leapfrogging his battalions, Bingham must push the 116th farther northward by nightfall to capture the minuscule farm settlements of Lützerath, Spenrath, Pesch, and finally Otzenrath. Fulfillment of Gerhardt's orders would ultimately require the men of the 116th to advance nearly ten miles from dawn to dusk—all of it on foot—an unthinkable progression by the standards of the recent past, but in the exhilarating days of Nazi Germany's imminent crack-up, such an accomplishment had abruptly become the norm.

At 9:02 A.M. on the twenty-seventh, Gerhardt phoned Bingham and asked, "What time did your column get underway?" When Bingham responded, "The 3rd Battalion pulled out at 0845," the general snapped: "That's fifteen minutes late! You've got to begin to produce. If it's going to be like this all day long, you've got to begin to show results. I think you picked your starting time [8:30 A.M.] way too late, and then you are late getting started."

Bingham had the temerity to answer back, "The order we got last night specified a time to be in a certain place"; the general rejoined: "I don't think so." An exasperated Bingham vowed, "We'll get there and get the job done." Still dissatisfied, Gerhardt concluded: "If you can't do it, we'll have to get somebody to do your job for you. You've got to begin to produce!"

The men of the 116th "produced"—and probably saved Bingham's job—by reaching their jump-off point at Holzweiler shortly before noon. It had been a tough slog, but as the 116th's February report noted, "There was to be no rest for the weary and sweat-stained troops; preparations for [the] attack were commenced immediately." The 3rd Battalion, commanded by Bill Puntenney—at twenty-five, one of the youngest infantry battalion commanders in the U.S. Army—opened the 116th's attack on Immerath at 1:30 P.M., moving eastward in a widely dispersed formation from Holzweiler across the familiar tabletop flatland toward the objective, one and a half miles away. Puntenney's impressive force included more than a dozen Shermans from Company B, 747th Tank Battalion, and at first it seemed that nothing could stop the American juggernaut. But the skimpy number of defenders holding Immerath, who even had two tanks of their own, resisted with astounding tenacity for a few hours and inflicted eleven casualties—including three killed—on Puntenney's leading unit, Capt. Arvid

Ree's Company L. The typical MOS-745 rifleman in Puntenney's battalion was just a few years beyond adolescence, but one of the dead Company L 29ers, PFC David Misky of New Haven, Connecticut, was unusual in that he was thirty-five years old, a college man, and married.

Capt. Berthier Hawks's Company I swept into Immerath in the wake of Company L and encountered equally resolute resistance. One of Hawks's veteran squad leaders, S/Sgt. Raymond George—who had been with Company I since June 16, 1944—led his men cautiously through the village and spotted an enemy tank in a cul-de-sac. A surprised German tanker standing beside his vehicle reached for a pistol, but was shot dead by one of George's riflemen. As George undertook the laborious procedure of affixing an antitank grenade to his M-1, PFC James Doyle Jones from Atkins, Arkansas, fired several rounds from a bazooka at the tank, but each shot missed. Return fire from the tank wounded PFC Herman Davis and Sergeant George—his third wound in eight months.

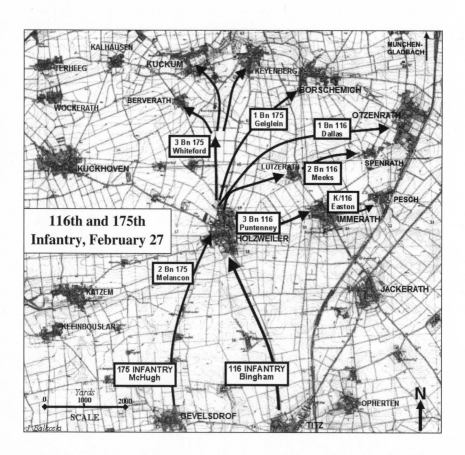

(Four days later, Davis died of his wounds; George never returned to Company I.) Jones, however, zeroed in on the tank with his bazooka and finally scored two hits, knocking it out. The Company I morning report for February 27 proudly noted that other company members destroyed a second enemy tank in Immerath and captured thirty-five prisoners by nightfall. In the hyperbolic words of the 116th's action report, the regiment had "added the town of Immerath to the territory wrested by main force from a desperate foe."

Meanwhile, Lt. Col. Lawrence Meeks's follow-on 2nd Battalion swung to the west around Puntenney's left and, virtually unopposed, pushed another 1,000 yards beyond Immerath to secure the Lützerath farm by 2:30 P.M.—less than an hour after Bingham had begun his attack. For the remainder of the afternoon, the 116th's steady and unimpeded progress triggered even greater hyperbole on the part of the anonymous report writer: "Following a quick and skillful reorganization [at about 3:00 P.M.], the embattled, land-hungry battalions of the 116th Infantry continued their relentless pursuit of the enemy. Before night had enveloped the dark and bloody ground, the 1st Battalion [Lt. Col. Tom Dallas, CO] had seized Otzenrath; the 2nd Battalion had forced its way into Spenrath; and the 3rd Battalion [actually just Capt. Elmer Reagor's Company K], aided by a preparatory air strike, had silenced enemy opposition in Pesch. The positions seized by the battalions were cleared of vestigial resistance and consolidated. The units buttoned up for the night, held fast, and made preparations for a renewed offensive in the morning."

Company K's clerk, thankful to have inserted on his daily morning report the name of only one soldier wounded (twenty-three-year-old Pvt. William Murphy, from Chicago, who had just joined the outfit as a replacement six days previously), revealed that his unit's biggest concern was no longer the enemy: "Men troubled with sore feet from marching in the continuing advance." In early evening an overjoyed Gerhardt phoned the 116th's command post and forgave Bingham for his supposed sluggishness that morning. "Congratulations!" the general announced. "Well done, all the way through. You did a fine job and finished up swell. It will be straight ahead tomorrow."

A Company K platoon leader, 1st Lt. Bob Easton, observed that in the enemy towns entered by the 116th Infantry, "As usual there were hastily improvised white flags, sheets, and tablecloths hanging from doors, windows. People watched us, women, children, old men, some with hostility, some crying, some turning away in utter hate—as I remember a large grotesquely pregnant woman we passed—some with curiosity and a smile. . . . The modernity of Germany, materially, is impressive. In architecture, construction, and machinery, what I've seen is superior to anything else over here [in Europe]. There are other tokens of advanced civilization. Books, plenty of them, if on the wrong subjects, the glories

of Nazism, etc.—yet with Goethe too; and pianos and Bach, Beethoven, Mozart.
. . . There is a disciplined, thrifty quality about the neat brick homes, evidence of
industry, self-respect, strength . . . but charm? Not much."

While the 115th and 116th plunged ahead across the Cologne Plain, Gerhardt
"threw the book" at the enemy, as he liked to say, by committing his third—and
last—regiment, the 175th Infantry, to the fight on the division's left flank, taking
over the front of the recently departed 330th Infantry. Hardly ever before had the
general committed all nine of his infantry battalions to a battle simultaneously,
but on February 27, 1945, with the scent of victory in the air, he did exactly that.

For some weary men who had expected to find glory in war but instead had
become inured to its unremitting violence, the events of February 27 provided
evidence that the imminent and crashing finale of the European war just might
yield a little glory after all. Following the same leapfrog pattern that had proven
so successful the previous two days, the 175th moved out before dawn and
headed north toward the front. This was no ordinary attack: the 2.6-mile interval
between the jump-off point at Gevelsdorf and the initial objective at
Holzweiler—as vacant as the Kansas prairie, with the usual barren pastures and

**White flags hang from German homes in a Rhineland village captured by the
29th Division.**

only three scattered farmhouses—would be recorded as one of the lengthiest assaults in 29th Division history, almost three times as long as the deadly ground crossed by Pickett's ill-fated charge at Gettysburg in July 1863. Holzweiler's defenders, however, demonstrated nowhere near the same determination to stand their ground as the Union soldiers who had held Cemetery Ridge against Pickett. The Germans in Holzweiler, in fact, offered almost no resistance at all and did not even attempt their normal "enthusiasm"—counterattack—after the Americans had cautiously penetrated into the village.

The 175th's assault actually began on a sour note when three Sherman tanks from Company A, 747th Tank Battalion, ran over mines in the dark and were disabled. "Paths had been cleared by engineers," a report commented, "but the tanks were unable to see the marking tape because of darkness. An engineer guide would have prevented loss of these tanks." Nevertheless the 2nd Battalion, led by Lt. Col. Claude Melancon, kept going, accompanied by the surviving tanks, and entered Holzweiler first, just two hours after jump-off. Then the follow-on 3rd Battalion, under Lt. Col. Roger Whiteford, pressed even farther ahead, traversing another two and a half miles of equally bleak farmland. Shortly after 10:00 A.M. it entered Keyenberg, Kuckum, and Berverath. Whiteford's battalion lost just one man wounded in the attack, and the only German soldiers in sight were those holding their hands high over their heads. Plenty of daylight remained on February 27 for the 175th Infantry to seize even more ground, so Maj. John Geiglein's 1st Battalion moved up from a reserve position at Mersch and plodded ahead on foot nearly nine miles on the right of the regiment's zone to capture Borschemich in late afternoon.

The regimental action report for February noted, "In assaulting enemy positions, assault fire—continuous rifle fire while closing in [also called "marching fire"]—has been proven effective and cuts down our casualties by keeping the enemy in their holes." But most German soldiers no longer dared to fight from those "holes"; by now they were retreating to the Rhine and beyond as fast as they could. During the 175th's astounding February 27 advance, scattered German fire and mines wounded fifteen 29ers; none died.

The German soldiers now striving to hold back the American tide on the Cologne Plain were a different breed than those who had stood up to the 175th in the Norman *bocage* at St. Lô. No menacing and immovable *Fallschirmjäger* here; the Americans' dramatic success in the opening phase of *Grenade* had so deadened the Germans' spirits that their meager ability to resist had evaporated almost entirely. Joe Ewing noted that the enemy "never had a chance to organize his positions. . . . Without communications or command, and without knowledge of what was going on, the Germans put up a futile and spiritless resistance. Wehrmacht troops, reinforced by a scattering of *Volkssturm*—civilian soldiers, the 'pitchfork army'—did not fight hard. At times they didn't fight at all, but just waited for the approaching Americans and then gave up. . . . The attack was too fast for the civilians. They were caught in the sweeping tide of the division's advance, and hundreds of them remained in each little town. They crouched in their cellars until the infantry yelled down and told them to come up. When they knew no German troops were in the vicinity, they overdid themselves in reassuring the Americans. . . . '*Nein*! *Nein*!' they kept exclaiming, waving their arms and pointing emphatically in the direction of München-Gladbach. '*Deutsch Soldaten weg*!' they would say. '*Aller weg*!'"

The German soldiers have gone away. Everyone has gone away.

SOME PRETTY FAST COMPANY

And so, more than four years after President Roosevelt had called up the 29th Division to carry out an unimaginably challenging task, the 29ers sensed the job was finally close to fulfillment. True, it had been a dirty and ruthless job. And for many veterans whose psyches had been sapped dry by countless close calls and the shock of more than 20,000 29th Division casualties since D-Day, the elation triggered by final victory—whenever it came—would be considerably muted.

When would that victory be gained? On February 28, 1945, with the Soviets only thirty miles from Berlin and the Western Front cracked wide open, it could not be far off. Meantime, the 29th Division must continue to fulfill its pivotal role in *Grenade*, which had shaped up as the U.S. Army's most successful offensive so far in the European war. Everywhere on the Ninth Army's front the enemy was in full retreat, and the Americans' renowned mobility was about to come into play. "Elements of three armored divisions [2nd, 5th, and 8th] were moving into the battle," Ninth Army's 1947 history noted. "Time was growing short for the German cause west of the Rhine; the juggernaut was gathering speed."

The 29th Division advance, Ewing wrote, "proceeded in a steady, unrelenting march up the flat roads, flanked by vacant foxholes, across the long fields, through brick stables and wagon sheds, into houses, upstairs in the bedrooms, and down in the cellar, in every single town on the division front." Since the 29th had pushed out of Jülich on February 24, it had smashed through dozens of minuscule villages and farms scattered across the vast Rhineland plain. But on the morning of February 28, 1945, when staff officers gazed at Gerhardt's situation map, even an amateur strategist could easily discern that the kind of war fought by the 29th Division was about to change thoroughly. The arrows on that map, all with dramatic and unswerving trajectories pointing due north, were trained directly on the 29th's next objective. To capture it, the 29ers would no longer fight across desolate farmland; they must instead wade through a dense, built-up landscape, fundamentally altering their battle methods.

The change would be abrupt. Urban islands in the middle of the agrarian Cologne Plain, München-Gladbach and its sister city, Rheydt—the boyhood home of Nazi propaganda minister Joseph Goebbels—manufactured vast amounts of textiles in their heyday for the Nazi war machine. One correspondent described Gladbach as "the first rich industrial prize in the Ruhr," even though more than 90 percent of the 200,000-plus citizens living in the city supposedly had already fled.

Had the German Army fled too? The 29ers fervently hoped so, since fighting through the tangle of bombed-out factories and workers' homes against determined opponents in the eight square miles encompassing the München-Gladbach area might develop into another Stalingrad. Happily, early on February 28, McLain reported to Gerhardt, "The field marshal [Montgomery, whose Twenty-First Army Group still included U.S. Ninth Army and the 29th Division] doesn't think there is anything in that town."

The accuracy of Monty's statement would be determined that very day, during which the field marshal had scheduled a tour of the Ninth Army sector. Simpson decided to show Montgomery Jülich's impressive but battered Citadel, and he directed Gerhardt to arrange a tour. Since it had been Lt. Col. Bill Puntenney's 3rd Battalion, 116th Infantry, that had captured the Citadel on February 24, the general phoned Puntenney in the morning and ordered him to leave command of his outfit to his executive, Capt. Adler Haaland, and make the ten-mile drive back to Jülich to provide commentary for the top brass—including Simpson and McLain—during Monty's visit.

"I was in some pretty fast company," Puntenney recalled. "[Gerhardt] took me over and introduced me to Field Marshal Bernard Montgomery and told him that I was the officer in charge of the assault on the Citadel. Here I was talking to one of the most famous commanders in World War II. He asked a lot of questions about the attack on the Citadel, and I accompanied him on a tour. . . . I later found out why Montgomery was interested in the Citadel. About a week later he escorted Winston Churchill through."

For a few hours on the last day of February, it seemed as if the enemy had proven Monty wrong. Bingham's 116th Infantry, on the right, and McHugh's 175th Infantry, on the left, resumed the attack toward München-Gladbach just before dawn, but they had not progressed far before the Germans fought back hard, forcing Witte to admit in a conversation with his G-3 counterpart at XIX Corps, "We are not making the speed we made yesterday." When the 116th's 1st Battalion advanced from Otzenrath to Hackhausen, and the 2nd Battalion to Hochneukirch, a staff officer reported to the war room, "They got a lot of direct fire getting in there and some casualties [about twenty-five in both battalions]. Pretty good resistance there." Similarly, on the 175th's front, a report noted that "the leading battalion [2nd] attacked Wanlo, moved through it with ease, and then ran into entrenched infantry just north of the town." A German prisoner brought in for interrogation revealed some disturbing news: his *Soldbuch* identified him as a member of the renowned Panzer-Lehr Division, supposedly assembling in Rheydt for a counterattack. Already, he claimed, the vanguard of the division, five tanks and 100 troops, had arrived.

But Panzer-Lehr had been decimated fighting the British and Canadians, and the German Fifteenth Army commander, General Gustav von Zangen, confessed

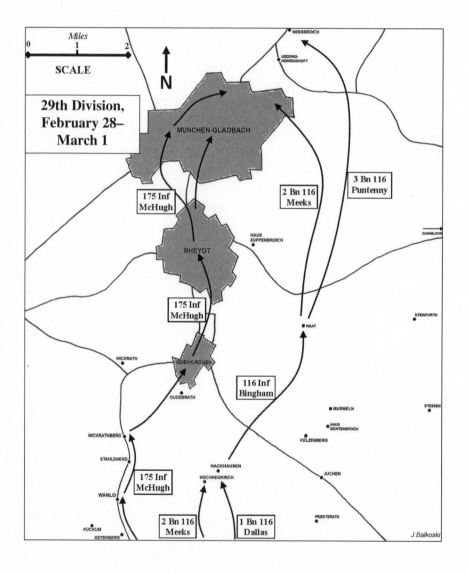

that "it was too weak for any mission. [Its] commitment, however, was very urgent in view of the present situation." But the urgency of the situation was beyond von Zangen's control, for all across Ninth Army's front the Americans were moving with greater force and rapidity than the Germans could handle; the deployment of Panzer-Lehr to Rheydt had less impact than inserting a pinkie in a dike about to rupture. No German enthusiasm, much to Gerhardt's delight, would develop that day—or the next. Monty had been right.

The enemy line, such as it was, cracked completely by noon on February 28. At 2:16 P.M., an ebullient Witte remarked to a staff officer—as he watched his minions wield black grease pencils on acetate map overlays to depict the 175th's surging movement beyond Wanlo into Wickrathberg, Güdderath, and all the way into the southern suburbs of Rheydt—that the "175th is moving up like a greased pig." Likewise, on the 175th's right flank, the 116th gushed forward—a report noted that "resistance crumbled rapidly"—as far north as Waat, just southeast of Rheydt. At 7:50 that evening, a proud Gerhardt phoned McLain and reported, "We took about 450 POWs today."

Holbrook Bradley accompanied the 175th's 3rd Battalion that day and reported to his Baltimore readers on the capture of some of those prisoners: "In an attic, Lt. Col. Roger Whiteford, of Ruxton [a Baltimore suburb], was checking over the ground his troops were about to cross to secure a toehold in Odenkirchen, which even then was under heavy artillery fire. . . . Up at a command post at the edge of town, we could look across the whole width of the field and see the other battalions of the regiment already on the high ground to the north. . . . [Then] we saw one of the strange sights of the war, when one, then a dozen, then more Germans stood up in the trenches, hesitated a moment, then dropped their weapons and started toward our lines, hands held high above their heads. Soon there was a line, more than sixty, moving at first slowly, then almost at a run to our men who stood with their rifles waiting to see what happened. The German first-line defenders gave up without firing a shot."

The events of February's final day had undeniably cast the 29ers into a positive mood. An anonymous GI artist prepared a cover drawing for the 116th's February 1945 action report, which would feature a cartoonish German soldier with his hands over his head, another soaring through the air as a result of a swift American uppercut, and a third about to be run over by a U.S. Army jeep. One of the smiling American occupants of that jeep, which has just snagged a German clothesline with attached ladies' undergarments, says to a comrade, "This has the characteristics of a breakthrough, don't it?"

It did. In fact, March 1, 1945, ended up one of the most glorious days in 29th Division history, not so much because of that breakthrough and stunning capture of München-Gladbach—an event that triggered a giant March 2 *New York Times* headline—but due to the plausible rumor floating among the 29ers that the 29th's war might soon be over. By nightfall on March 1, as Ewing reported, "The word spread like the wind through the division. The 29th was out of it. . . . We're through fighting! We're staying here!"

In the recent past, enemy soldiers had fought like tigers to retain inconsequential German towns much smaller than München-Gladbach, so the enemy's lack of resistance on March 1 amazed the 29ers, especially in a place a reporter described as "one of the cities which the Germans were expected to defend to the last . . . and is the key to Düsseldorf," just thirteen miles to the east across the Rhine. Gerhardt opened the March 1 attack at 7:00 A.M. by throwing the 116th Infantry in a flanking movement around the eastern periphery of Gladbach, while the 175th launched a direct assault on the city proper.

Maneuvering through open terrain rather than the urban wasteland of München-Gladbach, Bingham's 116th had the easier job. "Employing the village of Waat as a staging area," the 116th's action report noted, "the battalions surged forward with the 2nd on the left, the 3rd on the right and 1st following closely in support and having the additional mission of liquidating lurking remnants of the enemy." Ordinarily, after the usual high casualties inflicted by fanatical German defenders, the 29ers rarely were in the mood to boast about their accomplishments. But the war's tenor had changed, and with the enemy on the run and American casualties dropping to near zero, bragging over 29th Division triumphs now seemed appropriate. "Village after village fell before the irresistible onslaught of the hard-hitting soldiers of the 116th Infantry," a regimental combat summary declared. "Several tanks and self-propelled guns were the only heavy armament which the enemy was able to muster to meet the attack, which seemed to strike everywhere at once. So rapidly did the attackers move, both afoot and mounted on reconnaissance vehicles, that the enemy was never permitted to group or regroup his guns. Fast and powerful thrusts on the part of the assaulting battalions knocked the enemy off balance, allowing him neither respite nor the opportunity of concentrating his forces to meet slashing new attacks. . . . Another great struggle had been won by a unit inured to the horrors and hardships of battle as well as to the elation of hard-earned victories." The effusive writer proudly concluded that "this memorable first day of March, the culmination of the lightning offensive which had begun four short days before, saw a total of fifty-three inhabited localities fall into the hands of the 116th Infantry Regiment."

Bill Puntenney's 3rd Battalion swung around München-Gladbach's eastern periphery, moving so fast that when he phoned Bingham and reported that his outfit held the hamlets of Uedding-Herrenshoft and Neersbroich, two miles northeast of Gladbach, he recalled "[Bingham] couldn't believe it." A crossfire from two enemy machine guns held up Reagor's Company K for a while and wounded several men in the leading rifle squad, including the squad leader. But Pvt. Charles Van of Monroe, Louisiana, carrying a BAR, rose to the occasion, a *29 Let's Go* article observed, as "the Joe of the hour. He assumed command at once, directed the rescue of the squad leader and another casualty, and, when both had been taken to the comparative safety of a foxhole, administered first aid to them." Van thereupon arranged a textbook attack on the Germans by providing covering fire with his BAR while PFC Roger Schaefer armed his M-1 with a rifle grenade and crept around the enemy's flank. "Schaefer's first rifle grenade was a beautiful piece of marksmanship," *29 Let's Go* remarked, "landing smack in the middle of the enemy position. The Krauts manning the gun—those who were able to move—promptly scrambled out and waved a white flag." Immediately thereafter, Van and Schaefer watched in amazement as packs of German soldiers emerged from their holes with their hands over their heads, shouting the familiar "*Kamerad!*" "So this rifle squad, leaderless for a brief moment, turned over to the PW cage a total of thirty-two Supermen," the article concluded.

Two canal bridges a few miles northeast of Gladbach would be vital to the 29th's neighbor, the 2nd Armored Division, when it launched its imminent dash to the Rhine River—now within easy range of American artillery. Puntenney noticed that the enemy had prepared one of the bridges for demolition with six explosive charges connected by a wire leading to a plunger on the far side of the canal. "I sent a runner for some wire pliers," Puntenney noted, "and proceeded to cut the charges apart so the bridge couldn't be demolished. The [German] who was supposed to push the plunger had evidently gotten scared off with our fast approach. I didn't think much of it at the time, but if it had been booby-trapped, the bridge and I could have gone sky high."

That evening Puntenney had a remarkable chance meeting with an old friend he hadn't seen for years. The "big fellow" who all of a sudden stomped down the steps into Puntenney's battalion command post cellar turned out to be none other than a former classmate from the University of Arizona, Walter Nielsen, now Captain Nielsen of the 2nd Armored Division. Nicknamed "Hoss," Nielsen was an All-American fullback for the Arizona football team who once "carried a trio of Brigham Young University tacklers a good ten yards" at the end of a memorable run. As Puntenney remembered, "We had a brief visit because he was in a hurry."

During those exhilarating days, S/Sgt. Bob Slaughter of Company D remarked that he "became very wealthy for a short time" when he and his comrades entered a German bank that was carrying on business as if there was no war going on. "I couldn't believe that the safe's door was wide open," Slaughter recollected. "Neat stacks of brand-new reichsmarks sat in plain view. We didn't hesitate. After all, this was war, and we were the victors. While members of the section waved their M-1s in the air, each of us traded our haversack contents for stacks of new reichsmarks. . . . I carried my 'guilt-pack' for a few days until we were fired upon by an enemy ambush. I was so laden with reichsmarks that it was hard for me to find cover fast enough. I realized that staying alive was better than being a wealthy corpse." Eventually, Slaughter handed over the money to an aged man and his wife; he remembered they were "surprised and happy to get it."

Apparently every American soldier in the Rhineland on March 1, 1945, was in a hurry. Led by Geiglein's 1st Battalion, the 175th plunged into München-Gladbach from the south. An article in the *New York Times Magazine* on Sunday, March 18, noted: "Fire burned here and there where a shell had hit, although after three years of bombing, there wasn't much left of München-Gladbach [and] Rheydt to burn. . . . American infantrymen, wearing little gray and blue patches on their shoulders, arrived, and the short, ugly noises of street fighting moved for thirty-six hours northward through old Rheydt, down Horst Wesselstrasse and at length through the whole city." The 29ers trod past neatly painted signs proclaiming *Es lebe Adolf Hitler!*—Long live Adolf Hitler—and *Was hast du heute für das Vaterland getan?*—What have you done today for the Fatherland? As the GIs learned, the locals had not done much at all. A front-page *Times* article observed: "There were many signs that Propaganda Minister Goebbels hoped his old home town would put up a better scrap. . . . Storekeepers had boarded up their windows, and only scattered columns of refugees and a few curious citizens were abroad either to welcome or defy the American Army. There was no last-ditch defense by the *Volkssturm* [people's militia] as promised by Hitler, and most townspeople still remaining appeared relieved rather than disappointed. Several volunteered the belief that the war would be over in a month, saying regular Wehrmacht troops shared their view." Intelligence officer Krznarich commented, "The comparatively few enemy troops remaining in the town showed no strong desire to continue a fight." Geiglein concluded, "Our losses have been very light. . . . The only thing that has slowed us much is this rubble."

On March 1, the 175th nearly lost Lieutenant Colonel Melancon, a 1935 Louisiana State University graduate and an unrivaled and fearless combat leader who already held a Silver Star, four Bronze Stars, and a French *Croix de Guerre*. The thirty-year-old native of Baton Rouge was leading his 2nd Battalion toward Gladbach when a Ninth Air Force P-47 fighter, minus its pilot who had successfully bailed out, came plummeting down from the sky and crashed directly into one of the 747th's Sherman tanks, next to which Melancon was standing. A reporter noted that "Colonel Melancon was singed when showering oil from the crash caught fire. Four men in the tank were rescued, but severely burned." It was, the reporter noted, "a spectacular escape from death." Melancon shook it off—a morning report labeled his wound as "light"—and remained on duty. "I had a feeling everything was going to be all right," he said.

Ewing, who entered München-Gladbach with Company G, disagreed with the *Times* reporter's assertion that only "a few curious citizens" witnessed the American entry into the city. "Even as the troops were moving up the main street on the first day, German civilians crowded around the sidewalks, watching this combat operation as though it were a parade. It was a silent and curious, but unhostile crowd, in marked contrast to the civilian temper in earlier towns in Germany. Many civilians made general overtures of friendship, waving and smiling; some even raised their arms to make the V-for-Victory sign." During the 110th Field Artillery Battalion's entry into Rheydt, many Germans were hardly silent: "Masses of people lined the streets and cheered the column as it passed," the battalion history recorded, an astonishing sight to men who over the past nine months had come to despise all things German. "In accordance with non-fraternization orders, the cannoneers neither responded to nor recognized the welcome," noted the history.

Maj. Albert Hoffman, a staff officer at division headquarters, refused to be taken in by the locals' pleasantries. "The people must be taught that war does not pay, and that a few smiles and gifts are not what we came for," he wrote to his wife. "There may be a lot of good people, but we have no way of telling who they are, so everyone has to be a bad Nazi and not to be trusted because we can't take chances."

A three-man team from 1st Lt. William Howell's Company I, 175th Infantry, comprising Howell, radioman PFC George Hubbard, and a runner, PFC James Crawford, took no chances when they cautiously entered a Gladbach house to check for enemy soldiers and weapons. They encountered only a "meek German civilian . . . [who] stood in a corner while they minutely searched each room." Finding nothing but a Nazi flag, which the contemptuous 29ers hurled out a window, the GIs departed and headed down the street. No longer so timid, the German dashed down the front steps, gesturing to the Americans that they had left something important behind. "You can imagine PFC Hubbard's chagrin," a *29 Let's Go* article reported, "when he got back there to find the weapon they had overlooked was his own carbine."

On a hasty visit to Gladbach, Gerhardt encountered two members of the 747th Tank Battalion, Sgts. Robert Ackerman and Kendal Van Pelt, who evidently said or did something that caused the general to lose his temper. A fellow tanker said that Gerhardt claimed "they were drunk and disorderly [and] reduced them both to privates on the spot." But the 747th, despite its presence alongside the 29th since Normandy, was not a component of the division, and Gerhardt lacked the authority to undertake that punishment. According to the tanker, "Ackerman reported what had happened to Lieutenant Clauer [his platoon leader], then asked for reassignment as kitchen police." Instead, Clauer ignored the incident, and eventually Ackerman and Van Pelt were both promoted. Indeed, Van Pelt would soon gain the high honor of a battlefield commission to lieutenant.

Times reporter Clifton Daniel—Harry Truman's future son-in-law—noted that March 2 was "the greatest day for Allied arms in western Europe since last August." While the 29th Division consolidated its hold on Gladbach, the rest of Ninth Army raced east toward the Rhine as the Germans, according to Daniel, waged "a desperate struggle to rescue enough troops from the debacle to defend the Rhine and the Ruhr against inevitable Allied crossings." Ninth Army's 1947 history, *Conquer*, asserted that "the battle itself was won; now the pursuit and the mopping up remained. The objectives from here on were to inflict the maximum punishment on German forces attempting to withdraw across the Rhine and by bold, rapid pursuit to seize intact, if possible, at least one of the eight Rhine bridges in Ninth Army's zone."

Spring was still three weeks off, but the winter weather had improved dramatically and, more importantly, the GIs' spirits had too. The singing of birds and the nascent buds on the tousled shrubs and trees hinted at a more serene world ahead; this time, the confident 29ers fully expected they would live to see those buds sprout flowers; and by the time they did, assuming the Allies maintained their current momentum, Hitler would be dead and the American horde would be heading home. But for the next few days, maybe longer, the 29ers must make München-Gladbach and nearby Rheydt their homes away from home. That process, according to the 29th's second-in-command, Brig. Gen. Leroy Watson, would be simple: "Move the people out and put the soldiers in." Meantime, Gerhardt announced firmly to his minions, "Let's have no looting!"

The electrifying orders arrived at 9:05 P.M. on March 4 from Simpson's Ninth Army headquarters: "The 29th Infantry Division, with attached 821st Tank Destroyer Battalion, 554th Anti-Aircraft Artillery Battalion, and 747th Tank Battalion, is relieved from attachment to XIX Corps effective March 4 at 7:50 P.M. . . . The 29th Infantry Division will remain in place in army reserve pending further instructions. Conduct training with view to prepare future operations eastward. Rehabilitate personnel making maximum use of recreational facilities." No sweeter phrases in Army lingo existed for a combat soldier than "army reserve," "rehabilitate personnel," and "recreational facilities." The 29th Division would in all likelihood remain in the München-Gladbach area for a long while; by the time Ike figured out where to reinsert the 29th into the line, who knew how far the front would have progressed into central Germany?

For the wretched residents of München-Gladbach, the war was over. And maybe the 29ers' war was over too.

FOUR

Hitler—KAPUT

A STUDY IN CONTRASTS

Paul Joseph Goebbels could not go home again. Not even to the city that just a few years ago had changed the name of the street on which he was born from Prinz Eugenstrasse to Josef Goebbelsstrasse in his honor.

The 29th Infantry Division currently occupied Goebbels's hometown of Rheydt, a state of affairs that produced cracks in the emaciated Reich propaganda minister's rigid faith in Nazi ideology. The sycophant who had once gushed, "Adolf Hitler, I love you because you are both great and simple at the same time—what one calls a genius," had recently railed in his diary, "The news that the town of Rheydt received the Americans with white flags makes me blush. I can hardly realize it, especially not the fact that one of those white flags flew from the house where I was born."

Goebbels would blush even redder when he discovered that Schloss Rheydt, a sixteenth-century castle presented to the propaganda minister by the citizens of Rheydt at a time when the cult of Nazism was much more popular in the Rhineland than it was in March 1945, had been converted into a U.S. Army regimental command post. (The castle caretaker, Heinrich Furst, claimed, "Leaders of the [Nazi] party came around to the people of the city and said, 'The Reichsminister for Propaganda was born here, and you should be very grateful, so you will raise money to buy Schloss Rheydt and you will give it to Joseph Goebbels out of gratitude.'") Had Goebbels learned of the recent handiwork of a creative 29er in

147

Schloss Rheydt, he would have positively erupted in fury. Armed with a paint-brush, a can of black paint, and a wooden signboard, that anonymous GI had marched boldly into the castle's cavernous dining hall and headed straight to an enormous painting of Hitler, in martial pose and Nazi regalia, that hung over the fireplace. Stepping up onto a chair, he affixed the board across the painting and gleefully slathered paint on it, spelling out a German word that required no trans-lation: *KAPUT*. Later, he attached a large cardboard cutout of a scruffy 29th Divi-sion GI and hung it adjacent to *der Führer*'s portrait.

Schloss Rheydt was no longer the property of the Goebbels family; now it belonged to Lt. Col. William Blandford's 115th Infantry, the regiment formerly known as the 1st Maryland that just four years ago had been spread out in small-town armories all across the state: in Crisfield, Cumberland, Elkton, Frederick, Hagerstown, Salisbury, and others. If the regiment were to spend a rehabilitation

Maj. Gen. Charles Gerhardt (left), Brig. Gen. William Sands (center), and Brig. Gen. Leroy Watson (right) stand in front of Hitler's portrait in Joseph Goebbels's Schloss Rheydt.

period of indefinite length behind the front, Blandford could find no better command post than Schloss Rheydt, which a *Stars and Stripes* reporter described as "a sprawling country house with a stone-wall moat and scattered clumps of spring flowers like snowdrops." For at least the next several days, and with luck maybe even longer, the delighted Blandford and his staff would sleep in plush beds in carpeted second-floor bedrooms with spacious private bathrooms, warmed by immense fireplaces and lit by "ornate lamps which belonged in some New York hotel."

So impressive were the Schloss Rheydt accommodations, in fact, that on March 2 Gerhardt phoned Blandford and announced, "After seeing your establishment, I've decided to take it over for the division." The general, however, made the mistake of adding: "What do you think of that?" An alarmed Blandford promptly rejoined, "I don't think it's big enough, sir." The general reflected for a moment, then concluded with resignation, "I guess not."

Blandford soothed the general's disappointment by arranging for an elaborate dinner at Schloss Rheydt for 115th Infantry and 110th Field Artillery commanders on the evening of March 3, an event to which Gerhardt and two other general officers, Brig. Gens. Leroy Watson and William Sands, were also invited. As Rheydt was still officially in a combat zone—the men had only just had the chance to rid their bodies and uniforms of grime following ten consecutive days of intense combat—the dinner would be devoid of formality save for the enlisted personnel acting as servers, wearing formal top hats adorned with the 29th's yin-yang symbol. A few bright red Nazi flags with their loathsome black swastikas still lingered in the Gothic banquet hall, war trophies that Blandford would surely show off to Uncle Charlie, along with the Hitler—*Kaput* portrait.

The 115th's executive officer, Lt. Col. Anthony Miller, acted as mess president. A native of a modest west Baltimore neighborhood who had enlisted as a private in the Maryland National Guard in 1931, Miller stood, raised his glass, and according to Holbrook Bradley, "proposed a series of salutes to the personnel present and those men, wounded or dead, who have left the outfit." Those toasts were preceded, as Bradley described, by a repast "that ran from a fruit cup as a first course through southern-style ham, apple pie, and constantly flowing wine [while] the regimental orchestra played off to one side, starting with *Roll Out the Barrel* [the 29th's unofficial march, dating to its use at the conclusion of the La Cambe cemetery dedication in Normandy on July 23, 1944], and running through songs old and new as the hosts and guests joined in. . . . At a huge oak side table, white-coated enlisted men served champagne and gin in gleaming goblets monogrammed with Goebbels' initials."

Gerhardt thoroughly savored the evening; the next morning he phoned Blandford and inquired, "What time did the last [guest] leave?" Blandford replied: "Between 2230 and 2300, sir." The general remarked, "That was fine, and I certainly enjoyed it."

Brig. Gen. Leroy Watson gives a toast at the March 3 Schloss Rheydt dinner. Seated, facing the camera (left to right): Lt. Col. Tony Miller (obscured), Lt. Col. Randy Millholland, and Lt. Col. Purley Cooper. Seated at the head of the table: Col. William Blandford. Seated with backs to the camera (left to right): Maj. Gen. Charles Gerhardt, Brig. Gen. William Sands, and Lt. Col. Glover Johns. The two mess attendants in top hats are unidentified.

Two days later, the 115th Infantry carried out another event in the same dining hall that would generate headlines and photos, not to mention a sense of grim vengeance among American citizens on the home front, particularly those who adhered to the Jewish faith. According to Bradley's narrative of that affair, "German propaganda minister Joseph Goebbels should have a new headache tonight," a headache that would be set off by the astonishing news that the 29th Division had used Schloss Rheydt for a Jewish prayer service. For a man who had once declared, "The Jews are to blame for each German soldier who falls in this war," that news was supremely galling. The 29th Division's Jewish chaplain, Capt. Manuel Poliakoff—known by friends and family as Mendel—noted, "I'd much prefer holding a service in the city's synagogue, but the two here have long since been burned." A young Orthodox rabbi from Baltimore who had only recently joined the 29th Division, Poliakoff remembered, "They wanted services then and there, so I obliged, but—my God—there were tremendous swastikas hanging down from the ceiling, all the way down, and silk, pure silk!" Draped in the traditional *tallit* prayer shawl, Poliakoff stood behind a sturdy oak table, topped with two simple candles and a dark cloth featuring a prominent Star of David, and solemnly commenced the service. On the far side of the room, a witness recorded, "A log fire crackled noisily in one of those fireplaces you can stand up in."

Another Baltimorean, twenty-nine-year-old T/5 Martin Willen, acted as cantor and stunned the congregation with his operatic renditions of *piyutim*—Jewish liturgical poems—perfected by years of prewar practice at the city's renowned Peabody Conservatory of Music. Little more than fourteen months in the past, homefront Baltimoreans had heard Willen's tenor voice, as sonorous and commanding as Nelson Eddy's, on a special Christmas Day 1943 radio broadcast recorded in England, during which he masterfully performed a popular tune, "Just a Little Love, a Little Kiss," that he dedicated to his wife, Miriam. Willen's daughter later retold the story of how her father, a member of the 115th Infantry's Service Company since 1941, came to Colonel Blandford's attention: "Marty was in a foxhole in Germany when a jeep pulled up and carried him to the colonel's office. The colonel had heard that he had a wonderful tenor voice. He was asked

The March 5 Jewish prayer service at Schloss Rheydt. At left is PFC Ben Mermelstein, Capt. (Chaplain) Mendel Poliakoff is in the center, and at right is T/5 Martin Willen.

to perform Friday evening services for the Jewish soldiers; sing *Ave Maria* on Sunday mornings for the Catholic services; and sing the Lord's Prayer in Sunday afternoons for the Protestant services."

A member of the 115th Infantry's Company H, twenty-three-year-old PFC Abraham "Ben" Mermelstein of Newport News, Virginia, stood behind Poliakoff holding the *Torah*, the sacred scroll wrapped around two wooden poles and containing the Five Books of Moses. All U.S. Army soldiers of Jewish ethnicity dreaded falling into German hands, and just a few days after D-Day, Mermelstein had undergone that nerve-racking experience at Le Carrefour, Normandy. Fortunately his captivity lasted just a few hours, as he snuck away in the dark from a column of American prisoners being herded to the rear by their German captors along a lonely Norman road.

Jewish religious services require attendees to cover their heads, and Poliakoff, Willen, and Mermelstein satisfied that tradition according to entirely different methods. Poliakoff donned a *kippah*, the traditional Jewish head cover, but Mermelstein wore a simple G.I. olive-drab woolen cap. Willen sported the most utilitarian head cover of all, a plain U.S. Army steel helmet. Afterward, Poliakoff, Willen, Mermelstein, and all the Jewish GI-worshippers departed the castle and headed straight for the moat—into which they promptly urinated.

The Yanks' exultations at Goebbels's expense might have diminished had they known what caretaker Furst had told a *Stars and Stripes* reporter. "He never came here, Doctor Goebbels," Furst insisted. "Once a year, maybe a day or two at a time. Last year [1944], not at all. The [Nazi] party used the Schloss as a guest house for visiting men of importance in the Düsseldorf *Gau* [district], of which this is a part. Sometimes someone from Doctor Goebbels' office came with women, but the Reichsminister, no."

In their interactions with Rheydt's pathetic citizenry, irritated 29ers noticed that the servile *volk* regularly disavowed the Nazis, and Goebbels in particular. "Joseph Goebbels was never any good," a Rheydt police sergeant pronounced to the GIs. "A swine. Also a dog. And a big mouth." Goebbels had been a childhood schoolmate of the sergeant's wife, who related that he was "always trouble. He would tell the others that things weren't fair. It was always something. He talked too much, I guess." The policeman concluded: "He'd come back to München-Gladbach and Rheydt once a year or every other year. He'd stay one day or two days, and everyone would have to go to a party rally and shout *Sieg Heil*." Before the 29th Division's conquest of those twin cities, however, the 29ers deduced with absolute certainty that no German had openly described Joseph Goebbels as a "big mouth."

Two young women who tentatively approached a 29th Division command post on March 8 held a genuine loathing for Joseph Goebbels. Twenty-year-old

Gela Baser and her seventeen-year-old sister Rachel spoke no English, but when Captain Poliakoff conversed with them in Yiddish, he learned they were Jews from Rakow, Poland, who had somehow slipped free of the fatal net that had swept most of European Jewry into Hitler's "final solution." However, their parents, two brothers, and another sister had not been so fortunate. After hiding from the Germans in a sympathetic Polish farmer's stable through the winter of 1942–43, those family members had been discovered and shot; Gela and Rachel escaped only because they had been absent on a foraging expedition. The two girls forged birth certificates, establishing identities as Polish gentiles. The Germans bought the ruse and conveyed them both into Germany as slave laborers, although Gela confessed, "I lived in fear every moment of being recognized—by the Nazis or the Poles." Assigned to German families for household work, they overheard chilling conversation among their masters, one of whom once blurted, "I need a good, cold drink and a dead Jew."

Poliakoff, who in the interwar period had studied at a Polish *yeshiva* near the girls' birthplace, took pity on them and recalled that he eventually came "to love them like daughters." On March 18 a fellow Baltimorean who served on the 29th Division staff did Poliakoff a favor by arranging for Gela and Rachel's transportation to Brussels to live with a Jewish family; from there, Poliakoff hoped they could proceed to Palestine for resettlement. Gela, however, married a U.S. Army soldier from California in December 1945, and both girls moved to the United States. "When a German who lived through that time tells the world that they didn't know what their government was doing to the Jews, and others they deemed undesirable, don't believe it," Gela said in an interview. "I was there and lived among them and heard what they knew."

As the 29th settled into München-Gladbach, a city whose vast working-class districts of neat, brick row houses reminded the 29th Division's many Baltimoreans of their hometown, Lt. Joe Ewing witnessed the profusion of German civilians "riding bicycles, pulling wagons, pushing baby carriages. In this populous German city, stirring quietly, moving sober-faced in its defeat, one felt now the slow pulse of the German homeland. . . . Questions, interminable questions, were asked of the MPs and the sentries who stood before the billets, nearly all of them producing negative answers: The town-major said I could. . . . I must go back to the house and get . . . *Essen* [food]. . . . Can I cross the street?. . . . I must talk to the *Kommandant*."

A history of the U.S. Army in the occupation of Germany noted that München-Gladbach "was a study in contrasts—some districts badly damaged, others almost intact except for the windows. . . . Buildings were sliced in two, and frequently where a wall had collapsed, the furniture could be seen in place in rooms on the upper floors. . . . Here and there, grim-faced older civilians could be seen painting out the [Nazi] slogans with whitewash." The simple act of moving the people out of their homes and putting the soldiers in usually worked without a hitch, as the locals did not dare protest. However, Lt. Col. Purley Cooper recalled, "In Rheydt, Battery A notified the owner of a fine house that his home was to be requisitioned. Obviously a man of wealth and education, the owner replied in English and cordially invited the officers to be his guests. When informed that he would have to vacate the building and that enlisted men would be included in those to be housed, he was profoundly shocked."

The 116th's Lt. Bob Easton wrote to his wife: "The children stare, smile, wave—some of them—and I wonder if they won't always remember the straggly, wet, and dirty columns of GIs that passed lightheartedly through the streets of town, some carrying rifles muzzles down, some muzzles up, some wearing this garment, some that, all braced against come-what-may by the old American care-free and don't-give-a-damn. I wonder what the children will be thinking when they grow up and how long the ruined towns will remain ruined or what our American feet in the rich soil of this Rhine valley mean—slogging, slogging, occupying, bringing the indescribable feeling of home and place with us to a cellar for a few dark hours, and then out again into the attack, the occupation, the slogging on, and again the attack."

Sometimes German docility went too far. Once, when the 29ers of the 115th Infantry's 2nd Battalion queued up for chow, 1st Sgt. Floyd Wright, a veteran of the prewar Virginia National Guard, glanced behind him and noticed two German soldiers holding mess tins waiting patiently in line. "Seems they had been peering out of a cellar window and decided chow time would be as good as any to give up," noted a *29 Let's Go* article. "The more the sergeant questioned them, the more urgently they insisted they be fed. They kept pulling out 'safe conduct' passes from every conceivable place on their person. Before they had been marched off to a POW pen, still holding empty mess gear, the Krauts produced between them twenty-five safe conduct slips. They weren't taking any chances, those lads."

Puntenney's 3rd Battalion of the 116th took over an intact neighborhood in Gladbach that had somehow avoided the Americans' deluge of bombs and shells. The 29ers had not enjoyed such commodious and warm lodgings for a long time. "All we had to do," said Puntenney, "was to tell [the residents] to get out, and the Germans grabbed a few things and left. . . . [We] were unaccustomed to the luxuries of soft rugs on the floors, unbroken glass in the windows, soft mattresses on the beds, running water, and sometimes even electric lights." So agreeable were those accommodations that the 116th's after-action report for March 1945 featured a cover drawing of a euphoric 29er dressed in skivvies, slumped in a comfortable German easy chair, with his boots off and a cigar in his mouth. The caption read: "TO THE VICTORS BELONG . . ." Another cover drawing depicted an immaculate German bedroom with a made-up double bed, desk lamp, and dresser. The carpet at the foot of the bed is embroidered: "COURTESY OF MÜNCHEN-GLADBACH."

One day, Puntenney and his staff heard an unusual roar high above their heads and looked up as one to see some strange aircraft. They were German Me-262 jet fighters, the *Wunderwaffen*—wonder weapons—Hitler regularly bragged about but 29ers had almost never seen. "They came in very high and were lobbing bombs in the direction of the bridges over the Roer River," Puntenney recalled. "We made out the airplanes high overhead traveling much faster than anything we had seen before. I watched as a flight of P-51 Mustangs tried to cut them off, but the jets ran away with ease."

For Puntenney, who just four years in the past was riding a horse through the Chihuahuan Desert in west Texas as part of the legendary 7th Cavalry, warfare had changed faster than he thought possible.

SOMETHING TO THINK ABOUT

It was time to get cleaned up; Uncle Charlie would insist on that. Starting on March 2, 1945, Gerhardt's obsession with "personal hygiene," as Army manuals termed the soldierly art of caring for oneself, would trigger a procession of thousands of 29ers toward rear-area shower facilities. The general steadfastly held to the Army maxim "cleanliness comes first," as spelled out in the August 1944 War Department pamphlet *Army Life*: "No other single habit of hygiene is as important as keeping yourself clean. An unclean body is offensive to others. It may be a source of disease to you as well as to your buddies." Front-line troops who had not shaved for a few days must do so immediately; fingernails would be cut and cleaned; teeth would be brushed ("brush on both the inside and outside," *Army Life* advised); and hair would be trimmed since "long hair is often unsanitary and a source of infection." Combat had disrupted those sacred practices, but at Gerhardt's insistence, the 29th Division would soon resume its reputation as a spic-and-span outfit.

Cleanliness, of course, also applied to uniforms, field equipment, weapons, and vehicles. Accordingly, field jackets, trousers, and footgear soiled with Rhineland mud would soon be tossed onto heaps and replaced with fresh items, including snappy Ike jackets and new boots. Weapons would be stripped and thoroughly cleaned because, as a field manual asserted, "Very minor details of maintenance make a great deal of difference. . . . Proper oiling, cleaning, and stacking are completely necessary to the care of these precision mechanisms." Gerhardt himself occasionally made surprise visits to company and battery bivouacs to ensure the 29ers adhered to those principles, as he did one day in March in München-Gladbach at the apartment building occupied by the 115th

Infantry's Company K. "As [Gerhardt] was going down the line," remembered Jack Kussman, now a first lieutenant, "he said to one of my men, 'When was the last time your lieutenant inspected your rifle?' This soldier, to whom I will always be grateful, said without hesitation, 'Yesterday, sir.' The general had to forego a pleasure that I heard he enjoyed: chewing out a junior officer. I had not inspected the man's rifle the day before, and I don't think that I had ever done so."

On March 4 the 29th Division's artillery chief, Brig. Gen. William Sands, recommended to Gerhardt that all forty-eight of his 105-millimeter and 155-millimeter howitzers be carefully inspected and calibrated; since D-Day those pieces had fired hundreds of thousands of rounds, and Sands worried that their worn-out gun tubes might have deteriorated so badly that the pinpoint accuracy on which U.S. Army tactical doctrine depended would be ruined. Sands's concern was valid: when each of the 29th's three 105-millimeter artillery battalions fired on an open-plain test range near the village of Holzweiler, the cannoneers learned that many tubes were worn beyond repair; in both the 110th and 224th Field Artillery Battalions, four tubes were discarded and replaced with new ones. The much heavier twelve 155-millimeter howitzers of the 227th Artillery, however, all fired with near-perfect accuracy at a Wickrath test range and required no tube replacements. Cooper noted that after the 110th's final calibration, "The howitzers were regrouped to give each battery four guns of similar shooting strength. Battery A received the 'longs,' Battery B the 'mediums,' and Battery C the 'shorts.' The regrouping accounted for known differences in the guns and brought increased accuracy to the massing of fire on targets after an adjustment by a single gun or battery, but those cannoneers whose weapons changed hands were openly sentimental about losing the old ones that had served them so well."

Some of the busiest men in the 29th Division in March 1945 were the battalion and regimental surgeons, who at daily sick call were able to address their soldiers' maladies much more thoroughly than during periods of intense combat. The most prevalent problems were exhaustion and shaky nerves, both serious conditions, but by this stage of the war medical personal knew they would improve dramatically assuming the men could spend a week or more beyond the range of German guns and get a couple of consecutive nights of good sleep in a soft bed and a warm house, courtesy of its evicted owners. Even the 104th Medical Battalion's dentists got into the act by providing inspections that some 29ers with severe tooth pain probably dreaded almost as much as facing the enemy. While he was carrying out those checkups, the 29th's chief dental officer, Lt. Col. Douglas White, experienced a mini-family reunion when his son, Pvt. Douglas White, Jr., paid him a surprise visit. The younger White had joined the division a few days previously as a replacement, making them in all likelihood the only father-son duo in the 29th Division.

Twenty-ninth Division vehicles needed even more restoration than the 29ers' teeth, for the ubiquitous Rhineland mud that had caked on wheels and chassis seemed impossible to remove. The general was a stickler for immaculate vehicles, and his attitude had not even softened after the February episode in which his own beloved jeep, *Vixen Tor*, had gotten firmly stuck in a morass of mud on a Rhineland country road and had to be towed out by a passing vehicle. Those drivers who cared about the 29th Division's record so far in World War II proudly displayed a list of the division's battle honors in yellow or white paint on their vehicles—artillerymen also followed that practice on their gun shields—and the current rest period allowed the 29ers time to update the list. Indeed, Sgt. Bob Cuff, Gerhardt's driver, added three new names to *Vixen Tor*'s olive-drab front windscreen: Jülich, Titz, and München-Gladbach.

Members of a division in army reserve should have had plenty of free time, but Gerhardt resolved to take advantage of the break by molding his men into better soldiers. Training of all kinds would occur everyday, including road marches, tank-infantry tactics, forward observation methods, marksmanship, and, as one cynical 29er noted, "those perennial favorites, close-order drill, first aid and sanitation, [and] military customs and courtesy." Gerhardt's boss at XIX Corps, General McLain, warned him, "The main thing is to get comfortable and get some rest before the next operation. . . . Don't put in too many hours on [training]."

Gerhardt fretted that his men's unaccustomed comfort might tempt them into unsoldierly behavior. "We're bearing down," he told McLain, "on the question of looting, military discipline, drinking, etc." McLain responded: "That's good." The 29ers did not have to look hard to find plenty of German liquor, which a diplomatic GI observed "helped to add sparkle to the company parties held throughout the division." Rumors of prodigious binge-drinking swept through the division, but Cooper avowed, "For every man who got drunk on champagne, there were ten who took a few sips, wrote letters, went to the movies. Indiscriminate drinking was a direct result of looting, strictly prohibited and something to be ashamed of."

Most veteran GIs had long ago discovered the fine art of scrounging, and when it came to war trophies, military items such as enemy pistols, helmets, and field gear were always fair game. Civilian loot, however tempting, was different, and orders from division headquarters warned that anyone caught pillaging would suffer punishment. Nevertheless, the 29ers' uninvited presence in German homes—minus their owners—created opportunities to "liberate" spoils that were too good to pass up. When the 116th Infantry had first entered München-Gladbach, Colonel Bingham facetiously remarked, "We're advancing as fast as the looting will permit." As related by a 29er up the chain of command, "This remark was quoted direct to [XIX] Corps on the telephone, where it was duly transcribed onto the corps headquarters log. It caused much hilarity, where, fortunately, it was taken as a joke; but one staff officer there commented that maybe the famous slogan '29 Let's Go' would now be changed to 'two shooting and nine looting.'"

By-the-book company and battalion commanders strove to lessen looting opportunities by permitting evicted homeowners to take their most cherished items with them, and sometimes provided a room on an upper floor in which other valuables could be stored behind a locked door. The 110th Field Artillery's surgeon, Capt. John Ambler, learned the extent of the 29ers' temptations when, for just a few minutes, he left his cherished camera unattended in a basement aid station. When he returned, the camera had disappeared. "In a message to all batteries," the 110th's history noted, "the battalion commander stated that if the camera were returned to the battalion message center, no questions would be asked. Within a few hours, the 'Doc' received his camera together with an anonymous note advising him to label his property in the future."

Only a week had passed since the 29th Division had stormed across the Roer to seize Jülich, and compared to its previous combat record—six weeks slogging through the Norman hedgerows from Omaha Beach to St. Lô; three weeks battering down the defenses of Brest; and another three weeks grinding across the Rhineland to the Roer—the current campaign on the Cologne Plain had been easy. Much more importantly, the 29th Division, along with every other Ninth Army outfit and the British-Canadian units pushing hard toward the Americans from the north, had achieved one of the western Allies' most decisive victories of World War II, one that broke the German lines wide open, crushed enemy resistance west of the Rhine, and triggered a new, mobile phase of the war that would carry on relentlessly until Hitler was dead and Nazi Germany was no more.

Nine months of nearly continuous combat had dramatically matured the 29th Division, and its February 23 assault across the flood-swollen Roer proved it. That attack had been a model of U.S. Army efficiency, an operation that only a world-class military unit could carry out successfully. As always, however, the price had been high; the week of high-intensity combat from Jülich to München-Gladbach had cost the 29th more than 800 men, of whom about 100 died. Even more sobering was the detail revealed by division clerks when they added up the latest butcher's bill: the most recent casualty figures brought the 29th Division's grand total to more than 20,000 men lost since D-Day, not counting several thousand more who succumbed to disease, injuries, or combat exhaustion.

At 11:30 A.M. on March 2, Gerhardt proudly hosted a visit to the war room from his three immediate superiors, Generals McLain, Simpson, and Eisenhower. Just a few hours before, General Ike recalled in his postwar memoir, "For the only time in the war I put on a steel helmet." The episode unfolded when

Eisenhower and Simpson were crossing the Roer into Jülich by jeep, and a high-altitude German Me 262 suddenly appeared, triggering a heavy antiaircraft barrage by American batteries within a few hundred yards of the two generals. Ike recalled that "within a few seconds, fragments of exploding shells were dropping around us." A *New York Times* reporter in the entourage, noting that the jet proceeded to strafe a nearby American command post at which Ike arrived just a few minutes later, described the incident to his readers as a "narrow escape" for the supreme commander.

Gerhardt would have been pleased had he known what Eisenhower had told Simpson after visiting Jülich and observing the destructive results of the 29th Division's recent attack: "Jülich will be something for the Germans to think about in the future," Ike mused. His visit to the 29th, although highly satisfying to all, was rushed; he had his mind on other weighty matters, most notably the recent intelligence from the front confirming that a few bridges spanning the Rhine River were still intact. If the Americans could seize one and establish a strong bridgehead on the far side of the river, the enemy's ability to defend that formidable waterway would collapse.

Shortly after departing the 29th's war room, the SHAEF staff composed a message to German civilians, scheduled for broadcast by Eisenhower the next day on Radio Luxembourg. "The Allied armies have broken through the West Wall and are overrunning the territory west of the Rhine. . . . Any attempt to evacuate eastward will place you in mortal danger. All roads and railways to the Rhine and all Rhine crossings will henceforward be packed with retreating German troops under heavy air and artillery bombardment. Women, children, and old people who flee eastward will not only risk death from Allied aircraft and guns, but they will risk also being killed in the stampede of the defeated German Army or by German guns firing from the eastern bank of the Rhine. . . . Keep off the roads wherever you are. Take shelter and stay under cover. Tell the German soldiers to surrender and thus avert a senseless massacre in which both you and they will be killed."

War news became even more positive late on March 7 when the 9th Armored Division, a part of U.S. First Army, dashed into Remagen, Germany, seized the Ludendorff railroad bridge spanning the Rhine, and rushed troops and tanks across the river to establish a firm bridgehead on the far bank. It took a while for that momentous news to filter down to the 29th Division; the March 9 edition of the *29 Let's Go* newsletter observed, "There is a security blackout on official details." But when that blackout was lifted, Gerhardt's delighted GIs learned that tens of thousands of Yanks had already crossed to the Rhine's east bank. Yet another nail in the Nazis' proverbial coffin, the 29ers sneered.

It wouldn't be long now.

THE HELL WITH THIS MORALE

For a full, glorious week, the 29ers savored their absolute authority to evict Germans from their homes, a power that allowed the GIs to live inside warm buildings, eat at dining room tables, and sleep in cushiony beds. But late on March 8, the disheartening news arrived at division headquarters that the 29ers themselves would be evicted from their agreeable new habitats. The purveyor of that directive was U.S. Ninth Army, which at Simpson's order, would presently transfer its headquarters from Maastricht, Holland, to a city much closer to the front: München-Gladbach. It hardly seemed fair; the 29ers had only just settled into Gladbach, a prize they had seized with brute force, guile, and blood. An American army command post, however, was a massive organization—cynical front-line infantrymen would rather call it bloated—and with its plethora of two dozen headquarters sections; attached units such as military police, signal, and quartermaster outfits; and bountiful supply depots, it needed almost as much space as a combat division. The official U.S. Army table of organization for an army headquarters called for nine generals, thirty-two colonels, forty lieutenant colonels, sixty-one majors, and sixty-two captains; so top-heavy was the organization that its complement of full colonels equaled the number of buck sergeants.

The 29ers' disappointment was somewhat mollified when Simpson ordered Gerhardt to leave one infantry battalion behind in Gladbach to perform security duties for Ninth Army headquarters. The 115th Infantry's 3rd Battalion, under Lt. Col. Randolph Millholland, got the job and immediately embarked on the kind of work known to GIs as "palace guard" duties: manning checkpoints, controlling traffic, assembling barbed wire barriers, guarding depots, and safeguarding the top brass. Ordinarily that kind of duty, which required spotless uniforms, creased trousers, soldierly postures, and incessant saluting, would have been classified by that highly expressive new piece of Army slang—chickenshit—but with the war in its terminal phase and the horrors of combat starting to fade from the GIs' psyches, the security of rear-echelon work was far preferable to getting killed in a senseless German *Götterdämmerung*. The 175th's 3rd Battalion relieved Millholland's men on March 17; one week later, the 1st Battalion, 116th Infantry, took its turn.

The eviction of the 29th Division from Gladbach forced the men to shift back to the countryside into what one 29er referred to as "cow-towns," minuscule farming hamlets such as Jüchen, Murmeln, Kelzenberg, and Wanlo, large enough to provide quarters for a single company or battery of about 170 men, but no more than that. Those places, a 115th Infantry soldier noted, were "not unlike those [we] had come to know back on the western bank of the Roer, except the towns [we] now occupied were virtually undamaged by the war. Although in some cases the homes were not quite as modern as those in München-Gladbach, many of the men were glad to be out on their own again, away from constant supervision by the battalion and regimental staffs."

The 29ers quickly settled into a pleasant routine: a hearty breakfast, followed by morning calisthenics, various training exercises, lunch, athletic activities, dinner, and finally evening entertainment. The 116th Infantry's March 1945 monthly report described the schedule as "a judicious mixture of activities, some intended to relax and rest the men, the balance designed to make them fit, eager for the next mission, and technically adequate for it. Movies were shown daily, church services held at regular intervals, passes granted, parties held. Sports included softball, baseball, football, and even (in the 1st Battalion) a track meet consisting of nineteen events. Officers as well as enlisted men participated in the various activities." Best of all, those pursuits were undertaken beyond the range of German guns.

The best method to relax the men was neither softball nor films; it was a furlough to a destination far behind the front: Holland, France, or England, or in some cases even the United States. In March, Gerhardt awarded lengthy furloughs to the States to a lucky batch of long-service 29ers, almost all of whom were D-Day veterans with at least thirty months of overseas service. Their passes would not even begin to count down until they reported to a stateside Army post close to their homes; and they would not begin the journey back to Europe until their number of furlough days—usually thirty, but up to ninety—had expired. No one in their right mind believed that the European war would still be raging by the time they returned, assuming the Army would ever demand their return.

Other fortunate men received furloughs of three weeks to England, one week to Paris or the French Riviera, or—the most common of all—a forty-eight-hour pass to nearby Holland. A member of the Headquarters Company of the 115th's 2nd Battalion, 1st Lt. William Holberton, departed the 29th on March 26 for the Riviera and took up lodgings in the world-famous Hotel Carlton in Cannes, just a stone's throw from the beach, featuring rooms with glorious views of the Mediterranean. "It was hard to absorb the reality that was before us," Holberton wrote. "Each bedroom was a complete piece of heaven in itself. Running water, hot and cold, private toilet facilities, large, comfortable bed—it was all too much to absorb and believe." The celebrated casino at Cannes drew throngs of GIs, but Holberton's devotion to Catholic theology—he would take up the priesthood after the war—drew him instead to a tiny offshore island and its fifth-century *Abbaye de Lerins*, occupied by monks whom the Germans had left alone during the occupation. That sacred island provided a sense of tranquility, just the thing that Holberton needed to draw his mind away from the war.

During a Paris furlough, Maj. Robert Walker of the 29th Division's military government section—soon known as G-5—experienced anything but tranquility.

While enjoying a drink at the *Moulin Rouge*, the legendary haunt of the painter Henri de Toulouse-Lautrec and the birthplace of the erotic cancan dance, he recalled: "I met a gorgeous French girl named Frances. She was dark-haired, diminutive, shapely, English-speaking, and personable. I was entranced. She was a delightful conversationalist and seemed most interested in me. . . . She reached for my hand and said softly, 'I am 2,000 francs.' I said, 'What?' She repeated it, slightly louder. I, the debonair, big-spender, laughed and said, 'Oh, no, I can't afford it.' Disgustedly, she said, 'What do you think? *Pour l'amour*?' [For love?] I said, '*Oui*.' She made a sound of distaste, as if I had offended her. . . . [Later], as she stepped out the door, I heard her say to a couple of girlfriends, 'Well, I guess I sleep alone tonight.'"

Since October 1944, almost every 29er at one time or another had traveled to the town of Heerlen, Holland, for a break from the front. The combined efforts of the amiable residents and rear-echelon American Special Services personnel had produced a first-class rest center. The Hollandia Theater, featuring two picture shows per day of current Hollywood films, was probably the most popular attraction, but there was also the ice cream bar, Ruto's Café (for "deluxe meals"), free haircuts, a beer garden, showers, a pool, a Red Cross "Donut Dugout," a Friday night dance, a reading room, and a P.X.—"with Coca-Colas too!" Best of all, one of the rest center's "few, but important" regulations stipulated "Weapons or knives will not be carried or worn."

First Lt. Bob Easton described Heerlen as "immaculate, the brick houses universally trimmed with green or yellow window frames and planted with neat shrubbery and flowers." One afternoon two Dutch couples, who spoke little English, stopped Easton on the street and invited him into one of their homes for an "evening of beer, conversation, more beer, more conversation, [and] finally dining on bread and jam and fresh boiled eggs and coffee." Easton enjoyed the hospitality so much that he returned the next evening. "The Dutch are the most up-and-coming people I've met over here," Easton confessed in a letter to his wife. "For example, nobody in this family we visited spoke English before the Americans arrived on September 1. Now they all speak, read, and write it tolerably well and have taught themselves. . . . Wholesomeness and a good democratic air of independence shine from everyone you meet. They honor us as liberators."

Another person who honored the 29th Division by her presence was world-class opera singer Lily Pons, who performed a series of concerts on March 18 and 19 in the Ninth Army zone. The star of New York's Metropolitan Opera hardly seemed the type of performer who would please an audience of fighting men, but according to GI logic, any celebrity who came so close to the front to entertain soldiers and passed up much more lucrative stateside engagements was worthy of admiration. Indeed, Pons had only recently arrived in Europe from a three-month tour in the China–Burma–India theater, and it was the first time since her debut at the Met in 1931 that she had not scheduled any New York performances during an opera season. "They [soldiers] are my favorite audience," Pons asserted. "Much, much more fun than a typical opera group. They are all so appreciative and unrepressed." Pons's remarkable voice stunned the listeners, especially her jazzed-up rendition of *The Blue Danube*, in which she displayed her trademark soprano runs up and down the musical scale, interspersed with plenty of trills and pulsating notes held for ten seconds or more. According to a reporter, Pons was "backed by one of the finest all-soldier orchestras ever assembled," conducted by Pons's husband, Andre Kostelanetz. "Lots of them are better than my men back home," Kostelanetz said.

The 29th Division's nearly month-long period out of the line in March 1945 provided an opportunity for some officers to sample life in the Army Air Force. For Lt. Col. Randy Millholland of the 115th Infantry, his 3rd Battalion's duty as the "palace guard" at Simpson's headquarters in München-Gladbach allowed him to slip away to the Ninth Air Force for four days to examine how ground support by fighter-bombers worked from the airmen's perspective. A thirty-eight-year-old native of Cumberland, Maryland, Millholland had enlisted at age eighteen as a private in the Maryland National Guard and over the next twenty years evolved into one of the 29th Division's premier leaders. His short stint with the Ninth Air Force was more of a refresher course than an introduction, since he had already served a lengthy tour with the Ninth in England as a liaison officer prior to D-Day.

Another officer, Capt. Chester Slaughter of the 115th's Company B, took what he thought would be a short break from the 29th Division by traveling to an airfield outside Laon, France, the home base of the Ninth Air Force's 416th Bombardment Group. The 416th was a veteran outfit that had been flying missions for

Lily Pons, the star of New York's Metropolitan Opera, performed for the 29th Division on March 18 and 19, 1945.

more than a year, first with A-20 Havoc light bombers and more recently with A-26 Invaders. Slaughter decided he would not spend his short interval away from the front merely watching the 416th from the ground. On March 21, the 416th was ordered to attack a target just outside the town of Vreden, Germany, with fifty-one A-26s, each armed with a massive 1,000-pound bomb. At 3:00 P.M., Slaughter climbed aboard the lead ship in a flight of eighteen bombers, piloted by Capt. R. J. Rooney, who was about to fly his sixty-fifth mission before heading home to the States. Two hours later, from Rooney's cockpit, Slaughter watched the attack unfold from 10,000 feet; the 416th's summary described the mission as "excellent," with no losses. However, on the return trip, flying straight into the setting sun, an A-26 unexpectedly descended into Rooney's formation. "It was obvious something bad was about to happen," noted the pilot of the ship next to Rooney's. "The right side of the invasive ship struck the tip of Rooney's left wing. . . . I watched the left prop of Rooney's ship cut through the aft bomb bay of the invasive ship. Whirling away, that prop looked like a giant pair of scissors. . . . I hit the mike and called out, 'Rooney, for God's sake, jump, jump, go, go!'" Both A-26s were cut to ribbons and began their fatal, gyrating descent. Only one member of Rooney's crew parachuted to safety; the other three men aboard, including Chester Slaughter, perished in the fiery crash.

During its March recuperation, the 175th Infantry gained an exceptional soldier, but also lost one. In the summer of 1944, it had been forty-two-year-old Col. Edward McDaniel of Alabama who, as Gerhardt's chief of staff, kept the 29th Division running smoothly. A member of the West Point class of 1926, McDaniel had begun his career as an infantryman, but spent the first two years of World War II behind a desk in Washington working under Gen. George C. Marshall for the War Department General Staff. Transferred to the 29th Division in June 1944, his administrative expertise shone in September 1944 when, in Gerhardt's absence, he arranged in just a few days the incredibly complex 500-mile movement of the 29th by rail and truck from Brittany to Holland in compliance with an unexpected order from Lt. Gen. Omar Bradley. Shortly thereafter, McDaniel returned to his roots when Gerhardt appointed him commander of the 115th Infantry, a job he held until he suffered a serious wound on November 18. After nearly four months of convalescence, McDaniel returned to the 29th on March 11, 1945. Gerhardt promptly assigned him to the command of the 175th Infantry as a replacement for Col. Harry McHugh, who had been on loan to the 29th from the 80th Division for one month. As an esteemed member of the 29th Division family, it was good to have McDaniel back.

On March 18, the redoubtable commander of the 175th's 2nd Battalion, Lt. Col. Claude Melancon, received the tragic news that his twenty-three-year-old wife, Essie Ray, had died of an illness back home in Louisiana, leaving a six-year-old daughter, Claudia, in the care of her grandparents. Gerhardt promptly granted Melancon leave, and he departed for the States the following day, never to return to the 29th Division. Indeed, three months later the Army discharged him from duty. During his two-year period of overseas service, Melancon had first lost his father, then his brother—and now his wife.

That relentless booster of 29th Division esprit de corps, General Gerhardt, never failed to brag that his outfit was special, and during the division's March 1945 rest period, he finally had a chance to prove it. All three of the 29th's infantry regiments, as well as the 121st Engineer Combat Battalion, had been cited by the U.S. Army for "outstanding performance of duty" during the Normandy campaign and awarded the Distinguished Unit Citation, a prized commendation created by President Roosevelt's executive order in February 1942. The order specified that "an appropriate streamer, emblem, or guidon band . . . may be displayed by the organization to which such citation is issued," and "a suitable device identifying such citation shall be issued to all officers and enlisted men who are assigned or attached as members of such organization, the device to become a part of the uniform."

The general would savor the several formal ceremonies in March during which he would issue Distinguished Unit Citation streamers and ribbons to deserving units and personnel. The streamers, blue and about a yard long with white embroidery spelling out the sacred names of past battles, would be affixed by Gerhardt himself to regimental and battalion colors, as well as smaller, fork-tailed company guidons; the ribbons, plain blue rectangles little more than one inch long with eye-catching gold borders, would be pinned on the 29ers' shirts above their right-breast pockets. Even GIs who had not been members of the 29th Division in Normandy would receive the ribbons, but uniform regulations required their removal if they transferred to another outfit. However, those rare 29ers still with their units in March 1945 who had participated in the Normandy fighting were permitted to wear the Distinguished Unit Citation ribbons proudly for the rest of their military careers, regardless of what units they served in.

On Tuesday, March 13, 1945, Colonel Blandford of the 115th Infantry assembled about 150 of his men at *Haus Bontenbroich*, the regimental command post, three miles southeast of München-Gladbach. They formed up in perfect alignment on a pleasant green adjacent to the placid Kelzenberger Brook, spanned by a picturesque footbridge; Gerhardt would arrive at 3:00 P.M. to present streamers and ribbons to personnel representing all twenty companies of the regiment. Blandford had requested that personnel representing their units at the ceremony should be D-Day veterans since the Distinguished Unit Citation streamers soon to be attached to colors and guidons were embroidered "St. Laurent-sur-Mer," the first French village liberated by the 115th during the Omaha Beach invasion. But company first sergeants found it difficult to fulfill that request: when they looked over their rolls, they realized hardly any D-Day veterans were left, particularly in the nine rifle companies.

After attaching the streamers to the colors and walking down the line of troops to pin on the ribbons, Gerhardt saluted the thousands of 115th men no longer with the regiment: "It won't be long now before it will be finished over here," declared the general. "We've come a long way since the day we stormed the beaches. Lots of our men have given their lives. For them, as well as us, this citation is a tremendous honor."

The frequent close-order drills to which the 29ers were subjected in March seemed like a prime example of Army chickenshit, but they turned out to be worthwhile. Almost every 29th Division unit would carry out a review that month, and everyone who had read the inscrutable Field Manual 22-5, *Infantry Drill Regulations*, knew that formal U.S. Army parades were highly complex affairs. If a company did not comprehend and practice those regulations and

The 115th Infantry receives its Distinguished Unit Citation streamers, labeled "St. Laurent-sur-Mer," for its performance on Omaha Beach on D-Day. The event took place on March 13, 1945, at *Haus Bontenbroich*, Germany.

ultimately dissolved into a mob of Sad Sacks during a review, the whole outfit would be perceived as hopeless and would certainly draw irate attention from Uncle Charlie. It had to be done right.

In late March, on several occasions, witnesses took in the impressive sight of a 3,000-man U.S. Army infantry regiment marching in close order on a wide-open parade field, with colors and guidons flying, accompanied by the 29th Division band—the first time parades of regimental size had occurred since the division had landed on the Continent. Considering the 29ers were used to fighting, not marching, their performance was creditable; not up to the standards of the Army War Show, of course, but laudable nonetheless. Gerhardt took advantage of the 116th's March 28 review to issue Distinguished Unit Citation ribbons to the men and attach the streamers, labeled "Normandy Beachhead," to colors and guidons. The men of the 1st Battalion also gained an additional streamer, embroidered "Vire" in honor of the unit's daring seizure of that Norman city in August 1944. There were no Sad Sacks on the parade ground on that memorable day.

On three separate occasions in March, the 500-man 110th Field Artillery Battalion conducted much smaller but no less impressive reviews on an open field adjacent to battalion headquarters at *Haus Zoppenbroich*, a sixteenth-century manor house near Rheydt. "For each of the parades, the weather was excellent," noted Cooper, "and marching with beautiful precision to the music of the division band, the battalion passed in review while the sun shone brightly on Old Glory, the 110th standard, and [red] battery guidons. Each stirring scene was enhanced by the greenness of spring, and each was a perfect setting for men to receive well-deserved promotions and decorations. . . . These displays of a fine military team made up of tried and true fellow soldiers brought a thrilling pride to everyone present." The 29er who carried Battery B's guidon, T/4 Dick Herklotz of Baltimore, remarked, "We looked good, all right, like real garrison soldiers, but I wonder how many noticed our guidon—full of shrapnel holes?"

At the first review, Cooper bestowed the honor of battlefield commissions to two enlisted men, twenty-four-year-old Sgt. George Christofil of Youngstown, Ohio, and twenty-six-year-old Sgt. Nick Gregorio of Pittsburgh, Pennsylvania. In their roles as fresh shavetails—second lieutenants—Christofil was assigned as the battalion's munitions officer, and Gregorio assumed the role of motor transport officer.

As an anonymous soldier blurted: "The hell with this morale. Let's get the war won!"

I COULD THINK OF TOMORROW

On March 4, 1945, the date on which Simpson placed the 29th Division in that glorious status known as "army reserve," his Ninth Army units were already on the Rhine River, poised to cross the magnificent waterway either by amphibious assault or via one or more of the four Rhine bridges that still stood in the army zone. With the enemy in disarray, Simpson supposed that in the next few days he could get substantial numbers of Ninth Army troops over the Rhine by one means or the other, but to do so he needed permission from his boss, Montgomery, who had already concocted a set-piece offensive scheduled for March 24 that would, according to the British official campaign history, "assault the Rhine on a broad front with a well-prepared and coordinated plan." Monty therefore turned Simpson's much more impulsive scheme down. "It was a great opportunity for me and for all of us, really," a frustrated Simpson recalled. "Had I been allowed to cross then, I think I could have formed a bridgehead for my entire army to cross and then formed a bridgehead for the British. In my opinion, it would have ended the war a month earlier than it did."

Just how long the 29th Division would remain in Ninth Army reserve was anyone's guess. By the time that rest period ended, Gerhardt surmised, Ninth Army troops would already have jumped the Rhine and pressed on into central Germany toward Berlin. But three more weeks would pass before Monty initiated his meticulously planned Rhine crossing, Operation *Plunder*, the commencement of which the 29ers could not fail to discern because at 1:00 A.M. on March 24, they were awakened by the thunderous salvos of 2,070 Ninth Army cannon, 25 miles distant, which fired the astonishing total of 65,200 rounds in one hour at the hapless enemy defenders on the far side of the Rhine. The Germans, an enemy general observed, "could only pretend to resist" against such an overwhelming attack. To no one's surprise, Hitler's boast that the sacred Rhine would hold back the invaders proved empty; Ninth Army's 30th and 79th Divisions, along with two of Monty's corps to the north, slammed over the Rhine before dawn against such feeble opposition that a 30th Division soldier asserted, "There was no real fight to it. The artillery had done the job for us." At 10:00 A.M., the enemy's woes increased by a considerable factor when Allied transport aircraft deposited two airborne divisions behind German lines by parachute and glider. Ninth Army's official history observed: "The operation, as expected, became almost immediately more of an engineer construction task than a military tactical maneuver."

The 29th Division had only recently carried out a risky assault across a major river, so the 29ers were happy to leave the Rhine crossing to someone else. Eleven days before *Plunder*'s start, however, ten mystified 29ers received orders to report to a rear-area training site on the Maas River in Holland run by an outfit they had never heard of, the 1153rd Engineer Group. When they arrived, they learned Ninth Army had selected them, along with dozens of men from other units, to pilot assault craft across the Rhine for the first few days of *Plunder*; for a solid week beforehand, they would practice their boating skills on the Maas with the engineers. "We blew our stacks when we heard what the chore was," fumed Sgt. Leo Caporali of the 115th's Company E, a D-Day veteran. "No one was very happy about it, but we had a job to do, so we did it."

Actually, Ninth Army had plucked those unhappy 29ers out of their peaceful bivouacs because of the words they themselves had written on their *Soldier Qualification Cards*, known as War Department Form 20. Asked to provide their "Main Occupation" and a "Second Best Occupation," evidently all ten 29ers had been a little too eager to boast that they knew how to handle boats. One of the men, PFC Bill Kabakjian, surely regretted telling the army that he used to own a sixteen-foot launch and "scoot up and down the Delaware River" in it; now he would have to perform the much more hazardous job of "scooting" back and forth across the Rhine. All ten 29ers eventually performed their *Plunder* tasks flawlessly, and happily all returned safely to the 29th Division on March 26. "Actually, it was a cinch compared with the Roer crossing, although we didn't know it at the time," Kabakjian noted. On *Plunder*'s first day, when the 30th Division men in Kabakjian's boat saw the 29th's motto, "29 Let's Go," painted on his boat, they blurted, "Jeez, what are you guys doing up here?" It was a long story . . .

Plunder's object was to "cross the Rhine River north of the Ruhr industrial area and secure a firm bridgehead in order to develop operations to isolate the Ruhr and penetrate deeper into Germany." Since D-Day, Ike had been fixated on the Ruhr: the Germans could not hope to carry on the war without it, as its profuse factories produced the majority of the Fatherland's steel and coal, even under unrelenting attack by Allied bombers. There was nothing like the Ruhr anywhere in the world; historian Rick Atkinson depicted it as "a sooty ellipse that extended east from the Rhine for some sixty miles," as big as Rhode Island, featuring more than a half-dozen densely populated cities pulsing with the sounds and smells of round-the-clock war production.

The 29th Division would inevitably be drawn into a battle for this vital area of Nazi Germany, which Ike described in a late March 1945 press conference as "that extraordinary region." Would it be the 29ers' last fight? If there were anywhere in Germany for the enemy to make a last stand, it would be the Ruhr. "While there are many indications that the majority of German soldiers and civilians realize that Germany cannot win," Simpson warned, "the enemy, from habit and training, continues to fight well."

During the protracted wait for Ninth Army orders in the 29th Division war room, the fidgety Gerhardt received a surprising message from XIX Corps headquarters. The corps commander, McLain, would be absent for a while; as senior division commander, Gerhardt would take over. True, he would only hold command for two days, March 26 and 27, but it was a rung on a career ladder that Gerhardt had longed for since General Hodges had sacked Pete Corlett as XIX

Maj. Gen. John Anderson, commander of the U.S. Army's XVI Corps.

Corps commander last October and replaced him with McLain, a National Guard general. McLain's selection had mightily disappointed Gerhardt and other XIX Corps West Point generals, who could not comprehend how a guardsman could be selected over a professional soldier. But now, at least for a few days, Gerhardt could view the war from a loftier plane.

At 11:00 A.M. on March 29, back in his familiar folding chair in the 29th Division war room, Gerhardt learned that the 29th Division would immediately be transferred from McLain's XIX Corps to Maj. Gen. John Anderson's XVI Corps, which had just carried out the phenomenally successful Rhine crossing. The sixth corps commander under whom Gerhardt had served since D-Day, Anderson may have been the one Gerhardt admired most. Anderson had entered West Point from Iowa and graduated in 1914, when Gerhardt was a mere plebe and Ike Eisenhower a "cow," or junior. Known to his fellow cadets as "Swede," the fifty-four-year-old Anderson was one of the rare American soldiers on the Western Front who had participated in the U.S. Army's 1916 expedition to capture Pancho Villa in Mexico. (George Patton, Bill Simpson, and Alvan Gillem were three others.) He was a gunner to the core, and by the start of World War II he had grown into one of the U.S. Army's premier artillerymen.

Anderson's XVI Corps had fulfilled its tough trans-Rhine assault, but Simpson faced a daunting administrative challenge that surely reminded him of his advanced Command and General Staff School classes at Fort Leavenworth two decades ago. Presently, Simpson had to funnel 200,000 men and vast amounts of materiel across the Rhine on a narrow front, using only six hastily constructed bridges; five more bridges in Monty's sector, three of which were built by the Americans, had to be shared with British troops—and the Yanks had to yield priority to the British. In the closing days of March, Simpson could do little to avoid a bottleneck on the Rhine's west bank and congestion on the opposite side, an exasperating situation that threatened to suck the momentum out of Ninth Army's assault on the Ruhr and its imminent push into central Germany. "I was bottled up there," Simpson fumed. "Here I was, sitting there with twelve divisions in my army, but I only had two of them crossing the river and ten just sitting there. . . . Finally, once I got across, we started toward Berlin, but there had been a delay of three or four days."

So congested were the roads leading to the Rhine bridges that Anderson did not order the 29th Division to cross the river until March 31, a week after *Plunder* had begun. Bingham's 116th Infantry led the division's move, closing down its bivouacs near München-Gladbach before dawn and heading north by truck toward a treadway bridge near Rheinberg. Darkness and frequent halts imposed on the columns by MPs at road junctions, allowing convoys from other outfits to pass, prevented impatient drivers from opening their throttles to attain high speed; the fifty-mile journey to the 116th's new assembly area at Bruckhausen on the far side of the Rhine consumed nearly six hours. The regiment's monthly report noted that the movement was "orderly," but in the predawn darkness a deuce-and-a-half driver lost control of his truck and smashed into a roadside tree on the low ground adjacent to the Rhine. Sixteen 29ers from Company I were injured—three seriously. One of the injured, PFC John Meeg of Brooklyn, was a prewar veteran of the 245th Coast Artillery, a New York National Guard outfit whose 16-inch guns at Fort Tilden defended New York harbor.

The 115th Infantry's turn came next. Thanks to a start time of 10:00 A.M.— in daylight—its three-hour trip across the Rhine to an assembly area at Dinslaken was much smoother than the 116th's nighttime movement. "After a month of inactivity," a 115th soldier noted, "there was a decided stir of excitement and anticipation in the clear, crisp spring air." At dawn the next day, April 1—Easter

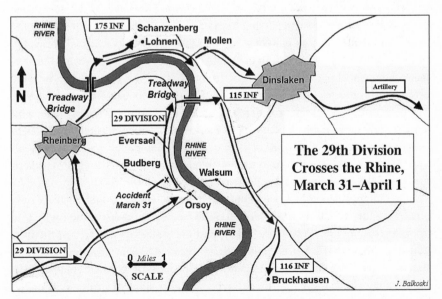

Sunday—the 175th moved out and reached the Rhine at 8:00 A.M. An hour later, the regiment's new commander, Colonel McDaniel, opened up his command post in a farm complex known as Schanzenberg, less than a mile north of an oxbow bend in the Rhine. All of the 29th Division had crossed the great river with little fanfare and virtually no notice in the hometown press.

Indeed, by March 31, 1945, the Rhine was old news; stateside newspaper readers now craved to know when the Allies would reach Berlin and Hitler would meet his dismal fate. Hundreds of thousands of Allied troops had already traversed the Rhine by that date, considerably lessening the melodrama of the 29th Division's crossing. Besides, the point where the 29ers crossed the river, between Rheinberg and Dinslaken, was not the Rhine of German legend—of Wagner and his valkyries; of the narrow Rhine Gorge and Lorelei; of mystical riverside castles. Rather, the 29th Division passed over a much more nondescript, 500-yard-wide watercourse that unhurriedly meandered like a slithering snake through an expansive, flat valley highly susceptible to flooding and erosion. Over time, locals had countered those evils by lining the river's curved banks with dikes, towering twelve feet or more above the adjacent landscape, and by erecting stone jetties and ripraps along the shore.

Still, the 29th Division's passage over the Rhine, an event to which Gerhardt had looked forward for months, was undeniably stirring. Indeed, such luminaries as Winston Churchill and George Patton had recently perceived so much symbolism in the Allies' crossing of the Rhine that they had both immodestly urinated in it. Pvt. Art Plaut wrote of the 115th Infantry's Rhine journey: "The scene of construction and road clearance at the bridge site was impressive, as the dust raised by numerous bulldozers and passing trucks rose into the blue skies over the river. Scores of silvery barrage balloons, reminiscent of England and the Normandy beaches, dotted the sky as part of elaborate precautions taken to prevent the Germans from knocking out the bridges from the air. Close to the shores were prisoner of war cages filled with hundreds of recently captured German prisoners. The trucks rolled across the river slowly, about noon [March 31], each man a bit tense for fear that an enemy plane might suddenly appear or an enemy shell might come screaming out of the east. The crossing was completely uneventful, however, and as the trucks rolled into a grassy rendezvous area on the eastern bank of the Rhine, the men breathed a collective sigh of relief."

The mighty Rhine had been conquered easily. Berlin would be Ike's next objective, but the cheery 29ers now looked far beyond that—all the way to a troopship sailing into New York harbor, past the Statue of Liberty, and finally a train ride home. "We felt a great elation," recalled D-Day veteran PFC John Barnes of the 116th Infantry's Company A. "The band of fear was gradually lifting from my chest. I felt almost glad to be alive, the signs of spring were on the land, and I could think of tomorrow. It was a strange feeling."

FIVE

The Great Migration

THE PAST WAS THE PAST

At 12:27 P.M. on March 31, 1945, when the 29th Division had only just begun to settle into its new bivouacs on the east side of the Rhine, the war room phone buzzed: XVI Corps headquarters was on the line with an urgent message for General Gerhardt. "We may want to use the 116th Infantry this afternoon in an offensive mission," a XVI corps staff officer declared. "They'll go by motor and will be attached to the 75th Infantry Division." That order was soon confirmed; the displeased men of the 116th, who that very day had carried out a bumpy six-hour nighttime journey by truck, must again climb aboard deuce-and-a-halves, this time for a twenty-five-mile trip to the east to join up with the 75th Division near a coal-mining town named Marl.

The 116th had been detached from the 29th and assigned to another division once before, and the experience had been excruciating. Indeed, the time spent with the 30th Division in October 1944 in the bitter fight to capture Aachen had been one of the regiment's toughest battles in World War II. Attachment to the 75th hinted that the 116th would soon enter combat for the first time in a month. With the Germans apparently on the run, however, the imminent battle hardly shaped up as a repeat of Aachen. Nevertheless, the enemy was now defending a vital piece of its heartland, the Ruhr industrial zone, and if Hitler still possessed his malicious ability to sway German minds, the fighting could be severe.

A twenty-five-mile journey by truck seemed effortless, but as always the top brass stressed that not a moment was to be lost, forcing the 116th yet again to travel at night. At 3:30 A.M. on April 1, the first truck serials moved out, despite the assertion by a 116th officer that as a consequence of the rush, "There will be a little confusion on the move." There was, and it was more than "a little." Navigating an unfamiliar road network in the dark, on roads crowded with vehicles going in both directions, slowed the truck convoys down to an average speed little faster than a jog. The journey lasted more than five hours, and for the second night in a row, exhausted members of the 116th attempted to sleep on uncomfortable benches within the unforgiving cargo beds of U.S. Army trucks, bouncing fitfully along on rutted roads toward a destination no one seemed to know anything about.

When the last elements of the 116th finally pulled into Marl shortly before noon on Sunday, April 1, someone in authority had mercifully decided that they no longer needed to rush the regiment into an "offensive mission"; the 29ers could therefore spend the rest of Easter Sunday resting and cleaning up. Meantime, Bingham reported to his new boss, fifty-three-year-old Maj. Gen. Ray Porter of the 75th Division, a holder of a Distinguished Service Cross from World War I and one of Ike's rare division commanders who had not learned his trade at a military college. What would be the role of the 116th? So rapidly were military events on the Western Front transpiring that Porter hardly knew where to begin. On the same day Bingham's 29ers had arrived at Marl, the U.S. First and Ninth Armies had linked up sixty miles to the east, completing what Ike called the "largest double envelopment in history." That accomplishment pocketed more than 300,000 enemy troops within the Ruhr, and if the Americans could force their surrender, the yield of prisoners would be greater than the Soviets had captured at Stalingrad.

The 75th Division, along with two other XVI Corps infantry divisions, held the northern shoulder of the pocket, with orders to press ahead into the heart of the Ruhr. More than two million souls resided in the great manufacturing cities of that region, a dense urban landscape of munitions plants, coal mines, iron ore beds, canals, countless rail lines and marshalling yards, and above all steel mills—including the renowned Krupp works in Essen. Allied bombers had reduced those cities to rubble, but somehow the Germans had sustained their production of war materiel. With the Ruhr now cut off from the rest of Germany, however, and the U.S. Army within artillery range of the industrial zone, production had just about ceased.

The 75th Division's objective was Dortmund, the easternmost of the Ruhr's manufacturing cities, inhabited by 540,000 people and depicted by a division booklet as the "Pittsburgh of Germany." To get there, the 75th, with the 116th Infantry on its left, would first have to traverse a major canal, then carry out an attack through a ten-mile terrain belt that abruptly changed from rural to urban. The closer the Americans approached Dortmund, the tougher the fight would be: XVI Corps's history described Dortmund, along with other Ruhr cities, as "veritable fortresses with elaborate shelters against shellfire and bombing, fixed anti-aircraft artillery emplacements capable of direct fire upon ground troops, and thousands of buildings providing ideal havens for enemy snipers."

By April 2, the quartermaster truck companies that had transported the 116th Infantry the past two days had disappeared, and the 29ers had to move toward the front the old-fashioned way, by foot. In three and a half hours, they marched eight miles from Marl to the town of Oer-Erkenschwick, a trek that seemed easy for those 116th soldiers who had prepared for D-Day only a year ago—it seemed like a decade—with four-hour, sixteen-mile speed marches or twenty-five-mile hikes across Dartmoor. At 5:30 P.M. the next day, April 3, Bingham's men marched three more miles and took their place at the front in between the 75th Division's 289th and 291st Infantry Regiments. During that march, Company K's Lieutenant Easton noticed that "a pretty German girl came toward us pushing a bicycle, wearing blue slacks and a brown corduroy jacket, a white scarf around her hair. Her face was splattered on one side with mud thrown up by our passing tanks, which were just ahead, and there was no expression but hatred on that face as it regarded us coldly. We passed carcasses of horses cleanly butchered—every scrap of meat removed, only the fresh entrails remaining. . . . In [a] house we saw the head and carcass of a half-eaten dog."

The 116th Infantry was about to rejoin the war in earnest. At 1:00 A.M. on April 4, following a thirty-minute artillery barrage, the attack toward Dortmund jumped off. Bingham's principal challenge at first was not the enemy; rather, it was moving his regiment across the Dortmund–Ems Canal, one of Germany's most magnificent artificial waterways, connecting the Ruhr industrial region with the North Sea, 150 miles distant. "The Dortmund–Ems Canal proved a much more formidable obstacle than the term 'canal' would lead a casual observer to believe," noted a 116th report. "The sides of the canal were perpendicular and thirty feet high; the canal was approximately thirty-five yards wide; and, while it had been partially drained [due to RAF bombing attacks], there was about three feet of water left."

The attack, Company A's PFC John Barnes noted, got off to "a bit of a confused start, but the initial move seemed unopposed." The relieved 29ers appreciated their good fortune; had the enemy offered the kind of resistance it displayed at Omaha Beach, St. Lô, Brest, Aachen, or Koslar, the excruciatingly slow canal crossing could have quickly turned bloody. "Scaling ladders, although they proved to be somewhat short, were an absolute necessity for descending the near bank and ascending the far bank," the regiment's April 1945 action report observed. "The water which remained in the canal was no great obstacle to the foot troops, but having to wade through it caused every man to be wet, muddy, and uncomfortable throughout a cloudy and chilly day."

After clearing the canal, the 116th pressed ahead at a brisk pace, Dallas's 1st Battalion on the right, Meeks's 2nd Battalion on the left. German resistance picked up as the Americans approached Waltrop, a typical Ruhr coal-mining town populated by 20,000 people. According to a 116th report, "enemy resistance was found to be poorly organized, but in spots it was effective and still tough." Barnes recalled that "each time we found an obstacle—buildings or woods—they would put up a fight." However, after a typical U.S. Army firepower display, consisting of every weapon at the infantrymen's disposal in addition to pinpoint artillery fire, Barnes noted, "They quickly retreated or surrendered."

Company F attacked Waltrop under the command of a mere second lieutenant, a rank toward which veteran infantrymen ordinarily did not offer much respect. But 2nd Lt. Dudley James of Florence, South Carolina, was one of the 29th Division's most expert soldiers, a man who, after graduating from college, had enlisted in the Regular army as a private in January 1940, months before President Roosevelt initiated the draft. By June 1944 he had risen to first sergeant, the senior noncommissioned officer slot in the 116th Infantry's Company G, and landed with that unit on Omaha Beach in the opening minutes of the D-Day invasion. First sergeants did not customarily spend much time in forward foxholes, but James was a soldier who felt a pressing need to be up front. He was wounded on June 17, 1944, during the 116th's attack toward St. Lô, and again on August 5, near Vire. He returned to the regiment in time to join in the 116th's effort to capture Aachen in October, during which he gained a Silver Star. As related by his citation, "James rushed forward across 200 yards of open terrain, which was covered by intense enemy fire, and pulled [a wounded soldier] from a flaming tank. After extinguishing the wounded man's clothes, James carried him to a place of safety." On November 2, he gained a battlefield commission as a second lieutenant and transferred to Company F.

Company F's assault on Waltrop evidently was in good hands, thanks to James's innovative methods for seizing and maintaining the initiative. James noted that he used "one platoon as a point or screen force, the platoon operating in front of the company by 400 yards in a scattered formation along the sides of the road. The remainder of the company [followed] in a column. [I] moved with the forward platoon, keeping in contact with the rest of the company by SCR-536 radio. . . . The platoon used as a point moved along the main road into the

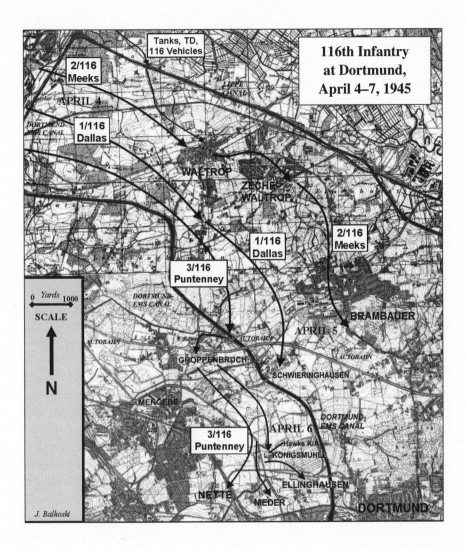

Tanks, TD,
116 Vehicles

2/116
Meeks

APRIL 4

LIPPE
CANAL

**116th Infantry
at Dortmund,
April 4–7, 1945**

DORTMUND-
EMS CANAL

1/116
Dallas

WALTROP

ZECHE
WALTROP

1/116
Dallas

2/116
Meeks

3/116
Puntenney

0   Yards   1000

SCALE

N

DORTMUND-
EMS CANAL

BRAMBAUER

AUTOBAHN

AUTOBAHN

APRIL 5

AUTOBAHN

GROPPENBRUCH

SCHWIERINGHAUSEN

MENGEDE

DORTMUND-
EMS CANAL

3/116
Puntenney

APRIL 6

Hawks KIA

L. KONIGSMUHLE

ELLINGHAUSEN

NETTE

NIEDER

DORTMUND

J. Balkoski

outskirts of the village and was fired upon from the right flank. The platoon leader moved over to the left of the woods, which provided cover, and continued to move into the village, occupying the first houses. . . . [I] radioed the platoon leader of the platoon leading the remainder of the company and ordered it to move to the right flank, taking up a marching fire position when it came within range of the village; when reaching the edge of town, to move to the left in buildings that had already been cleared. This was done, and the marching fire proved very successful, keeping the number of casualties down to two slightly wounded

[PFC Archie Ivey and Pvt. Warner Hamlett, for both their second wounds of the war], while at the same time destroying the enemy opposition and enabling the company to continue on its mission."

Obviously the enemy troops standing between the 116th and Dortmund could no longer resist with the fanaticism the 29ers had coped with in the past. Bingham's men hauled in hundreds of prisoners—Capt. James Rabbitt's Company A alone took 135 on April 4—and once S-2 officers interrogated them, the extent of the pandemonium within the enemy camp became clear: a hodge-podge of seventy-one different German units was represented among the prisoners, including two standard infantry divisions, the 180th and 190th, but also the apathetic 106th Balloon Battalion, 473rd Convalescent Company, 1180th Regimental Supply Company, and 477th Home Guard Battalion, among others. The 29ers also encountered their first examples of Hitler's "people's militia," the *Volkssturm*, labeled by a February 1945 U.S. Army intelligence bulletin as "definitely a bottom-of-the-barrel organization." Populated by teenagers and, much more commonly, middle-aged men up to sixty years old, the *Volkssturm* received little training and wore no uniforms save for a black-and-red armband featuring two Nazi eagles. Not surprisingly, as a 116th report related, "The *Volkssturm* troops proved ineffective. Most of these civilian soldiers had no weapons; those who were issued arms discarded the same and refused to fight."

By sunset on April 4, the 29ers had advanced four miles, a one-day terrain gain that in Normandy would have been considered spectacular. In April 1945, however, far more lengthy daily advances all across the Western Front had become the norm as Nazi Germany disintegrated.

One detail that deeply troubled Bingham, however, was the American engineers' struggle to bridge the canal. With no water in the channel, floating bridges could not be employed; an attempt to fill the canal with earth shoved in by bulldozers got nowhere on April 4 due to the stout construction of the side walls. If the engineers did not solve that problem soon, the 116th would have to fight with no support from armored vehicles, and even worse, food and ammunition would have to be brought forward on foot. "Since it was my job [in Company A] to lead the ration parties from the rear areas to the front-line troops," Barnes recalled, "I was very busy that day and the next. I don't know how many times I climbed down and up those ladders to cross the canal. It wasn't particularly dangerous, just tiring." At one point, Dallas's need for ammunition was so great that a 75th Division artillery observation pilot flew his diminutive L-4 aircraft to the front, loaded with what limited amounts of ammunition it could carry, and landed in a field next to the 1st Battalion command post near Waltrop. "This landing permitted him to evacuate a wounded officer [probably 1st Lt. Samuel Conrad of Company B] on the return trip," noted the 29th's history. "The plane came back three more times with supplies and ammunition during a day which also saw four ammunition trucks winched across the canal."

Bingham finally solved the problem when he and his operations officer, Capt. Carroll Smith—both decorated D-Day veterans—scouted the canal and located a small bridge still standing a few hundred yards beyond the regiment's northern boundary. Just before sunset on April 4, a 116th account noted, "tank and tank destroyer units, impatient at the long delay, poured across the canal and sped on their way to join and support the assaulting foot troops." The next day, trucks and jeeps crammed with supplies would follow.

At 7:00 A.M. on April 5, the 1st and 2nd Battalions jumped off and again made impressive progress toward Dortmund. Meeks's 2nd Battalion cleared yet another expansive coal-mining town, Brambauer, with little difficulty and lost only one man slightly wounded; Dallas's 1st Battalion advanced three miles through a much more pastoral landscape dotted with woods and picturesque Westphalian farms. Despite a Company C clerk's morning-report description of German resistance as "light [with] moderate mortar and occasional self-propelled artillery fire," Dallas lost more than a dozen men wounded and one man killed. No one yet knew that the unfortunate fatality, a radioman named PFC C. J. Galloway who had joined Company A at Brest, would be that unit's last GI killed in action during World War II. (The first had occurred at H-Hour on Omaha Beach almost exactly ten months before.) His comrade, PFC Barnes, claimed that Galloway's death was caused by fratricide when an American howitzer shell fell short of its target.

Lt. Verne Morse's Company C had orders to capture Schwieringhausen by the afternoon of April 5, and as his men warily approached that place from the north at 11:00 A.M., they got their first look at that celebrated example of German ingenuity, the *Reichsautobahn*. A straight-as-an-arrow stretch of one of those controlled-access highways, consisting of two parallel paved roads, each twenty-five feet wide and separated by a grassy median, cut directly across Company C's route into Schwieringhausen. Constructed in the late 1930s with cutting-edge cloverleaf interchanges, overpasses, underpasses, and bridges, the highway provided a direct connection between the Ruhr and Berlin, 270 miles to the northeast. For now, of course, not a single automobile was traveling in either direction. That state of affairs, however, would soon change; Ninth Army had no intention of letting such a progressive piece of engineering go to waste. If Adolf Hitler's last-known address was somewhere in Berlin, the *Reichsautobahn* would provide a convenient means of getting there.

On April 6, Bingham decided to hold Dallas's and Meeks's 1st and 2nd Battalions in place, allowing time for those fatigued units to rest, while swinging Puntenney's fresh 3rd Battalion in an end run around the 116th's western flank. That convoluted maneuver required the 29ers to perform a three-mile nighttime approach march from their reserve bivouacs, starting around 4:30 A.M., and cross the Dortmund–Ems Canal on a seventy-foot footbridge constructed by a platoon from Company B, 121st Engineer Combat Battalion, near Groppenbruch. Then, at 7:00 A.M., Puntenney's men were to begin their attack, directed at the western fringe of Dortmund's industrial district, three miles south. The plucky engineers began their taxing task in the inky gloom at 1:30 A.M. "At 0515 hours the work was completed, and the infantry started to cross at 0525 hours," noted the sappers' report. "In a short while the entire battalion had crossed and the platoon's mission was successfully completed."

Led by Capt. Berthier Hawks's Company I, the 3rd Battalion fanned out on the far side of the canal and warily headed south just as the first pink hints of dawn appeared on the eastern horizon. Company K's Lieutenant Easton recalled, "It was a little like attacking New York City. Imagine a long meadow resembling Central Park, but V-shaped, its apex pointing from the suburbs into the heart of downtown." The 29ers crossed the empty *Reichsautobahn* at one of its distinctive cloverleaf junctions and headed south, giving the Dortmund suburb of Mengede a wide berth on their right. Unfortunately, that move exposed the battalion's right flank, and according to a report, "The enemy seized the opportunity and began to throw in an increasing volume of artillery." Also, as Easton related in a letter to his wife, "The German FOs [forward artillery observers] were up in the skyscrapers and had a truly beautiful view of us."

The 116th's action report remarked that German resistance was "overpowered with a violent barrage from every mortar and artillery piece in the supporting units." A vital element of that support was provided by Company B, 747th Tank Battalion, and a light tank platoon from Company D, both of which had crossed the canal at the autobahn bridge at dawn, joined up with the dogfaces as they trudged southward, and opened fire with 75-millimeter shells and machine guns on any German who dared to offer resistance. A 747th account reported that resistance "ceased as soon as the tanks closed in."

Puntenney's men pressed on. "We advanced rather grandly if absurdly in a broad skirmish line down the meadow toward the rising sun, dew on the grass, shot and shell flying around," wrote Easton. "Really it was fantastic, a covey of brown-clothed men scattered over the meadow, those skyscrapers rearing up in front of us like mountain peaks with the sun coming over their summits." By the end of the day, the 3rd Battalion had gained the three miles stipulated in Bingham's orders and settled in for the night in the Dortmund suburbs of Nette, Nieder, and Ellinghausen, alongside a major rail artery running into Dortmund.

Puntenney paid a high price for that three-mile gain, as during the attack enemy howitzer and mortar fire inflicted thirteen casualties on his outfit, including three dead: two from Company K and one from Company I. Pvt. Attilio Simone of Camden, New Jersey, twenty-seven years old, had been in the Army less than a year and had joined Company K as a replacement only a month ago. At the close of the day, Easton "saw him lying in a plowed field in a drizzle of gray rain. They had laid his poncho over him and marked him with his own rifle, stuck in by the muzzle with his helmet over the butt. . . . I had led him where he was. He was following me. Perhaps the bullet intended for me hit him. If I live a hundred years, the thought of him will never leave me."

Easton knew the other Company K fatality intimately. Pvt. Donald Bryant, a twenty-six-year-old Illinois native, had joined the 29th Division at Brest in September and suffered a slight wound at Koslar two months later. He abruptly walked away from the company on November 22, 1944, and disappeared, causing the clerk to list his status as "missing in action" and later as "absent without official leave." Bryant remained in hiding behind the lines in Holland for more than two months before he was picked up by MPs and dumped unceremoniously in the stockade. In cases such as Bryant's, the U.S. Army invariably returned the offender to the front, and when the MPs dropped him off at Company K's bivouac on February 1, Easton noted, "Already he looked like a man condemned to Fort Leavenworth for 99 years."

Members of the 116th Infantry's Company K after receiving decorations for valor at a January 1945 ceremony.

Bryant strove mightily to make up for his transgression. The kindhearted Easton recalled, "I'd talked to [him] heart-to-heart the night he came back to us from detention, advising him not to worry, the past was the past." Despite a frosty reception from the platoon, his steady conduct during the February 23 Roer assault and the subsequent battles across the Cologne Plain all the way to München-Gladbach impressed his comrades and redeemed his reputation. Easton categorized him as a "character" and remembered: "Nothing he didn't know. A walking dictionary." When Bryant was killed by a shell a few miles short of Dortmund, Easton mused, "He'd made good, stayed in there solidly. . . . And I'd seen the pride and manhood return to his eyes and spine. And then this. It was heartbreaking, really."

The final 3rd Battalion fatality was a man Puntenney described as "a good friend," twenty-five-year-old Capt. Berthier Hawks of Virginia, a bona fide D-Day hero who had helped crack enemy resistance on Omaha Beach by slipping his Company C up the steep coastal bluffs between deadly German strongpoints. His landing craft's ramp, however, had nearly crushed his foot, an injury that cut short his combat career in Normandy four days later and resulted in six months of recovery time in England. Hawks had returned to the 116th on December 9 and assumed command of Company I. During the April 6 attack, Company I men had just passed a set of sturdy buildings, labeled "*Königsmühle*" (King's Mill) on Hawks's map, and pressed ahead across a nearby railroad track. "Captain Hawks was on the second floor of a large brick barn, peering through a small window to observe the enemy's action in the fields ahead," Puntenney wrote, "when an 88 shell hit the building near where he was standing." The dejected Puntenney concluded: "All casualties are hard to lose, especially so when it is a close friend."

So far the three-day effort to capture Dortmund had cost the 116th 124 casualties, one-third of whom were of the "non-battle" variety, including combat exhaustion, illnesses, and accidents. One casualty that occurred the next day, April 7, epitomized the pitiless fortunes of war. Lt. Francis Turton, a thirty-three-year-old native of Ontario, Canada, who led a platoon of five M5 Stuart light tanks in the 747th (attached to the 116th) was described by a comrade as "an efficient officer, respected by his men as an excellent combat leader and all-around honorable person." Turton had survived months of severe combat, most notably in the 175th Infantry's epic stand at Bourheim, Germany, in November 1944. A mile behind the front, his life was snuffed out in a moment by a tragic mishap when a tanker, pushing himself out of an M5 hatch, accidentally knocked into a fully primed machine gun and caused it to open fire. The unlucky Turton, standing directly in front of the gun, was killed. A fellow tanker, 1st Lt. Homer Wilkes, stated the obvious when he noted, "His death under those circumstances saddened all who knew him."

Bingham may have lost 124 men, but Ninth Army soon compensated for that loss with exactly 124 men fresh out of rear-area camps, whose designations the U.S. Army had recently changed, somewhat euphemistically, from "replacement depots" to "reinforcement depots." That name change, according to Army logic, was intended to enhance the shaky morale of those frightened rookies thrust abruptly into veteran units with little knowledge of their surroundings and no familiarity with their new comrades-in-arms.

The skyscrapers of Dortmund loomed close ahead, but the men of the 116th would take no further part in the 75th Division's effort to conquer the Pittsburgh of Germany. That city would finally fall one week later, on April 13. A few hours after Puntenney's 3rd Battalion had pushed to within sight of the city on April 6, General Anderson at XVI Corps provided Bingham with the delightful news that as of 11:30 P.M. the 116th Infantry would be reattached to the 29th Division, following just three days of combat with the 75th. Pulling a unit out of the line in an active combat zone and relieving it with another, however, was always a highly complicated endeavor; in Bingham's case, it was made much more complicated, as his S-3, Captain Smith, reported to the 29th's war room, because "the unit that relieves us [the 320th Infantry, 35th Division] has to be relieved themselves." Also, when a frustrated Bingham learned that his men would have to march out of the line on foot in the dark to a rear assembly area several miles away, he brusquely informed the war room that the move was "quite a haul, and we have lots of stuff: overshoes, overcoats, etc. How about getting the trucks over here?" But the war had reached a stage at which most of the American army was on the move; neither Ninth Army nor XVI Corps had any trucks available.

A burst of frantic phone calls from Gerhardt's logisticians yielded an impromptu solution: the 29th's four artillery battalions would loan the 116th twenty-four trucks, which would pick up Bingham's men no later than 8:00 A.M. the next day, April 7. The usual snafus ensued: Dallas's 1st Battalion, Smith reported at 8:42 A.M., was "still in the line"; another officer stated, "Some of their people [320th Infantry] got lost coming down here. . . . 10:00 A.M. would be an optimistic estimate of when we'll be able to start." But veteran soldiers knew it was much easier departing the front lines than entering them. By noon, the snafus had been worked out. The 116th Infantry had left the capture of Dortmund to others and, as the regiment's April 1945 action report noted, "it was with some relief that the men of the 116th Infantry reverted to the seasoned Blue and Gray 29th Infantry Division."

JUST LIKE A MOVIE

Cannoneers from all four of the 29th Division's artillery battalions had coped with severe ammunition shortages for months in the aftermath of D-Day. Ike's logisticians had sorted out those supply troubles by late 1944, but by April 1, 1945, the frustrated 29ers, eager to display what they could achieve when unfettered by shell shortages, promptly discovered that the number of decent enemy targets was dwindling by the day. The war was moving fast, and to keep up with it, 29th Division artillery—equipped with a total of thirty-six 105-millimeter howitzers and twelve much more hard-hitting 155s—needed to move to the front and find something to shoot at. As a 29th Division gunner observed, "The great chase to the east was on . . . [and] the cannoneers fully expected to share in it."

By Easter Sunday, April 1, the 29ers had not fired their howitzers against the enemy for a month. But General Anderson of XVI Corps abruptly terminated that dormant period by attaching all four artillery battalions to the 79th Division, one of two corps units that had stormed across the Rhine on March 24 and was now engaged in static, almost siegelike operations along the Rhine–Herne Canal just north of the great industrial city of Duisburg, populated by nearly half a million people. The Germans defending Duisburg were surrounded, along with more than 300,000 others in the Ruhr pocket; so bleak was their future that on April 2, a 79th Division officer crossed the canal under a white flag to suggest that they give up. "It was just like a movie," a *New York Times* reporter wrote, "with all sorts of salutes, heel-clicking, and *Heil Hitlers*, but the bemedaled German commandant refused to surrender Duisburg. . . . 'We have no other choice but to fight on in the name of our Führer and the fatherland,' the German said." If that was what the Germans wanted, the 29ers would give it to them.

The 29th Division gunners unlimbered their pieces in Duisburg's northern suburbs, in terrain unlike anyplace they had fought before. Not much open ground was available around the factory towns of Holten and Hamborn, and as forward observers and liaison teams moved to the front, closer to Duisburg, they noticed that the landscape turned entirely urban. "This was like fighting in industrial areas of Pittsburgh, Philadelphia, or Baltimore—manufacturing areas were almost solidly continuous, with just an open field here or there between built-up centers," a 29er emphasized. The men, Cooper observed, "experienced strange feelings as they drove through areas of brick row dwellings and through a metropolitan business district [of Hamborn] where thousands of German civilians bustled about, seemingly paying scant attention to either the warriors or the war." Cooper recalled that the 110th Field Artillery "established headquarters in an office building of the huge Linde oxygen plant; the plant itself, like all others in the neighborhood, having been wrecked beyond description by Allied aerial bombing. . . . [The 110th] manned a battalion observation post on a 200-foot brick chimney rising from the roof of one of the oxygen plant buildings."

From Easter Sunday through Thursday, April 5, the artillerymen fired into Duisburg in support of the 79th Division. For four of those five days, the weather,

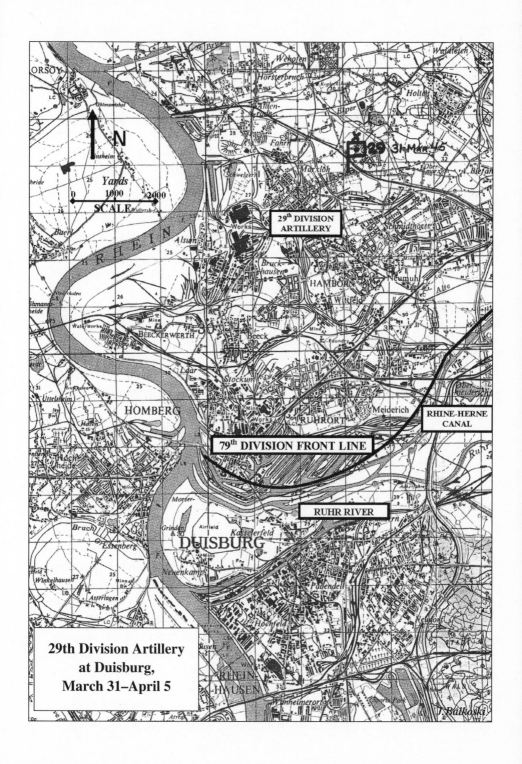

**29th Division Artillery
at Duisburg,
March 31–April 5**

as a report noted, "was extremely bad," so air and ground observation in daytime was limited. Accordingly, most of the fire was of the unobserved harassing variety and typically undertaken after sunset. All 29th Division gunners could not fail to note the irony that they were stuck in one of the most stagnant operations they had ever experienced in World War II while other Allied units had broken the Western Front wide open and were racing into central Germany. But they would not be stuck for long. On April 6 at 11:00 A.M., Anderson reattached all four artillery battalions to the 29th Division, and two hours later, they were on their way by truck to the division's latest assembly area just south of Münster, sixty-five miles away.

The brass hats did not seem to know for the moment what to do with the 29th Division. Aside from snipping away the 116th Infantry and the division artillery for temporary missions with other outfits, Simpson had not passed on any imperative missions to the 29th since it had crossed the Rhine and assembled around Dinslaken starting on March 31. That passivity may have annoyed the division's atypical glory seekers, since other divisions—most notably the 29th's old running mates, the 2nd Armored and 30th Divisions—were currently racing toward Berlin. However, the Blue and Gray Division, most 29ers concurred, had already achieved more than its share of glory; how could anyone think otherwise given the 29th's casualty toll of more than 20,000 men in ten months of combat, starting on D-Day? Besides, with a safe return to the States imminent, who wanted to be among the last American casualties of the European war?

The 29th Division's April 6 transfer to the Münster vicinity was its third major change of position in six days. After crossing the Rhine and settling into camps on the east bank on April 1, the division shifted just two days later to the coal-mining town of Dorsten, twenty miles to the northeast, with no major mission save to defend several bridges spanning the Lippe River, guard a vast synthetic rubber plant in Marl, and provide an infantry battalion to perform "palace guard" duties at Ninth Army headquarters at Haltern. That dull duty lasted only seventy-two hours; early on Friday, April 6, the 29ers packed up items that had only just been unpacked and headed in vast truck convoys toward Münster, forty miles northeast. Gerhardt chose the village of Sendenhorst, twelve miles south of Münster, for his headquarters. The next day, April 7, the 116th Infantry rejoined their comrades; the 29th Division was finally in one piece again, poised to play a role, as yet undefined, in the final downfall of Nazi Germany.

Whatever it was that Ninth Army wanted Gerhardt to do, evidently it would not involve combat. The events of the past week, however, provided a strong hint about the 29th Division's future role in the war. The moment the division had crossed the Rhine, it entered an appalling new world unlike anything the 29ers had seen before. It seemed that all of central Europe was on the move; the landscape teemed with huddled masses of pathetic people whom the Anglo-American armies now categorized dispassionately as "displaced persons"—known to the 29ers simply as "DPs." The 29th Division found some DPs in slave labor camps of indescribable filth in the Dinslaken area, but in early April 1945 most DPs were mobile, thronging the roads of central Germany, trudging inexorably westward toward a salvation they hoped the western Allies would bestow. They consisted chiefly of slave laborers, mainly eastern Europeans—women as well as men—heartlessly cast aside by their masters as German industry disintegrated. "In the Ruhr area alone," a Ninth Army report observed, "300,000 displaced persons were liberated from their enforced slavery. . . . They were on the road twenty-four hours a day, columns of people loaded in charcoal-burning vehicles, riding bicycles, pushing wheelbarrows, pulling carts and wagons and every possible kind of homemade contraption that could be made to travel on wheels—anything to relieve the burden that most of them had to carry on their backs." Mixed in with those hordes were thousands of bedraggled and starving men who had been cut loose from German prisoner-of-war camps, a few Americans, British, and Canadians, but mostly French, Belgians, Dutch, Soviets, Poles, Czechs, Yugoslavs, Greeks, and even former German allies such as Italians, Hungarians, and Romanians.

Easton scrutinized those masses of humanity and portrayed them in an April 3 letter to his wife: "Many liberated slave workers came streaming toward us—Poles and Russians mostly—calling out to us as we pass, laughing, exchanging brief phrases with our Polish and Russian boys. They are a motley assortment, wearing a patchwork of ragged clothes . . . sometimes singing—men and women linked arm in arm—and sometimes they run to us and walk alongside, the girls linking arms with a soldier they like. I saw one [woman], Polish or Ukrainian, walking between two men, full-lipped, full-bosomed, wearing dark slacks and a tailored blouse and no hat, probably just free a few hours, and she was shy and afraid like a creature long caged."

When at 6:12 P.M. on April 1, XVI Corps ordered the 29th Division to provide a single rifle platoon to guard the first of the corps' DP camps, Gerhardt in all likelihood inferred what the future held in store. That platoon, drawn from the 115th's Company A, was directed to report to a fenced-in camp near Buschmannshof, little more than a mile from the Rhine, and "to be prepared to mount guard for a week to ten days." An officer in the war room replied, "It is OK to use that platoon any way they [XVI Corps G-5 personnel] want to."

What started out with a 40-man rifle platoon, as Gerhardt learned from Ninth Army on the evening of April 7, was about to expand to a 14,000-man division. At a 9:00 A.M. meeting in the 29th's war room on April 8, the general discussed with his senior commanders what he described as "a mission to take over a security job. . . . The move involves the whole works, including division head-quarters. We will make the best of it. . . . Alert your people." The scope of that mission astonished Gerhardt's minions; no U.S. Army unit of division size had ever attempted anything like it. The 29th Division was to cover an area bordered by the Rhine in the west to beyond Münster in the east, a vast oblong amounting to more than 1,000 square miles, and to be prepared to expand that oblong much farther to the east upon Ninth Army order.

Above all other of its new responsibilities, the 29ers must keep the main east–west supply arteries in its zone clear; failure to do so could halt Ninth Army's lightning advance into central Germany toward Berlin. Simpson therefore demanded that the 29th Division keep DPs off the roads and herd them into areas where the wretched multitudes could be cared for, sorted out, and eventually dis-patched home. Additionally, the 29th had to carry out another essential duty by implementing military government within the German districts they occupied. Ever since they had first entered Germany in October 1944, the Yanks had become proficient at those functions: Nazi officials were rooted out, order among the civilian population was maintained, sabotage was prevented, and the infra-structure was gradually restored.

There was no time to lose: within twenty-four hours of Gerhardt's receipt of the Ninth Army order, the 29ers were expected to be on the new job. The general divided his sector into four zones: division artillery in the west, alongside the Rhine, encompassing the city of Wesel; 116th Infantry in the east, in and around Gütersloh; and 115th and 175th in the center, near Dülmen and Münster. To reach their new sectors, most 29ers had to backtrack westward over the same roads they had only recently traveled in the opposite direction. It seemed like yet another

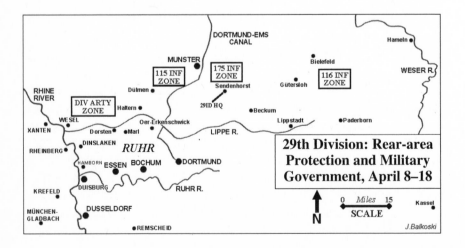

29th Division: Rear-area Protection and Military Government, April 8–18

Army snafu—but whatever the reason for those inscrutable back-and-forth move-ments, it would quickly be forgotten as Gerhardt's men tackled the new and bewildering duties for which none of them had been trained. They must do their best, so as always—29, let's go!

The 29ers did indeed go; and when they went, the amazed GIs took in what one observer described as "the great migration." Herding those wandering DPs into camps, either decrepit ones built months ago by the Germans or new ones hastily erected by the Allies, was the easy part; there they would be sorted into groups separated by nationalities—a historian noted "the designation DP turned out to be almost synonymous with Russian"—and sprayed with a DDT power-duster to kill insects that could quickly turn the camps into typhus death traps. Already existing camps must be cleaned up; new and much cleaner camps would have to be established by the dozens. Sanitation was far and away the most pressing issue; for soldiers used to the fastidious Gerhardt and the 29th's spotless barracks, mess halls, and kitchens, the spectacle of a DP camp came as a shock. "Most established camps were in a horrible state of filth," noted a 29th Division summary. "Camps became almost nauseating in short order unless strenuous and continuous regulations were enforced. . . . Garbage was thrown about indiscriminately in buildings, out of windows, in piles about entrances to buildings. . . . Human waste received much the same treatment. Indoor toilets were filled and overrun, defecation continued in these rooms, even in sleeping quarters."

The GIs would be challenged to impart the 29th Division's high standards of cleanliness to throngs of apathetic, anxious refugees; nonetheless, they must try. "The first step taken was to have a general cleanup campaign," the summary noted. "Buildings were cleaned out [by the refugees themselves] and sleeping quarters reallocated and rearranged. . . . Kitchens were established and mess halls set up. . . . Toilets were cleaned out or closed. . . . Frequent washing was encour-aged." The 29ers met the nearly unmanageable challenge of the DPs' dehydration and malnutrition head-on by trucking in plentiful food and clean water; by mid-April, Ninth Army was passing out 200,000 rations per day to the DP camps. Allied ex-prisoners of war, however, were provided with C- and K-rations straight from the 29th Division's own supplies. The GIs also addressed the equally daunting problem of disease by setting up aid stations and hospitals, run not only by the 29th's medical personnel but also by doctors who emerged from the hordes of refugees. One ad hoc 29th Division hospital was "staffed by two Belgian physicians, a Polish nurse, and a small American medical unit attached to the local British military government detachment."

The DP work was of course not as hazardous as combat, but a 29er noted that "the ingenuity and patience of every soldier directly connected with a camp was taxed to the utmost." Happily, as a 29th Division report remarked, "What appeared to be an insurmountable problem at first gradually began to dwindle in size." Indeed, one of the 29th Division's most important goals during this period was to ensure that capable leaders within the various ethnic groups in the DP camps would come forth to control their own people without constant oversight from the American army. One thing with which the 29th Division rarely had to contend was concerted defiance among the refugees; that would come later, after V-E Day. At a collection point run by the 115th's 2nd Battalion, 1st Lt. William Holberton recalled, "Once the people understood what we were trying to do for them, they, for the most part, cooperated very well." A SHAEF G-5 report corroborated that sentiment: "The truth is that the Eastern workers are astonishingly well-behaved."

Such a vast and complex process could not be devoid of problems. A member of Holberton's company, PFC Thomas Malia—a thirty-three-year-old D-Day veteran from Maine—declared: "Notice was given to the German civilians to vacate certain sections [of the town of Beckum] so that we could quarter the displaced persons there. We planned to house the Russian DPs in one block, the Italians in another, the Poles in a third, and so on. Trouble started when the Russian

Eastern European "displaced persons" at a camp in Germany.

and Italian DPs made themselves at home and started helping themselves to whatever they wished. Orders came down to the platoon to handle the trouble that was brewing. Lieutenant Holberton instructed us to keep everyone out of these specified blocks. . . . I had every imaginable kind of hard-luck story presented to me by German civilians trying to get into their homes. One woman even tried to bribe me to get her a pass. I gave her a dirty look and said to her in German: '*Nichts— eintritt verboten.*' [No—entry prohibited.] A fairly attractive girl walked up to me and made a gesture of familiarity. I gave her the same answer. . . . We worked late that evening and maintained guard details throughout the night. The next day we housed the Russians, Italians, Poles, and French in separate quarters."

No unit had a tougher job during this dreary period than Cooper's 110th Field Artillery, which covered the 29th Division's westernmost zone in and around the battered city of Wesel. Several Rhine bridges were situated in Cooper's area of responsibility, and he held orders to prevent displaced persons from passing over the river, save for French, Belgian, or Dutch ex-prisoners on their way home. An inordinate number of refugees therefore crammed into the 110th's zone, mostly in Wesel, with nowhere to go and nothing else to do but wait. "Little did [we] realize the problems that would occur from taking over and setting up military government," the 110th's April 1945 monthly report stated. Over the next nine days, the 500-man 110th collected a total of 13,917 people, 16 percent of the 86,000 gathered by the division as a whole. In addition, Cooper's men pulled together 6,204 ex-prisoners of war. "The sanitary conditions in Wesel beggared description," Cooper asserted. "Still remaining under the rubble, according to the burgomeister's estimate, were the bodies of over 1,000 people who had been killed in air raids. Though attempts were made to burn the debris in places where the sickly stench of human decay was worst, they were only partially successful because of the preponderance of masonry." The artillerymen gathered 1,900 Italians struggling to survive and transported them to the much healthier confines of a new camp at Brünen, one of ten camps run by the battalion. Those Italians willing to work—and there were hundreds—received cigarettes and food in compensation for their efforts in completing a new wooden railroad bridge over the Rhine near Wesel, an act that Cooper noted "immediately reduced the tremendous highway supply traffic."

The 29ers' authority over the throngs of displaced persons depended on forceful communication, expressed in language the refugees could understand. Given the assortment of languages spoken by the DPs, however, and the fact that only a tiny percentage spoke English, productive interactions between soldiers and refugees seemed problematic. But the U.S. Army melting pot almost never failed to overcome linguistic challenges; as Holberton noted, "Most of the displaced workers knew enough German to understand simple commands and to answer routine questions. Within [my] platoon there were a couple of men who could handle Italian, and one who could speak Polish. Usually, the Russians could understand Polish. I could speak German, so all in all we made out reasonably well. . . . There were a few Dutch civilians, but they easily understood either German or English, or both. There was a Greek sailor who had somehow been caught up in the Nazi net and ended up in the middle of the German heartland. Trying to get information from him was a real obstacle. Finally, we worked out a slow but effective path through the language forest. I spoke German to an Italian, who then spoke Italian to another Italian, who could also speak Greek."

The 29ers spent hours—day and night, rain or shine—manning roadblocks to divert "the motley traffic," as one GI called it, away from the American army's main supply routes. Orders stipulated that the 29ers must comb through those "motley" multitudes and separate civilians from the soldiers whom the Germans had captured in battle, in some cases nearly five years earlier. Making that distinction was trickier than the GIs imagined, for years in German captivity had taken a toll on the prisoners' clothing, not to mention their psyches. "Many wear shabby green uniforms," a report noted. "They are Red Army PWs. Frenchmen and Belgians also still wear their old army uniforms, now almost in tatters. Poles and Dutchmen and Serbs wear any kind of rags. Their German masters had not kept them in clothes." The 116th Infantry alone maintained thirty-six camps for ex-prisoners of war, which gathered 23,883 men, over three-quarters of whom were Soviets. Indeed, one overflowing camp near Lippstadt held 10,789 Red Army members. "Normally the officer or non-commissioned officer of highest rank in the respective Allied POW camps was appointed commander," declared a 29th Division report. "This contributed materially to the maintenance of discipline [and] dissemination of directives and information." Although western Europeans were permitted to head home after benefitting from a steady diet and basic medical care for a few days, the 29th Division could not yet release Soviet and Polish ex-prisoners because their eastward path to freedom passed through German-controlled territory. They were promised freedom to go when the war ended, an event they hoped could not be far off.

In one camp occupied by 300 French soldiers, a mere U.S. Army buck sergeant, Dewey Ray of the 115th Infantry's Company E, provided the management the ex-prisoners desperately needed. A native of Waco, Texas, Ray was described as "a tall, husky, soft-spoken lad with a worried look that makes him seem a decade older than his 20 years." Ray indeed had much to worry about: he did not speak French, and only three fellow Americans, one of whom was a doctor, were on hand to provide help. A senior French *sous-officier* (noncommissioned officer) named Baron, who had been captured when Ray was still an adolescent, maintained discipline and passed on Ray's directives to the men.

One morning, an observer noted, the French "stood their first formation in five years when a GI bugler blew 'To the Color,' as Sergeant Baron ran up a home-made tricolor. The 300 soldiers of the French Republic stood at attention with tears of joy in their eyes. The night before the boys had made the red, white, and blue flag out of German tablecloths." At the close of the poignant ceremony, Baron concluded, "These German people will tell you they don't want war any-more. They didn't feel like that four or five years ago. They were all good Nazis when they were winning."

From time to time, a small, disheveled group of soldiers would approach a roadblock and address the incredulous GIs in perfect English, expressed in accents that divulged their homelands—Great Britain, Canada, the United States. British and Canadian ex-captives, some of whom had been in confinement since Dunkirk in May 1940, were promptly conveyed to nearby Commonwealth units. According to one 29er, when two U.S. Army Rangers who had been captured in Italy trudged into the 29th Division's zone, "They were suffering so much from hunger that they could not eat normally. Under the surgeon's care, they were fed and rested and then evacuated to an Army hospital."

So focused were the 29ers on the refugee issue that it was easy for them to forget they were currently situated in what had only recently been the heart of Nazi Germany. The closest armed enemy troops were miles away; as for German civilians, Holberton commented: "They realized the tables had been turned, and that these 'undesirable' workers were now in a favored position. The Germans themselves were relegated to the lowest rank in the pecking order." Still, the enemy noncombatants had to be governed, and that governing power within each of the 29th Division's four districts was vested in Gerhardt's four senior com-manders: Bingham of the 116th, McDaniel of the 175th, Blandford of the 115th, and Sands of the artillery.

Maj. Robert Walker's 29th Division military government (G-5) section, con-sisting of only five officers and eleven enlisted men, provided vital, if over-stretched, support to those four experienced combat leaders, all of whom had spent the war learning how to kill Germans, not govern them. Walker had gradu-ated from law school in 1941 and spoke fluent German; his senior noncommis-sioned officer, T/Sgt. George Curtiss (born George Kertesz), grew up in several European countries and resettled in New York City as a teenager in 1938. In addi-tion to English, he spoke fluent German, French, and Hungarian and performed decently at Spanish, Italian, and Russian, too. In the environment in which the 29th Division currently found itself, those language skills were critical.

"For the initial phase, we go slow, feel our way out," Walker told an inter-viewer. "We never put a Nazi in a position of trust. . . . We haven't had to arrest many Germans. . . . The big dilemma for military government now is: Do we use the civilian administrations we find in each county? I think it's better that we do. But that is up to higher authorities to decide."

Would the Nazis commit acts of sabotage behind the front? For a time, the Americans worried they would, but that anxiety quickly evaporated. Instead, the 29ers worried most about keeping the DPs and Germans apart. The 29th Division was doing its best to corral the tens of thousands of DPs and ex-prisoners who roamed the countryside in search of sustenance, but as an Allied G-5 report noted, "German farmers say the eastern workers are stealing their chickens. German workers say that the Russians are breaking into homes and helping themselves to necessities." That report drew a blunt conclusion: "German middle-class people say the Russians are animals." In one disquieting instance, an outraged burgomeister met with 29th Division authorities to complain that roving bands of Russians were using weapons to rob local German farmers of their produce and poultry. The ad hoc military government had to admit that his grievance was valid, and said it would do what it could to stop the looting. "In one such case," a 29er recalled, "the investigators found that the 'weapons' used in the holdup had not been tommy guns, as the victims believed, but grease guns used for lubricating vehicles."

The 29th Division's constabulary role in Germany could turn ugly in a hurry if local residents remained firmly committed to fascism. During a series of home inspections in a German town, the 116th Infantry's S/Sgt. Bob Slaughter discovered to his surprise that some of the natives would have trouble weaning themselves from Hitler and the Nazis. A D-Day veteran and prewar guardsman from Roanoke, Virginia, Slaughter remembered "an aristocratic young man, about 13 years old," who opened his front door in response to the Americans' pounding. "Jokingly, I said that my men and I were looking for *Herr* Adolf Hitler, and that when we found him, we would hang him from the nearest lamppost." The youngster ardently replied, "No, no. . . . That will never be! He is our Führer!" Concluded Slaughter: "I found the incident amusing, but it also showed me just how deeply the Nazi movement had penetrated German society."

On the other hand, during its recent period of attachment to the 75th Division, the 116th Infantry had learned that many German civilians were assuredly tired of the Nazis. As Company K entered Oer-Erkenschwick, a woman approached Lieutenant Easton and tentatively asked what the Americans did with "people who killed German people?" The intrigued Easton learned that "her boyfriend threw a hand grenade in the burgomeister's window and killed him 'because he was a Nazi swine, and everybody hated him—he joined the Party and became burgomeister only to put money in his pocket and drink schnapps and sleep with pretty women.'" The 29ers eventually learned that her narrative had more complex origins: when the Americans had first approached the undefended town, the burgomeister demanded the *Volkssturm* fight "to the last man," an order that understandably disturbed the young and old male civilians who must carry it out. A senior member of the community informed him, "With such men I cannot fight." According to the gist of the natives' account, "The irate burgomeister began to destroy installations, blowing up the shaft of the coal mine in which most of the villagers earned their living. He cut off the water supply and ordered everyone to flee into the remnants of Nazi Germany." In the lead story of the April 11, 1945, edition of *29 Let's Go*, editor Jean Lowenthal wrote, "When the 'Hitler boy' threatened to blow up the bunkers in which the villagers took refuge, they did a little blowing up of their own." (According to the 116th's monthly report, the burgomeister was shot dead by his fellow citizens, not blown up.) Lowenthal concluded: "The citizens of Oer-Erkenschwick apparently can read the writing on what's left of the West Wall."

Some hard-up Germans, anxious to restart their lives, bombarded the 29ers with curious requests. One day, PFC Ernest Menkel of Queens, New York, was taking a break outside a derelict Wesel factory that housed the command post for the 110th Artillery's Headquarters Battery. Three German male civilians approached him and, luckily for them, discovered that Menkel spoke fluent German, owing to his birth in Danzig in 1920. "Menkel explained to his buddies that the Jerries had asked him for the superintendent of the plant," Lowenthal noted in the April 12 *29 Let's Go*. "They were looking, they said, for a job. Menkel referred them to the military government."

So efficiently had the 29ers opened the golden door for the huddled masses yearning to be free that on April 19, Simpson penned a laudatory letter to Gerhardt. "I was greatly impressed with the speed and thoroughness with which you carried out this new and unusual mission," he wrote. "It was a real pleasure to me to note the enthusiasm and energy with which you and your staff, and the commanders and staffs of your subordinate units quickly analyzed the task and fashioned a plan which I consider a model for the performance of this type of mission. . . . I am happy to share your pride in the record built up by the division. Please accept my sincere congratulations upon your past performances and my heartiest best wishes for continued success. May I ask that you communicate these remarks to the officers and men of your command?" As one of Gerhardt's "past performances" had caused his corps commander to demand his relief—a demand approved by Simpson but vetoed by Ike—the 29th Division's superb execution of its military government role, and before that its bold assault across the flood-swollen Roer, had evidently redeemed Gerhardt's reputation. Maybe Ike had been right in rejecting Gerhardt's relief: not many U.S. Army generals could match Charlie Gerhardt's boundless optimism and energy, even if he occasionally misused those traits. "I never saw him when he was low," Simpson remarked.

Now that the fantasy of leading victorious troops down Berlin's *Unter den Linden* was growing more plausible by the day, how could any American general on the Western Front be low? The 29th's longtime combat partner, the 2nd Armored Division, had reached the Elbe River on April 11 after a glorious one-day dash of sixty miles. The next day, the 2nd Armored crossed the river: Berlin was another sixty miles distant. Given the speed of the American blitzkrieg, visions of the Stars and Stripes flying over the Reich Chancellery began to dance in the heads of the U.S. Army's senior leaders.

On Friday, April 13, 1945, however, a newsflash fresh from the States triggered a shock wave that permeated every worldwide front in which Americans served: President Franklin Delano Roosevelt was dead. Roosevelt had only recently commenced his thirteenth consecutive year in the White House; the youngest 29ers could hardly recall a time in which someone else had been president. The April 13 edition of *29 Let's Go* featured a front-page story, encased in a thick black mourning border, with the headline, "President Roosevelt Dies Suddenly." So unfamiliar were the 29ers with FDR's replacement that the article referred to the new president simply as "Senator Truman" without even using his first name.

When Ike learned the news shortly after midnight, he recalled that he "went to bed depressed and sad." The next day he wrote to FDR's cherished friend Harry Hopkins, "I bitterly regret that he could not have been spared to see the final day of victory." In Berlin, Joseph Goebbels had an entirely different reaction: "My Führer," Goebbels announced, "I congratulate you! Roosevelt is dead!"

The war must of course go on. Eisenhower issued an order that adhered to the War Department's recent directive: "Wearing of mourning badges, firing of salutes, dropping national and regimental colors and standards will be dispensed with in view of war conditions."

SIX

Something to Write Home About

GIVING THE WOODS A HAIRCUT

Even the shocking news of Roosevelt's death could not shove the exhilarating war reports from Europe out of stateside newspaper headlines. In its first edition since Roosevelt's death had been broadcast to the nation the previous afternoon, the April 13, 1945, *New York Times* featured a front-page banner that blared:

> *PRESIDENT ROOSEVELT IS DEAD;*
> *TRUMAN TO CONTINUE POLICIES;*
> *9TH CROSSES ELBE, NEARS BERLIN*

The "Great Crusade," as Eisenhower called it, in which the 29th Infantry Division had played such a pivotal role, was finally close to fulfillment. The 29th had expended thousands of lives, and far greater numbers of broken bodies and souls, to reach this point. The 29ers deserved a break; everyone, even Ike, agreed with that sentiment. Several times in the past, implausible rumors had swept through the ranks, alleging that the Blue and Gray Division had fought its last battle; this time, five days into its military government mission in the Ruhr, those rumors seemed wholly credible. How could they not be when Ninth Army's leading elements were poised to reach Berlin within twenty-four hours? "It was incredible to us how quickly the war seemed to be ending, the enemy collapsing like a giant balloon," wrote PFC John Barnes of the 116th Infantry. Always an astute observer of his battalion's morale, Lt. Col. Purley Cooper recalled, "Many members of the 110th [Field Artillery] thought that they would never move farther east, and that the 29th Division would see no more fighting."

What the 29ers did not grasp, however—and in fact no one on the Western Front knew except those in the highest reaches of the Anglo-American command—was that on March 28 Eisenhower had made the momentous decision to erase Berlin from its first-place standing on his list of strategic objectives and redirect his armies toward other significant targets in Germany and Czechoslovakia. As of that date, when the Soviets were only thirty miles from Berlin and the western Allies nearly ten times that distance, Ike's decision made perfect sense. Two weeks later, as Ninth Army raced to and beyond the Elbe, and the Soviets had not yet begun their Berlin offensive, Eisenhower may have been tempted to place the German capital on top of his objective list again, but much to the regret of some American and British generals, and even more politicians, he steadfastly held to his initial judgment, asserting, "So far as I am concerned, that place [Berlin] has become nothing but a geographical location; I have never been interested in those." Instead, the Red Army, which would commence its final grand assault toward Berlin on April 16, would inevitably gain the laurels of seizing the Fatherland's sacred city and hoisting the hammer and sickle over the Reichstag.

Simpson's Ninth Army, of which the 29th Division was still an integral part, would advance no farther toward Berlin for the rest of World War II. Rather, it would stand fast on the Elbe and fight a mop-up war behind the front, a curious struggle in which the front lines, as the astonished Americans soon discovered, were anything but symmetrical, and Germans could appear out of nowhere to offer resolute resistance and in some cases even launch robust counterattacks.

Would the 29th Division be drawn away from its vital military government mission and sucked into that last clean-up mission against the enemy? All 29ers hoped that it would not. Yet gossip suggested that the 17th Airborne, 79th, and 95th Divisions would soon take over the 29th's constabulary duties: one rumor declared that the division would join Patton's Third Army in its advance into Czechoslovakia; another more likely possibility was that it would transfer to the U.S. First Army and move immediately to Nordhausen, the site of a Nazi death camp recently liberated by the 104th Division, to mop up nearby pockets of recalcitrant German troops. Whatever it was that the high command finally decided, one detail was certain: the 29th Division would not end up in Berlin, as Gerhardt had hoped.

Not until Tuesday, April 17, did the 29th Division's future crystallize. At 12:15 P.M. a Ninth Army order arrived at the war room, directing the 29th to move

eastward by truck and join Simpson's effort to mop up isolated enemy units west of the Elbe River. Gerhardt's summary of that order left no doubt in the 29ers' minds that they would soon be fighting again: "Upon closing in assembly area, prepare for possible tactical employment," he commanded. Led by Blandford's 115th Infantry, the 29th Division moved out early on April 18 to an assembly area in a rural and heavily forested region east of Celle, some thirty-five miles west of the Elbe. A few 29th Division units manning DP camps near Wesel on the Rhine had to travel more than 200 miles to reach their destination and, thanks to their use of a wide-open autobahn for part of the journey, they completed the trip in the comparatively short time of thirteen hours. At 4:30 P.M. on April 19, Gerhardt set up his new command post in Uetze; by the afternoon of the next day, April 20, the 29th Division, "like an old war horse who has lived in clover long enough," as an anonymous 29er noted, was in its assigned position, ready to wage war again.

A frustrated 116th Infantry soldier who thought he had seen the last of armed Germans remarked that the regiment was relieved of its military government work "just as it had developed an efficient organization, had become accustomed to the work, and had begun to enjoy it." A 115th Infantry GI echoed that emotion when he recalled, "The [military government] experience had been a new one, but a pleasant one for the men of the regiment, and it was not with a great deal of joy and enthusiasm that they gave up their new duties for a return to the more familiar but hardly well-liked tasks of returning to combat."

Simpson's reassignment of the 29th Division from Anderson's XVI Corps to Maj. Gen. Alvan Gillem's XIII Corps, an organization to which the 29th had belonged for a month over the winter, hinted at tough times ahead for the 29ers. Gillem commanded the northernmost American corps on the Western Front, a detail that caused him immense headaches because his mission differed fundamentally from the British units under Montgomery on his left flank. In the week prior to the 29th Division's attachment to XIII Corps, Gillem's leading unit, the 5th Armored Division, had dashed eastward to the Elbe and reached that river by April 12. As Monty and Ike had previously agreed, however, the British units to Gillem's left had abruptly turned 90 degrees and headed north toward Hamburg. The gaping hole on Gillem's left flank, patrolled only by small American and British cavalry units, eventually widened to sixty miles as the British overran crumbling German units on the roads heading toward the Baltic Sea. The 29th Division's movement to Celle, Gillem presumed, would help plug that gap, and in doing so the 29th would become the northernmost U.S. Army division in Europe.

Gillem had to extend his left to cover that zone, which was far from secure even though British troops had recently overrun it. "Half in jest, half in earnest," reported Charles MacDonald, the U.S. Army's official historian of the campaign, "service troops complained that it was safer on the front line at the Elbe than in the rear echelon." The 29th Division would soon learn that judgment was entirely accurate. Early on April 16, two days before the 29ers' arrival, "a force estimated at a thousand men and thirty tanks [from the enemy's newly raised Clausewitz Panzer Division] cut the main supply route of the XIII Corps near Gillem's command post at Klötze," MacDonald noted. "For four more days, contingents of the new panzer division turned up at various points in the rear of the corps. . . . Telephone communications and motor messenger service between the XIII Corps and the Ninth Army were disrupted for two days."

So concerned was Gillem over the hodgepodge of German units roaming among his vital lines of communication back to the Rhine that on April 20 he detached McDaniel's 175th Infantry from the 29th Division and directed it to restore order behind the front. Some 500 enemy soldiers, mostly from the mediocre Clausewitz Panzer Division, reportedly had taken refuge in the immense forests adjacent to Klötze, some twenty miles south of the corridors through which the 115th and 116th Infantry were poised to sweep to the Elbe. As related by the 29th Division's official history, "At night small parties would come out on the roads and ambush the last vehicles of American supply columns and return again into the woods." To cut short that practice, Gillem ordered McDaniel "to give Klötze Forest a real haircut," suggesting that the only German soldiers he wished to see emerging from those woods over the next few days would be dead or prisoners.

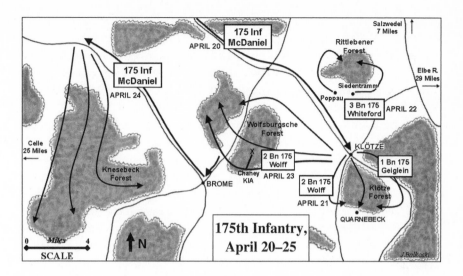

175th Infantry, April 20–25

"The air was full of conflicting stories, and nobody seemed to know the exact strength or location of the German battle groups," a 175th member noted. Operating directly under Gillem's control, McDaniel blocked off all escape routes from the woods and, during a heavy downpour, commenced his attack from the north at 10:24 A.M. on April 21 with the 1st and 2nd Battalions, led by Majors John Geiglein and Edward Wolff. Holbrook Bradley equated the operation to "a wild-game hunt, in which the beaters drove the animals into range of the waiting hunters," an apt comparison since for the first hour the 29ers flushed out almost as many deer as Germans. "For men who had seen fighting at its roughest and toughest," Bradley added, "the most amazing contrast of this engagement was the complete quiet. Only occasionally was there the sound of rifle fire, and that more often than not was when some rifleman took a shot at an animal bounding through the underbrush." By sunset, after a four-mile sweep, Geiglein's and Wolff's units emerged from the forest at the village of Quarnebeck without a single casualty. According to the 175th's April 1945 action report, "nearly 400 prisoners were captured," four 88-millimeter guns taken, and seven U.S. Army trucks loaded with gasoline liberated. Bradley concluded: "[We] thought how tough Jerry could have made it if he had the stuff and wanted to."

The next day, April 22, Whiteford's 3rd Battalion deployed to nearby Poppau and Siedentramm and plunged northward at 2:00 P.M. into the dense *Rittlebener Forst*, which supposedly held more lurking members of the Clausewitz Division. "Company K [1st Lt. Clyde Reed, CO] held the center of the line," a report noted, "while Company L [Capt. Ernest Burkhartt] was on the left and

Company I [1st Lt. William Howell] on the right. The heavy weapons company [Company M, Capt. John Crane] was posted at strategic points to cover and support the riflemen. The companies marched through the wooded area and covered all of it on the march. The woods yielded nineteen Germans and were made completely secure in the operation. The task was fully accomplished by 5:00 P.M." Not a single 29er was injured.

On April 23, Wolff's 2nd Battalion advanced into yet another wilderness, the eight-square-mile *Wolfsburgsche Forst* west of Klötze, but this time the task abruptly turned ugly when a hidden pack of Germans the 29ers had bypassed ambushed 1st Lt. Harold Chaney's thirty-three-man Antitank Platoon and killed three of its members, including Chaney, T/Sgt. John Kardos, and T/5 William Miller. Those losses, Ewing remembered, broke "the easy-going atmosphere that had hung over the operation, [and] brought a vigor and aggressiveness to the 2nd Battalion troops, who continued through the forest using small-arms fire freely." The 29ers' overpowering reaction to the death of their comrades continued for the rest of the day and most of the next, including several intense artillery and mortar barrages and the commitment of both the 1st and 3rd Battalions to the fight. According to a combat summary, forty-three Germans were killed in the two-day sweep, and when McDaniel ordered forward a "bullshit wagon," a truck equipped with a massive loudspeaker that could reportedly project the sound of a human voice for over two miles, most of the remaining defenders emerged from their hiding places with their hands up. By 6:00 P.M. on April 24, *Wolfsburgsche Forst* was under full American control.

After four straight days of clean-up operations in the gloomy woods adjacent to Klötze, McDaniel's 29ers could hardly believe Gillem would require any further work of that kind. The Clausewitz Division had turned out to be a cipher and no longer posed any substantive threat to XIII Corps supply lines. But intelligence reports intimated that one more forest still needed to be cleaned out, the fifteen-square-mile *Knesebeck Forst*, twenty miles west of Klötze. Early on April 25, the 175th Infantry moved by truck to the northern periphery of the woods, and at 11:00 A.M. all three battalions

First Lt. Harold Chaney of the 175th Infantry, one of the last 29ers killed in action during World War II.

plunged southward into the gloom to commence a methodical hunt for wayward Germans, a process to which the 29ers had recently become absolutely accustomed. "The density of the woods and the thoroughness of the search necessitated a slow but steady march, during which the woods were swept to flush out any concealed enemy," the 175th's April 1945 action report noted. "Twenty-four Germans were captured." Smack in the middle of the woods, according to the report, was some sort of "rocket test range," as well as vast stores of enemy materiel that provided plenty of opportunities for souvenirs that would impress the folks once the 29ers returned home. So easy was the operation—mercifully no casualties were suffered—that the 175th's morning reports do not even mention any contact with the enemy that day.

OLD ENOUGH TO KILL

The 29th Division's new sector at Celle was a foreboding place. British Army units had recently passed through the area, and ten miles north of Celle, just outside the placid farming village of Bergen, the Tommies had uncovered another Nazi death camp, one in which two sisters from Amsterdam named Margot and Anne Frank had died of typhus just a few weeks earlier. But the 29ers were too busy undertaking their first tentative forays into the vast pine forests east of Celle, searching for skulking German troops, to absorb any knowledge of yet another example of Nazi horror. "Living conditions in the area were the most primitive yet seen in Germany," a 29er recollected. "Open water wells, with their buckets raised or lowered by long poles used as levers, recalled some of the more backward regions of the United States. . . . [The] little farm villages [were] barely supported by the poor sandy soil of the clearings."

If enemy troops wished to hide, this was the place to do it. "The situation was none too clear," a report stated. "Enemy strength and disposition were unknown; reports of enemy mobile guns, tanks, and troops were vague and conflicting. . . . The [British] armor had raced through the sector so fast that only roads and shoulders had been cleared of the enemy." But the 115th and 116th Infantry found no enemy troops hiding in the Sprakensehl and Klosterforst woods surrounding their assembly areas east of Celle. If the Germans were not there, however, Gillem's orders stipulated that the 29ers must look for them someplace else.

Finding the elusive enemy in that heavily forested region could turn into a needle-in-a-haystack search unless the GIs promptly came up with novel tactics to search out and destroy the Germans as the 29th Division swept eastward toward the Elbe. By this stage of the war, veteran 29ers had grown thoroughly accustomed to adapting their war-fighting methods to the rapidly changing nature of the conflict. Indeed, in the past the 29ers had been forced to alter their tactics fundamentally every time the high command committed them to a new battle. On

D-Day, they had learned how to storm a heavily fortified coastline from the sea; in Normandy, more than a month passed before they had grasped how to fight effectively in the constrictive *bocage*; in Brittany, they had mastered siege warfare, including attacks against formidable eighteenth-century forts; in Germany, they had found out by trial and error how to carry out attacks across the deadly, wide-open Rhineland flatland; at the Roer River, they had overcome the daunting challenge of an assault across a flood-swollen river; on the Cologne Plain, they had absorbed on the fly how to carry out lightning warfare; and most recently, in the Ruhr, they had skillfully practiced the much more peaceful art of military government. The point that even the greenest 29er could not fail to appreciate was that in the past the 29th Division had successfully adapted to a highly fluid war. True, it had paid a terrible price in human lives to do so; but if once more Gerhardt demanded an essential tactical transformation, the 29ers would adjust just as effectively as they had before.

Now the 29ers had to learn how to carry out mop-up warfare, searching out and destroying Germans troops who refused to give up, and Gerhardt came up with an ingenious way to do it. Starting on April 20, the 29th Division—less the 175th Infantry, which was performing its similar operation under XIII Corps at Klötze—would commence a northeastward movement toward the Elbe River, nearly fifty miles away; with the 115th Infantry on the left and the 116th on the right, the 29th would methodically sweep through a corridor, starting out twelve miles wide but steadily expanding to twice that distance, an extraordinarily lengthy frontage for a single division. On their headquarters maps, staff officers set out daily objectives known as "phase lines," designated by feminine names in alphabetical order: Doris, Ethel, Fanny, Genie, Helen, Ida, Jane, Kay, and Lottie. Speed was of critical importance, so time did not permit the infantrymen to carry out the job the old-fashioned way, by walking; instead, Gerhardt motorized both the 115th and 116th by borrowing more than 100 deuce-and-a-half trucks from the division's non-infantry units. When combined with the 115th's and 116th's normal quota of thirty-four trucks apiece, that loan was more than sufficient to maintain an impressive speed of advance as long as the infantry encountered no obstinate enemy resistance. "This type of warfare was something entirely new to the regiment," observed the 115th's history, "for it involved rapid, motorized movement coupled with a wide fanning-out to cover and search large areas, including many sizable forests."

On Friday morning, April 20, on the 29th Division's right flank, the 116th Infantry "thrust forward into the unknown," led by forty men of the 29th Cavalry Recon Troop's 3rd Platoon. (One of the M8 Greyhound armored cars in that dashing outfit was christened "Ike," another "Monty.") What those advance scouts found that Friday in the "unknown" was . . . nothing. Even better, as the

116th's monthly report noted, the next three days were no different: "The probing and clearing operations of April 21, 22, and 23, 1945, were virtually unopposed, and the regiment swept forward, gathering in scattered groups of prisoners from time to time. The advance rather closely resembled a march, so light was the resistance from a dispirited and disorganized enemy. For once the 'Ever Forward' [the 116th's motto] 116th Infantry, which had slugged it out bitterly with a savage foe in such engagements as St. Lô, Vire, Fort Montbarey, Setterich, and Koslar, and had paid a dear price in dead and wounded for its relentless progress—for once, the 116th Infantry found the going easy and the cost low." Through country that Company K's Lieutenant Easton described as "absolutely flat and quite densely wooded, with smallish pines that grow out of sandy red soil," the 116th advanced nearly forty-five miles over four days and, best of all, suffered virtually no casualties. That success brought the regiment to a point just seven miles from the Elbe; the next day, April 24, 116th members expected to wade in that great river and gaze across it, hoping to catch a glimpse of a Red Army soldier coming from the opposite direction. All in all, if one had to fight a war, this was the way to do it.

Maj. Charles Cawthon had just returned to the executive officer slot in the 116th Infantry's 2nd Battalion following recovery from an October 1944 wound he had suffered at Würselen. (He was amused at one staff officer's reaction to his return; scuttlebutt among the battalion staff was that Cawthon was dead.) Within the 29th Division, "All was still ordered and businesslike," Cawthon observed,

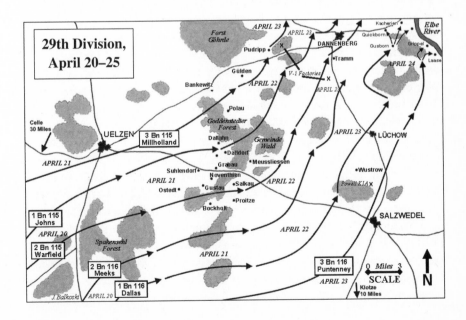

"but somehow easier. . . . There was a comfortable feeling of being back in surroundings I knew so well." Cawthon, like any 116th veteran, found the push to
the Elbe a "cushy" war: "Houses invariably had bed sheets hung from the windows as rumor spread among the inhabitants that this sign of surrender would
forestall destruction of their property," he remarked. "I do not think there was as
much thought of destruction as there was of acquisition. . . . In one house was a
bed-ridden elderly woman, and a note in rough English asking that she not be
harmed as she was a good person and had always thought highly of Americans.
We were surprised that we should be considered a menace to flee, and that we had
to be importuned not to harm an invalid."

On the 29th Division's left flank, the 115th Infantry was not nearly as lucky.
The early-morning advance on Friday began well enough, and for most of the day
the 29ers encountered no opposition as they rolled through Phase Lines Doris,
Ethel, Fanny, and Genie. This was textbook work for the scouts of the 1st
Platoon, 29th Cavalry Recon Troop, who led the advance in jeeps and armored
cars. Their commander, Capt. Ed Jones, remarked that his troopers' scouting
"greatly facilitated the advance of the infantry, as the [infantry] battalion commander did not have to do his own reconnaissance or plan an attack for every
objective. The platoon also investigated the area adjacent to the battalions' axis of
attack, thereby insuring against any surprise action from the flank." The 115th
rolled on for twenty-five miles and encountered not the slightest opposition. The
29ers checked every minuscule village along the route, and when they found no
enemy troops, they reported that detail back to regimental headquarters, where
diligent staff officers circled the villages on a map to indicate they were secure:
Ostedt, Bockholt, Kolau, Güstau, Suhlendorf, Proitze, Salkau, and many more.
Near sunset, however, as Johns's 1st Battalion neared Phase Line Helen, the
29ers encountered British 6th Airborne Division troops heading north, who
reported that a jumble of enemy troops, including parts of the Clausewitz Panzer
Division, intended to make a stand in three tiny hamlets on the western edge of
the vast Goddenstedter woods: Grabau, Dalldorf, and Dallahn.

The Tommies were right: the next day, April 21, would mark the 115th's
first full-fledged battle in nearly eight weeks. There would be no rides in deuce-
and-a-half trucks that morning; Grabau reportedly contained an entire company
of German infantry and three armored vehicles armed with deadly 75-millimeter
guns, and as 1st Lt. Julian Stoen's Company C cautiously approached the village
on foot from the west at 11:15 A.M., it came under heavy fire. After the 110th
Field Artillery and the attached Company A, 89th Chemical Mortar Battalion,
dropped a few salvos on the village, Johns ordered up a "bullshit wagon," and a
German-speaking 29er warned the enemy defenders that if they did not surrender
immediately, they would all be killed by the Americans' overwhelming firepower;

they had five minutes to think it over. "When the five minutes passed without any action on the part of the enemy," the division history reported, "another artillery and mortar concentration was placed on the town. Once again the surrender was demanded, again without any success." This time the howitzers and mortars included smoke shells in their bombardment, and Stoen's men, all of whom were fully conscious that World War II in Europe could only last for another week or two, rose and warily pressed on toward Grabau. As difficult as it was for the 29ers to believe, plenty of German diehards still existed who were willing to face death for the Führer as long as they could kill just a few more Americans.

"We found ourselves in a hell of a spot, and we called back for tank [actually tank destroyer] support," PFC Walter Vanatta related. "When two TDs arrived [from Company A, 821st Tank Destroyer Battalion], someone hollered, 'Let's Go!' and that was the first time I ever saw things happen by the book. Our marching fire was pretty good, and we threw plenty of lead at them, causing the Jerries to pull back. . . . A real tank battle developed between our units and three German tanks. Shells were hitting all around us, and we were between the two sides. Tree bursts showered us with shell fragments, and there were a number of casualties. One of our TDs was damaged. PFC Joseph Blanchard [a Texan], whose hole was directly in front of the tank [destroyer], was killed. Later the [American] tankers who had been forced out of their vehicle came back and continued firing. They certainly had guts."

During a lull in the battle, a jeep occupied by a few 29th Division medics, oblivious to the situation, drove straight into Grabau. "The men who observed the incident were amazed by it, and they were even more amazed a short time later when the jeep drove out again, carrying a wounded German soldier and a nurse," the regimental history reported. "[The Germans] were as anxious that their wounded man be given attention as the American aid men were to return to our lines, and an arrangement was made that satisfied both sides."

Presently, shelling from the 110th's howitzers and 89th's mortars swelled to a crescendo, and at 1:30 P.M. Stoen's men stormed into Grabau. The battered enemy finally gave way, leaving behind, according to Vanatta, seventeen dead. Dozens of Germans surrendered; the divisional history reported "that they had wanted to surrender all the time, but they were forced to resist by the German lieutenant in charge of the assault guns. [He] reportedly escaped to the neighboring town of Dalldorf during the barrage." In addition to the death of PFC Blanchard, Company C lost six men wounded.

After Grabau's capture, Company A under Capt. Mack Hays charged across 1,000 yards of open ground toward Dalldorf, but according to Johns, Hays's men discovered "an almost empty town." The 29ers discerned that the enemy had fled a mile farther to the north, taking refuge in Dallahn, which 1st Lt. Eugene

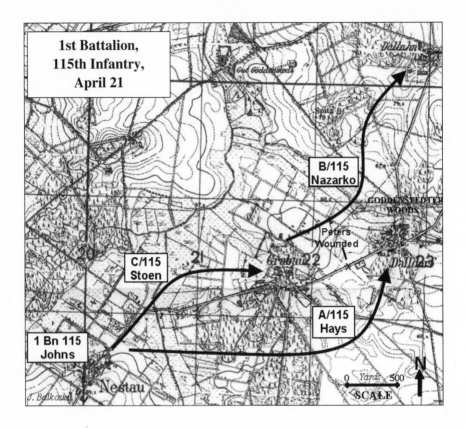

Nazarko's Company B was about to attack. At 4:45 P.M., as Nazarko's men approached Dallahn in the dispersed formation prescribed in field manuals, disaster struck when several well-camouflaged German 20-millimeter guns opened fire on the vulnerable 29ers caught in the wide-open fields west of town. In just minutes, three of Nazarko's men were killed and many more wounded. The three dead 29ers were S/Sgt. Carl Davis, twenty-four, of Kentucky; Sgt. Alphonse Berducci, nineteen, of Philadelphia; and PFC Grover Thomas, twenty-four, of Wisconsin. Thomas was a D-Day veteran who had twice before been wounded and had served with Company B for so long that in December 1944, Gerhardt had granted him an extended leave in the United States, from which he had returned to the front only on April 6. His comrades later learned that when Thomas departed the States to return to Europe, his wife was pregnant.

For some time, Company B survivors, lying prone on the exposed ground, were paralyzed; if the enemy could drop a few mortar rounds on the 29ers, many more would be killed. "The men looked around for cover," Johns remembered.

"There wasn't any. . . . None of the men were anxious to get killed so late in the game. But they didn't stay down for long. Lieutenant Nazarko jumped to his feet and yelled, 'C'mon, goddammit, let's go!' and started off for the guns, firing his carbine. Not a man in the company hesitated. It was too much for the Germans. When the whole company kept coming, they came out from behind their guns and surrendered. Nazarko received a Silver Star."

The death of three men "so late in the game," however, was a tragedy that would take Company B some time from which to recover. Nine men also suffered wounds, including 1st Lt. John Hatch, a platoon leader, and PFC John Payton, who had enlisted in the Maryland National Guard at Hagerstown on January 21, 1941. Payton had been busted from technical sergeant to private, a significant reduction in rank, for an undisclosed infraction during a lengthy stay in the replacement pipeline following a July 1944 wound. Another disturbing disciplinary issue surfaced just hours before the April 21 attack when a troubled Company B soldier, PFC Ralph Chutnicutt, failed to report for roll call. A thirty-two-year-old Indian from California, Chutnicutt had joined the company as a replacement in November. Four days later he returned to duty, but once more within the next month would go AWOL and end his 29th Division service confined in the 115th's guardhouse.

Maj. Al Warfield's 2nd Battalion, advancing on Johns's right, experienced a much easier day, as the battalion journal for April 21 revealed: "0700—Companies began moving out according to plan; 0820—Company F reported that Objective 1, Bockholt, taken; 0900—Recon elements of Company E approached Gustau; 0908—Company E reported Kolau cleared at 0848; 0910—Division recon reported two 20-millimeter antiaircraft guns and one antitank gun in woods west of Noventhien. One man wounded by fire. Two 20-millimeter antiaircraft guns captured." Company E's executive officer, 1st Lt. Sanford Reamey, who had transferred out of Company G on March 16, recalled that the 29ers captured much more than that. "Reports from higher headquarters informed us to be on the alert for seven Tiger tanks and a German general who was supposed to be in the [Noventhien] vicinity. . . . Company E [Capt. Earl Palmer, CO] was sent up to attack. . . . It took almost a half hour to get into position, and then [an enemy] vehicle which was supposed to be a tank turned out to be a mobile flak gun. Sergeant Herbert Sokill [actually Sokol], PFC [actually Private] William O'Connell, a BAR man, and PFCs Vincent [Vicente] Franco and Joseph Cataldo [both of whom had been arrested in late 1944 for lengthy AWOL infractions] were in position to note that the Germans had an entire company or battery of these guns, but the men were moving out and not manning them. We opened fire on them and wounded five. The rest were scared as hell and surrendered. Company E that day took a captain and thirty-two men. Our booty included one tractor pulling four units, each mounted with a 20-millimeter flak gun, three quadruple-barreled mounts, and a trailer loaded with ammunition. The German captain, seeing that his situation was hopeless, told us that he had some twenty men in the woods, some of them wounded, and asked to contact them to arrange for their surrender."

Warfield's battalion experienced an unfortunate friendly-fire incident that night after Palmer's Company E settled into Meussliessen and Company G, led by 1st Lt. James Larson—who had just assumed command the previous day—set up camp in and around Solkau, three miles south. Warfield ordered Larson to run a patrol with two jeeps to contact Company E in Meussliessen, but as the regimental history noted, "communication between the two [companies] was not what it should have been." Larson and Palmer were separated by a vast forest, *Gemeinde Wald*, which at night was a sinister place in which the 29ers knew German troops still lurked. "The Company E outposts didn't know that Company G was making the patrol, and when the two jeeps came into the lines in the middle of the night, the Company E men opened up on them," an account noted. "The Company G troops were confused and believed that they had run into a German outpost. One jeep got away, but the other was hit and abandoned. One man was wounded in the neck and another reported missing."

The corridor through which the 115th Infantry had orders to advance was much too wide—eight-and-a-half miles—to be covered by only two 800-man infantry battalions, so in early afternoon of April 21, Blandford ordered his 3rd Battalion, led by one of the 29th Division's most redoubtable soldiers, Lt. Col. Randy Millholland, to take over the regiment's leftmost sector and join in the sweep to the Elbe. While Millholland's men were preparing to move out, there was a scare that "a [German] mustard gas dump" had blown up, but whatever it was that actually transpired ultimately amounted to nothing. A Company K platoon leader, 1st Lt. Jack Kussman, recalled that the movement was "almost always unopposed, through small towns and villages which were undamaged by bombs or artillery. . . . I did not have any enthusiasm for getting back into combat at this time; however, it was generally easy going." Kussman confessed, "We all knew that the war was about over, and it was difficult to accept the thought of casualties so close to the end."

On Sunday, April 22, 1945, the 29th Division was indeed "close to the end," so close that the Soviets were pounding Berlin with artillery and, for the first time ever, a tormented Hitler had blurted, "The war is lost!" The 115th Infantry's regimental journal noted, much too optimistically, "Russians getting close; expect to meet any hour." Even so, on April 22 the 29th Division endured a distressing day when many unfortunate 29ers unexpectedly became victims of the German Army's latest devious method to postpone its demise. A hint of what was soon to erupt on the twenty-second occurred the previous evening when a jeep driven by

T/5 James Peters, who had been Johns's driver since June 1944, was moving up a road toward Dalldorf. "No mines had previously been encountered," Johns remembered. "Peters drove calmly down the road to a point about halfway to Dalldorf. The next thing he knew, [I] was picking him up off the side of the road. His jeep was hardly recognizable as such. He had hit two stacks of three Teller mines each." Peters survived, but an infantryman who had hitched a ride to the front with him, Company B's PFC Edward Wolicki, twenty-seven, of Buffalo, New York, was grievously wounded and died shortly thereafter. Later, another jeep occupied by the commander of the 115th Infantry's Company M, 1st Lt. David Woodhouse, and his driver, PFC Herman Mumford, was moving from Bankewitz toward the neighboring hamlet of Gülden. "The jeep passed over a suspicious bump in the road," the 115th's history reported. "Upon investigation, the men unearthed a patterned series of mines that would have blown them to bits had not the jeep miraculously passed through a gap in the field."

The 29ers were about to discover that all across the division's front, on both major and minor roads, the enemy had expertly planted thousands of anti-vehicle mines, which would soon inflict far more deaths and injuries on Americans in this

Lt. Col. Glover Johns, CO of 1st Battalion, 115th Infantry, examines his jeep, destroyed by a German mine on April 21, 1945, near Dalldorf, Germany. His driver, T/5 James Peters, was injured, and a member of Company B, PFC Edward Wolicki, was killed.

sector than bullets and shells. As an anxious Blandford remarked in a phone call to the war room, "We are going so fast that we don't have enough people to sweep the roads." Every U.S. Army vehicle, large or small, was a potential target, and the 29ers by necessity would soon learn to drive with extreme caution, often with a man sitting on the hood of a jeep or truck to scrutinize the road ahead for raised or disturbed earth, the telltale signs of hidden mines.

On April 22 the 554th Antiaircraft Artillery Battalion, commanded by Lt. Col. Lawrence Linderer, experienced its costliest day of combat since it had been attached to the 29th Division in December. The men of the 554th were still recovering from a dreadful April 11 accident in which two Battery B members had died from electrical shock caused by a short circuit in a telephone line. Eleven days later, two Battery A weapons carriers were moving on a narrow dirt trail near Polau when they detonated mines. Eight men were wounded and both vehicles destroyed.

In the absence of Shermans from the 747th Tank Battalion, the 821st Tank Destroyer Battalion, led by Lt. Col. Howard Arbury, was providing de facto tank support for the 29th Division in the drive for the Elbe, but no one could have imagined that Arbury's unit was also about to undergo one of its toughest periods in World War II; in a four-day span, five 821st men were killed and fourteen wounded by mines. The problem became so alarming that a frustrated Arbury radioed the 115th's command post: "Would like to know if anyone is sweeping the roads?"

The men of the 121st Engineers responsible for sweeping those roads were overwhelmed not only by the scope of the task—a battalion report estimated that "a total of 850 miles of road were swept for mines" that week—but also by the challenge posed by the mines themselves, many of which were evidently of a new variety the 29ers had not seen before, made exceptionally deadly by magnetic activation. "The slight attraction of the magnetic substance in the mine to any metal on a vehicle or a person could cause the prompt demolition of a mine," the report noted. Those mines, according to Ewing's *29 Let's Go*, were "about two feet square in a wooden case, buried about four to five feet below the surface of the road, and [they] could not be discovered by mine detectors. A mechanism in the mine enabled the enemy to set it so that it would explode after it had been passed over a desired number of times by metallic objects. Thus, if the mine were set at number 7, half-a-dozen vehicles could pass over the road unharmed, but the seventh would blow up. One of these mines, exploding under a tank destroyer, threw it into the air and turned it completely over."

No one had seen anything like it before. "You better do something about them," a concerned 116th officer radioed the war room. "[It is] a new type of mine that has a very sensitive apparatus; you can't walk close to them with a rifle because the metal in the rifle sets them off. We have the area roped off. The engineers said they couldn't handle them. The Germans themselves don't know how to deactivate them. There is a German civilian who seems to know something about them, and we are making him mark the location of them." A few days later Bingham told the war room, "They say they're not magnetic mines, but electric."

A catastrophe occurred near Wustrow at 2:30 P.M. on April 24 when the 121st's commander, twenty-nine-year-old Lt. Col. Raleigh Powell from Petersburg, Virginia, was, according to Glover Johns, "last seen examining a mine with a bayonet [and] was blown to bits." Another account noted that "there were three or four Teller mines in a handcart . . . [and] he [Powell] wanted to look at them." PFC Glenn Dickerson of the 121st's Company C wrote home that Powell "fooled with the new type [of mines], which are not to be fooled with. . . . We picked up his body—meat—over a whole acre of ground. Never did find it all." Powell's death and the obvious hazard posed to the 29ers by the magnetic mines—or were they electric?—caused a concerned Gerhardt to issue an order on April 29, halting the engineers' attempts to defuse or destroy them and instructing them "to keep out of the danger area. The erection of 'Danger' signs and barricades at the entrances to the area started at the end of the [April] period." The general telephoned Powell's replacement, Maj. Robert Stewart, and pronounced with as much sympathy as he could muster, "Well, you are it. Keep them going now. . . . Bad luck, but that is the way it goes."

The sheer scope of the Germans' mine-laying effort, and their seemingly limitless supply of mines and other kinds of explosives, amazed the American engineers. One day, a platoon from the 121st Engineers' Company B came across a small culvert east of Lüchow that the enemy had prepared for destruction. "Further investigation of the charge as it was being removed showed it to consist of 210 pack charges labeled 'SP MNT 43,' total estimated charge: 3,000 pounds," an engineer report stated. "The charge was stacked four deep in the culvert directly in the center of the road. Its priming consisted of one pack charge with a push-and-pull-type firing device connected to a pull wire and another pack charge with a time fuse inserted. . . . No booby traps were found around the charge. All the pack charges were removed to an isolated point, where they were promptly blown and destroyed. If this 3,000-pound charge had been set off in place by the enemy, it would have caused a crater sixty feet across and twenty-five feet deep."

On April 22, a German mine slew one of the 115th Infantry's most esteemed soldiers, 2nd Lt. Miller Cassell, known to one and all as "Joe." "Even in this war, where men die by the thousands," a comrade wrote, "Lieutenant Cassell's death is *one* that will not be forgotten." The twenty-six-year-old Cassell was a prewar member of the 1st Maryland Infantry (later the 115th), a bookkeeper by trade, who excelled at the military profession from the moment of his enlistment. By

June 1942 he had risen to the Army's senior noncommissioned officer rank, master sergeant, only five of whom were included in the table of organization for a 3,200-man infantry regiment. During the 29th Division's twenty-month training period in England, Cassell assumed the 115th's senior NCO slot, the regimental sergeant major, and remained a pivotal figure in regimental headquarters, even after he gained a commission, until his death from a mine in the lonely woods near the Elbe. As related by Lowenthal in the *29 Let's Go* newsletter, Cassell's demise "left a hollow, aching feeling among his many friends in the 115th Infantry. They remembered Joe when he was at [Fort] Meade, his wedding overseas to a pretty English girl [Dorothy] at Bodmin, his being made sergeant major at regiment, and his battlefield commission last October [1944]. They recalled, too, how happy he was when his British bride arrived safely to live with his parents in Frederick, Maryland. [Dorothy was reported to be the first English bride of an American soldier to arrive in western Maryland.] He was a swell guy, liked by everyone who knew him. He was great fun at a party—never too noisy or too quiet, his pals reminisced."

Lt. William Holberton of the 2nd Battalion's Headquarters Company nearly became another victim of the same minefield that caused Cassell's death when his platoon moved to the scene with orders to extract the destroyed jeep and remove any remaining mines. "The first thing we started to do," Holberton remarked, "was to move the remains of the jeep to the side of the road. A group of us tipped it over and began to let it settle. I suddenly noticed the triple prongs of a mine right where my part of the jeep was to rest! Needless to say we reversed the procedure very carefully and gently. A careful inspection of the area revealed a Z-shaped mine pattern across the road. Carefully, we removed some twelve or fourteen mines and just as carefully placed them in a sort of natural sinkhole several yards off the road. . . . A block of TNT was placed with the mines, the fuse lighted, and in seconds we had a tremendous explosion. The noise was so great that regimental headquarters called battalion to inquire of the source of the explosion."

If any fretful 29ers believed that enemy mines would slow down or even paralyze the division's advance to the Elbe, those notions were swiftly dispelled by the unyielding reaction of their commanders. "It is impossible to clear mines in front of attacking units in a fast-moving situation," Blandford pronounced. "Attacking troops have to take chances—a minefield is one of them." In the closing days of April 1945, the dutiful 29ers took those chances, and unfortunately many of them paid with their lives.

Blandford's 115th Infantry pressed ahead on April 23 at 9:00 A.M. from Phase Line Ida, mines or no mines. Ninety minutes later, a 2nd Battalion officer reported to the war room: "The reconnaissance [platoon] is at Phase Line Jane and will be on it shortly. The companies are following it up. They are getting quite a few prisoners. Very little [resistance]; going very good." An hour later, Blandford phoned Gerhardt and asked for "authority to go up to 'Lottie.' I can get up there and get settled early today." The general replied: "That's fine. It's working out just right." So right, in fact, that the fulfillment of the regiment's current mission seemed imminent when Blandford radioed Millholland and ordered, "Be prepared to make a reconnaissance to [Elbe] river and relieve elements of 5th Armored Division in your sector tomorrow morning [April 24]." As the 115th approached Pudripp, a diminutive hamlet on the western periphery of the vast *Dannenberg Forst*, the immensity of American military might became evident to the amazed 29ers of Capt. Robert Armstrong's Company K, who stood by the roadside and watched a 5th Armored Division vehicular column roar past toward the Elbe. According to the regimental history, the column was so lengthy that it took two hours to clear Pudripp.

The sprawling Hanoverian pine forests through which the 115th Infantry passed held some staggering surprises. A railroad line running straight into the seemingly uninhabited *Dannenberg Forst* aroused sufficient suspicion in Armstrong that he ordered 1st Lt. Jack Kussman to take two platoons to investigate. "As we got deep into the woods—I may have been lost—we came upon a very high chain-link fence," Kussman recollected. "To see a fence like this in the middle of a dense forest made us very cautious. A couple of us crawled up to the fence, and we could then see several buildings down in a valley. . . . Everything was quiet; there seemed to be no activity in or around the buildings. The whole thing gave us an eerie feeling. . . . We cut the wire fencing and with extreme caution started down the hill toward the buildings. We checked what appeared to be a guardhouse and found it empty. Before we had a chance to check the other buildings, about 200 or so young women burst out of the buildings, yelling and screaming when they saw us."

The 29ers had stumbled into an expertly camouflaged factory that seemed, after a hasty appraisal, to be devoted to the production of parts for Nazi Germany's notorious V-1 jet-powered flying bombs, popularly known to Britons—of whom nearly 23,000 had become victims in ten months—as "buzz bombs" or "doodlebugs." Kussman later speculated that since "all the workers we saw were women, this was probably an assembly line for timing devices [fuses] or other internal parts for either (or both) V-1s and V-2s." Whatever it was the factory produced made no difference. "I contacted Captain Armstrong by radio," Kussman continued, "and he passed the information on to battalion. I knew the installation would have to be secured, so I was more interested in that than what was inside the buildings." However, Kussman confessed, "I quickly lost control of my platoon. . . . The GIs soon had [railroad] cars filled with girls and were having a great time. . . . It was not too long before a jeep with officers from 3rd Battalion headquarters came driving down the railroad track, which I think was the only entrance to the factory. The staff officers told me they were taking over, and that I should finish my mission of clearing the rest of the forest. . . . Naturally I thought this was a bit unfair since we were the ones who had found the plant that the Germans had been able to successfully hide from the Allies during the entire war, but we had to move on. I told the sergeants to assemble the men and after quite a while were able to account for all except two who could not be found." Kussman remembered: "Had it been a real combat situation, I would have passed the case of the two missing men to Captain Armstrong. But after discussing the matter with my platoon sergeant and a squad leader, we decided to handle the matter within the platoon. I had good NCOs, and one in particular was alleged to have settled a discipline problem with his fists."

Warfield's 2nd Battalion bumped into another nearby V-1 facility that afternoon just outside of Tramm, and when the 29ers guardedly entered the compound, they saw something no Allied solider had yet seen during World War II. The enemy had parked rows of the familiar V-1s in hangers, but as the surprised GIs performing up-close examinations soon learned, those models differed dramatically from the originals because the Germans had taken the extraordinary step of adding cockpits. Piloting a 400-mile-per-hour flying bomb packed with nearly 2,000 pounds of explosives and flying a kamikaze mission against a vital Allied target demonstrated the enemy's current level of desperation: the Germans could think of no better way to achieve pinpoint accuracy. Like so many Nazi schemes, however, the idea went nowhere. So to the 29th Division's checklist of captured enemy equipment now could be added a few dozen unique flying bombs, into which happy 29ers piled for souvenir photos. The enemy's propensity to booby trap equipment, however, triggered an abrupt warning from the war room that "a possibility exists that some of the buzz bombs have 21-day delay fuses attached," advice that caused the 29ers to hastily abandon any further merriment until engineers could inspect the V-1s. Indeed, the next day, according to a report, the sappers "found and deactivated several delayed action bombs," thankfully before anyone was injured.

Waging a campaign in a heavily forested region in which the enemy made no attempt to establish a conventional front generated some peculiar incidents. One day, twenty-six-year-old PFC Fernand Lambert, a native of southeastern Maine and known to his Company K comrades as "Frenchy," captured a German *Hauptmann* (captain) in the village of Wedderien and brought him in for interrogation. As related by the regimental history, "The German captain led Captain Armstrong and some of his men to a building in town and into a room, where the Yanks were amazed to find the headquarters staff of the German corps assigned to the defense of the entire Hannover area. The prisoner bag included two colonels, four majors, six captains, seventeen lieutenants, and one sergeant. The Company K men found all of the enemy weapons neatly stacked in wooden boxes, which facilitated the proper distribution of those valued souvenirs."

In the 2nd Battalion's zone, Holberton noted the unceasing flow of German prisoners "making their way westward to the safety of the Allied rear areas. These prisoners were like none we had ever seen: there were no guards! The Germans were desperate to get away from the oncoming Russians, so they crossed over the Elbe and headed west. Day and night we saw thousands of these soldiers, some in commandeered vehicles, some on foot, but all moving away from the Russians."

"There were more than enough grisly sights if you cared to look for them," a 29er noted. "Along one road members of the 2nd Battalion saw the unforgettable sight of a German driver sitting bolt upright in the seat of a burned-out halftrack. His hands still clutched the steering wheel, but the man could hardly tell where he was going. He had no head."

At 1:00 P.M. on April 23, as the 2nd Battalion pushed north toward the Elbe from the doodlebug plant at Tramm, scouts "reported hearing sounds of troop activity as they advanced steadily but cautiously forward." Friendly troops from the 5th Armored Division were supposed to be located somewhere ahead, but no one seemed to know exactly where—until now. "Coming out on one side of a road," the 115th history observed, "the scouts were surprised to find themselves across from one of the several kitchens of a 5th Armored Division unit. [Journals indicate that this was probably the 771st Tank Destroyer Battalion, a XIII Corps unit attached to the 5th Armored.] Tanks [probably tank destroyers] and guns and trucks were scattered somewhat indifferently throughout the area, and the tankers themselves were in a chow line, mess kits in hand." Such gross lapses in security, the flabbergasted 29ers reckoned, could not be forgiven even at this late stage of the war.

On Tuesday, April 24—described by one 29er as "a beautiful spring day"— the 29th Division's curious five-day offensive, indisputably its easiest of World War II, came to an end when both the 115th and 116th Infantry reached their objective, the Elbe River. That offensive, Cawthon noted, "was hardly started before it was over." Somewhere on the far side of the 400-yard-wide Elbe, the GIs expected the Red Army to make an appearance soon. As the disappointed 29ers would soon discern, however, fanatical Germans still populated the neighborhood on both banks of the river.

The high command informed the 29ers that the Elbe was more than a river; it was "an international boundary line between U.S. and British troops [on the west] and Russian troops [on the east]. No unobserved firing over the river." Cooper described the 29th Division's new zone as "sandy ridges and rounded bluffs covered with pine and rising 200 or more feet above the river. On the German, or northeast side, the terrain of the state of Mecklenburg was almost flat as far as the eye could see." From his Dannenberg bivouac, Easton said, "We can smell the Baltic Sea when the wind is right."

The 115th progressed to the Elbe on April 24 against no opposition; the last five days, noted the regimental history, "seemed quite unreal. . . . In many of the towns it was impossible to believe that there was a war going on. It seemed almost like Tennessee or Carolina maneuvers, with the civilians coming out on the streets to watch the men go by. It must have been an impressive sight to the farmers." A throng of Germans hidden in the woods east of Dannenberg, however, made that Tuesday a much more daunting day for Bingham's 116th Infantry. Backed up against the Elbe with no line of retreat, those enemy troops still holding faith in the Führer, probably about five hundred in number, no longer had any choice but to fight or surrender. The most intractable among them took refuge in five riverside towns—Quickborn, Langendorf, Kacherien, Grippel, and Laase—and prepared to block the 116th's advance to the Elbe. At about 11:30 A.M. on the twenty-fourth, 1st Lt. Thomas Fernley's platoon from the 29th Recon Troop, consisting of four M8 armored cars and a few jeeps, came under heavy German fire as it emerged from a forest and sped toward Quickborn, just a mile south of the Elbe. Fernley opened up on the enemy with a .50-caliber machine gun and directed his platoon to do the same as it swung from column into line. Soon after he dismounted from his M8 to more closely direct his troopers, an act that his troop commander, Capt. Edward Jones, observed was performed with "the ease, calmness, and thoroughness that was his nature." After returning to his armored car, Jones recalled, "Fernley was wounded in the left side by a sniper and died half an hour later in an aid station." In a May 1945 consolation letter to Fernley's father, Jones added that Fernley's platoon "would follow him anywhere. . . . We had soldiered together for almost three years, and to say that I thought a great deal of him is a very meager expression. . . . He did not suffer, as he was unconscious for most of the time."

For about two hours, as the 29th Division's operations journal noted, "resistance was heavy in the entire sector, consisting of small-arms fire, *Nebelwerfers* [rocket launchers], and mines." However, when 1st Lt. Verne Morse's Company C approached Quickborn and poured into it the cumulative firepower of the entire 1st Battalion, the 111th Field Artillery Battalion, Company B of the 89th Chemical Mortar Battalion, and Battery B of the 554th Antiaircraft Battalion, the German garrison quickly lost its inclination to fight; Morse's men swarmed into the village without the loss of a man and captured more than 100 Germans. The attack on Langendorf, just 500 yards short of the Elbe, was much tougher: driving the enemy out of that village cost Company B, led by 1st Lt. George Magner, four casualties, including two dead. Both slain 29ers, PFCs James Ewing and James

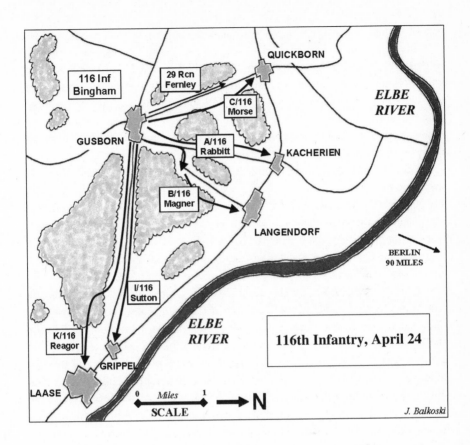

Roberts, were among the last men to join Company B during World War II when they arrived from a replacement depot in early March 1945. A native of rural Vernon County, Missouri, south of Kansas City, Ewing had graduated from high school less than a year before. He had not reached his nineteenth birthday by the time of his death and thus became one of the youngest 29ers killed in action. Ewing and Roberts were nearly the last of the 1,298 men of the 116th Infantry to die in eleven months of combat starting on Omaha Beach; only one more member of the regiment would lose his life before V-E Day.

Reporter Holbrook Bradley noted in a front-page story in the *Baltimore Sun* that the "cold, cloudy weather during the last few days has given way to a bright, warm spring day." In midafternoon, Bradley accompanied Capt. James Rabbitt's Company A and a few 821st Tank Destroyer Battalion M10s as they moved through a forest clearing toward Kacherien, 1,200 yards west of Langendorf, which reportedly harbored several enemy *Nebelwerfers*. "There was the familiar roar of the tank destroyer's heavy motor and the usual flying dirt and dust as we ground up through the sand, passed a burned-out German self-propelled gun, then rolled through the pines to the open space which marked the front," Bradley wrote. "Suddenly there was a cracking report 300 yards ahead of us, and before we could duck, a *panzerfaust* [antitank rocket] screamed through the air not more than a couple of yards overhead. . . . The next moment a gunner slammed five rounds from a 76 [-millimeter gun] into the spot, while an assistant gunner turned on the deafening heat of a .50-caliber machine gun."

Rabbitt's men dashed across the clearing in the widely dispersed formation the 29ers had learned in training and pressed ahead into the woods adjacent to Kacherien. The demoralized Germans surrendered in hordes, including "one fat, perspiring Kraut, a lieutenant colonel . . . whose name was Leptihn, [who] asked that we not radio his name because he had a wife and daughter in Berlin." Still, a few resolute Germans in Kacherien fought on, lobbing mortar shells into the advancing Americans. "There was nothing any of us could do," wrote Bradley, "for there were no foxholes and no shelter anywhere. Worse still, the heavy woods on our right flank meant tree bursts if the shells came in there. The only thing we could do was sweat it out." The 29ers indeed sweated it out, but the shells wounded three men, including Pvt. Bruce White, a D-Day veteran of the 116th's Service Company. Rabbitt ordered his men forward; soon, as Bradley reported, "we were in the edge of town. German resistance had collapsed. . . . The only noise of battle now was the rolling fire of our attacking infantry and the droning roar above, as squadrons of Thunderbolts, on patrol for the Luftwaffe that wasn't there, wheeled and turned in the blue sky."

Three miles south, near the base of a great horseshoe bend in the Elbe, 1st Lt. Sears Sutton's Company I assailed Grippel and quickly seized 123 Germans as prisoners. The 29ers penetrated all the way to a riverside bluff that offered a majestic view of the great river, flowing 680 miles from Czechoslovakia to the North Sea. Enemy die-hards, however, inflicted six casualties among Sutton's men; happily, none of them died. Twenty-ninth Division infantrymen regularly teased second lieutenants about their predictably brief careers in combat, and one of Company I's six wounded, 2nd Lt. Henry O'Karma of Wilkes-Barre, Pennsylvania, seemed to validate those barbs. O'Karma had joined Company I in Normandy on July 17 and was wounded two weeks later at Vire. He returned to duty as a platoon leader on November 19, only to be wounded again five days later at Koslar. Once again O'Karma came back to duty on February 27, only to gain his third Purple Heart of the war on April 24 at Grippel.

Ever since the dreadful battles in Normandy's *bocage*, Gerhardt had made routine visits to front-line command posts. However, his participation in Company K's April 24 assault on the riverside village of Laase nearly caused the general's name to be added to the 29th Division's lengthy casualty list, already some 21,000 names long. Laase's defenders, defined by a Company K morning report as "German riflemen, well dug in on the outskirts of town," managed to inflict non-fatal wounds on three 29ers, but they could not stop the company's relentless progression into the village and beyond to the Elbe. Company K, led by Capt. Elmer Reagor, thereupon corralled 163 German captives—more than Reagor's current complement of men—and freed three American prisoners of war, in addition to liberating a U.S. Army truck.

"The boys really sat up and paid attention when they saw a man with two stars on his helmet," a *29 Let's Go* article noted. "T/Sgt. Bernard Lipscomb of Richmond, Virginia [a D-Day veteran], testifies to the general's coolness under fire and to his infantry 'know-how.' When a sniper's bullet cut the fence a yard from where they stood, the general calmly headed for cover and directed the capture of the sharpshooter." Lieutenant Easton recalled: "I rounded the corner of a house with carbine ready to fire and came face to face with a major general with a .45 automatic pistol ready to fire, apparently at me. It was Uncle Charlie himself come to help us clear the village. I couldn't think what to say, so I just grinned. He grinned back. We proceeded to clear the house together. On its dirt floor lay a kid in German uniform aged about fourteen ripped nearly in two by an M-1 bullet. One of our medics was already treating him." Pvt. John Ratliff of Mississippi eventually captured the sniper and shoved him toward Gerhardt for interrogation. He was another "mere youth—just sixteen; he'd been in the Wehrmacht only a month," *29 Let's Go* reported. The general lamented, "Not yet old enough to vote, but old enough to kill." Soon afterward, Gerhardt "returned to wherever major generals are supposed to stay."

Four days later, Captain Reagor departed Company K on a ten-day furlough to the Riviera. He had been with the outfit since Brest, and Easton described him as "one of those rare humans with all the qualities of greatness: complete simplicity, complete modesty, complete courtesy. . . . He has told me in deepest confidence and soul-baring of trying to get himself killed during his first days in combat. When he discovered his wife's unfaithfulness, he lost all desire to live. . . . Finally he decided he wasn't meant to die but to live, and he began to live for the men."

The Elbe, Cawthon recalled, was "wide, muddy, and rushing. This was a demarcation line, along which the Iron Curtain of communism was soon to descend. On that April 24, 1945, the far shore showed only the misty green curtain of early spring." Green was also the color of the flares that had been provided in profusion to front-line 29ers according to an arrangement Eisenhower had made with the Red Army to avoid accidental clashes between same-side troops: the Soviets would fire red flares as they approached Anglo-American units, whose members would reply with green flares. The impatient 29ers peered across the Elbe, ready to pop their flares—but not a single Soviet soldier was in sight. Gerhardt's men must wait on the riverbank for the Red Army to come to them. By now, every member of the 29th Division knew that waiting was the most prevalent fact of life in the U.S. Army, and the wait for the Russians would endure for more than a week.

Starting on April 25, the GIs methodically carried out Gillem's order to evacuate all German civilians living within three miles of the Elbe in the 29th Division's zone to villages farther to the west, where local residents must make efforts to accommodate them. The division's management of that movement, according to Gerhardt, "was very well handled—organized and going along in good style." From the soldiers' perspective, the civilian evacuation provided almost every 29er on the Elbe front with comfortable abodes, which generally featured serviceable electric and telephone lines as well as indoor plumbing. However, one incredulous 110th Field Artillery officer, 1st Lt. Robert Davis, observed the low thresholds: "Must have small people around here." On the Elbe, the 115th's Lieutenant Kussman recollected, "We [Company K members] were quartered in a large, upscale house; it had a big, winding open stairway, beautiful wood floors, plumbing that worked, and I had a large private bedroom. . . . I was always a little uneasy about kicking people out of their homes. However, this was our policy."

The Elbe River in the 115th Infantry's sector, April 1945.

For German civilians, the trauma of widespread home evictions by the U.S. Army was tempered somewhat by the gradual realization that relocation under American administration was infinitely preferable to the fates they would have suffered at the hands of the onrushing Red Army. As of May 1, 1945, the Elbe already divided two vastly different worlds: west of the river, Anglo-American military government staffs released edicts announcing that displaced German families could move their livestock and food supplies with them, a policy to which Gerhardt insisted his 29ers must adhere; on the opposite side of the Elbe, shocked German civilians would learn that Soviet troops did not observe such niceties and in fact pitilessly hauled away as much loot as they could carry while wreaking nearly unrestrained barbarities on the local population.

The 29ers settled into comfortable German homes in the riverside villages, populated, Easton remembered, by civilians who had "been warned we would rape and burn and murder [and] they cannot show enough appreciation when we don't, wanting to cook for us, scrub the floor, make up beds with sheets— one old woman, still unbelieving, asking: 'When you leave will you burn the house down?'"

At 8:00 A.M. on April 26, McDaniel's 175th Infantry was released from Gillem's XIII Corps control and reassigned back to its rightful owner, Gerhardt. The members of the Dandy Fifth piled into trucks and spent most of the day bouncing over the rutted roads of Hannover, rolling eastward for some seventy-five miles until they reached the "international boundary" of the Elbe. There, McDaniel's men relieved the 335th Infantry of the 84th Division and took position on the right of the 116th, with Wolff's 2nd Battalion on the left, Whiteford's 3rd Battalion on the right, and Geiglein's 1st in reserve, occupying picturesque riverside villages such as Gorleben, Vietze, Holtorf, and Schnackenburg.

Glenn Dickerson, a perceptive young PFC of the 121st Engineers, attached to the 175th, penned an April 26 letter to his parents from an unnamed German village he identified only as "Krautland." "These Krauts still employ a town crier—bell and all," he

A sketch of PFC Glenn Dickerson, Company C, 121st Engineer Combat Battalion, drawn in 1945 in Germany.

wrote. "He walks down the streets ringing his bell, and when a crowd collects, he makes his speech, then repeats the process farther down the street. After he is gone, all the Krauts gather and buzz, buzz about what the crier said. In one town, the first time I saw one, he did his job on a bicycle. The next time I saw him, he was walking, indicating some GI 'needed' his bike. We were getting ready to go in to supper from a job today, standing by the truck, when a Kraut babe comes by carrying two cameras. . . . I just watched her stroll by and into the military government office with them and turn them in. It would have been perfectly OK to have taken them away from her, and they were nifty cameras, but I just let her go. Now some jerk in the military government has two good cameras. . . . Am I dumb! There will never be another opportunity like that one."

VENTY-NOIN, LET'S GOOT

At 11:30 A.M. on April 25, 1945, the event the free world had anticipated for weeks finally transpired when GIs from the U.S. Army's 273rd Infantry, 69th Division, met Red Army troops at the historic Saxon city of Torgau on the Elbe River. That news may have electrified Truman, Churchill, and Stalin, but 160 miles to the northwest, where the 29th Division currently held an extraordinarily lengthy front of nearly forty miles along the Elbe, it triggered barely a ripple. Gerhardt fully expected his 29ers to pop their green flares momentarily as a recognition symbol for approaching Soviet troops, so the 69th Division's accomplishment hardly seemed momentous. Indeed, the 29 Let's Go newsletter did not mention the Torgau linkup for three days, and even then devoted only a single paragraph to it, topped with an unexceptional headline.

Some 29ers, decidedly in the minority, agreed with Purley Cooper of the 110th Field Artillery, who recalled that "it was hard merely to sit and wait for the Russians—a continued pursuit of the Germans seemed much more inviting." Most of Gerhardt's doughboys, however, held the much more pedestrian viewpoint that Hitler was surely doomed, and that other, less-bloodied outfits could ensure his inevitable downfall. "We were only too painfully aware," wrote Lieutenant Holberton, "that a round from a sniper's rifle, a booby trap exploded unawares, a mine detonated in a roadway or field, could kill or seriously wound just as effectively as ever they did in Normandy or the Rhineland. The Germans were just about defeated, but their bite was still effective. While we were relaxed to a certain extent, knowing that organized resistance was a thing of the past, we were still alert to the ever-present dangers of a still fanatical people." The 116th's Cawthon concluded: "The distinction of being the last casualty was widely unsought."

Plenty of evidence of Nazi fanaticism remained. Rumors had recently drifted into 29th Division command posts along the Elbe of a shocking incident at the Saxon town of Gardelegen, forty miles south. In and around a large barn on the town's outskirts, another XIII Corps outfit, the 102nd Division, had discovered the charred corpses of nearly a thousand displaced persons, burned alive and gunned down by SS guards on Friday, April 13. Only a handful of men from the throng of slave laborers and prisoners of war had managed to escape. A XIII Corps liaison officer, 1st Lt. Harold Leinbaugh, who visited the massacre site and met with one of the survivors, an ex-French commando, observed that "he knows the only solution is practically annihilation of the Krauts. They've degenerated into a state lower than animals. . . . I never knew what hate was until I saw what remains of those poor devils."

The seventeen agents of the 29th Division's counterintelligence corps detachment, led by an El Paso attorney named Capt. Ellis Mayfield, were greatly overworked investigating local Nazi leaders and their alleged sabotage or war crimes. Mayfield adhered to the U.S. Army's strict "automatic arrest" rule whenever his men encountered high-ranking officials of the *Ortsgruppen*, the Nazi political leaders of local municipalities, and threw twenty of them in jail during April 1945. "A considerable number of war crimes were investigated," Mayfield reported, "and seven persons were placed under arrest for trial by JA [judge advocates, U.S. Army lawyers]. Included were two men who admittedly shot five American flyers after they had been captured."

Happily for the 29ers, the Germans on the Elbe front displayed a lingering zeal for Nazism only with an occasional artillery barrage and an even more infrequent nighttime raid across the river. For several consecutive days at the close of April, enemy gunners fired intense bursts of shells, usually about sixty in number, from medium- or heavy-caliber howitzers located miles away east of the Elbe. Typically opening fire shortly after midnight, most of the time the Germans failed to achieve pinpoint accuracy, but periodically they scored a few lucky hits. Cooper recalled that on April 25 a British Royal Artillery regiment a few miles north of the 110th Field Artillery at Bahrendorf "got the devil shelled out of it, suffered several casualties, and was forced to shift to a new location." The next day another barrage hit the 224th Field Artillery hard in its encampment near Meudelfitz, a mile west of the Elbe, and wounded Maj. Sherwood Collins, who had held the battalion's executive officer slot since the lengthy training period in England. Even the nearly extinct German Air Force entered the fray: "At night," Cooper recalled, "lone Luftwaffe planes persistently reminded the cannoneers that the war was still on by dropping anti-personnel bombs. One night a bomber dumped its load between the trails of Battery B's guns without harming the artillerymen who, fortunately, had sought the safety of nearby slit trenches."

Rules imposed by the Anglo-American high command restricted the 29th Division's frustrated gunners from retaliating against their German counterparts for fear of hitting approaching Red Army troops. A XIII Corps order demanded,

"No harassing or interdiction missions will be fired." However, if "positive iden-tification" of an enemy target on the far side of the Elbe could be obtained by direct observation, the 29th Division's gunners were free to open fire, but "par-ticular care will be taken not to fire on parties bearing flags of truce [and] all fir-ing will cease upon receipt of the designated identification signal [a red flare, later changed to white] from Russian forces." Opportunities to hit back at Ger-man artillery, however, were rare. In the last week of April, the 110th Field Artillery fired only 21 missions, totaling 411 rounds; in contrast, the 110th had recently fired 151 fire missions, amounting to 2,988 shells, in a single day, Feb-ruary 23, 1945, the jump-off date for the 29th Division's assault across the Roer River at Jülich.

At 3:45 A.M. on April 30, a die-hard German soldier, accompanied by a hand-ful of like-minded comrades, stealthily rowed across the Elbe and stormed into an outpost manned by the 116th Infantry's Company G, commanded by Capt. Daniel Keyes. The enemy raiders, who evidently had no goal except to kill a few Americans before Germany's inevitable demise, caught the 29ers by surprise. Cawthon suspected "that the entire outpost had been confidently asleep," but Bingham reported to the war room that "when [the Germans] were challenged by the boy in the foxhole, they threw a grenade. It killed one man [twenty-year-old PFC Richard Urenn from Detroit] and wounded four." The Germans then disap-peared into the darkness. Urenn, a veteran of the Normandy campaign, was the very last of 1,298 members of the 116th Infantry killed in action during World War II in eleven months of combat from Omaha Beach to a lonely outpost on the Elbe River. An astonished Gerhardt blurted: "I didn't expect the Germans to do anything like that."

The most ironic detail of the tragic affair was that for every German soldier still willing to fight, there were thousands of others fixated only on displaying white handkerchiefs, rowing—or even swimming—across the Elbe, and checking into a U.S. Army prisoner-of-war camp. That option, according to those prudent men, was far preferable to dying for a lost cause or ending up a captive of the Red Army. "It was obvious that the fighting spirit of the Wehrma-cht was 'kaput,'" the 116th's monthly report noted. "Never before had prisoners been so easily obtained."

A perplexing directive from XIII Corps on this matter reached Gerhardt's war room: "The basic idea is we don't want to give civilians or individual [Ger-man] soldiers on the other side [of the Elbe] any idea that we are going to offer sanctuary over here from the Russians," Lt. Col. Paul Krznarich, the 29th Divi-sion's chief intelligence officer, remarked on April 26. "We don't want to go across the river and negotiate any surrender whatsoever. Moreover, we don't want civilians coming over. If they swim across, we can take them. But if they are in a boat or on a raft, we want to turn them back. If they come across with a white flag in a group and attempt to surrender, we can accept them as POWs." A member of the 116th's Company A, PFC John Barnes, recalled that the directive was completely ignored. "A regular ferry system was set up to bring the Germans desperately seeking escape from the feared Russians to surrender to the suddenly friendly hands of the Americans," he noted. "Some of the Company A boys manning makeshift ferries earned a bundle of loot from German civilians eager to pay anything to escape the Russians."

One could hardly believe that a war still raged. Joe Ewing noted that the 29ers on the Elbe "walked about freely, unconcerned at the thought that they were in plain sight of the enemy across the river." He added, "There was hardly a sight or sound of war along the Elbe, an incongruous 'front line.' A soldier, with a BAR and a fishing pole over his shoulder, whistled as he walked leisurely down the road to the outpost line at the river. It was a quiet and peaceful scene, with the trees white in their blossoms and cattle grazing on the river's grassy banks. For the man on the line, the war as he knew it was really over."

For a few days, Cooper's 110th Field Artillery Battalion was the northernmost U.S. Army unit on the Western Front, the far left flank of a mighty American battle line that stretched 550 miles southward to the Swiss border. On April 25, Cooper set out by jeep from Bahrendorf and about six miles to the north came across the command post of a British brigade from the 5th Infantry Division, poised to launch an attack across the Elbe toward the Baltic Sea coastline. On April 29 the 110th was supplanted as the northernmost American unit in Germany by three U.S. Army divisions Eisenhower loaned to the British for their offensive, which successfully reached the Baltic on May 2.

Five miles south of the 110th's encampment at Bahrendorf, Cooper's cannoneers stumbled on an amazing spectacle in the nearby Göhrde forest, a vast woodland broken up by occasional heaths and featuring some rustic hunting lodges favored by the German royal family before World War I. There, in the middle of the woods near the village of Göhrde, a couple dozen double-decker buses from the *Berliner Verkehrsbetriebe* transit system were neatly lined up under a tract of pine trees. Although the Berlin bus system had been in a shambles for a year or more due to gas shortages and Allied bombing attacks, evidently the Nazis did not wish the buses to fall into Soviet hands and had recently shifted them to a safer spot west of the Elbe. As related by Cooper, "Remembering the tremendous transportation problems encountered in handling the freed allied people at Wesel, and with an eye to the future, a group of mechanics under M/Sgt. Randall Conoway, the battalion motor sergeant, later returned to see if the buses were usable. They found that the Germans had removed identical essential parts from each motor."

Meantime, on April 30, 125 miles away, the Wagnerian *Götterdämmerung* of Nazi Germany played out in Berlin's Führerbunker. Eva Braun, Adolf Hitler's wife of just one day, bequeathed her favorite fur coat to Hitler's young secretary and prepared for the end. "Now it has gone so far; it is finished," Hitler mumbled to the secretary. "Goodbye." Then he and his new wife withdrew to their private quarters; Braun took a cyanide capsule shortly thereafter, and Hitler shot himself. Thirty-six hours later the stunning development made it into the May 2 edition of *29 Let's Go* with an all-caps headline: "HITLER REPORTED DEAD." There was some confusion, however, concerning how the Führer had died. The next day, *29 Let's Go* reported that Germany's new president, Adm. Karl Dönitz, had claimed that "[Hitler] had been killed in action in Berlin." Another rumor surfaced in a May 2 stateside newspaper headline that declared, "A brain stroke killed Hitler, Eisenhower's evidence indicates." That fabrication, as a member of the SHAEF staff recalled, was issued "to give the German people in the world facts to disabuse their minds that Hitler died a hero." The 29ers, however, cared not how their reviled foe had expired; the only question that mattered to them was that, if Hitler was indeed in his grave, how could the war go on any longer?

The fundamental task of 29th Division intelligence officers was to judge the current state of enemy morale, and for the past several weeks that task had become entirely straightforward. Months had passed since the division had captured strapping young Aryan *Fallschirmjäger* or arrogant Waffen-SS troops; the current throng of compliant prisoners possessed none of those formidable soldiers' defiance, as the members of 1st Lt. Eugene Nazarko's Company B, 115th Infantry, learned in late April when they captured several dozen Germans near the Elbe. The 115th's prisoner-of-war enclosure was miles behind the front, so for the moment the captives accompanied Nazarko's men as they carried out their daily chores. As a May 3 *29 Let's Go* article observed, a 29th Division officer, 1st Lt. Paul Anderson [actually a 110th Artillery observer with the 115th], recruited "two strapping Krauts" to carry his SCR-300 backpack radio. "It wasn't long before the Wehrmacht men got the hang of the Yank way of doing things," the reporter noted. "As the scattered doughs halted for a break, the two 'supermen' would set up the radio the way the 'looey' [lieutenant] had shown them. When the ten minutes were up, the Jerries would let out with the same command Anderson had uttered. As shouted out by the Krauts, it came out: 'Venty-Noin, Let's Goot.'"

ALL FEAR WAS GONE

In late afternoon on April 30, 1945, a few 29ers from Company G, 175th Infantry, manning a lonely outpost on the Elbe near Gorleben, spotted some suspicious enemy activity on the far side of the river. Earlier that day, a German cross-river raid had killed a member of the neighboring 116th Infantry, and Capt. Hugh Brady's Company G men were understandably a little jumpy. The wary GIs fired several mortar rounds, prompting three German soldiers on the opposite bank to yell unintelligibly and wave a large white flag. Binoculars established that two of the three men were at least field grade officers. Brady's men signaled them to cross, and they paddled over in a rowboat. One of them, in halting English, asked to speak to "the commanding officer" without delay. Brady phoned the 2nd Battalion, and the battalion commander, Capt. Sam Dinerman—actually the executive, but in temporary command while Maj. Edward Wolff was on leave in England—immediately traveled down to Brady's command post to discern his foes' purpose.

The intrigued 29ers thereupon gathered an astounding story from those three Germans, so remarkable that Dinerman grasped at once that what the enemy intended to do soared far above the command level of a mere U.S. Army captain. Dinerman phoned the 175th's commander, Col. Edward McDaniel, who instantly concurred that this was indeed big news. At 9:10 P.M., McDaniel contacted the war room and told Gerhardt: "It seems that there is a lieutenant colonel from a V-2 Rocket Division [known as *Division z.V.* within the German Army] who wants to discuss surrendering to us. I am going to check on it further." Ninety minutes later McDaniel reported to the flabbergasted Gerhardt: "There are about 10,000 men. They are northwest of Berlin, facing east. . . . [The division] consists primarily of highly trained personnel. The reason they give for [the surrender] is they have so much technical information that they don't want to fall into the hands of the Russians." A skeptical Gerhardt declared, "We don't want to get involved in any political business now. I will call [XIII] Corps and then call you back." But a few minutes later, Gillem and Gerhardt agreed that, regardless of pesky inter-Allied "political business," if the V-2 Division could "be taken totally like that without a fight, it will be so much to the good." Gerhardt concluded: "We will tell McDaniel that it is OK, and he can go ahead and tell them to come in."

The senior of the three enemy officers, SS *Obersturmbannführer* (Lieutenant Colonel) Wolfgang Wetzling, explained to McDaniel that at its peak, *Division z.V.* (*zur Vergeltung*, or "Retaliation" Division) consisted of more than 11,000 men, both Army and SS, all devoted to launching deadly V-2 rockets from their bases in Holland against Allied population centers, chiefly Antwerp and London. As Anglo-American armies neared and eventually traversed the Rhine, *Division z.V.* withdrew into Germany, destroyed most of its remaining rockets, and hastily retrained its dispirited personnel to fight as conventional infantrymen or artillerymen. The delusional Wehrmacht high command then ordered the division to move eastward across most of central Germany to join in the hopeless battle for Berlin, and by late April the reluctant ex-rocketeers were on the verge of entering the fray against the vastly superior Red Army in a vain effort to hold open a corridor from the German capital to the west.

Wetzling claimed to McDaniel that just a few days ago he had approached the *Division z.V.* commander, Col. Gerlach von Gaudecker, and urged him to pull the division out of the line posthaste and retreat westward to surrender to the Americans. Wetzling assured his superior that the outfit's surviving rocket equipment would electrify the western Allies, so he urged von Gaudecker that it must be preserved and carried back to the American lines. With their country in the midst of a calamitous collapse, all German soldiers would soon be forced to make crucial decisions about their future, and although Wetzling was assuredly a fanatical SS man—he would be implicated in war crimes after the war—he knew that die-hard Nazis would view his scheme as perfidious; should Hitler, who was still living at the time, learn of it, he would certainly order the instant execution of Wetzling and any like-minded *Division z.V.* members.

On April 29, the day before Wetzling's entry into 29th Division lines, von Gaudecker consented to carry out the capitulation as clandestinely as possible. He ordered Wetzling, a staff officer named Maj. Günter Matheis who spoke some English, and Lt. Wolfram Lucke, a divisional signal officer, to travel westward to the Elbe to negotiate an immediate surrender to the 29th Division, issuing them bogus papers in the event German military policemen stopped them en route and became suspicious about their intent. Although Matheis was slightly wounded by Company G's April 30 mortar barrage, the three Germans eventually made it across the Elbe to bring McDaniel in on their plot. Wetzling promptly displayed a note from von Gaudecker to McDaniel in badly fractured

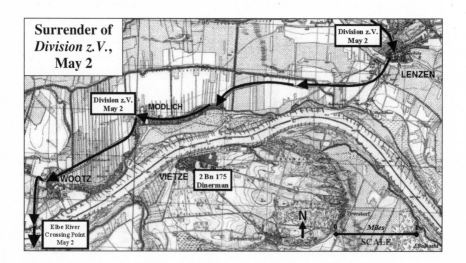

Col. Edward McDaniel, commander of the 175th Infantry, negotiates surrender terms on May 1, 1945, with Maj. Günter Matheis of the V-2 Rocket Division.

English: "*Obersturmbannführer* Wetzling and Major Matheis have the order and the right to have a speach [*sic*] with the General Commander of the military power on bord [*sic*] of the west Elbe about a leading of the Division z.V. (V-2 Rocket Division) to the victory army." McDaniel acknowledged receipt of this message by signing it, but mistakenly noted "May 30, 1945" as the date.

After three hours of negotiations, ending at 1:45 A.M. on May 1, Capt. John Hirschmann, the 175th's intelligence officer, radioed the 29th Division war room with spectacular news: "The two senior [German] officers of the delegation [Wetzling and Matheis] have returned to their division with Colonel McDaniel's decision to accept the surrender of *Division z.V.* in accordance with the policy laid down by higher headquarters [specifying that the surrender must be 'unconditional']. The lieutenant [Lucke] is remaining here at the 175th command post with a radio and will be notified by prearranged message when *Division z.V.* leaves their present area. . . . It has 1,500 vehicles and wheeled weapons. The nearest elements are twenty-five miles east of the Elbe River."

At midday on May 1, when Wetzling arrived back at *Division z.V.* headquarters thirty miles northwest of Berlin, he consulted with von Gaudecker, and the two men immediately issued an astonishing order to their men: "All troops should immediately disengage the [Red Army] and travel to the area of Lenzen, near the Elbe River. Our surrender to the western Allies is agreed upon. In addition, all existing V-2 materiel and documents are to be transported and surrendered." Turning their backs on one enemy and moving into the arms of another within a single day would be an arduous challenge. Some of von Gaudecker's men currently in contact with the Red Army must disengage and travel seventy miles to Lenzen over roads jammed with disconsolate soldiers and panicked civilians, and for at least part of that movement they would be under air attack by Soviet fighter-bombers. (McDaniel had guaranteed Wetzling that he would contact the U.S. Ninth Air Force to ensure no American aircraft attacked *Division z.V.*) Assuming the German troops could successfully reach Lenzen, they would then have to move six miles farther down the Elbe on a narrow riverside road to arrive at Wootz, the point opposite Company G's outposts designated by McDaniel for the river crossing. There the Germans would be met by American engineers manning boats, rafts, and amphibious trucks to ferry *Division z.V.* and as much of its equipment as possible across the Elbe.

How could a unit as untested and downhearted as *Division z.V.* carry out such a complex, speedy, and covert operation? In addition to holding off the Soviets, von Gaudecker faced the real danger that intransigent German fighters positioned between his division and the Elbe would fight back against his apparent treachery. Seemingly it would have been easier for von Gaudecker to disband his division and announce that every man must fend for himself. But unlike most German units in the current catastrophe, *Division z.V.* was fully motorized, so it could move rapidly—no man would have to walk. Above all, every one of von Gaudecker's men was motivated by an intense desire to avoid falling into the hands of the Russians. The astute McDaniel recognized this when he commented: "They are all interested in saving their hides."

McDaniel had ordered Wetzling to demonstrate *Division z.V.*'s readiness to begin the Elbe crossing by displaying four hefty white flags, fifty yards apart, on the Elbe's east bank near Wootz. At 7:14 A.M. on May 2, 1st Lt. George Harris of the 175th's Headquarters Company notified the war room by phone, "The Krauts have put the white flags up." By 9:00 A.M., as the 175th's May 1945 monthly report noted, "Hundreds of German vehicles lined the road [on the east bank] for miles, while [German] troops marched along the road and assembled in nearby fields prior to crossing the river. Company C, 121st Engineers, furnished boats and crews to ferry the German prisoners across the river, while the regimental commander [McDaniel] and his staff supervised the operation. It was a tremendous job to expedite the movement of the prisoners across the river and assemble them in the fields prior to shipping them to the rear by truck."

Other German soldiers involved in the hopeless fighting in and around Berlin had reached the same conclusion as those in *Division z.V.* Streaming westward as fast as they could away from the Red Army, many of those men hopped into the boats and rafts operated by U.S. Army engineers and gladly crossed the Elbe into American captivity. The prisoners included a German lieutenant general and his staff, conveyed in several automobiles and twelve motorcycles. It was a point of honor for a German general to surrender only to an opponent of equal or higher rank, so when a patrol leader from the 175th's Company M, Sgt. Donald Robertson, encountered the enemy entourage on the Elbe's east side, Robertson described the general's attitude as "arrogant beyond belief." Included in the enemy mob surging across the Elbe, Ewing remembered, "were about thirty German shepherd dogs, some of which were later to find homes in the United States."

Division z.V.'s capitulation could not be strictly categorized as the "unconditional" kind McDaniel had insisted upon. Hitler's cronies were notorious for inflicting ghastly punishments on the families of disloyal Germans, and to ensure that those fanatic Nazis did not retaliate against the relations of *Division z.V.* soldiers, McDaniel agreed to keep the news of the surrender as discreet as possible. He kept his word: neither stateside newspapers nor the American military press took much notice of it. McDaniel also promised Wetzling that German prisoners would be treated according to the dictates of the Hague Conventions, promptly transported into U.S. Army prisoner-of-war enclosures, and not handed over to the Red Army—despite the undeniable detail that Wetzling's men had only recently engaged the Soviets in battle. German SS men were not known for according promises to their enemies, but Wetzling, in exchange for gaining American assurances that the Russians would remain uninvolved, pledged to McDaniel that *Division z.V.* would hand over to the western Allies as much of its top-secret rocket equipment as possible rather than destroying it.

Almost as soon as the American engineers began ferrying the gloomy Germans over the Elbe, Gerhardt received the unwelcome news from Gillem that within the next two days the 29th Division would be transferred out of XIII Corps and shifted to a new sector. That development, Uncle Charlie fretted, "puts a different outlook on the thing [the surrender]," and he speculated that the 29th would have neither adequate time nor sufficient trucks to move the swelling mob of enemy troops to the rear before the 84th Division arrived to take over his sector. A disappointed McDaniel opined, "I think we should do what we can," to which Gerhardt rejoined: "We'll proceed then—but don't drum up any more trade than we have to." Happily, the general's worries were unfounded; over the next thirty-six hours, the 175th herded 10,367 prisoners over the Elbe, ushering them into the wide-open fields west of the river for eventual transfer to the 84th Division and ultimately corps- and army-level military police outfits.

The last of the 29th Division's 3,720 World War II fatalities occurred during the river-crossing operation when twenty-one-year-old PFC Harry Short of Company A, 121st Engineers, a native of Lake County, Florida, drowned in the Elbe. His comrades never recovered his body, and Short's name is listed today on the Tablets of the Missing at the Netherlands American Cemetery at Margraten.

The *Division z.V.* episode represented one of the 29th Division's finest moments in World War II. Only sixty hours after Wetzling had contacted McDaniel, the 29th Division, without firing a shot, had arranged for the surrender of a full enemy division—manned by personnel whom earnest Anglo-American scientists and soldiers would presently want to meet—and organized its movement across a major water obstacle while the onrushing Red Army nipped at its heels. "Lord, what a sight!" recalled PFC Harold Gordon, whose proficiency in German helped him gain authorization to row over to the enemy's side of the river. "The banks were black with men. We processed them as fast as we could and still seemed to make no dent at all upon the new hordes that poured in. It was like a dream. For miles and miles a winding river of vehicles and men in field gray stretched along the chief roads, overflowed into the fields, into the side roads, onto the dike beside the river. . . . Trucks, tanks, Jerry jeeps, assault guns, wagons, everything—all crammed with guns, armed Jerries, women, cognac, food, bazookas, typewriters, and every bit of equipment you could think of. I collected two Jerry sergeants, who were standing by the side of the road, and told them what to tell the soldiers to do. . . . German officers came up, I gave them instructions, and passed on. God, you've never heard of anything like it. The ditches were jammed with discarded equipment. Tanks with loaded guns idled along the road, most of their crews sitting on top. Command cars full of officers sat around. And here we were, a handful of about twenty Americans spread over a mile or more." PFC Dickerson of the 121st noted in a letter home to his parents that his foxhole buddy, PFC Marvin Gutknecht—who spoke fluent German— "went over [the Elbe], without permission, and stayed a day and a half. He slept under a blanket with two Kraut soldiers that night, got drunk with a Kraut colonel, and came back with armfuls of pistols and binoculars." Later, Gutknecht presented Dickerson with one of the pairs of binoculars as a gift.

Future 29th Division historian Ewing, then a member of the 175th's Service Company, witnessed the spectacle from start to finish and wrote: "The impending surrender of the German division with its prospect of souvenirs, sent the men of the 175th, and especially those of its 2nd Battalion, into a state of great expectation. But spirits were considerably dampened when the order came down that the 2nd Battalion's Ammunition and Pioneer Platoon [an element of the battalion Headquarters Company] would be detailed to guard and direct the Germans on the riverbank. All other infantry troops were ordered to remain in their positions."

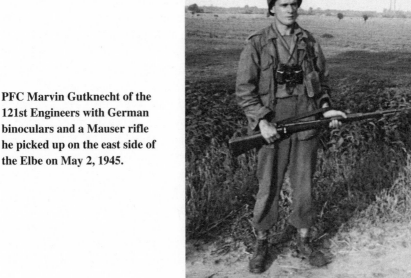

PFC Marvin Gutknecht of the 121st Engineers with German binoculars and a Mauser rifle he picked up on the east side of the Elbe on May 2, 1945.

The scene, Ewing remembered, cast the 29ers into "a state of happy excitement. All fear was gone. Danger was gone. . . . The whole situation seemed to symbolize the end of the war."

Any 175th Infantry GI who desired a souvenir would have no trouble appropriating one: a German helmet, a Walther P38 pistol, a Wehrmacht dagger, a *Gott Mit Uns* (God With Us) belt buckle, a pair of top-notch binoculars. But one lucky 29er, Captain Hirschmann, came upon the Comstock Lode of war souvenirs entirely by accident. Hirschmann spent all of May 2 at McDaniel's order on the enemy's side of the Elbe, helping to organize German troops for their movement across the river. Unlike many intelligence officers, Hirschmann was not fluent in the enemy's language, and he therefore gladly accepted the assistance of a congenial and dapper German civilian who claimed to have attended a British school prior to the war. (Whether that civilian's assertion that he also had social contacts within the British royal family was genuine, the 29ers did not yet know—nor did they care.)

According to a postwar War Department report that investigated the event about to unfold, "While assisting in the ferrying operations, the civilian said he had some silver he wanted the Americans to have to prevent its destruction or loss. He described it as having belonged formerly to the German imperial family and later [after World War I] confiscated by the German government. At first skeptical, Hirschmann questioned the civilian as to how much silver he had. He said two or three trucks would be required to transport it." No longer skeptical, Hirschmann was staggered to learn that prior to the Great War, the vast silver dining set had been the property of Crown Prince Wilhelm and Duchess Cecilie, the eldest son and daughter-in-law of the notorious Kaiser Wilhelm II. McDaniel informed Hirschmann that he could ship the silver across the Elbe, "providing the operation did not interfere with the movement of the surrendered troops."

"Captain Hirschmann advised the civilian to have some German soldiers load the silver on trucks, and it would be ferried across the river," the War Department report continued. "About two or three hours later, he reappeared with two truck loads containing wooden boxes, which he said contained the silver. Colonel McDaniel took possession of the silver under the provisions of the Seventy-ninth Article of War." According to the War Department's 1920 version of those articles, the Seventy-ninth, titled "Captured Property to be Secured for Public Service," declared: "All public property taken from the enemy is the property of the United States. . . . Any person subject to military law who neglects to secure such property or is guilty of wrongful appropriation thereof shall be punished as a court-martial may direct."

So far, so good. . . . But McDaniel and his staff were much too busy supervising the *Division z.V.* surrender and, immediately thereafter, the 29th Division's withdrawal from the Elbe to bother about the vast silver banquet set now in the 175th Infantry's possession. Only a week later, in Bremen, Germany, after a thorough examination and inventory of the forty-four wooden crates, did McDaniel grasp the extent of the treasure trove in his hands. Stamped *Kronprinzliche Silberkammer Stadte Silber* (Crown Prince's Silver Collection) and large enough to provide place settings for 500 people at a formal feast, initial appraisals by experts valued the set at nearly one million dollars. After the war the 175th Infantry conveyed the silver to the regiment's home station at the Fifth Regiment Armory in Baltimore and planned to display the magnificent collection in a new regimental museum.

Momentous events in Europe were developing so swiftly that Gerhardt had no time to savor his capture of *Division z.V.* In a few days the 29ers would be on their way to a different region of Germany, and they displayed not the slightest interest in the fate of their prisoners. American and British generals, however, held an acute interest in the Germans' supposed skills in rocket science and ordered the captives shipped westward by truck to prison camps in Belgium for thorough interrogation by Allied intelligence officers. During that journey, fuming Belgian citizens took every opportunity to pelt the passing Germans with rocks and bottles. By July 1945, the British had established a camp for their special prisoners on Germany's North Sea coast, and three months later, after the Germans had managed to assemble and fuel several V-2s under the vigilant eyes of their captors, the prisoners carried out three successful rocket launches.

Happily, those V-2s were aimed not at London or Antwerp, but only at the sea.

WE ARE FRIENDS!

By the first day of May 1945, the GIs of the 175th Infantry had expected they would be swapping souvenirs with Soviet Cossacks, the prospect of which, as Ewing recalled, was "the staple of discussion at this time. . . . Men who spoke Russian were in great demand, and 'Russian liaison' groups appeared in front-line units. General Gerhardt directed that the American flag be flown atop the highest flagpole on the west bank of the river for the benefit of any Red Army patrols which might be trying to find us. Russian artillery could be heard across the Elbe, and units on the front line commenced shooting up green flares to signal their presence."

Instead, the 175th's disappointed doughboys saw nothing but a multitude of disconsolate German soldiers on the far side of the Elbe, all endeavoring to end World War II in a U.S. Army prisoner-of-war camp. A rock-solid rumor from regimental headquarters indicated that the 29th Division would shortly be on its way to a new rear-echelon job miles behind the front. If the 29ers would soon leave the Elbe behind them, and the war's end was imminent, would they ever see a Red Army "Ivan?"

They would. Irrefutable evidence of the Russians' proximity surfaced on the evening of May 2 on the front of Whiteford's 3rd Battalion, nine miles upstream from the Germans' Elbe crossing point at Wootz. A 7:03 P.M. phone call to Gerhardt's war room reported, "There is a lot of firing going on down in front of the 3rd Battalion. . . . [German] people are jumping in the river and swimming across." Only one thing could make German soldiers and civilians so desperate, Whiteford's men surmised, and that was the closeness of the Red Army. They were right: twenty minutes later, an artillery L-4 observation aircraft pilot remarked that "something very unusual is going on in the little town of Lanz [two miles away on the opposite side of the river]. [I] saw civilians scattering and coming toward the river. [I] saw a white flare [the Soviets' prearranged recognition signal] over there also." At 8:54 P.M. another pilot made a definitive identification with the enthusiastic report: "The Russians are here! They are on the river just to the southeast of the little town of Lanz. . . . Their tanks with the [red] stars are up to the river, jeeps painted gray, shooting white flares—and quite a few horsemen there."

The moment had come at last. Whiteford contacted the Company L command post in Schnackenburg and ordered Capt. Ernest Burkhartt to "go out and find the Russians" immediately. For that exhilarating but still hazardous task,

Burkhartt selected a six-man patrol led by twenty-six-year-old Pittsburgh native 2nd Lt. Kenneth Rohyans, a Normandy combat veteran who held a Silver Star for valor. One of the patrol members, thirty-year-old PFC Russell Frederick of Niles, Ohio, spoke Russian. Another, twenty-two-year-old T/Sgt. Olger "Ole" Raaum from western North Dakota, had in early 1940 enlisted at age seventeen in the Regular army and also had earned a Silver Star. The other three patrol members included S/Sgt. Ralph Stecklein, twenty, from the high plains of northwestern Kansas; Sgt. George Taktekos, nineteen, from Brooklyn; and PFC Palmer Loro, twenty-one, also from Niles, near Cleveland.

Rohyans and his five followers crossed the Elbe at Schnackenburg at about 9:15 P.M. and proceeded eastward along the riverbank toward Lütkenwisch, leaving Raaum behind to guard the rowboat. Just fifteen minutes later, in the muted light provided by a moon just a few days short of full, the 29ers spotted some figures who, according to the divisional history, wore "long gray coats and round furred hats." A team of horses was herded nearby. "Moving out in front, PFC Frederick shouted in Russian: 'We are friends! We are American soldiers!' After a pause, someone answered, 'Come on!' The patrol found one Russian officer and five enlisted men in the group. There was a great round of handshaking. . . . There were things to drink, of course, the first drink being a powerful mixture of vodka and brandy in tall water glasses."

The 29ers learned that the Soviets, dressed like Cossacks of yore, were part of a mounted troop commanded by Capt. Mikhail Kravienko and formed part of the 28th Cavalry Regiment of the 6th Guards Cavalry Division, a highly distinguished outfit whose commander and staff had gained the exalted Order of

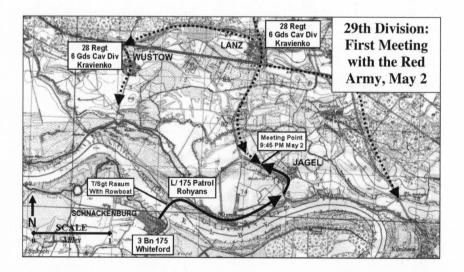

Suvorov, 2nd Class, for operations against the Germans in 1943. After several rounds of pleasantries, Rohyans escorted Kravienko back across the Elbe to Whiteford's command post, an impressive fifteenth-century edifice on the outskirts of Gartow owned by Count von Bernstorff. There the assembled officers drank more toasts and reviewed the military situation. Whiteford learned that Kravienko's troop represented a "very limited" cavalry screen far ahead of the advancing main body of the Red Army's 2nd Belorussian Front, the Soviet version of an army group. "There will be more [cavalry] in tomorrow," a phone message to Gerhardt's war room observed, "[but] the infantry will not catch up for about four days."

Dawn on May 3, a beautiful spring day, brought festive members of both armies down to the riverbank, where, as the *29 Let's Go* newsletter reported, "Blue and Grayers were crossing eastward and Joe Stalin's cavalrymen were reversing the process. [May 3] was a day for the books, something to write home about." Corporal Lowenthal, the *29 Let's Go* editor, crossed over to the far side of the Elbe and noted: "Like our Joes, [the Soviets] rode up and down the roads on German bikes and drank whatever they could find. . . . They were smoking American cigarettes and trying to learn to chew the gum given them by the Yanks. The wrapping paper on the gum threw them for a loop at first until they got the knack of stripping it off. Some of the Rooskies posed laughingly with Joes for the photographers, swapping their black lambskin toppers for helmets. All of them had their medals on. Most of the men had the Red Army equivalent of the Purple Heart. Like an American outfit, the troop was composed of youngsters and gray-haired men. . . . Some of the men were shoeing their horses in the stables back of the CP. The captain's horse, Darian, a big brown stallion, had fought with him since 1939 and had been nicked by shrapnel at Leningrad. . . . There was a copy of the Moscow daily, *Pravda*, on the table. And no fire in the room. The Russians, many dressed in fatigues, didn't seem to mind the cold. They fired M-1s and carbines and were amazed they didn't have to pull the bolt back after each shot."

A supernumerary colonel at 29th Division headquarters, Alexander George—categorized in reports as "assistant to the assistant division commander"—was seeking a useful role, and on the morning of May 3, he found one. At 1:00 A.M., George crossed the Elbe and, escorted by several Russian horsemen, traveled six miles beyond the river to the command post of another Red Army outfit, the 5th Guards Cavalry Division, which along with the 6th comprised the point of the Soviets' blitzkrieg into central Germany. Gerhardt had instructed George to locate a senior Russian officer so that a suitable ceremony could be arranged between the Red Army and the 29th Division; George found one in Maj. Gen. Nikolai Chepurkin, the 5th's commander. A 29er described Chepurkin as "a very good man; they say he is a very well-liked gentleman, and the 5th is a crack division." George radioed the war room and arranged for Chepurkin and his entourage—including a *Pravda* reporter—to travel to Whiteford's command post at the von Bernstorff mansion, where Brig. Gen. William Sands, Gerhardt's artillery chief, would meet them. Despite Gillem's avowal to Gerhardt that in any ceremony the Russians would "like equal rank," Uncle Charlie was too busy getting ready for the 29th Division's forthcoming withdrawal from the Elbe to attend; he did, however, provide Sands a Thompson submachine gun, featuring the division's blue-and-gray yin-yang symbol and inscribed "Elbe River, 1945," for presentation to the Russians.

The ceremony kicked off at 6:00 P.M. on May 3, in the midst of the 29th Division's hectic preparations to depart the area the following morning. After a formal exchange of salutes, Sands and his aide, Capt. Bruce Bliven—a 1937 Harvard graduate who after the war would become a celebrated New York writer—removed their helmets as a mark of respect to their allies. "Inevitable toasts to the president, the late FDR, and continued friendship of the Allies were drunk," Lowenthal reported, adding that "General Sands presented the noted Russian general with the stars of his rank." Sands also bestowed upon Chepurkin Gerhardt's Tommy gun in addition to an M1911 .45-caliber Colt pistol in the name of General Simpson of U.S. Ninth Army.

Brig. Gen. William Sands and Maj. Gen. Nikolai Chepurkin of the 5th Guards Cavalry Division meet on May 3, 1945, at Count von Bernstorff's mansion near Gartow, Germany.

Chepurkin gratefully returned the Americans' hospitality, and that evening Sands and his staff crossed the Elbe for another ceremony at the 5th Guards Cavalry Division's command post. Lowenthal wrote that the Soviets entertained the 29ers in "lavish fashion," including stirring Russian music provided by a Red Army band. Chepurkin presented Sands with a beautiful Cossack saber and a PPSH-41 submachine gun, a weapon Red Army infantrymen cherished just as much as U.S. Army dogfaces treasured the Tommy gun. Both Soviet weapons are now displayed in the 29th Infantry Division Museum at the Fifth Regiment Armory in Baltimore.

It was time to go; the 29th Division had an appointment elsewhere in Germany. Lowenthal noticed, "The Red Joes were feeding their horses when we left."

SEVEN

The Last Act

VICTORY IN EUROPE

The 29ers, those lucky soldiers who had survived months of combat on the road from Omaha Beach to the Elbe, were about to take their first steps on the long journey home.

The Great Men of the Anglo-American high command had long ago reached a decision that would dispatch the 29ers on the initial leg of that glorious voyage. Nearly eight months before the 29th Division met the Red Army on the Elbe, Roosevelt and Churchill had met in Quebec's austere and windswept Citadel, with its stunning views of the St. Lawrence River, and had begun the highly satisfying process of Nazi Germany's dismemberment. Although Eisenhower's troops occupied only insignificant amounts of German soil by September 15, 1944, the supremely confident president and prime minister spent hours that day poring over maps to fashion a provisional plan for Allied occupation of Germany once Hitler's inevitable defeat was achieved. That victory could not be far off, Roosevelt and Churchill agreed, and when it transpired, the Allies must ensure German militarism would never rise again. The momentous accord reached that day "assigned the southwestern zone of occupation in Germany to United States forces and the northwestern zone to British forces."

The next day, September 16, the American Joint Chiefs of Staff met in the magnificent Château Frontenac in the heart of Quebec's *Haute-Ville* to mull over the plan and seek a solution to their overriding concern that the U.S. occupation zone in Germany was landlocked. Army Chief of Staff Gen. George C. Marshall came straight to the point: "It would be desirable," he said, "to specify one port [within the British zone] that would be controlled by the United States. . . . One port would be enough provided the United States had complete control of it and the port had sufficient capacity to handle approximately 10,000 tons of supplies daily." Adm. Ernest King, the U.S. Navy's senior officer, "concurred," stating "that Bremen and vicinity be proposed for United States control." An hour later, when the Americans put forward that arrangement to their allies, the British immediately agreed—and even went a step further. Adm. Andrew Cunningham, the Royal Navy's First Sea Lord, "suggested that the American area should also include Bremerhaven, some forty or fifty miles down the [Weser] river," the stenographer recorded. "Bremerhaven was, he understood, the port where large ships had to berth."

So the 29th Division would soon begin occupation duty in northwestern Germany in the area now designated the Bremen Enclave, a vast 1,500-square-mile district encompassing not only Bremen and Bremerhaven, but also dozens of small towns in the lower Weser River basin. Gerhardt learned of this surprising development in midafternoon on May 3; at 4:21 P.M. he phoned Witte in the war room and informed him: "They have changed our mission, and instead of taking over the zone [in and around Gütersloh, an area the 29th had occupied for a short time in April], we are going into a concentration area in the zone around Münster. We are taking over the job the 95th Division had [and shifting from Gillem's XIII Corps back to Anderson's XVI Corps]. It looks like a pretty good deal to me." A concerned Witte remarked that the Bremen job sounded like it would require the addition of "a lot of specialists." He was right: so many new men and units would eventually be attached to the 29th that the division would become known as "Task Force Bremen," while Gerhardt would gain the exalted title of "Commander, Enclave Military District."

With a consummate efficiency that by this phase of the war had become the norm, just before dawn on May 4 the 29th Division began to roll westward away from the Elbe, bouncing over the now-familiar roads and autobahns in multitudinous trucks and jeeps toward Münster. The forwardmost 29th Division outfits, manning outposts along the Elbe, faced an arduous journey over 220 miles of clogged roads, which they completed with barely a hitch in little more than nine hours during a gloomy day defined by the division's operations journal as "overcast with occasional rain." Cooper's 110th Field Artillery Battalion led the way "via Luchow, Uelzen, Celle, Hannover, Minden, and Warrendorf"; Cooper boasted that throughout the journey not one of the 110th's 124 overworked vehicles broke down. The 115th Infantry did not fare as well: at 3:45 P.M. on May 4, Blandford reported to Witte that due to a slight shortage of vehicles, "we overloaded some trucks and lost them. On the next move [from Münster to Bremen] we would like to have a minimum of 110 trucks, but 115 or 120 would be better. We want to only put about twenty men in a truck." (As many as twenty-five 29ers had been packed into some vehicles.) The always helpful Witte responded, "I think it can be arranged."

During the journey, the 29ers' progression through several major road intersections revealed the amazing spectacle of German military policemen directing traffic, a sight that caused the bemused Cooper to confess, "The situation was becoming too complicated." So complicated, in fact, that Cooper noted his men "were forced to refuse the surrender of large bodies of German troops, which had been bypassed or had remained hidden during the recent blitz to the Elbe. In order to maintain the march schedule and to prevent blocking a large part of the division column, the Blue and Gray officers simply directed their German counterparts either to surrender to the nearest stationary American unit, or if the troops came from a given area and had transportation, to take them home and report to Allied authorities there." In the course of just a few weeks, the Germans had changed from detested and dangerous enemies to harmless and pitiable bystanders. Under the extraordinary conditions of Nazi Germany's collapse, many 29ers could no longer maintain the hatred of all things German to which they had grown accustomed over the past several months. In one curious incident during the 110th's withdrawal toward Münster, "German civilians apparently cheered the battalion column and tossed flowers at the men." Cooper figured out later, however, that "the tributes were for German soldiers bearing passes to proceed to various points of surrender and crowded into German vehicles which had sandwiched between units of the 110th's column. Politely they were ordered to fall back and keep an interval to the rear."

As the 29ers settled into their temporary bivouacs around Münster at nightfall on May 4, the latest war news hinted that they had seen their last battle. Near Lüneburg, 170 miles northeast, Field Marshal Sir Bernard Montgomery— that old friend of the 29th Division under whom the 29ers had served for more than half their period in combat—had just accepted the unconditional surrender of all German forces within his command area, covering much of Holland and northwestern Germany, including the entire Bremen Enclave. Monty had defined the event as "the last act" and spoke for all 29ers when he pronounced: "This is a great moment." A great moment indeed, for if the 29th Division was about to move into the Enclave, it would be entering a zone at peace, with no blackouts, no armed German soldiers, and above all no combat.

Following a day of rest and cleanup on May 5, Blandford's 115th Infantry paved the 29th Division's path to Bremen on Sunday, May 6. The 100-mile journey to the northeast was easy; what happened afterward was not. Scheduled to relieve the 95th Division's 378th Infantry in Bremen at 9:00 A.M. on May 7—the

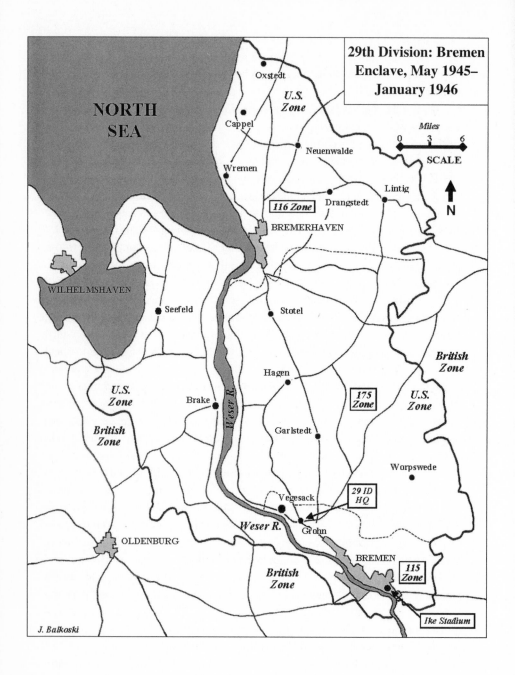

**29th Division: Bremen
Enclave, May 1945–
January 1946**

NORTH
SEA

Oxstedt

*U.S.
Zone*

Cappel

Neuenwalde

Miles

0   3   6

SCALE

N

Wremen

Lintig

Drangstedt

116 Zone

BREMERHAVEN

WILHELMSHAVEN

Seefeld

Stotel

*British
Zone*

Hagen

*U.S.
Zone*

Brake

Weser R.

*175
Zone*

*U.S.
Zone*

*British
Zone*

Garlstedt

Worpswede

Vegesack

*29 ID
HQ*

Weser R.

Grohn

OLDENBURG

*British
Zone*

BREMEN

*115
Zone*

Ike Stadium

J. Balkoski

378th had been guarding the city's harbor facilities for nearly a week—the 115th's arrival at 7:00 P.M. the previous evening triggered a brief housing predicament, forcing the 29ers to share cramped quarters with their 95th Division comrades-in-arms for one highly uncomfortable night.

The 121st Engineer's Company A, led by Capt. Leland Moring, accompanied the 115th Infantry into Bremen with two primary missions—"mine clearance and opening of roads"—but Moring reported back to the war room that he needed immediate help. As Gerhardt bluntly remarked to his new boss, Maj. Gen. John Anderson of XVI Corps, "The bridge situation [over the Weser] is bad." Two weeks previously, as the Tommies fought their way into Bremen, the Germans had demolished the city's main Weser span, the *Kaiserbrücke* (Kaiser's Bridge), but British sappers promptly constructed a Bailey bridge nearby. The British span, however, could carry only one-way traffic; Gerhardt stated the obvious when he told Anderson, "It slows things up."

Since Lt. Col. Raleigh Powell's death from a mine blast on April 24, the 121st Engineers were now led by one of the last field grade officers to join the 29th Division in World War II, Lt. Col. Marvin Jacobs, a thirty-year-old Marylander who had graduated from West Point less than five years in the past. Gerhardt ordered Jacobs to move the rest of his battalion into Bremen right away to help out Moring; Jacobs completed the shift on May 8, and Company C, commanded by Capt. Herbert Williams, punctually set out to build another bridge—a "Class 40 steel treadway bridge, floating"—over the Weser a half-mile upstream from the British span. Jacobs set up "a definite traffic circulation plan" in which "the Bailey bridge would handle all one-way traffic flowing out of Bremen, and the treadway would take all one-way traffic coming into Bremen." Meantime, Company B, under Capt. Sidney Smith, embarked on a weeklong effort to repair the main roads emanating from the city.

The most troublesome issue of all for Blandford was the ill-defined chain of command under which he must carry out his occupation duties. An anonymous 115th officer complained that there was "considerable confusion as to who is authorized to give orders. The 115th Infantry is attached for operations to the British 52nd Division, [but] the 1st Battalion is apparently to take orders from the naval commander in charge of the docks." Untangling the command muddle would take time. The British unquestionably still held the reins of authority within the Enclave—they had only recently captured Bremen by force—and when they would depart was anyone's guess. An impatient Anderson complained to Gerhardt, "What they need up there is you—a directing hand to coordinate." Gerhardt answered, "The sooner the better from my viewpoint. You'll talk to [U.S. Ninth] Army about it?" Anderson answered back: "Army can't do anything about it. The British will have to say, 'All right. Take over.'"

The next day, after looking into the matter, Gerhardt reported to Anderson: "The people down below with the [52nd] Division are ready to have us take over at any time. It is a case of getting the area cleared, taking care of German prisoners, etc. If we could get the bulk of our headquarters up there, it would help when we begin to take over." Anderson asserted: "We'll take it up with Army this morning and let you know."

But the British were still a long way from proclaiming "Take over." The designated Grand Poobah of the Bremen Enclave, Charles H. Gerhardt, would have to wait nearly two more weeks for his installation.

Minus Blandford's 115th Infantry, already on occupation duties in Bremen, the 29th Division had only just begun to settle into its new bivouacs in and around Münster when an electrifying message from Eisenhower's forward headquarters at Reims, France, arrived at Gerhardt's war room in Warrendorf at 8:05 A.M. on May 7. "A representative of the German high command signed the unconditional surrender of all German land, sea, and air forces in Europe to the Allied Expeditionary Force and simultaneously to the Soviet high command at 0141 hours Central European Time, May 7, under which all forces will cease active operations at 12:01 A.M., May 9," the communiqué began. "Effective immediately all offensive operations by Allied Expeditionary Forces will cease and troops will remain in present positions. Moves involved in occupational duties will continue. Due to difficulties in communication, there may be some delay in similar orders reaching enemy troops, so full defensive precautions will be taken. All informed, down to and including divisions, tactical air commands and groups, base sections and equivalent. No release will be made to the press pending an announcement by the heads of the three governments." The 29ers were not privy to another much more succinct message Ike had just sent to the Anglo-American Combined Chiefs of Staff: "The mission of this Allied force was fulfilled at 0241, local time, May 7, 1945."

Later that day, an anonymous clerk typed an historic sentence into the "Incidents, Messages, and Orders" column of the 29th Division's "Journal of Latitude Advance," otherwise known as the war room journal ("Latitude" was the 29th's code name). The last of tens of thousands of entries that had been recorded since June 6, 1944, on Omaha Beach read: "The war room as such and the war room journal are discontinued." As he had done every evening since D-Day, Gerhardt penciled in his initials, "CHG," in the lower right corner of the page, indicating his approval.

It was over.

IT'S BEEN A LONG WAY

Gerhardt composed a simple but eloquent message for the 29ers, to be included in the following day's edition of *29 Let's Go.* "Omaha Beach to the Elbe River," he began. "Isigny, St. Lô, Vire, Brest, Siegfried Line, Roer River—the objectives taken on the way. We trained hard for a difficult task, have high standards and a record of all missions accomplished. Our success is a direct result of the efforts of all individuals throughout. WELL DONE! 29 LET'S GO!"

Dissemination of the surrender news down the chain of command triggered a brief outburst of celebratory clatter: the crack of gunshots fired into the air; the bellow of vehicle sirens and horns; the banging of metallic pots and pans; the whoops of exultant 29ers. But "V-E Day," as the prospective event had been designated in the civilian and military press well before the German surrender, triggered far more muted emotions within the 29th Division than on the home front. The 116th Infantry's Maj. Charles Cawthon theorized that a 29er's typical low-key reaction to the news was in "keeping with the mood in which he had fought the war: conviction, determination, unstinted effort, no little courage and sacrifice—and little exultation." PFC Art Plaut of the 115th noted that "somehow the entire event seemed anticlimactic. . . . For almost a month the average soldier had been able to see that the end was not far away, and the fact that the regiment was not engaged in actual combat at the time of the surrender contributed to the lack of enthusiasm. The men were relieved, but they were not overly excited. They had seen too much of war, and they were tired. . . . The attitude seemed to be, 'Let the folks at home celebrate if they want to. We'll wait until we're sure that we have something to celebrate.' The memories of the fighting were still too fresh, the taste of the hardships endured still too bitter, the comforts of home still too remote for any real celebration."

The 175th's Colonel McDaniel phoned the war room and noted, "I suggest we mount the [29th Division] band on trucks and let them visit the various battalions and regimental command post areas to play some martial music." But that was not nearly good enough for Gerhardt. During the general's tenure as 29th Division commander—now twenty-two months—he had always insisted that an essential element of any 29ers' life must be close-order drill, but that requirement infuriated many combat veterans, who did not see the point of toy-soldier rigamarole in their rare respites from front-line duty. But the U.S. Army was assuredly not a democracy, and like it or not, 29ers had learned how to march in perfect step, execute sharp right- and left-wheel turns, and stand at rigid attention in flawless alignment while the brass made speeches. Now was the time, Uncle Charlie proclaimed, for his men to demonstrate those traits; V-E Day provided plenty of opportunities, and after witnessing or participating in a couple of impressive parades, most 29ers had to admit that Gerhardt had been right when he avowed: "It is those superficial things that you are judged by." Nothing radiated the 29th Division's soul better than a triumphal review in the heart of the enemy's country, carried out by hundreds—sometimes thousands—

of combat veterans marching in perfect step behind fluttering colors and guidons to the beat of the top-notch music of the 29th Division band. "I never liked parading in the States," Lieutenant Easton wrote to his wife, "but I do now. Marching with these fellows with whom I've shared so much brings us all closer, like good conversation, only much, much better. And we all feel this and silently respect it. In step, easy, tested, strong, we are right as never before and perhaps never again."

The word came down from Ike's headquarters that American units on the Western Front would observe Wednesday, May 9, as Victory-in-Europe Day. As the 116th's May 1945 monthly report remarked with a twinge of contriteness, "It was, after all, a great day," and every unit in the 29th Division must therefore put on some form of martial display that fittingly would include memorial services honoring all 29ers who had lost their lives since D-Day—a total of 3,720 men, not counting hundreds more still unaccounted for on the voluminous roles of the missing, as well as those many GIs who had died from non-combat causes.

At 3:45 P.M. on May 9, "a brilliantly sunny day," the full 500-man complement of Cooper's 110th Field Artillery Battalion paraded in "a fine meadow" just outside Hoetmar, twelve miles southeast of Münster. The event, Cooper remembered, "was a dramatic and fitting end to the long fight. The most prevalent feeling was one of gratitude to God for a victorious peace in Europe at last and an end to the slaughter." In the presence of Gerhardt's chief artilleryman, Brig. Gen. William Sands—who had worn the blue-and-gray yin-yang patch longer than anyone in the 29th Division—the 110th's adjutant, Capt. Bill Boykin, read Cooper's General Order Number 6 to the rapt cannoneers. "On February 3, 1941, this battalion, then the 1st Battalion, 110th Field Artillery Regiment, Maryland National Guard, was inducted into the service of the United States," Boykin intoned. "Since the assault landing in Normandy on June 6, 1944, the officers and men of the battalion have maintained relentless pressure toward the defeat of Germany and carried out their primary mission, support of the 115th Infantry Regiment, to the utmost of their ability. Never in history has the infantry of our army, which bears the brunt of land warfare, received such fast, accurate, and massive artillery support when and where needed, than in this war. Never has an enemy been more relentlessly pounded around the clock. . . . Remember our comrades who have made the supreme sacrifice and upheld the standards and ideals for which they died. You are a member of a fine division and a fine battalion. I am proud of you, and I know that your generals and the nation share that pride. As to the past: Well done! As to the future, tackle it with the spirit of the division's old battle cry: 29, Let's Go!"

The ceremony concluded with a perfect march-past by the battalion's five batteries—Headquarters, A, B, C, and Service—as the 29th Division band blared

"Maryland, My Maryland." Led by an officer and a veteran enlisted man carrying a forktailed red guidon, each battery passed Cooper and Sands on the reviewing stand with a perfect "eyes right," as the guidon dipped in salute. An emotional Cooper noted that the moment "created a memory that never can be erased." Later, each battery organized a party, "with schnapps from a nearby plant at Freckenhorst supplied with the compliments of the burgomeister."

The 121st Engineer Battalion's V-E Day affair in Bremen was more of a somber memorial service than a triumphal review. The 121st had come a long way since its days as a District of Columbia National Guard outfit, as its executive officer, Capt. Henry Lewis, noted with some emotion at the event: "This battalion, with the 116th and 115th, assaulted Hun-infested Europe. From Omaha Beach to Les Foulons, where, after blowing hedgerows, clearing mines, performing night and day every engineer task possible to assist the doughboy, you went into the line as infantry—through all of Jerry's machine gun fire, burp guns, mortars, and 88s, plus rain, cold, and mud—and you held this line until relieved. . . . The 121st Engineer Battalion performed every engineer task in the book and many not covered in the book. V-E Day, May 9, 1945, finds us on the outskirts of Bremen. On this Memorial Day we are assembled here first to give thanks to God in heaven for the victory; second, to pay solemn tribute in honor of those men of the battalion who paid the supreme sacrifice in breaking the bonds of the enslaved nations in order for all peoples to have the inalienable rights of liberty, freedom, and the pursuit of happiness. May you and I always remember that only by the grace of God and the sacrifices of such men are we present here today. May we and those at home ever be worthy of the cause for which these ninety-two men gave their very lives."

In a pasture outside Isselhorst, Bingham's 116th Infantry—"3,000 men standing with bowed heads," according to Easton—sang hymns and listened to psalms read by solemn Protestant, Catholic, and Jewish chaplains before tramping in review past Gerhardt, "by columns of companies so he could get a good look." Later, in the gloomy Lutheran church in Isselhorst, Easton's 3rd Battalion held a memorial service, which kicked off with a rendition of the stirring 1756 hymn "Come, Thou Almighty King."

Come, Thou almighty King,
Help us Thy name to sing,
Help us to praise!
Father, all glorious,
O'er all victorious,
Come and reign over us,
Ancient of days!

In one pew Easton noticed two Company K members—whom he categorized as "boys"—reading from the same hymnal. "I saw them sharing the same frozen foxhole on an outpost along the Roer River," Easton wrote, "and when we jumped off and crossed the river, they came one behind the other on the foot-bridge. . . . These two men have eaten, slept, prayed, gotten drunk, argued, laughed, bitched about the Army, and gone to the latrine together for six months, and they've fought together, if there is such a thing."

A chaplain closed the service with "My Country 'Tis of Thee," and as Easton filed out of the church, he overheard two veterans reminiscing about the old days at Fort Meade when the 29th Division had been mobilized in early 1941. One vet-eran murmured, "It's been a long way."

Replied the other: "Yeah."

HOW MANY POINTS DO *YOU* HAVE?

When U.S. Army Chief of Staff George C. Marshall learned of the German sur-render at Reims, he cabled Eisenhower straight away: "You have completed your mission with the greatest victory in the history of warfare. You have commanded with outstanding success the most powerful military force that has ever been assembled. You have met and successfully disposed of every conceivable diffi-culty incident to varied national interests and international political problems of unprecedented complications. You have triumphed over inconceivable logistical problems and military obstacles, and you have played a major role in the complete destruction of German military power. . . . You have made history, great history, for the good of all mankind."

Marshall had shared a big secret with Ike since October 1944, and now that Hitler was dead and the Nazis eliminated, it was time to let every GI all over the world in on it. In the summer of 1944, Marshall's staff had concocted a plan to arrange for the massive redeployment of U.S. Army soldiers in Europe once the war in that theater was over, a scheme that would discharge some men from serv-ice, send others home for eventual deployment to the Pacific, and leave some on occupation duty in Germany. To introduce the redeployment plan to the GIs, Marshall had obtained the services of several luminaries in the stateside entertain-ment industry to create a top-notch film titled *Two Down and One to Go!* Col. Frank Capra, director of the legendary 1934 film *It Happened One Night*, and Walt Disney, the animator who had created Mickey Mouse, completed the project in September 1944, and when Marshall saw it for the first time, he confided to Ike that it would be "a vital stimulus to morale." However, he decreed that the film's existence must be kept secret until Germany had surrendered, "otherwise we shall have an extremely serious morale reaction."

With the great victory now a reality, U.S. Army commanders worldwide had to take immediate action to fulfill Marshall's firm order: "The showing of this film will take precedence over all activities of troops except for combat." Stateside civilians, Marshall presumed, would expect immediate action by the War Department to send American soldiers home from Europe, and among the sixty-one U.S. Army divisions in Eisenhower's command, that order was carried out with celerity; dozens of silver metal film reel cases containing copies of *Two Down and One to Go!* arrived in the 29th Division's bivouacs shortly after V-E Day, and on May 11 and 12 all 29ers got a chance to view the movie. It began with an image of the imperious Secretary of War Henry Stimson while a band rendered a stirring version of "Columbia, the Gem of the Ocean," followed quickly thereafter with cartoon visages of Hitler, Mussolini, and Tojo—the first two blotted out by a bold **X**. Seated at a desk underneath a massive portrait of his mentor, Gen. John J. Pershing, Marshall then looked intently into the camera and saluted "the armed forces of the United States for courage and complete devotion to duty," affirming: "Now that the United Nations have delivered Europe from the Nazis"—he pronounced it "Nah-zees"—"two of our three enemies lie among the ruins of their own evil ambitions. . . . We've won the battle of Europe, but the war—the global war—will not be won until we have exterminated Japanese military power. . . . Now, together with our allies, we shall concentrate devastating power against this treacherous enemy and rid the world permanently of this menace of barbarism. We can do this if every American, in or out of uniform, keeps in heart and mind the plain fact that we will not have won this war, nor can we enjoy any peace, until Japan is completely crushed."

What followed, as explained by officers in an "Information and Education Orientation Hour" as well as by a *Two Down and One to Go!* pamphlet, drew the 29ers' attention much more intently than patriotic music, caricatures of tyrants, and speeches by generals. The pressing question in the mind of every 29th Division soldier was whether he would be obligated to remain in uniform for possible redeployment to the Pacific Theater to help crush Japanese "barbarism," or discharged from the Army and returned to civilian life. That question, the 29ers were about to learn, would soon be addressed by the U.S. Army's stunningly simple method to determine who must continue in military service and who could go home. Each enlisted 29er would be issued an "Adjusted Service Rating Card," which would be filled out by members of the S-1 (Personnel) section of his unit and sent up the chain of command, ultimately ending up at the adjutant general's office in Washington. Every man would be assigned a point total in four categories: one point for each month in Army service; one point for each month in overseas service; five points for each campaign star and each decoration, including the Purple Heart; and twelve points for each dependent child under eighteen. The higher a soldier's grand total, the greater the chance of his discharge from the Army—but exactly how many points would it take? According to the current issue of *Stars and Stripes*, "The Army said that the first men with eighty-five points or more would start for separation centers next week, and also that it might be possible for a soldier with fewer than eighty-five points to get out."

Stars and Stripes noted with amusement that the Adjusted Service Rating Card could thus turn into either a soldier's "Trip Ticket Home" or a "T.S. ['tough shit,' or more delicately 'tough situation'] Slip," and warned that the cards must be "checked by YOU before they're sent in. Before you sign the card, make sure your time in service, time overseas, and number of children are correct—and make sure all your awards are entered." The Army froze a soldier's point total on May 12, 1945, a date designated as "R-Day" or "Readjustment Day"; a GI just short of eighty-five points, therefore, would truly be in a "T.S." quandary, since no one could accumulate any more points after that day, with the exception that the Army would eventually award one more five-point campaign star to those men who had participated in the conquest of Germany from the Rhineland to the Elbe.

Holders of the Medal of Honor who wished to be discharged from the Army would be permitted to do so regardless of point totals, but by May 1945, only one 29er—the 175th's S/Sgt. Sherwood Hallman—had been granted that exalted decoration, and he was dead. Similarly, enlisted men age forty-two or older who desired a discharge would be granted it even if they lacked eighty-five points— but the 29th Division had only a handful of such men. As strange as it seemed to most 29ers, some enlisted men wished to remain in uniform and make the Army a career; Maj. Gen. William Tompkins, head of the Special Planning Commission

Trip Ticket Home—or TS Slip

ADJUSTED SERVICE RATING CARD

NAME ESTOFF   WILLIAM   T.   ASN 32491687   ARM or SERVICE Engrs.

UNIT 999th Combat Engr Bn.   MOS

TYPE OF CREDIT :	NUMBER	MULTIPLY BY	CREDITS
1. SERVICE CREDIT — Number of months in Army since 16 Sep 40	40	1	40
2 OVERSEA CREDIT — Number of months served overseas since 16 Sep 40	26	1	26
3. COMBAT CREDIT — Number of decorations and Bronze Service Stars since 16 Sep 40	4	5	20
4. PARENTHOOD CREDIT — Number of children under 18 years old	2	12	24

TOTAL CREDITS   110

W.D., A.G.O. Form No. 163.

Here's sample of card which is Step One of the long voyage home. Cards are to be filled out by personnel offices and checked by YOU before they're sent in. Before you sign the card, make sure your time in service, time overseas, and number of children are correct, and make sure all your awards are en'ered.

An Adjusted Service Rating Card, as introduced to the GIs by a May 1945 edition of *Stars and Stripes*.

on Marshall's War Department Special Staff and the prime architect of the discharge plan, affirmed that if they had a "satisfactory record," they would be retained in the postwar Army.

The discharge scheme for officers, according to the War Department, would be "tougher than the plan for enlisted personnel, primarily because officers have received additional training, have heavier responsibilities, and have developed specialized skills and the capacity of leadership." Although officers would be allotted point scores according to the same method as enlisted men, Tompkins asserted: "The return of officers to the United States will be controlled by theater commanders. . . . [but] if an officer is declared surplus by his theater commander, he may still be retained if he is needed by a unit of the Army Air Forces, Army Ground Forces, or Army Service Forces." That obfuscatory language boiled down to the fact that the U.S. Army could retain officers indefinitely even if they had amassed eighty-five or more points.

On May 15, the War Department provided an addendum to the discharge plan that listed forty-one Military Occupational Specialties (MOS); if a soldier held one of those MOS, he would not be eligible for demobilization regardless of how many points he had. Speakers of Asiatic languages, marine engineers, diesel and radar mechanics, telephone and radio repairmen, teletype operators, telephone and telegraph linemen, telephone switchboard operators, and cryptographers, among many other specialties, would evidently be needed in the Pacific for the impending invasion of Japan. Fortunately for the 29ers, only a handful of GIs among the 14,000-plus men currently in the division held those MOS.

Most 29ers had to admit that the enlisted men's discharge method was fair, a sentiment corroborated by a May 12 stateside newspaper editorial: "[The plan] seems to satisfy most of the men in uniform, and that is the most important point." Tompkins remarked that the rules "will apply equally to soldiers all over the world, and they embody the desires of the soldiers themselves as expressed in polls taken by the War Department among thousands of enlisted men in this country and overseas. More than 90 percent of the men interviewed said they believed the men to be released first should be those who had been overseas and in combat longest, and those with children. . . . Men with combat experience make up a little over one-third of the Army but constitute nearly three-quarters of the number to be released. Fathers represent 19 percent of the Army and 26 percent of the group returning to civilian life."

Nothing the Army did could fail to produce plenty of naysayers, a point acknowledged in a blunt Army report that declared: "A small and perhaps irreducible minority of men . . . are so disaffected in general that they probably would complain about any plan which did not release them at once." One of those disaffected men wrote to his senator that the plan was "a long ways from being fair. This is not only my opinion, but almost every GI you talk to, so when you read that old baloney about it is the way the GIs wanted it, then it burns you up, as I have not yet run into a GI that was ever asked before the point system went into effect."

A 29er's satisfaction or disenchantment with the discharge plan of course depended on whether the Army had credited him with eighty-five points or more. President Roosevelt had activated the 29th Division on February 3, 1941, and any Maryland, Virginia, and District of Columbia National Guard members or pre–Pearl Harbor draftees who had been a part of that mobilization and had served continuously in the division since were assured of discharge: their point credits for months in service and months overseas were close to eighty-five, and five points for each of the 29th Division's three (soon to be four) officially credited campaigns—Normandy, Northern France, and the Rhineland (Central Germany would soon be added)—provided another fifteen, more than enough to put them over the eighty-five point goal even if they had no decorations and no children. However, combat and other forms of attrition over four-plus years had caused the number of such long-service men, especially in the infantry, to dwindle to paltry numbers.

Similarly, men drafted in 1942 who joined the 29th Division in the States or in England, and who later participated in the D-Day invasion and all four of the division's subsequent European campaigns, were likely to have amassed sufficient points for discharge, although they may have needed one or more Purple Hearts or other medals to put them above eighty-five points. Men conscripted in 1943 or 1944, however, were unlikely to reach eighty-five, even if they joined the 29th Division in England prior to D-Day and stuck with the division from Omaha Beach to the Elbe River. For example, a 29er drafted in June 1943 who joined the 29th Division in England in March 1944 would have twenty-four points for service time, fifteen for overseas service, and twenty for the 29th's four European campaigns—a total of fifty-nine points. He could break the eighty-five barrier only if he was the father of three or held six decorations—or any other combination of fatherhood and awards credits totaling at least twenty-six—but not many 29ers in May 1945 could count on such a large number of supplemental points, especially given the 29th Division's well-known reputation for stinginess in the matter of combat medals.

A 29er who fell just a handful of points shy of eighty-five could hardly be blamed for wondering if inequities in the system would thwart his prompt discharge. As a member of a division that had suffered more than 20,000 casualties in eleven months of nearly continuous combat, at first glance some of those inequities seemed flagrantly biased against the front-line soldiers who had borne the brunt of the battle. Aside from an infantryman's greater likelihood of collecting five points for a Purple Heart or combat decoration, a rear-echelon GI who had never been within thirty miles of the front accumulated points identically to a rifleman. "What gripes me," one irritated 29er wrote, "is that combat time—and I mean combat where the shells are flying and men are dying—doesn't count for a tinker's damn. Oh, yes—five points for each battle star; but even the SOS [Services of Supply] can get them. . . . But those poor doughs [infantrymen]! What chance have they got? They don't live long enough to pile up points."

In October 1943, the Army had acknowledged the infantryman's key wartime role by establishing the Combat Infantryman's Badge (CIB), an award that front-line soldiers valued highly, featuring a musket framed inside a blue rectangle and encased in a wreath of oak leaves. Only infantrymen—the men Ernie Pyle had labeled the "mud, rain, frost, and wind boys"—could gain that exalted badge, which drew plenty of respectful stares while on leave and entitled the owners to an extra ten dollars per month. Then why, 29th Division infantrymen wondered, did the discharge system grant no points for the CIB, the one and only award that symbolized the U.S. Army branch that suffered by far the most combat deaths during World War II? Even General Eisenhower reportedly favored bestowing five points to men who held it. If so, Ike's recommendation was overruled; to grant five points to infantrymen for their CIBs, Tompkins's commission decided, while snubbing other men who served routinely in the front lines—medics, artillery forward observers, combat engineers, tank and tank destroyer crews—would be unfair to the other branches.

Another sore point: the 29th Division had played a vital role in Operation *Overlord* on June 6, 1944, which the War Department had officially recognized by allowing the division's D-Day veterans to affix an "assault arrowhead" icon on their European-African-Middle Eastern campaign ribbons. The prestige imparted by that tiny arrowhead was out of all proportion to its one-quarter-inch size, for it established at a glance that the wearer had landed on Omaha Beach in the most crucial operation of World War II. Yet the War Department did not allot any points at all to a 29er who proudly wore the arrowhead, while a campaign star for Normandy was worth five points even for a replacement who had joined the 29th Division weeks after D-Day.

The discharge plan's twelve-point credit per child—roughly two and a half times the value of a combat medal—rankled many 29ers who had no children. "Twelve points for a no-good brat," a 29er griped. "Sure, give points for children, but for heaven's sake why should they count more (and so much more) than combat time?" The same 29er noted in a letter home that he had sixty-one points, adding that "an SOS (son of a b——) who had the same thing . . . who hadn't even smelled powder or got within twenty miles of the front lines, but who had two kids, would go home and I wouldn't, even though I've been in combat for ten months, and he was as safe as in his wife's or mother's arms. . . . Fair? The Army says so."

With the initiation of the large-scale discharge plan, the U.S. Army could no longer sustain sixty-one divisions in Eisenhower's command, so the War Department formulated a redeployment scheme that assigned each of Ike's divisions to one of four categories. Category I, as the War Department proclaimed, included "those units to be retained as occupational troops." Category II encompassed those units scheduled for transfer to the United States for eventual deployment to the Pacific; Category III incorporated divisions to be "converted or reorganized"; and Category IV absorbed all divisions designated for deactivation.

Ike assigned the 29th Division to Category I, indicating that the imminent occupation of the Bremen Enclave would be for the long haul. However, with so many long-service combat veterans on its rolls, many of whom possessed more than eighty-five points, the 29th Division would soon be so severely depopulated that it obviously could not carry out its vital occupation duties. The brass intended to solve that predicament by pairing the 29th with a Category IV division, the 69th, marked for shipment home and prompt deactivation. According to that plan, the 29th Division's high-point men would be transferred to the 69th and corresponding numbers of low-point GIs from the 69th would be shifted to the 29th. When that process began at some indefinite date in the future, old-time 29ers grasped that their division's distinctive spirit must inevitably dissipate; it would surely mark the end of a storied era in 29th Division history. Such a huge influx of new men could not possibly absorb the strict directives of the "29th Division Bible": the chinstrap rule, the "correct sight picture" for aiming a rifle, hands out of pockets, the prohibition on rain covers on vehicles, the proper disposal of cigarette butts, "I don't know, but I'll find out," and of course the sacred motto, "29, Let's Go!"

Happily, whatever fate lay in store for the 29ers would apparently be considerably safer than combat. How long the GIs would have to wait for the Army to sort out the demobilization process was anyone's guess, but in the meantime, as a 29th Division report noted, "Whenever two or more men got as close together as shouting distance," they inquired: "How many points do *you* have?"

ILLUSIONS MAKE ME IMPREGNABLE

The 29th Division could carry out grand military reviews as well as any outfit in the U.S. Army, but nothing the 29ers had ever done on a parade ground could match the resplendent victory parade put on by the British Army's 51st Highland Division in Bremerhaven in May 1945 upon the turnover of the Bremen Enclave to the Americans. The 51st had been in combat far longer than the 29th: in October 1942, when the 29ers had only just begun to settle into their new English bivouacs, the 51st Division launched a pivotal attack in the turning-point battle at El Alamein. The Highlanders then fought across the sands of North Africa all the way to Tunisia, partook in the July 1943 Sicily invasion, landed in Normandy as part of Operation *Overlord*, and battled across France and the Low Countries into northern Germany, ending the war in Bremerhaven.

The 51st's massed pipes and drums, amounting to more than a hundred pipers and sixty drummers dressed in Ike jackets, Tam O'Shanters, regimental kilts adorned with sporrans, and knee-high hose, led the parade with a rousing pipe march, wheeling right and halting near the reviewing stand to provide music for the rest of the Highlanders to pass in review. Then came the infantry: the storied regiments such as the Black Watch and Gordon Highlanders, whose immaculate troops marched past in impeccable cadence and alignment to regimental marches like "Highland Laddie" and "Cock o' the North," as the Jocks flaunted an inspiring military comportment that cloaked their war weariness.

The 29th Division's 116th Infantry had trickled into Bremerhaven over the past few days to relieve the British, and its 2nd Battalion under Lt. Col. Lawrence Meeks turned out in force to participate in the parade. PFC Arden Earll of Company H, however, recalled that the Yanks found it difficult to muster the Tommies' impressive martial demeanor. "We had not practiced close-order drill very much," he recalled, "and compared to them we didn't put on a very good show." With their minds on Adjusted Service Rating Cards and point totals, a little slackness was understandable; the 29ers might be out of uniform within a few weeks. Besides, even with practice it would have been hard to match the British: when General Patton had watched an Allied victory parade in Tunis in May 1943, he observed that the British "understand the art of ceremonial marching. . . . There was one sergeant-major who should be immortalized in a painting. He typified all that is great in the British non-commissioned officer, and he certainly knew it. I have never seen a man strut more."

Gerhardt's men may have been indifferent strutters, but the general doggedly resolved that the 29th Division's last mission in World War II would be carried out without blemish. The 115th Infantry and 121st Engineers had begun the move to Bremen on May 6, but the rest of the 29th Division had to wait in its camps around Münster for a week before Ninth Army finally ordered Gerhardt to relocate his men to the Enclave. Letter of Instruction 120 noted that "Task Force Bremen [as the reinforced 29th Division was labeled] would initiate the relief of the elements of British XXX Corps in the Enclave Military District, that the relief would be conducted progressively from south to north, and that it would be completed by May 25." The 115th Infantry, which already occupied Bremen, would remain there and would be joined by division headquarters; the 175th Infantry would occupy a considerably larger area on the east side of the Weser River between Bremen and Bremerhaven; the 116th would take charge of Bremerhaven and the adjacent coastal belt to the north along the North Sea; the 29th Division's four artillery battalions would garrison the area west of the Weser.

That thirty-five-mile stretch of the Weser from Bremen to the river's mouth at Bremerhaven could handle more shipping than any German port except Hamburg. The U.S. Army commander of the Enclave's port facilities, Maj. Gen. Harry B. Vaughan, remarked that "nothing better than Bremerhaven had ever been dreamed of by the American port commanders." Ocean-going vessels could dock at Bremerhaven's nineteen deep-draft wharves, which *Baltimore Sun* reporter Philip Whitcomb noted "surpassed anything found in other ports the American Army has yet used." Indeed, berthed at one of Bremerhaven's nineteen docks when the Americans arrived was SS *Europa*, a 50,000-ton Norddeutscher Lloyd Company ocean liner placed in service in 1930 that once held the record for the fastest trans-Atlantic crossing; soon it would be returned to service to convey American servicemen home from Europe. Whitcomb also observed that Bremerhaven possessed the "world's largest floating cranes [and] complete equipment for handling refrigerated goods, wheat, or coal." True, the silted-up Weser must be dredged and swept of mines, but when that work was completed, Whitcomb concluded, "the endless wrangling with French workers and authorities [at French ports] . . . is almost ended. The Germans don't dare to squabble. If things continue the way they have begun, the Germans will work and like it."

The upriver port facilities at Bremen handled lighter-draft vessels and canal barges and included elevators capable of handling as much as 70,000 tons of grain. Much more significant to Hitler, however, had been Bremen's vast capacity for war production, which made it a primary target of Anglo-American bombing raids over a period of nearly five years. Three different Bremen shipyards had produced 252 U-boats for war service; three aircraft factories had manufactured hundreds of Focke-Wulf 190 fighters; other plants had churned out tanks and trucks; and refineries scattered alongside the Weser purified oil. By the time the Americans arrived in May 1945, all of those production centers had ceased to exist.

Beyond Bremerhaven and Bremen, one 29er described the lowlands on both sides of the Weser "as level as a table top"; another depicted the region as "a flat country of small towns and small farms," adding that the land bordering the Weser had been "reclaimed by the maze of drainage ditches that crisscrossed it." According to Howard Norton, a *Baltimore Sun* scribe accompanying the 29th Division into Bremen, in the rural areas outside the city "the water level is just eighteen inches below the surface." Nevertheless, the 29ers noticed that, despite the obvious ravages of war throughout the region, the countryside was highly productive. In another *Sun* article, Whitcomb noted that "the section from Bremen to Hamburg was mixed wheat and cattle country. The cattle were numerous and the wheat in fine condition."

The British handed over control of the Enclave to Gerhardt on May 20, but five more days passed before the 29th Division relieved the last British and Canadian garrisons. In addition to his own division, Gerhardt's considerably augmented command now took in twenty-five supplementary units, including military government detachments, bomb disposal squads, a searchlight battery, an ambulance company, an entire evacuation hospital, and even an eight-man dental prosthetic detachment to manufacture false teeth. Gerhardt had to coordinate his activities with three other major commands also operating within the Enclave: the Bremen Port Command, the U.S. Navy's Task Force 126, and Air Task Force Bremen. Gerhardt's instructions mandated that naval and air matters within the Enclave must be left to the other commanders, while his own 29ers handled security, established military government, disarmed German prisoners, hunted down Nazis, and cared for displaced persons. Those missions became considerably more difficult when 1,000 high-point 29ers were dispatched home for demobilization just a few days after the 29th Division took over the Bremen Enclave.

The 29th Division faced an acute challenge. True, compared to battling German *Fallschirmjäger* in the Norman hedgerows, the Bremen mission was a cinch; but how could 13,000 war-weary 29ers hope to govern a 1,400-square-mile zone populated by more than 630,000 bewildered, pathetic, and famished inhabitants, many of whom supposedly remained intractable Nazis? The Germans were no longer the 29ers' enemies; would the GIs now behave as condescending conquerors or benevolent benefactors? The problem, as Secretary of War Henry Stimson told President Truman, was that "Germany has created, and twice misused, a swollen war industry—one substantially beyond her peaceful needs. . . . Certain physical steps can and should be taken to hamper the regrowth of her industrial capacity to more than reasonable peacetime needs. On the other hand, from the point of view of general European recovery, it seems even more important that the area again be made useful and productive. . . . While it is our object to disarm Germany, it should not be our purpose to make it impossible for the German people to live and work. We should not remove their capacity for aiding in the restoration of stable conditions in Europe and the world. . . . The problem which presents itself therefore is how to render Germany harmless as a potential aggressor, and at the same time enable her to play her part in the necessary rehabilitation of Europe."

The 29ers had endured many senseless Army directives over the years, but none struck them as more absurd than the non-fraternization policy. That injunction prohibited the GIs from speaking or socializing with German civilians—even children—except on official business and authorized hefty fines for even minor offenses. Every 29er had recently received a brown leaflet on stiff cardstock with a facsimile of Gen. Omar Bradley's signature, warning the troops "never to trust

Germans, collectively or individually," "to defeat German efforts to poison my thoughts or influence my attitude," and finally to "never associate with Germans." Flagrant violations of non-fraternization rules, such as "cohabitation" with German women or conducting clandestine business deals with civilians, could result in courts-martial; those found guilty would be confined in a stockade with reduction in rank and near-total loss of pay. Even general officers were not immune: in one bizarre case, three notable U.S. Army generals were found to have "engaged in friendly contact" after V-E Day with the aged Prussian icon Field Marshal Gerd von Rundstedt, in violation of the non-fraternization policy, although the Army did not impose a punishment.

A mindless adherence to the non-fraternization policy, the 29ers presumed, would prolong the ordeal faced by the subjugated and downtrodden German civilians within the Bremen Enclave and seriously complicate the 29th Division's efforts to rehabilitate them by getting them back to work. On May 5, a U.S. Army colonel who had just completed a two-week inspection tour of Germany's occupied areas concluded in a report to Ike's headquarters that "a non-fraternization policy anywhere with any people with whom we are not at war will appear

The Allies' non-fraternization policy prohibited GIs from speaking with German civilians. U.S. ARMY SIGNAL CORPS

childish, senseless, and in a very short time all of us will be ashamed that we ever behaved in such a manner. . . . Germany's military power is destroyed. The Nazi Party is dead. More than 20 million Germans are homeless or without adequate shelter. The average basic ration is less than 1,000 calories."

More than a month passed after V-E Day before Ike modified the non-fraternization policy, but even then the change was limited to revoking the ban on American interactions with German juveniles. On July 14, 1945, nearly ten weeks after the German surrender, Eisenhower finally proclaimed that "it is believed desirable and timely to permit personnel of my command to engage in conversation with adult Germans on the streets and in public places."

But the victorious 29ers and the vanquished locals evidently would need plenty of time to overlook the fact that they were recently mortal enemies. For the Germans, tolerance of their conquerors would be difficult, as the 29th Division still held the godlike authority to shove homeowners out of their residences to provide comfortable housing for the troops. A member of the 29th Military Police Platoon, PFC Ugo Giannini, wrote to his brother that "the Germans regard American MPs as SS troopers. I certainly won't break down and laugh—their illusions make me impregnable." Lieutenant Easton noted in a June 1945 letter to his wife, "The dereliction here is ghastly: husbandless women, fatherless children, people without houses, men returning from prison camps to find both house and family gone." He concluded: "It is a dreadful horror, actually, and yet in the streets the life of everyday goes on."

Two days after Ike had lifted the non-fraternization ban, a *New York Times* reporter observed that "there were a lot more Germans fraternizing with Germans than with Americans. Furthermore, there were as many Americans not fraternizing as there were fraternizing. There was no sign of any concerted effort by German femininity to beguile the GIs ideologically or otherwise . . . [despite] the traditionally high-powered American overtures." Another reporter in Berlin noted on the same day that citizens of that city, just like every other devastated locale in Germany, "were too preoccupied searching for food, clothing, and a place to live to care much whether [American] troops talked to them. Fraternization seemed like a minor problem."

In Bremerhaven, Easton noted, "You can't organize Americanism into a program and impose it. It must be learned day by day as people casually intermingle." Months could pass before effortless social interactions between the 29ers and the Germans became the norm. But in the 115th's occupation zone in and around Bremen, Johns's 1st Battalion tried to spark some "intermingling" in July 1945, and it worked beautifully. Johns wrote: "The first organized, officially sanctioned dance with GIs and German Fräuleins was held three days after the fraternization ban was lifted in the 'GI Joe's' pavilion at Vegesack [a Bremen suburb twelve miles north of the city]. This erstwhile beer hall had been taken over by the 1st Battalion and made into an enormous club for enlisted men, before any such clubs were installed for officers. The crack 1st Battalion dance band, 'Big Red's Low Pointers,' played every night, relieved occasionally by a German fourteen-piece orchestra that had played in the pavilion in more peaceful times. The battalion's special service officer, 1st Lt. David [actually Daniel] Inskeep, arranged for free beer, served by some forty-odd German waiters, and up to 10:00 P.M. each evening the men of the battalion and nearby units had all the fun of a nightclub with none of the expense. Then, when the dancing started, they really had themselves a time, as dancing was permitted four times weekly."

Presently, the Fräuleins were seen with the 29ers at many places besides dance halls. A member of the 115th Infantry observed that "the most famous, or infamous, meeting place during the summer months, was the beautiful Bürger-park, not far from the 2nd Battalion's area. The weather was consistently mild, the park was big, the girls were numerous and willing, and with a D-bar [a U.S. Army emergency chocolate ration] or a few cigarettes, a soldier could get anything he wanted." Fraternization of that kind continued to flourish throughout the summer of 1945 despite occasional handbills that appeared on walls over-night, affixed by ex-German servicemen, providing a warning "to German girls who associate with American soldiers that their heads will be shaved."

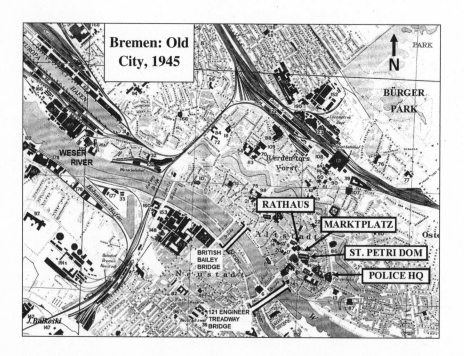

The Bremen locals had feared retribution from their conquerors, but in comparison with the tales of horror emerging from the east in areas of Germany occupied by the Red Army, the Germans eventually learned that the overwhelming majority of the 29ers did not have malice in their hearts. In the summer of 1945, 1st Lt. Malvin Walker of the 115th Infantry's Company L, a twenty-four-year-old native of Indianapolis who had landed on D-Day and suffered two wounds since, learned that getting the natives' minds off the war and finding common interests with their occupiers could help bring both sides together. An expert cello player and graduate of an Indianapolis music conservatory, Walker learned in June that the Bremen Philharmonic Orchestra was seeking permission from the U.S. Army to perform again. In 1943, the Nazis had forced the orchestra's well-known conductor, Hellmut Schnackenburg, to resign after he had refused to play the Nazi anthem, the "Horst Wessel Song," and subsequently led several performances of music written by Jewish composers such as Felix Mendelssohn and Gustav Mahler. The U.S. Army reinstalled Schnackenburg as conductor in July, and with Walker's unwavering assistance, brought together as many top-notch players as they could to begin rehearsals.

Schnackenburg decided on Johannes Brahms's *Ein Deutsches Requiem* (*A German Requiem*) for the Bremen Philharmonic's grand opening performance, which would take place in Bremen's eleventh-century *St. Petri Dom* (St. Peter's Cathedral). Both the composition and the location held profound meaning to Bremen residents, as Brahms himself had conducted the premiere of that piece in that very cathedral on April 10, 1868, an event that his good friend Clara Schumann wrote "has moved me as no other." The Bremen audience approved of the 1868 premiere so heartily that a Brahms biographer observed that the *Requiem* "marked a watershed for his bank account as well as for his fame."

The 115th Infantry's 1st Lt. Malvin Walker, shown here before his entry into the Army, helped to reinstate the Bremen Philharmonic Orchestra after World War II.

Allied bombing had scarred the cathedral, but the site was sufficiently sacred in Bremen's musical history that Schnackenburg did not dare seek an alternate site for the grand opening. The premiere went over so well with Germans and 29ers alike that Walker later remarked, "The part of my World War II military career I was most proud of was my effort to help bring the Bremen Philharmonic back together for its opening performance of Brahms."

St. Peter's Cathedral and the adjacent *Rathaus* (City Hall), a magnificent sixteenth-century Gothic edifice in front of which stood the renowned 1404 limestone statue of the Frankish hero Roland, framed an expansive *Marktplatz* (Market Square) that had been the center of municipal life in Bremen for centuries. During the interminable summer evenings of 1945—darkness did not fall over Bremen in June and July until after 11:00 P.M.—jaded Germans, overwhelmingly males, gathered in the *Marktplatz* and traded rumors. Some of those rumors alarmed the locals and, true or not, they occasionally provoked anger among the multitudes. The Americans and British were already fighting the Russians along the Elbe; the "Amis" were about to draft German males to fight the Soviets; the Red Army was about to take over the Bremen Enclave; the Russians would be allowed to seize German women for their brothels. "The rumors passed quickly," Ewing wrote, "from the *Frau* who did the soldier laundry, to the bake shop and grocery, and then, in an increasingly fast and broadening current, to the stores and bars and railroad stations and to other parts of the Enclave."

One evening, 1st Lt. Robert Henne of the 115th Infantry observed a "stuttering and shit-scared" major stagger into the 2nd Battalion office to announce that 10,000 Germans were rioting in the *Marktplatz*; Henne was to collect a nearby rifle company immediately and proceed to the square to investigate. Henne did so and found that the major's story was exaggerated, but not by much. In the square, Henne spoke with a dejected civilian, a former officer, who explained that the Germans would never stand for conscription to fight an Anglo-American war against the Russians, as the latest rumor hinted. The "riot" boiled over only after repeated American denials that such an idea existed.

With the Americans holding a near-total monopoly on weaponry and ammunition within the Enclave, even hordes of irate Germans could not have hoped to accomplish anything with violence. The 29ers ensured that they would maintain that monopoly by conducting random, unannounced house-to-house searches for illicit weapons. "Search parties unearthed a few unauthorized arms and ammunition caches, mostly shotguns, hunting rifles, and a few shells," Cooper reported. "In all such matters the civilian population was docile and cooperative."

Yet the Anglo-American high command worried incessantly that a clandestine German partisan movement would eventually arise, triggering a swelling wave of sabotage and even overt attacks against Allied troops and installations.

As late as November 1945, an anxious Eisenhower warned that Germany was "just one step" away from initiating an organized resistance movement. Ike's report to Washington, according to a November 1 *Times* article, noted that "groups of idle German youths and returning German soldiers were becoming increasingly and dangerously restless and were being watched closely for any sign of organized resistance. [Eisenhower] reported that while some attacks had been made on individual American soldiers [none were reported against 29ers], the activity of the German youths consisted mainly of distributing handbills and posters warning 'faithless' German girls who were fraternizing with Americans and displaced persons." In the event the Germans triggered any problems within the Enclave, Gerhardt ordered that each battalion in the 29th Division must maintain one company or battery on alert, fully armed and ready to travel on short notice to any spot where trouble might be brewing. Furthermore, U.S. Army rules for the occupation mandated that all American troops on duty must be armed at all times.

On June 4 a catastrophe occurred in Bremen that seemed to confirm Eisenhower's worst fears. At 11:00 that morning a massive explosion demolished the four-story *Polizeipräsidium* (police headquarters) in the heart of the city, killing thirty-five people, including four Americans, and causing windows to rattle in buildings ten miles away. Most of the 500 people working in the building were German, but the workforce also included two dozen American "G-men in khaki" from the counterintelligence corps and several other GIs from a military government contingent. "Two walls facing the building's inner courtyard collapsed in a burning heap of debris, engulfing nearly a dozen military vehicles parked there," a June 5 *Baltimore Sun* article reported. "[The building] was shattered as though it had been struck by a blockbuster [aerial bomb] . . . and confiscated German ammunition which had been stored in a ground-floor room continued to explode for half an hour." Based on the comments of surviving Americans, the reporter speculated that the disaster was an act of sabotage "caused by a delayed-action bomb—the Germans are known to have developed demolition charges with fuses delayed up to sixty-four days." Ten days later, however, a report drawn up by the German police concluded that the blast was not an act of terror, but an accident caused by "a slow gas leak [and] an accumulation of gas."

The 29ers suspected that Bremen harbored plenty of sullen young men capable of such a heinous act of sabotage. Those former members of the *Hitler Jugend* (Hitler Youth), according to Ewing, were "moulded in the Nazi philosophy since kindergarten days—[they] carried arrogance in their faces as they stood about sullenly on street corners throughout the Enclave. There was contempt in their eyes for the occupation forces." One of the only overt acts of sabotage occurred in late May when someone cut several gaps through a barbed wire perimeter in the 116th's zone. The 29ers could not fathom the purpose of that deed, but according to the 29th Division's monthly summary for May 1945, it was the type of action that "was taught in the *Hitler Jugend* schools." Bingham's 29ers strove to crack down firmly on the perpetrators, but "several possible suspects were investigated and interrogated with negative results." Gerhardt insisted that "German civil officials were made accountable for any recurrence of this incident, and the investigation was continued to determine the source of the acts." That investigation, however, fizzled out within a few weeks, and the guilty parties were never found.

In Bremen, a couple of 115th Infantry GIs teamed up with a U.S. Navy intelligence team that held an abiding interest in German U-boats. Bremen had been a major center of U-boat construction—dozens of unfinished boats still moldered in its shipyards—and the Navy men wondered whether they could pick up some secrets from a close examination of the battered submarine works. Lt. Bill Holberton recalled: "Sergeant [Warren] Rifenbark [a twenty-six-year-old Marylander who had been one of the first draftees to join the 29th Division in early 1941] and I loaded up with plastic explosives, detonators, primacord, and anything else we thought we would need. We met the naval personnel and then proceeded to blast a path of open safes, strongrooms, vaults, and so forth in the submarine works. We enjoyed it and jokingly suggested that perhaps we were preparing for a civilian life of crime. We spent about two days with the Navy in this work."

One summer evening a tragic incident unfolded outside the Liberty Theater in downtown Bremen when a few dozen GIs emerged after watching a film. A 29er, described by a witness as "very aggressive," swaggered down the sidewalk and bumped into two German boys, about fifteen years old, coming from the opposite direction. The GI angrily shoved the teens off the sidewalk into the street, an action that induced one of the boys to pull a P-38 pistol from his pocket and aim it at his tormenter. It was a fatal gesture: Lieutenant Henne observed that the unfortunate teen "was promptly shot about thirty times" by nearby 29ers. "When we examined the P-38," Henne recalled, "the firing pin had been removed, so it couldn't fire."

Standing orders within the Enclave prescribed the "automatic arrest" of all persons who had been members of the SS, Gestapo, or German General Staff (even non-Nazis), as well as senior civil servants, paramilitary officers, suspected war criminals, and Nazi Party officials. Most of those people, however, had disappeared, and if the 29ers hoped to root them out from their hiding places, accurate intelligence provided by willing local residents would be a necessity. The typical German male brought in for interrogation, a 29er wrote, "denied with vigor that he was or ever had been a Nazi. The people next door were Nazi, however, and the people up the street, but the German with whom you spoke was rarely, if ever, a party member. Actual non-party members were quick to report their party neighbors . . . thereby releasing their pent-up urge to deliver retribution to their former Nazi rulers. These voluntary informers were of considerable help to the division, whose CIC [counterintelligence] teams were combing the Enclave for 'big Nazis' and Germans in the 'automatic arrest' category." According to the 29th Division's June 1945 monthly report, "A total of 387 arrests were made [in June], of which 37 were arrests of Gestapo members, 23 *Sicherheitsdienst* [the Nazi Party's intelligence arm], 10 *Abwehr* [the German military intelligence branch], 18 war criminals, 45 *Bundschuh* [an underground cell of young Bremen males who supposedly would carry out guerrilla operations], and 254 who were in 'automatic arrest' categories." The report concluded: "Although the total figure is fairly high, there were no persons of outstanding interest taken, the most important arrest perhaps being that of one Dr. Alfred Vaatz, an expert on the construction of V-1 jet bombs."

Some of the more pragmatic German residents of the Enclave, who grasped that Nazi Germany was dead and would never rise again, tried to ingratiate themselves with their American occupiers. As the senior American officer within the Bremen Enclave, Gerhardt learned how far some locals would go to please him when in late May he established the 29th Division's command post in a former Luftwaffe barracks in Grohn, described as "the most modern and elaborate headquarters it had ever occupied in either Europe or the United States. Paved roads, concrete walks, spacious lawns, and well-kept hedges lent the Grohn Barracks the appearance of a college campus"—which in 1999 it would become. Maj. Albert Hoffman of the division staff depicted the setup as "the most comfortable place I've been since leaving the U.S." Grohn was just a short walk from Vegesack, the attractive Bremen suburb whose shipyards had churned out seventy-four U-boats during World War II.

By the time Gerhardt arrived at Grohn, the citizens of Vegesack had already begun the protracted process of restoring their city. Carefully scrutinized by U.S. Army military government officers to ensure no Nazis would regain positions of power, Vegesack had established an effective city council that met regularly to ponder how to work most effectively with their American masters. The council's "most active and visible member," according to Maj. Robert Walker, the 29th Division's chief military government officer, was Vegesack's police chief. "He was a caricature of authority," Walker observed, "but always willing to cooperate and do whatever could be done for the 29th Division. I was told by our Headquarters Company CO that the police chief had sponsored a resolution in the council for renaming a couple of thoroughfares in Vegesack in honor of important American officers. The resolution passed. The main boulevard was to be named 'General Gerhardt Strasse,' and the road leading from the boulevard to the division headquarters building was to be renamed 'Major Walker Strasse.' Painted signs were duly made and posted. Within a day or two, the 'Major Walker Strasse' sign was noted by General Gerhardt himself while traveling in his jeep from Bremen to Vegesack. 'Who put those signs up there?' he demanded. Upon learning of the city council's action, he abruptly said, 'Take 'em down!' The general was told that his own name had been posted on the beautiful landscaped boulevard running through Vegesack, but he quickly said, 'Take 'em all down!' And there ended Vegesack's effort to honor Americans with street names."

A few weeks later, the 29th Division's chief of staff, Lt. Col. Louis Smith, passed a letter on to Walker from the mayor of Bremen. According to the mayor, a priceless oriental carpet that had graced his office in the *Rathaus* for years was gone, no one knew where. Did any 29th Division soldiers know where it was, and if so, could it be promptly returned? Walker took immediate steps to investigate, as he noticed that Gerhardt had scribbled at the top of the mayor's letter: "1. What happened to the rug? 2. Where is it? 3. Steps taken for its return." Shortly thereafter, the 29th Division Headquarters Company commander, Capt. Frederick Johnston, approached Walker and inquired: "You want to know where the rug is? The general's desk is sitting on it!"

Walker recalled: "I laughed uproariously; he didn't. I told him to do nothing more unless he heard from me. Then I told the story to [Colonel Smith], who told me, 'Do nothing more.' The rug, I heard, was quickly returned to the grateful German mayor. No one ever mentioned it again."

On June 14, 1945, the 29th Division and all other Ninth Army units were transferred to Lt. Gen. Wade Haislip's U.S. Seventh Army when the War Department shipped General Simpson and his Ninth Army staff home to prepare for deployment to the Pacific. Gerhardt, who had developed a close relationship with Simpson over nearly nine months of severe combat, probably would have preferred to accompany Ninth Army if it meant a continuation of active campaigning. He would not develop nearly as close a rapport with Haislip, whose Seventh Army headquarters at Heidelberg was over 300 miles south of the Bremen Enclave. Happily, that lengthy distance hinted that Gerhardt for the most part would not be troubled by meddlesome Seventh Army staff officers.

At 4:30 A.M. on July 21, the 29th Division carried out an ambitious operation code-named *Tally Ho*, "designed as a security check to uncover black market activities, contraband, and to effect a meticulous check of the credentials of civilians and Allied military personnel." *Tally Ho* had been planned in secrecy for weeks, and the speed and intensity with which the GIs carried it out stunned the half-million residents of the Bremen Enclave impacted by it. The 29ers intended to check virtually every occupied residence within their zone, and before sunrise on the twenty-first, thousands of 29ers began pounding on doors to catch the locals by surprise. The perplexed residents received the "Amis" with drowsy stares, but the 29th's summary of the operation noted that, in general, "the populace was extremely cooperative and seemed to realize the necessity for the search." More than 1,600 Germans were detained for failure to carry proper identification papers, but of the hundreds of thousands of local residents questioned, only six "black market suspects" and two former SS men were arrested. A mere thirteen Germans were caught with illicit firearms. Also, sixty-one American GIs were picked up for various offenses, including possession of German weapons, AWOL status, and even "operation of unauthorized civilian cars under the influence of alcohol." Among the items of contraband confiscated by the 29ers were one can of grapefruit juice, one tin of corned beef, five cartons of cheese, two pairs of brass knuckles, one British Army uniform, fifteen radio transmitters, one GI field jacket, six books of Nazi propaganda, ten pounds of sugar, nine hundred pounds of salt, and forty-four *Panzerfaust* antitank weapons. One unfortunate civilian "was taken into custody when he could not explain a large stock of jewelry in his possession." According to a 29th Division report, "The behavior of the troops as they searched from house to house was uniformly excellent." Furthermore, concluded the account, "Although the operation uncovered no large stocks of contraband . . . the psychological effect alone [on the civilians] made it well worthwhile." In November 1945, an identical operation known as *Double-Check* was carried out with analogous results.

The 29th Division had more than enough firepower to suppress anyone who dared to challenge the U.S. Army's supremacy within the Bremen Enclave. However, Germany had changed so rapidly that during the last few episodes in the summer of 1945 in which the 29th Division employed that firepower, the intent was to defend Germans, not to kill them. Since the 29th had shifted to Bremen, the GIs had grasped that whenever the hordes of displaced persons—"DPs"—came into close proximity with German civilians, there would be trouble. With the European war at an end, the DPs—mostly Poles and Russians who had been worked nearly to death by the Nazis as slave laborers—were homeless; although the Allies cared for them and sought means for their repatriation, the ex-slaves carried an understandable hatred of everything German. The inevitable result, as Ike reported to the War Department, was that "cases of murder and organized looting occurred at an unpleasant rate." Housed in four teeming camps on the peripheries of Bremen and Bremerhaven, the DPs were at first subjected to a minimum of rules by the Americans, but as a *Baltimore Sun* reporter noted, "The German populace has become increasingly bitter as a result of the increased lawlessness," which reached such a low point in the summer that "after dark, maulings and knifings occurred in the shadows of the buildings and in the streets by the docks along the Weser River." Gerhardt realized that the situation, which the U.S. Army admitted had reached "serious proportions," could devolve into anarchy if the Americans continued to coddle the DPs.

"In an effort to curb these disorders," Ewing related, "three of the four [DP] camps were fenced in with barbed wire, and passes were issued on a regular military basis for those who wished to leave the enclosures." Still, some ruffians attacked a German man and his wife one night in Bremerhaven, and according to a 29er, the Americans engaged in "a short but furious battle with BARs and machine guns" against the DP outlaws—"the first of a long series of such skirmishes." Such "battles," of course, were entirely one-sided, as one party had an abundance of firearms and the other hardly any.

The 29ers also took drastic measures to prevent the DPs from obtaining liquor. At one vast storage tank of alcohol intended for industrial use, a 29er observed that the ex-slave laborers had appeared regularly "with bottles and buckets to carry it away"; the 175th Infantry put a stop to that by posting guards twenty-four hours per day. It took three months, but by late August 1945 the 29th Division's crackdown on the mayhem finally solved the problem. On August 26, a *Times* article noted: "Our latest report from Bremen is that the situation now is well in hand. [This] reflected a general reduction in crimes against German civilians throughout the U.S. occupation zone."

DISARMED ENEMY FORCES

On the evening of July 23, five shabby German cargo vessels—*Wesermarsch*, *Sardinien*, *Erpel*, *Nogat*, and *Warthe*—tied up to the Bremerhaven docks, watched intently from the quayside by a large contingent of 29ers from the 116th Infantry. More than 1,000 German prisoners of war were crammed into each vessel—a total of 5,345 men—the first batch of more than 180,000 Wehrmacht captives conveyed by the Allies back to the Fatherland from Norway, which had recently been freed from five years of Nazi occupation. Orders specified that the 29th Division "would be responsible for establishing a staging area and for guarding DEF [Disarmed Enemy Forces] on trains from the staging area to destinations in southern Germany and Austria." Delighted to be heading home at last, the Germans filed down the gangplanks in groups of 100 for the protracted identification checks and head counts to which they had become thoroughly accustomed in captivity. Still carrying themselves like military men, they formed up on the quay in orderly columns of three and tramped four miles north of town to an unused airfield on the banks of the Weser. There the Americans had established four camps, one of which was reserved for officers, and inside those barbed wire enclosures, under the vigilant guard of 29th Division men, the docile Germans would wait for trains to take them to U.S. Army reception stations near their homes so they could begin a new phase of their lives devoid of war.

World War II in Europe was over, and like it or not, the GIs of the 116th Infantry now must allow some compassion to creep into their psyches for men they only recently had striven to kill. "At the docks in Bremerhaven," a 29th Division report noted, "representatives from the 116th Infantry medical detachment met each ship to inspect all DEF onboard who had been declared sick by the ship's doctor. Those whose illness was of a serious nature were taken by ambulance to the hospital in Drangstedt [five miles east of the camps, where a hospital annex had been set up to receive ailing prisoners]. At the staging area a dispensary was maintained and operated by German medical personnel under the supervision of the surgeon, 116th Infantry. Medical and first aid supplies were always available. Sick call was held every morning and minor cases were treated at the dispensary."

A cadre of about thirty Germans stayed on at the camps for months to assist the 29ers in the onerous task of separating the captives into groups based on their ultimate destinations in Germany, Austria, or in a few cases Czechoslovakia. After detaining those in "automatic arrest" categories—hardly any of those were left—Germans who lived within the Bremen Enclave were trucked to one of three reception centers and, assuming all their papers were in order, promptly processed for discharge. Those living farther away had to remain in the staging area until 2,500 others, heading to the same destination, were grouped together for transportation by a train of immense length, in which each open gondola car carried fifty tightly packed passengers. (In the autumn, enclosed box cars were used instead, with a capacity of thirty-five men.) The Allies permitted Norwegian women married to German servicemen to accompany their husbands on the homeward journey, including those with young children and infants, a decision for which the downhearted couples were grateful: those unfortunate women would have been objects of contempt had they remained alone in Norway. In the staging areas, however, women and children were separated from the men "with screened latrines and washing facilities." The Americans also provided special train cars for the women, on which those with infants were permitted to take their perambulators.

Before departing camp for the train, parked on a siding just a few hundred yards away, the prisoners waited patiently in interminable lines to receive "discharge pay" from a German Army paymaster seated behind a table. Afterward, the German cadre sprayed their comrades with DDT insecticide to prevent the spread of malaria and typhus. Finally, in groups of fifty, the throng of prisoners, so heavily weighed down with personal belongings that they looked like an unending procession of hunchbacks, gladly plodded toward the siding to board the train that would take them one step closer to home.

As soon as the Germans hopped aboard the train, the 116th Infantry's guard mission ended and the 175th's began. Assigned to watch over the prisoners from Bremerhaven until the train reached its destination at a reception station, each

**When German servicemen were evacuated from Norway to Bremerhaven, they
were permitted to bring their wives (mostly Norwegians) and children. These
women are embarking on a train with their husbands for the final leg of the journey
to their new homes in Germany.**

train's forty-one-man guard platoon, fully armed and including one officer, was
outnumbered by more than sixty to one by the 2,500 captives, but the members of
the 175th correctly assumed that their herd, so eager to get the war over with,
would cause no trouble. The 29ers did not mix with their former opponents; five
boxcars—one in the front, one in the rear, and three interspersed among the rest of
the train—were reserved for the Americans, who, at only eight enlisted men per
car, enjoyed much more breathing space than the prisoners crammed into the gon-
dolas. A report noted that "periodic stops were made to allow the DEF to relieve
themselves and to obtain water for their canteens. When the train halted, sufficient
guards were dismounted to prevent escape of the DEF and to keep civilians away
from the train." Of the 187,355 disarmed troops guarded by the 175th over a four-
month span, only one man was fatally shot trying to escape. Another died when he
accidentally tumbled off the train. Supposedly only a single German successfully
escaped; the 29ers found it difficult to believe he would want to.

More than two-thirds of the prisoners—128,788 men and women—were
conveyed to three U.S. Army reception centers in the Rhine valley near Mainz.
The rest traveled to one of seven other centers: three in Germany, three in
Austria, and one at Pilsen, Czechoslovakia. The trains did not travel with impressive velocity; the one-way, 580-mile trip to Innsbruck, Austria, typically consumed six days, an average of only ninety-seven miles per day. But for the

relieved Germans, the end of their dismal war experience was almost over. Once a train arrived at its destination, the 29ers performed another head count, checked identification papers yet again, and handed over their prisoners to a fresh group of GIs. As long as no new snags surfaced, the Germans would shortly be released, and they would finally begin the last leg of their homeward journey.

The 29ers wondered when their turn would come.

THANKS FOR THE MEMORY

Major Walker, head of the 29th Division's military government section, spoke for all 29ers when he declared, "We were all just marking time until we returned to the United States." For the thousands of 29th Division enlisted men posted to long-term guard duties within the Bremen Enclave, however, "marking time" could be an agonizingly slow process. In the 116th Infantry's sector alone, situated in the northern part of the Enclave, the high command established eighty-seven sites "of military significance," including canal locks, a refrigeration plant, banks, hospitals, motor pools, a rifle range, machine shops, a compass factory, fishing boats, airfields, the renowned ocean liner SS *Europa*, and dozens of ammunition dumps. Orders stipulated that each post must be manned by at least two guards; some, such as airfields, required over thirty. Throughout the late spring and summer of 1945, the Enclave's thoroughly subjugated residents displayed virtually no belligerence toward any 29th Division guard post, and since no 29er in his right mind desired any more violence than he had already witnessed in World War II, the Germans' passivity was assuredly a good thing. True, passing hour after hour on monotonous guard duty while waiting for the trip home could be an ordeal; but as the 29th Division settled into the Enclave in their first weeks of the occupation, as long as the 29ers made it through their duty hours until the changing of the guard, they would have plenty of opportunities for enjoyment and recreation that could make "marking time" much more pleasurable.

The glorious realization that they would in all probability survive the global cataclysm had finally sunk in; with that pleasant thought entrenched in their heads, the 29ers could enjoy more stability in their lives than they had experienced since they were shipped overseas. The 115th Infantry's 1st Lt. Bill Holberton commented, "I slept in the same room and bed [in Bremen] from May 6 until I left the 29th Division in December." According to Walker, his stay in Bremerhaven "gave me a memorable chance to see how victorious conquerors could live in an occupied country, when their commanders made every effort to have them be comfortable and happy. . . . I saw that unit messes were serving meals on china from the liner *Europa* along with its silver and crystal. Civilians were glad to work in the mess halls just to get some food—and it also helped GIs to avoid KP. Entertainment and athletic programs were set up. I even played a couple of games on the [116th] regimental baseball team coached by Phil Sahara, who reportedly had been under contract to the Detroit Tigers." (Sahara played three years in the minors before the war, including one in the Cape Breton Colliery League.)

The 29ers did not take long to learn that the renowned Beck's *Brauerei* (brewery) was situated in Bremen and happily had continued to produce a first-class pilsner until shortly before Nazi Germany's surrender. Hence, as some delighted members of the 115th Infantry's Company L discovered in late May 1945 in a subterranean Beck's facility, millions of gallons of beer stored in classic wooden casks—ice cold—had somehow survived intact until the 29th Division's arrival in Bremen. It would have been wise to keep that discovery a secret, but soon every company in the 115th Infantry—and many more besides—were making unannounced visits to Beck's to "liberate" their share of one of the best beers in the world. Unfortunately, as Company L's 1st Lt. Malvin Walker noted regretfully, Maj. Gen. Harry Vaughan, head of the Bremen Port Command, found out about the 29ers' surreptitious visits and put an end to them immediately. According to Walker, Vaughan huffily announced to the 115th Infantry's commander: "Beck's is my brewery!"

Beer sales to 29ers within the Enclave, however, ran into a snag when, as Robert Walker reported, "the authorities declared that beer could not be sold to GIs as it exceeded 3.2 [percent] alcoholic content." Colonel Bingham, commander of the 116th Infantry, neatly got around that restriction by allowing beer in limited quantities to be handed out—not sold—to spectators at the plethora of sporting events that took place in the summer of 1945 in the 116th's zone. Gerhardt apparently never raised an objection to that practice.

As soon as the 29th Division moved into the Bremen Enclave, all 29ers with athletic inclinations were delighted to discover that they would have plenty of opportunities to get the war off their minds by playing sports. Those with advanced skills joined varsity baseball, football, soccer, track, swimming, tennis, and boxing teams and competed against American and Canadian squads from all over occupied Germany; the more numerous 29ers with less ambitious athletic goals participated in informal sports, such as softball, ping-pong, bowling, volleyball, handball, and golf. So fervently did the 29th Division embark on a sports program that on June 6, 1945—the first anniversary of D-Day—a *Baltimore Sun* article reported, "The 121st Engineer Battalion, which received a [Distinguished Unit] Citation for clearing mines from Omaha Beach and worked with the infantry all the way across Germany, is spending most of its time building baseball diamonds and soccer fields." For the next six months, the 29ers developed a sports passion, both as participants and observers. For any acquaintance of Charlie

Gerhardt—one of the finest athletes of his generation at the U.S. Military Academy—that development was hardly a surprise. The general himself engaged in exercise daily and regularly challenged members of the headquarters staff to a game of handball in the nearby gym. Despite the fact that Gerhardt was one of the oldest members of the 29th Division—he turned fifty on June 6, 1945—he almost always won. One of the opponents he habitually dominated, Major Walker, described him as "very competitive [and] in excellent shape. . . . He was slim, wiry, and lightning quick in his moves. He prided himself on staying fit." Each time he encountered Gerhardt thereafter, Walker recalled, the general blurted: "There's the guy with the tough hands!"

The 29th Division had a legacy of excellence in baseball dating back to its 1943 Plymouth Yankees team that won twenty-seven games without a loss to take the championship in the twenty-team U.S. Army league in England. The 29th's 1945 version of that team did not contain a single member from the 1943 club—three had died on Omaha Beach—but the 1945 squad lived up to that legacy by winning the Seventh Army championship against even tougher opposition, only to lose the European Theater "Little World Series" to the 71st Division Red Circlers team from Third Army that included major leaguers Harry Walker of the Cardinals and Ewell Blackwell of the Reds.

Starting in September 1945, thousands of 29ers came out to watch the 29th Division's top-notch football team play in Bremen's Ike Stadium, the former *Weserstadion*, built in 1922. Following Hitler's 1933 ascension to power, the stadium had been regularly used, as a 29th Division report noted, for "huge [Nazi] party demonstrations . . . with the football field feeling the iron boots of heel-clicking storm troopers." Clad in home uniforms of dark blue with gray numerals, the 29ers won five games (including a forfeit win against an 82nd Airborne Division team that failed to show up), lost four, and tied one. The last game of the year drew 20,000 fans to Ike Stadium on Thanksgiving Day, November 22, 1945, as the 29th played Vaughan's Bremen Port Command Bears, an integrated team containing both black and white servicemen. The game ended in a 7–7 tie. A histrionic "Thanksgiving Message" from Gerhardt on the first page of the game program proclaimed: "This first Thanksgiving since the end of the war finds the 29th Division fighting a battle totally different from the one we fought one year ago today. At that time the men of the Blue and Gray were moving forward, their bayonets pointed at Jülich and the Roer River. Riflemen of the 116th Infantry were moving toward the football field of the *Sportplätze* at Jülich in deadly quick opening plays that gained lives instead of first downs; a rain of shells, K-rations and turkey too, was their Thanksgiving dinner. Today, in peace and in the land they helped to conquer, these same Blue and Gray take to the field, but this time the weapons have been changed and the foe is friendly."

Those 29ers wishing to enjoy other kinds of entertainment within the Enclave had ample choices. Ten movie theaters ran several showings per day of first-run Hollywood films. Among those pictures reaching the Enclave that summer were a Philip Marlowe detective thriller, *Murder, My Sweet*, with Dick Powell and Claire Trevor; *Keep Your Powder Dry*, a film starring Lana Turner about three girls who join the Women's Army Corps; and Abbott and Costello's comedy *Here Come the Co-eds*.

Those 29ers who preferred live performances also had abundant opportunities to attend first-rate theatrical productions and concerts. An all-GI musical farce called *Fall Out for Fun*, supposedly concocted by bored GIs in a Third Army replacement depot just after V-E Day, proved popular not only in the Enclave but also throughout Europe and the Pacific. The troupe's musicians and singers opened up with "Sentimental Journey," a Doris Day stateside hit, and then plowed through thirteen more tunes in three scenes, including "The Trolley Song," made famous by Judy Garland in *Meet Me in St. Louis*, and Cole Porter's "Thick and Thin."

In the spring of 1945, the United Service Organizations (USO), a group founded in 1941 to boost the morale of American servicemen, sponsored traveling productions of eighteen past and current Broadway hits for tours throughout the American occupation zones in Europe, including *Night Must Fall*, *Arsenic and Old Lace*, *Our Town*, and *Boy Meets Girl*. The first play to hit the Bremen Enclave was *Night Must Fall*, a three-act British murder mystery that was, according to the USO playbill, "The New York and London Dramatic Hit." A review noted that the play "was something the boys could get their teeth into, something that would keep them on the edge of their seats as not to miss the blood-curdling screams, the little jokes in the midst of disaster, and the murder of old Mrs. Bramson." To the delight of the 29ers, the play's main character, a cad by the name of Dan, was played by the actor Dorman Leonard, who spoke with a perfect British accent; as a reporter noted, however, "actually he's from Brooklyn and can speak a Brooklynese accent at the drop of a hat."

The most popular USO productions of all within the Enclave were the shows put on by Bob Hope during his two-month tour of Europe. Hope and his troupe sailed from New York to England on the *Queen Mary*—the same liner on which part of the 29th Division had crossed the Atlantic in 1942—and gave a few performances in Britain and France before flying to Bremen on a C-47. During the flight he and his cast made a short recording that was broadcast that evening on Gen. Hap Arnold's *The Fighting AAF* radio show—"their first radio appearance from a moving plane," according to the *Washington Post*. When Hope landed at Bremen, the 399th Army Service Forces Band—an all-black outfit—greeted him with his theme song, "Thanks for the Memory," as a sailor treated him to a bottle of Beck's "with the compliments of all the guys in town." After attending Hope's premiere that night, an impressed *29 Let's Go* reporter wrote, "The first performance under the klieg lights at Ike Stadium was played to an estimated 7,000 GIs—absolute capacity," of whom, Hope conjectured, "ninety percent wore the Purple Heart." Hope did another performance at Bremerhaven; as noted in the 116th Infantry's July 1945 monthly report, "[It] was witnessed by practically 100% of the soldiers of this command." The 29ers, Hope recalled, "were a great audience. Their motto was 'Let's Go!' And they kept hollering it all during my show. . . . They were pretty cocky and had a right to be. What an outfit!"

Hope's opening schtick, delivered with his typical self-deprecating, deadpan spontaneity, never failed to bring the house down, mostly due to his uncanny ability to spew one joke or slapstick caper after another that played directly to the 29ers' current moods. After thoroughly warming up the audience, Hope bantered with his sidekick, Jerry Colonna, to whom he referred as "The Professor," after one of Colonna's idiotic personas. The 29ers particularly looked forward to Patti Thomas, the gorgeous blonde dancer who, clothed in a seductive black leotard and net stockings, did can-can and bump dances on the stage with blushing GIs chosen randomly from the audience. To ecstatic applause Hope and the cast closed, as always, with "Thanks for the Memory."

Anyplace in which 29ers lived or worked within the Bremen Enclave most likely had a radio tuned to the Armed Forces Radio Service's "AFN (American Forces Network) Bremen" radio station—1348 kilocycles on the tuning dial— from the station's sign-on at 6:00 A.M. to sign-off twenty hours later at 2:00 A.M. "The microphones and turntables of AFN Bremen bring you daily the best in American entertainment," declared a station leaflet. "Through your loudspeakers come the voices and music of the stars of the show world. And for every big sporting event in the Enclave, the sports staff of AFN Bremen is on the job, ready to bring to sports fans play-by-play, blow-by-blow descriptions of the action." The station featured a five-minute news broadcast every hour on the hour, followed by music programs such as "Date with Duke Ellington," "GI Jive," "Reveille Rhythms," "Bedlam in Bremen," and "Symphony Hour." AFN Bremen also featured occasional comedy and drama shows—"Burns and Allen" and "Mystery Playhouse," for example. One of the most popular programs was the "Morning After" show, during which comedian Bob Burns entertained his listeners with a corny monologue and occasionally played his bizarre homemade instrument, the "bazooka," after which the U.S. Army's antitank rocket launcher had been named.

On July 4, 1945, a 29th Division artillery battery lined up its four howitzers near Gerhardt's headquarters at Grohn and fired a forty-eight-gun salute precisely at noon in honor of the forty-eight states of the union. The booming reverberations drew the attention of the anxious locals. "When the smoke cleared away," noted Major Hoffman, "the civilians were hanging out of every window across the street. Now they know that we celebrate our independence."

On August 1, the 29th Division kicked off its impressive "Information and Education Program," a component of an ambitious instructional agenda concocted by Ike's headquarters in early June that would be instituted throughout the American occupation zone. The 115th Infantry's 1946 official history described it as "one of the most basically sound programs that the Army ever instituted . . . A great system of schools, reaching down to battalion level, and designed to carry courses appealing to every man, no matter what his interests and previous amount of education." The 29th Division's I&E program had been meticulously prepared for months by forty-three-year-old Maj. Albert Hoffman, who had enlisted as a private in the Texas National Guard in 1919. On active duty since November 1940, Hoffman joined the 29th Division in England a month before D-Day and was wounded at St. Lô. The Army considered Hoffman's work on the education scheme vital enough to retain him in Germany, even though his 123 points were more than enough for him to presume an early discharge would come soon. As a glum Hoffman observed, however, a point total "doesn't mean much for officers."

Hoffman's curriculum comprised college-level courses, vocational training, foreign-language instruction—German was the most popular—and just about any other subject in which 29ers expressed interest. For each class, he had to locate skilled teachers, order appropriate textbooks direct from the States, and, as he wrote home, worry about "a thousand other matters." One of his biggest worries was basic literacy courses. "We have nearly 500 men," he noted, "who have had less than a 5th grade education."

At one point, a frustrated Hoffman noted that his demanding work schedule was interrupted four or five times per hour by questions, requests, and suggestions submitted by curious 29ers. "One Jewish chaplain wants a course in farming," Hoffman wrote to his wife, Adelaide, "and it took me two hours to convince him that there was a lot more to farming than throwing a few seeds on the ground and waiting for the bankroll to grow to watermelon size."

Bob Hope recalled the profound change he had noted in the GIs since the last time he had entertained in Europe, when "the men who'd seen our shows had been all hopped up with anticipation of impending combat, and they wanted to like everything. But in 1945 they listened to our routines while packing."

TOUCHING HEARTS AND SOULS

So it was true. Family members and friends of the 29ers had presumed from their daily perusals of stateside newspapers that the 29th Division had been involved in the thick of the fighting in the European Theater. The reporters had told countless stories of battlefield triumphs, but suggested that casualties had been heavy. Just how many 29th Division men had been lost since D-Day? An appalling front-page article in the May 30, 1945, edition of the *Baltimore Sun* answered that question: according to the U.S. Army's official count, as the *Sun*'s headline related, the 29th had suffered "20,688 casualties, 130 percent of average strength," adding that "this is believed to be about the largest divisional casualty total of the war in Europe." Joe Ewing's book *29 Let's Go*, published in 1948, concluded that 3,653 of those men died in combat, and the Army eventually raised that figure to 3,720. Another 8,665 suffered non-battle injuries or illnesses, primarily trench foot and the psychological disorder euphemistically labeled "combat exhaustion."

On Wednesday, May 30, 1945, Memorial Day, General Simpson's Ninth Army headquarters staff arranged for a memorial service at the U.S. Military Cemetery near the village of Margraten, in the beautiful Limburg region of south Holland. Since November 1944, the 611th Quartermaster Graves Registration Company had buried 10,328 Americans—of whom some 950 were unidentified—and about 1,000 Britons and Canadians in forty-plus acres of former turnip fields. In separate plots several hundred yards away lay more than 3,000 Germans, only 300 of whom were known by name. At the end of September 1944, only six weeks before the 611th broke ground at the cemetery, a few 29th Division units had bivouacked in those same fields following the 29th's long journey from Brittany to Holland; now nearly 600 29ers reposed there, and many more were listed on the rolls of the missing.

Even three weeks after V-E Day, the 611th was still receiving a large number of American dead at Margraten every day due to the War Department's firm decree that all GIs buried in temporary graves in Germany must be exhumed posthaste from the soil of that former enemy country. A few weeks before Memorial Day, the 611th's commander, Capt. Joseph Shomon, noted, "The odor from the bodies was getting worse and could be smelled all the way to the village." Shomon eventually employed dozens of agreeable Dutch civilians, who worked diligently alongside the men of the 611th, and by the eve of the ceremony, the cemetery was ready to receive its distinguished guests.

The cemetery workers had sculpted many of the most recent Margraten graves into raised rectangular mounds of earth and stone, about eight inches high, with wooden crosses or Stars of David at their head. "Our main problem was getting enough flowers to cover all of the graves," Shomon remarked. "Once more the good people of Margraten came to our rescue. . . . The day before the [Memorial Day] services, our twenty trucks collected flowers from sixty villages and brought them in great piles to the cemetery. Nearly two hundred men, women, and children worked all night long, placing wreaths and flowers on the graves. Morning came, and with it a beautiful sight. Here were acres of colorful fresh flowers; here were acres of clean white crosses, aligned straight in every direction."

Just a few hours after dawn on Memorial Day, throngs of Dutch civilians totaling 30,000 people filled the roads leading to the cemetery; most of them carried flowers, some in large baskets that had to be hauled by two or more people. Despite years of privation under Nazi rule, the Dutch had turned out in their finest attire: men in formal black funeral wear with old-fashioned top hats; women in long black overcoats; boys in prim shorts, knee-high socks, and neat blazers; young girls with brightly colored bows in their hair. They filed into the grounds, nodded respectfully at the pair of helmeted U.S. Army MPs guarding the gate, proceeded down the cemetery's immaculate gravel paths, and took their assigned place around the perimeter of the cemetery. Shomon remarked that the Dutch were "two hundred deep in places."

The ceremony began just after Simpson's arrival at 11:00 A.M. In addition to Simpson, the commanding general of every corps and division that had fought with Ninth Army, including Gerhardt, would lay a wreath on the grave of a soldier from his command. A small contingent of British and Canadian generals

Dutch children march into Margraten Cemetery for the May 30, 1945, Memorial Day ceremony. U.S. ARMY SIGNAL CORPS

also attended. Simpson, Shomon recalled, was "filled with deep emotion. His words were terse, yet gentle. Now and then he looked up at all the crosses and flowers and hesitated a moment. The humbleness of the good Dutch people profoundly and visibly stirred him." Simpson laid the first wreath and chose a grave in Plot C of an unidentified "comrade-in-arms known but to God." Gerhardt and the other generals went next, and after each had deposited a wreath on the grave of one of his former soldiers, he stepped back, came to attention, and snapped a perfect salute toward the wooden cross. Catholic, Protestant, and Jewish U.S. Army chaplains followed Simpson to the microphone; according to Shomon, the Jewish chaplain, Capt. Joseph Shubow, "touched the heart and soul of everyone present. The Dutch people who understood English were perceptibly stirred [and] wept in bowed reverence."

The ceremony closed with a twenty-one-gun salute fired by a four-gun field artillery battery from the 79th Division, followed by "Taps" and a chaplain's final prayer. Every GI present came to attention and saluted when the white-helmeted Ninth Army band broke into "The Star Spangled Banner." Afterward, a Dutch priest conducted a Catholic mass on the cemetery grounds attended by thousands of civilians from the surrounding communities. "When mass started," Shomon wrote, "I felt an even greater gratitude to the people of Holland for their magnificent tribute to our dead comrades."

One of the nearly 600 29ers interred at Margraten was Pvt. Edward Jordan of the 175th Infantry's Company M, who was killed in the terrible struggle at Bourheim, Germany, on November 25, 1944. A New Yorker with a wife and one-year-old child at home, Jordan had been drafted in 1943 and joined the 29th Division as a replacement on September 19, 1944, following the siege of Brest. His career in the 29th lasted little more than nine weeks. On April 5, 1945, Jordan's grieving widow, Marie, invited three other war widows over to her West 20th Street Manhattan apartment. That meeting resulted in the formation of an organization known as Widows of World War II; two years later its name was changed to Gold Star Wives of World War II, after the red-bordered banner with a prominent gold star that families commonly hung in a window or on a door upon the death of a loved one during the war. The group still exists today as the Gold Star Wives of America.

In the summer of 1945, the most prominent widow in the United States, former First Lady Eleanor Roosevelt, inquired if she could join the group, and Marie Jordan welcomed her heartily. Eleanor was, after all, a war widow too, since her husband had been commander-in-chief of the American Armed Forces. In September Eleanor traveled down to Manhattan from her Val-Kill cottage in Dutchess County for her first meeting with an organization that still had only eighty members. "These women are, for the most part, very young," Eleanor wrote, "and for many of them renewal of a family life may come in the future. But this new organization may give them, during a very difficult period of their lives, the companionship and sense of backing which every woman needs and which her husband usually provides." Eleanor was touched when one young woman informed the group that she had nearly broken down in the aftermath of her husband's death. "Her health had been affected," Eleanor noted, "and she realized that she was not giving her two small children the kind of care and companionship they needed. She wondered if, for her own well-being and for her children's sake, she should try to find some sort of boarding school. . . . Suggestions were made that the group might find some member in her neighborhood who could help out and thereby give her more free time. It was heartening to see how general was the realization that both she and her children would lose something very valuable if, so early in their lives, the latter were separated from their mother and their own home." Eleanor noted the need for lobbying Congress when Marie mentioned that the share of her husband's $10,000 life insurance policy "amounted to $55 per month"—of which her mother-in-law got half.

On Memorial Day, May 30, 1946, exactly a year after the Ninth Army ceremony, Marie Jordan visited her husband's grave at Margraten on a trip sponsored by the Royal Dutch KLM Airline. She remarked that "the cemetery was in excellent condition. . . . Each grave was decorated with an American flag and strewn with fresh flowers brought by the Dutch people." Marie encountered a U.S. Army sergeant working on the grounds, who blurted to her: "But for the grace of God, we'd be lying out there now. There's not much we can do, but at least we can keep the cemeteries over here the way the folks back home would want them." A few years later, after the War Department allowed grieving families to choose whether their servicemen would be disinterred for reburial in the States or remain buried overseas, Marie chose the former option, and Private Jordan was eventually shipped home on a U.S. Army transport with thousands of other war dead for interment in hometown cemeteries.

The 29ers who listened regularly to AFN Bremen's hourly news broadcasts learned that the world beyond the Enclave was changing with astonishing rapidity. On June 26, 1945, the representatives of fifty nations signed the United Nations Charter after a two-month assembly in San Francisco. According to the opening phrase of the charter's preamble, the principal object of the United Nations must be "to save succeeding generations from the scourge of war, which twice in our lifetime has brought untold sorrow to mankind." On July 17 the United Nations' three foremost members—the United States, the Soviet Union, and the United Kingdom—commenced a two-week summit in the Berlin suburb of Potsdam to debate the terms of Germany's subjugation, redraw international borders, and thrash out the final defeat of Japan. Ten days into the summit, shocking news arrived from Britain that Prime Minister Winston Churchill had been deposed in a lopsided vote in favor of the Labour Party leader, Clement Attlee, who immediately replaced Churchill as the British representative at Potsdam.

Just four days after the close of the Potsdam conference, a B-29 bomber of the U.S. Twentieth Air Force dropped a single atomic bomb on Hiroshima, Japan; three days later another B-29 struck Nagasaki with a similar weapon. Less than one week hence, Emperor Hirohito announced Japan's surrender in a radio speech, and that capitulation became official on the deck of the U.S. Navy battleship *Missouri* on September 2.

In Bremen, the 29ers finally concluded with certainty that they would not see combat again in World War II.

A BED WAS A BED

A lucky group numbering more than 1,000 29ers never experienced life in the Bremen Enclave in any meaningful way because just days after the 29th Division's arrival, the Army dispatched those men home due to their high point scores on their Adjusted Service Rating Cards. With those transfers, almost all of the remaining 29ers who had served in the prewar Maryland and Virginia National Guard, as well as most of those in the first batch of draftees to join the 29th Division in the spring of 1941 at Fort Meade, departed the division for good. A May 29 *Baltimore Sun* article reported that a contingent of 500 GIs departing the 29th in late May included 150 Marylanders, of whom 61 were Baltimoreans. One of those men was Lt. Col. Roger Whiteford, who had joined the Maryland National Guard as a private in 1922, rose to the rank of lieutenant colonel, and led the 175th Infantry's 1st Battalion in its epic stand on Hill 108—"Purple Heart Hill"— outside St. Lô on June 18, 1944.

Virtually all the initial groups of 29th Division men dispatched for home had to travel to the United States by ship. Four 29ers, however, got extraordinarily lucky and were selected by the Army to make the homeward journey by airplane. The first two were Lt. Col. John Purley Cooper, commander of the 110th Field Artillery Battalion for nearly three years, and M/Sgt. Robert Brand, sergeant major of the 175th Infantry and one of the first draftees to join the regiment in April 1941; they left Bremen for Paris by air on May 28. Cooper and Brand had orders to report to Paris's Orly Airport on June 2 and rendezvous with about twenty-five officers and an equal number of enlisted men representing many of the divisions that had served in Omar Bradley's Twelfth Army Group. Joining them at the airfield would be a distinguished cluster of U.S. Army general officers, including Bradley himself, Clarence Huebner, Elwood Quesada, Leland Hobbs, Maxwell Taylor, Anthony McAuliffe, and many others. Three U.S. Army Air Force four-engine C-54 Skymaster transport aircraft would be waiting on the runways, fueled and ready to make the thirty-hour flight across the Atlantic in three stages: first to the Azores, then to Bermuda, and finally to LaGuardia Airport in Queens, New York.

Cooper and Brand arrived in Paris early, so they had a chance to see the city and stay in the renowned Ritz Hotel on the Place Vendôme for a night. When they checked in at the Ritz, however, an apologetic concierge confessed that all rooms were booked: would Cooper and Brand mind staying in one of the old servants' rooms in the attic? They would not mind; as Cooper recalled, "a bed was a bed," and since D-Day he had hardly slept in one. That afternoon, Cooper looked up his sister Hannah, a Red Cross worker who had a room at the Crillon Hotel on the Place de la Concorde, just a short walk from the Ritz. The two later walked back to the Ritz for dinner in its swanky dining room, filled mostly with Allied brass. During their meal, General Bradley entered the room and visited the Coopers' table; after introducing himself and chatting a few minutes, Bradley asked Hannah, "Well, young lady, is there anything I can do for you?" Hannah replied, "Well, yes, general, my brother is leaving for the States tomorrow morning, and I'd like to see him off at the airport. Could someone drive me?" Without a moment of hesitation, Bradley replied: "Done."

The next morning, with Hannah waving goodbye from a waiting room, the three Skymasters took off in what Cooper depicted as "a driving rainstorm." Cooper was delighted to find a friend on his airplane, Maj. Gen. Anthony McAuliffe, current commander of the 103rd Division but much more famous for his stirring response—"Nuts!"—to a German surrender demand in Bastogne during the Battle of the Bulge, when he had been acting commander of the 101st Airborne Division. Cooper and McAuliffe were both longtime artillerists; in the interwar period, McAuliffe had been a battery commander in the 6th Field Artillery at Fort Hoyle, near Baltimore, and he had gotten to know Cooper when the 6th's polo team played matches against the Maryland National Guard's 110th Field Artillery.

The three C-54s landed at LaGuardia at 2:00 P.M. on June 3. New York City officials at once thrust the passengers into cars and formed them into a convoy that headed through Queens into Manhattan by way of the magnificent Triborough Bridge to the Waldorf-Astoria Hotel on Park Avenue. Bradley forthwith gave a short press conference in the hotel lobby; the next day, a *Times* reporter described him in a front-page story as "erect and soldierly in his bearing, but so modest and soft-spoken that he seemed more like the mathematics instructor he once was at West Point than the commanding general of the Twelfth Army Group." The Waldorf then treated every soldier in the party to a steak dinner. The next day, June 4, the group boarded a train at Penn Station and headed for a victory parade in Philadelphia.

The "small band of conquerors," as a *Times* reporter described them, were driven in a motorcade through twenty-five miles of Philadelphia streets, cheered on by more than one million "riotous" citizens. Bradley commented that the reception was "overwhelming," and one could understand why: "Six scout cars, firing blank ammunition in their machine guns, led the procession," the *Times* noted. "Just before the parade swung into the downtown district, a battery of 75 [millimeter guns] on the parkway roared a 17-gun salute. In one of the residential areas a number of Nazi flags were stretched across the roadbed so that the entire motorcade rolled over them." The cavalcade turned onto Chestnut Street and finally came to a stop outside Independence Hall. After Bradley gave a short talk, the group proceeded a few blocks to the west for its last pageant together, a festive dinner at the Bellevue-Stratford Hotel. Bradley departed that night for West Point to speak at the graduation ceremony the following day. Cooper and Brand stayed overnight and took the train to Baltimore in the morning. A few days hence, the U.S. Army discharged both of them at Fort Meade.

The Army Air Forces had the trans-Atlantic procedure down to a science, and two other 29ers, General Gerhardt and his aide-de-camp of two years, Capt. Bob Wallis, were about to take advantage of that service. For the general, how-ever, it would be a round-trip journey, as orders specified that he must return to duty in the Enclave within one month. Just like Cooper and Brand four days ear-lier, Gerhardt and his trusted aide reported to Orly at dawn on June 6—the first anniversary of D-Day and the general's fiftieth birthday—to join the eminent grandee of the three-plane flight, Gen. George Patton, who was traveling with about 120 officers and enlisted men from his beloved Third Army. Headed for a celebration in Boston by way of the Azores and Newfoundland, they would arrive on the seventh, then fly across the United States, with a stopover at Denver, for a final grand fête in Los Angeles on the ninth.

The Skymasters touched down at Bedford Army Airfield, just two miles from where the American Revolution began at Lexington in 1775. "Over a route covered in reverse by Paul Revere," a *Times* reporter noted, Patton and his entourage, including Gerhardt and Wallis, drove into Boston "along a twenty-mile lane of humanity," consisting of more than one million elated Massachusetts citizens. At a grand banquet that night, Patton gave the kind of speech for which he was famous. He wanted "to go and take on those Japanese," he bellowed; then, "with misty eyes," concluded: "It is foolish and wrong to mourn the men who died. Rather, we should thank God that such men lived."

On June 9, more than a million Angelenos replicated the ecstatic reception already offered to returning veterans in East Coast cities. They lined Pico Boule-vard, cheering as the procession from Los Angeles Airport to City Hall drove by. When the motorcade turned left from Pico onto Broadway and passed the legendary downtown movie palaces—the Roxie, Rialto, Orpheum, and others—the locals' elation and applause surged as Patton, Gerhardt, and all the other servicemen—including California native Jimmy Doolittle—stood in their open command cars and signaled their gratitude to the crowds. That night Hollywood threw a grand celebration for Patton's group at the Los Angeles Memorial Coliseum, a venue with which Gerhardt was entirely familiar since he had served as a judge in Los Angeles's 1932 Olympics. Dedicated in 1921 to the American dead of World War I, the Coliseum could hold 100,000 people, and every seat was filled as master of ceremonies Jack Benny introduced the men on the stage while a dozen searchlights threw their beams skyward behind the memorial façade, adorned with a huge American eagle and the neon-light names "PATTON" and "DOOLITTLE." After Humphrey Bogart and Edward G. Robinson came on to provide still more tributes, all of which were broadcast live on radio, Gerhardt remembered that the lights were turned out and, "at a given signal, every person there lighted a match."

Two days later, on June 11, the group split up. Wallis set out for home and demobilization in Baltimore. Gerhardt flew to Macon, Georgia, to spend more than two weeks with his wife, Nina, and his progeny, a daughter—also named Nina—and a son, Chuck. In early July he flew back to Germany and was on duty again in Bremen on July 6 with a new aide-de-camp, 1st Lt. William Pinson.

Only five years previously, with the United States at peace and a robust core of isolationists clamoring for America to stay out of war, a uniformed U.S. Army soldier on the streets of Los Angeles, Boston, or Philadelphia had been an object of curiosity rather than one of adulation. In those days the left-shoulder patch sewn onto a soldier's uniform served only to identify the unit to which he belonged. In the summer of 1945, however, that simple piece of cloth held a much more profound meaning. It signified wordlessly the history of a soldier's outfit: where it had fought; what it had accomplished; how its men had died. The 29th Division's blue-and-gray yin-yang patch told a powerful tale of combat and loss from Omaha Beach to the Elbe, a story in which most veteran 29ers took immense pride: not a boastful conceit in themselves, but a solemn appreciation that thousands of comrades, living and dead, had changed the world for the better. Within the American occupation forces in Germany, a 29er's left-shoulder patch commonly drew stares from passing GIs, gazes of not only deep respect but also pity, accompanied by the sober comprehension that the doomed dogface soldiers at the tip of the U.S. Army spear—a tiny fraction of the Army as a whole—had borne the brunt of the battle, suffered and died in numbers incomprehensible to stateside civilians, and contributed mightily to Hitler's downfall.

So many GIs had developed a fierce pride in their unit patches that in the summer of 1945 the U.S. Army had to amend its uniform regulations. In the vast shuffle of men heading to the States from Germany for reassignment or demobilization, tens of thousands had been transferred to new outfits for the homeward journey, an infuriating experience for many who had been forced to rip off the patch they had worn in combat for months and sew on a new and wholly unfamiliar one. The high command had to admit that when a proud fighting man was involuntarily reassigned to a new unit and finally shipped home, it was fitting he should wear the same patch he had worn in combat. True, he still must always wear his current unit's symbol on his left shoulder; but the Army decreed that a GI could sew on his right shoulder the patch of the unit he had belonged to on active military operations—the one to which he afforded his strongest emotional attachment.

When Gerhardt returned to Bremen after his monthlong sojourn to the States, he perceived plenty of evidence of the new uniform regulation. To his amazement, the division he came back to on July 5 was radically different from the one he had departed on June 3. On June 28, 292 officers and 3,495 enlisted men from the 29th Division with 85 or more points on their Adjusted Service Rating Cards—nearly one-third of the division's current manpower—had departed in 249 trucks for Leipzig, Germany, in and around which the 69th Infantry Division was encamped. That fifteen-hour journey of 300 miles delighted the affected 29ers—most of whom were D-Day veterans—since the 69th was scheduled for redeployment to the United States much sooner than the 29th. According to the *Fighting 69th Sentinel* newsletter, "Red Cross girls were on hand with 23,000 doughnuts, 22,500 cups of coffee, 8,000 sticks of gum, and 8,000 cigarettes to welcome the newcomers." When would the 29ers come home? A *Baltimore Sun* article speculated that "it will likely be at least several weeks before this group arrives in the United States. They will go with the 69th Division to a redeployment center in France, where they probably will require two weeks to twenty-five days to go through the necessary processing. Then there will be a brief stop at an embarkation point before the actual voyage home begins."

The next day, June 29, those same trucks made the return trip from Leipzig to the Bremen Enclave, conveying an equivalent number of low-point 69th Division men to serve in the 29th under their new commander, Gerhardt. Like it or not, after removing the left-shoulder patch from their new Ike jackets, more than 7,000 men in Leipzig and within the Enclave abruptly embarked on the aggravating task of sewing their old patch onto the right shoulder of their uniforms and the new patch to the left. "Troops newly arrived from the 69th brought a new atmosphere to the Enclave," Ewing noted. "Everywhere the red, white, and blue 69th Division patch could be seen on right shoulders, and combat talk now included references to 'Leipzig' and 'the Siegfried Line.'"

Personnel exchanges between the Blue and Gray and the "Fighting 69th" Division—also known as the "Contact Division" due to its initial linkup with the

Red Army on the Elbe—continued for the rest of the summer as the Army gradually lowered the eighty-five-point score a GI needed to gain a ticket home. "The men who came in from the 69th felt pretty lucky," one 29er remembered, "for the word was that after reorganization in the States, that outfit would go to the Pacific." The Japanese surrender, however, made that issue moot. By the end of the summer of 1945, ex–69th Division men vastly outnumbered the original 29ers who had fought with the 29th Division across France, Holland, and Germany.

Since the revocation of the non-fraternization order, many bored 29ers decided that meeting German members of the opposite sex would be a good way to pass the interminable wait for a ship home. "It wasn't very difficult to meet the girls on the street," observed PFC Art Plaut of the 115th. "*Wue geht es, Fräulein*? [How are you, miss?], *Wo gehen sie*? [Where are you going?], *Kommen sie hier* [Come here], were generally sufficient to open a conversation and a friendship. Most Yanks accepted people at their face value, and there were only a few who allowed their active hatred of the Germans borne from combat or pre-combat days to prevent them from fraternizing. Unfortunately, too many men were willing to excuse the civilians for their responsibility in allowing a government to wage aggressive war against its neighbors. . . . The civilians offered the excuse that 'We didn't know what was going on,' and the GIs accepted it."

The 29ers learned that Bremen in October and November was not nearly as pleasant as it had been in the summer. The number of daylight hours shrank dramatically; the weather abruptly turned cold, and due to an insufficient supply of coal, the cold permeated almost every home and office. With Japan's surrender, World War II was over, and the 29th Division turned into little more than a U.S. Army clearinghouse for troops headed someplace else. "The division dropped down to its lowest strength in years, and many guard posts and other installations had to be dropped because of lack of sufficient personnel to man them," the 115th history noted. Amid that astonishing personnel turnover, a positive piece of news arrived in mid-October, providing a glimmer of hope for those yearning to get home. The 29th Division would be shifted from Category I to Category IV, the high command declared, indicating that the entire division's trans-Atlantic shipment home was imminent. How long would the 29ers have to wait? Much longer than they wanted to, given the Americans' propensity to make decisions at an agonizingly slow pace. Six more weeks passed until, on December 1, 1945, the U.S. Army finally transferred a new outfit, the 78th Division's 311th Infantry, to the Enclave to carry on the 29th's occupation duties. Finally the 29th Division, no longer responsible for governing and policing the zone in which it had dwelled for more than six months, could focus entirely on its forthcoming journey to the States; no one, however, seemed to know exactly when it would take place.

Before they headed home, the 29ers would have to adhere to the stupefying rigamarole of paperwork that the U.S. Army habitually churned out, but as Plaut mentioned, "No one minded, really, for all of the work pointed toward a speedier and less confused journey home." The "Clothing and Equipment Adjustment Form" demanded that a 29er list the quantity of items in his possession in thirty-eight different categories, including Drawers, Cotton; Handkerchiefs; Forks; Knives; Spoons; Undershirts, Cotton; Cans—Meat; and Cups. Then an officer had to check the list and sign it. On the "Certificates, Affidavits, and Customs Declarations Form," a 29er must "certify and declare that the following items of government property"—to be filled in as needed—"were purchased by me and are my personal property." Also, any captured German articles were to be listed, as well as "evidence of the right to possess the items of British, Canadian, or Russian government material." Finally, on a Customs Declaration, a GI was required to list all "personal or household effects, either taken abroad by me or acquired abroad for personal use."

Some 29ers harbored a hope they would be back home with their families for Christmas, and when headquarters released the order of departure of the regiments—116th first, 175th next, and finally the 115th—those hopes soared, especially when the GIs learned that the 29th Division would leave for home directly from Bremerhaven rather than moving hundreds of miles to a French port, as other departing divisions had done. A plausible rumor indicated that the first transport, *Lejeune*, would arrive in Bremerhaven by December 10 to take on the 116th, but as Ewing wrote, "Tentative sailing dates were continually being pushed back, as one delay after another was announced at division headquarters. . . . Winter made the restless, waiting Blue-and-Gray soldiers see the Enclave with a new drabness. Every day brought a new delay, a new date, and nobody knew for sure when the ships would arrive." The possibility of a Christmas arrival in New York evaporated. "Men who had transferred into the Blue and Gray because the 29th was supposed to have a high priority were chagrined as they read that the outfits they had left were further along toward the States than the 29th was," Plaut remarked.

Gerhardt at last released a "Letter of Instruction" on December 17, ordering the movement of all 29th Division units starting the following morning from their bivouacs within the Enclave to staging areas near the port of Bremerhaven. The wait couldn't be much longer now, the impatient 29ers presumed, as the letter denoted transport assignments and sailing dates down to company or battery level. However, the orders emphasized: "These moves are tentative [underlined in original] and are entirely dependent upon the arrival dates of ship transportation." The letter also warned: "Effective immediately, no transfers will be made between or within subordinate units of the division without prior approval of the G-3."

Nearly another week passed until the 116th Infantry boarded the U.S. Navy troopship *Lejeune* at Bremerhaven on December 24 and finally set sail for New York on Christmas Day. The 175th embarked over the next week, split among four Liberty ships—*Daniel H. Lownsdale, A. P. Hill, John L. Sullivan,* and *John E. Schmeltzer*—and two transports, *Bienville* and *United States Victory.* The last troopship to head home from Bremerhaven, *John Ericsson*—formerly the Swedish luxury liner *Kungsholm*—sailed on January 3, 1946, carrying the entire 115th Infantry. With the *Ericsson*'s departure, the colors of the 29th Infantry Division were no longer situated in Europe for the first time in thirty-nine months.

Of the eight vessels conveying the 29th Division home, *Lejeune*, as the elated members of the 116th discovered, not only departed Bremerhaven first but also was the fastest. Sailing at a top speed of eighteen knots, *Lejeune*—formerly the German liner *Windhuk*—could make the trans-Atlantic journey in nine days in good weather, and with the world at peace, her skipper, Capt. Frank MacDonald of the U.S. Navy, could dispense with zig-zagging and blackouts. Evidently, *Lejeune* was a lucky ship, as she had already crossed the Atlantic fifteen times without a scratch and had transported 91,429 American servicemen both to and from Europe. Mid-Atlantic January storms, however, almost guaranteed a harsh journey, during which a ship could only rarely attain top speed. "This was [*Lejeune*'s] roughest trip in almost a year," a seasick 29er learned from a sailor, "a fact of which too many of us are already aware." Nevertheless, the soldier added, "For the more seaworthy of us, there will be lots of pleasant memories. The thrilling sight of a heaving ocean, the cleanliness of the ship's lines, the entertainment provided by a sincere Special Service Corps, and the good Navy food, served in the efficiently operated mess."

Not nearly as many "pleasant memories" emerged among 175th men as they crossed the Atlantic in their six transports, all considerably smaller and more spartan than *Lejeune*. Atlantic storms and the Liberty ships' eleven-knot top speed promised a homeward journey of at least two weeks, during which, as a *Baltimore Sun* reporter wrote, the 29ers' "biggest complaint was boredom . . . which was slightly alleviated with a continuous series of poker and dice games." Boredom turned into fear when several ships plunged directly into a ferocious January 13 nor'easter off the east coast of the United States, triggering "mountainous seas that sent water and sleet over the bridge and caused a high rate of seasickness among the passengers and crew. . . . The only casualty listed was one small German dog, which was washed overboard during the height of the storm." Frigid temperatures froze the incessant spray and caked topside decks and equipment with ice. Even worse, the unfortunate *Bienville*, carrying 1,800 anxious 29ers, suffered an engine breakdown and was forced to ride out the tempest by heaving to while repairs were initiated. The miserable GIs aboard *Bienville* wondered whether the Statue of Liberty would ever come into view.

On New Year's Day, 1946, Gerhardt decided it was his time to come home. He had already seen off most of the 29th Division at the Bremerhaven docks; only the 115th Infantry remained in the Enclave, scheduled to depart on the *John Ericsson* on January 3. Uncle Charlie hoped to be back in the States by that date to greet the first of his 29ers to walk down a transport's gangplank in New York. Befitting his two-star rank, however, he planned to use a much faster and more comfortable means of transportation than a troopship. In June he had flown out of Paris on a C-54 Skymaster and reached Boston in thirty hours. If Gerhardt left Germany on January 1 and matched that rate of travel, he would arrive in New York well ahead of the troop transport *Lejeune*, which had departed Bremerhaven on December 25.

This time, however, would be different. He would not be returning to Germany, and within a few weeks of his return to the United States, Gerhardt knew with certainty he would be looking for a new job.

EIGHT

They Never Die

TOMORROW I'LL BE A GODDAMN CIVILIAN

The first lights of Long Island twinkled off the starboard bow after midnight; before long, there were too many to count, and their radiance intensified by the minute. *Lejeune*'s long voyage across the Atlantic was nearly over.

By sunrise on January 4, 1946—7:20 A.M.—hundreds of expectant 29ers, most of them puffing on cigarettes, lined the rails for a look. The day broke as most days did in New York City in January, with cloud cover so heavy that the sun was invisible. Happily an arctic air mass that had pervaded the northeast for days had just been pushed out by much warmer southwest winds, bringing on temperatures that weathermen predicted would hit 42 degrees by early afternoon. Presently, recognizable land features came into focus: first, the prominent Atlantic Highlands headland of New Jersey, off the port bow; then the south shore of Long Island on the starboard side; Sandy Hook; Rockaway; Coney Island; and finally Brooklyn and Staten Island, between which *Lejeune* would soon pass via the Narrows to enter the glorious harbor of New York.

The 29ers had prepared for this moment. A team of creative GIs had fashioned two banners, so big they could be seen a mile away. At dawn they hung them over the starboard side so the citizens of Manhattan could not miss them when *Lejeune* sailed up the Hudson that afternoon to her berth. One of them featured the blue-and-gray yin-yang symbol of the 29th Division; the other, the crest of the 116th Infantry, adorned with a fleur-de-lis and the regimental motto, "Ever

295

Forward." It no longer mattered that most of the men wore right-shoulder patches of other outfits, indicating they had come to the 29th Division after V-E Day; they all belonged to the 29th Infantry Division now.

As the 29ers approached the Narrows shortly after 2:00 P.M., a modest cruising yacht sped down the bay, drew near *Lejeune*, and swung around 180 degrees to sail alongside the huge transport on a parallel course. Curious . . . probably some sort of pilot vessel. But when the smattering of old-time 29ers peered into the boat, they made an astonishing discovery: there, standing in the open on the diminutive yacht's aft deck, was a compact U.S. Army officer with two-star rank on his garrison cap, attired in a dapper woolen overcoat and armed with a swagger stick, which he waved enthusiastically toward the puzzled GIs staring down at him from the transport's rails. Could it be? The word spread like wildfire among *Lejeune*'s 4,600 29ers: General Gerhardt! Under ordinary circumstances, whether in combat or in the more tranquil environment of the Bremen Enclave, an encounter with the general habitually triggered paralyzing anxiety, but this time the surprised 29ers expressed spontaneous joy to see him in this most unexpected of places. Some of the more exuberant GIs breached U.S. Army protocol by cupping their hands to their mouths and shouting down: "Yeah! Uncle Charlie!" Gerhardt displayed no signs of fatigue despite more than three days of continuous travel starting on New Year's Day in Bremen, including a twenty-four-hour round-trip journey from New York to Macon, Georgia, to pick up his wife, Nina, now standing at his side with a broad smile fixed on her face.

The frenzied 29ers could not fail to notice the general's retinue, which stood deferentially a few paces behind him. It included several uniformed staff officers and a much more alluring bevy of attractive young females, the first American women the GIs had laid eyes on within the confines of the United States for a long time—in some cases, years. Many men could not restrain themselves, bellowing "Hi, babe!" at the top of their lungs; others yelled imploringly, "Who are the women?"

Col. Bill Witte, the brainy officer who had been a fixture on Gerhardt's staff for thirty months, grabbed a megaphone and, to the disappointment of the animated troops lining *Lejeune*'s starboard side, identified each woman by name: they were all married, Witte emphasized, and their husbands were standing by their sides. Included in that group was Witte's own spouse, Nancy, a stunner dressed in an eye-catching white coat with enormous black lapels and a stylish hat featuring a flimsy piece of black netting drooped alluringly over her eyes.

Shortly thereafter, a reporter noted, "An Army tug, with a band and two girl singers, pulled alongside *Lejeune*, still making her way through the Narrows. They played and sang *Sentimental Journey* and *Roll Out the Barrel* [the 29th

Division's signature tune]. Soldiers crowded the rails of the transport, many with their feet hanging over the side, to listen and roar applause." In Bremerhaven, the final edition of *29 Let's Go* had warned the 29ers to be prepared for a muted reaction to their return: "Welcoming committees are a thing of the past. The war is many months gone (not that people have forgotten), and there are newer, more important things on the horizon." Evidently, the enraptured 29ers gathered, at least one welcoming committee was still functional.

Gerhardt's yacht eventually pulled away and sped back to Manhattan, allowing the 29ers to savor every moment of *Lejeune's* stately progression into the protected waters of the great seaport. Within the hour virtually every 29er had shifted from the starboard to the port side to take in a sight they had yearned to see for years: the Statue of Liberty. Sunset came early in New York at this time of year—4:42 P.M.—and by the time *Lejeune* approached Bedloe's Island, upon which the great statue sat, darkness was gradually setting in. No raucous clamor this time—rather, the GIs stared wordlessly at the magnificent icon, pondering the good fortune that had kept them alive to see it; nearly 4,000 unlucky 29ers lying deep in European soil never would, and they were profoundly missed.

Lejeune pressed on past Ellis Island and into the Hudson, decelerating to a crawl as two tugboats came down the river to shove her into her home berth at Pier 51 in lower Manhattan. "All the windows of the skyscrapers in lower Manhattan were lighted up with gold," wrote the *Baltimore Sun's* Lee McCardell. "A Negro orchestra from Camp Shanks [in Orangeburg, New York] was on Pier 51 to play the transport in. General Gerhardt, who had come ahead, was waiting to go aboard as soon as the gangplank should be secure. Pretty Mrs. Nancy Witte, the colonel's lady, standing on the end of the pier and listening to the soldiers yell as the tugs pushed the transport into the slip, said she wanted to cry."

Gerhardt strode up the gangplank and exchanged salutes with Lt. Col. Jim Hays, formerly of the 175th Infantry, currently the 29th Division's chief personnel officer. Three men in Gerhardt's entourage were attired in civilian clothes, and according to McCardell, Hays "yelped when he saw them—the clothes. One man had a velvet collar on his overcoat. The colonel wanted to feel that with his hand." Gerhardt warmly greeted every soldier he knew—and many he didn't. (One passenger with whom he had no desire to socialize, however, was Lt. Col. Harold Donovan, known as "Father Mike," the 29th's head chaplain. In autumn 1944, Donovan had loudly complained about Gerhardt's endorsement of a house of prostitution for 29th Division use, causing the general to remark caustically that Donovan "was disloyal and a troublemaker throughout.") Gerhardt knew that the War Department would deactivate the 29th Division within the next few weeks, and this was one of his last opportunities to say goodbye and offer his thanks to men who had served him devotedly.

Meantime, burdened with their heavy baggage, the 29ers formed lines of immense length along *Lejeune*'s gangways and began to debark. PFC Arden Earll of Company H, 116th Infantry—a D-Day veteran—recalled that as he waited for the line to move, New York longshoremen subtly opened their overcoats, revealing bottles of liquor to the returning troops. "They didn't offer the liquor for free, and I'll tell you that the going price was not cheap," Earll remarked.

"Down the gangplank they went," McCardell wrote, "barracks bags over their shoulders, calling out their first names in response as their last was called out by a man checking the passenger lists at the foot of the gangplank. . . . Women workers of the American Red Cross were waiting on the pier to distribute milk, coffee, doughnuts. Each disembarking unit dropped its barracks bags and halted long enough to be served. Then they moved on, to the end of the pier, and aboard the waiting ferry boats that shuttled them across the Hudson River—4,600 men when the last ferry pulled away at one o'clock this morning."

The ten-minute ferry ride brought the 29ers to Hoboken, New Jersey, where they boarded trains parked at austere platforms just a short march from the pier. They had hardly settled into their seats when they arrived fifty minutes later at Camp Kilmer, the same location from which the 29th Division had departed for Europe in September 1942. "Welcome home and welcome to Camp Kilmer," the 29ers read on a pamphlet thrust into their hands as they stepped off the trains. "You'll be out of here before you can say 'Jack Robinson.' . . . Most of you will move from here to a Separation Center for discharge. . . . We've got a lot of things to do for you, and you have a lot of things to do yourself before you can get on your way. There is no way that any visitors could see you. . . . Liquor is prohibited both on the Post and on the train and will be confiscated. . . . Stay on the ball. If you go 'goofing off' so that you miss your processing or miss a meeting that is essential, you not only jeopardize your chances of leaving, but the chances of all the men in your group. . . . We insist on military courtesy on this Post. . . . You're the 'returning hero' to your family, friends, and community. They'll be looking at you as the Army's representative. You will be on display, so to speak. So don't be a 'Sad Sack.' You've been through a lot—why spoil it by looking like anything but what you are—a good soldier."

The next contingent of 29ers from Bremerhaven, 550 men, arrived at Pier 84 in Manhattan on the Liberty ship *Lownsdale* on January 10, 1946, after a fifteen-day voyage. As an Army band on the pier played lively swing tunes, Gerhardt, his wife, and Witte marched up the gangplank to greet the exultant troops. (It was Witte's second time aboard: he had been invited to Christmas dinner on *Lownsdale* in Bremerhaven the day before her departure for home.) After longshoremen distributed newspapers to the troops, however, many of the GIs were no longer exultant. Not a single reference to the 29th Division's proud return home could be found; instead, the 29ers were bombarded with front-page articles on the labor disputes currently sweeping the United States, including major strikes by Western Union telegraph operators and Western Electric telephone workers. Just a few miles from Pier 84, in fact, 1,000 picketers were currently marching outside the Western Union headquarters at 60 Hudson Street, and a page-one *Times* article noted that the picketers that day were "joined by Representative Vito Marcantonio [a member of the American Labor Party] and two communist City Council members." The president of the Transport Workers Union, the reporter wrote, "addressed a special appeal to the police and other municipal workers to join the picketing when their hours of duty were over." A 29th Division sergeant complained loudly: "This is certainly a fine way to be greeted after three years overseas. My mom lives out in Chicago, and I can't even tell her I'm home."

The last six troopships carrying the remainder of the 29th Division to New York arrived over the next week. All but one of the vessels docked at Staten Island rather than Manhattan, and the troops consequently missed out on the glorious experience of sailing directly past the Statue of Liberty. The weather had turned bitterly cold again: when *Schmeltzer*, *Victory*, and *Ericsson* pulled into New York harbor on January 16, the thermometer read 18 degrees at noon, causing almost every topside item onboard to be encrusted in ice. Far more depressing than the frigid temperatures and a distant glimpse of the Statue of Liberty, however, was the current state of the United States. Reading the newspapers, it seemed almost all of America was on strike: in addition to the telegraph and telephone workers, strikers currently included bus drivers, bakers, steel workers, plumbers, coffin makers, automobile workers, meat packers, and electricians.

Of the roughly 12,000 29th Division troops conveyed home on eight transports, the authorities discovered two stowaways. The first, uncovered on *Ericsson*, was not a human at all, but a dog. Back in Bremerhaven, benevolent officers in charge of loading the ships typically did not object if a 29er wished to bring a dog back to the States on a troopship; there was one particular dog, however, who had been banned at Uncle Charlie's order. When Gerhardt departed for home on New Year's Day, he had directed Col. Alexander George, the 29th Division's chief military government officer, to find a home in Germany for "D-Day," his pet spaniel and constant companion since the general had picked up the stray in Normandy a few days after the invasion. George, a classmate of Gerhardt's at the Academy who succeeded the general as West Point quarterback, decided to surprise his old friend by taking D-Day home with him on *Ericsson*. "He ignored anyone who told him Gerhardt wanted the dog left behind," Major Walker recalled. "I was not present when George and D-Day landed in New York, but General Gerhardt was there to meet the ship. I did hear he was furious with Colonel George, but he kept the dog." D-Day remained a loyal friend to the general and died in the mid-fifties in Winter Park, Florida, shortly after his master's retirement from the Army. Gerhardt buried him in his backyard.

The other stowaway, a much more serious case, was discovered onboard *Lejeune* halfway between Bremerhaven and New York: a nine-year-old Ukrainian boy named Fredor Nichichuk, known to all members of the 116th Infantry's Company E aboard *Lejeune* as "Eddie," or sometimes "Ruski." Reporter Paul Saunier of the *Richmond Times-Dispatch* noted that the four-foot-tall, sixty-seven-pound Eddie "is not made like a boy at all; he's built like a full-chested, brawny Russian blacksmith, but in miniature." When an outraged officer on *Lejeune* demanded an explanation for Eddie's presence, Sgt. Ben Cook, a veteran of the first-wave landing on Omaha Beach who had been wounded at Würselen in October 1944, confessed that he had sneaked Eddie aboard in a duffel bag. Eddie had been with Company E continuously since April 1945, when the 116th managed a displaced persons camp near Lippstadt, Germany. Eddie and his parents had been forcibly removed by the Germans from their home in the Ukraine in 1942 to work as slave laborers in Germany. "Three years of beating and starvation diets followed," Saunier wrote, "before his parents were killed in an American bombing raid. The Germans then decided to finish the job, and a scar on the top of Eddie's head shows where a Wehrmacht soldier's bullet barely missed its mark."

The amazed senior officer aboard *Lejeune* ordered an immediate special court-martial for Cook "for carrying an alien civilian aboard." Cook explained to the board, consisting of a judge and four other officers, that Company E loved the kid; one 29er in particular, S/Sgt. George Smiley—another D-Day veteran who had enlisted in the Virginia National Guard at Company E's Chase City armory in the late thirties—loved him so much, in fact, that he wanted to adopt Eddie and add him to his family, which included his wife, Donna May, and a four-year-old daughter, Nancy. As a high-point man, Smiley had gone home in June to Boydton, Virginia, for his discharge. Almost every Company E GI knew of the plan and, according to Cook, many volunteered to adopt Eddie if Smiley could not. The judge called Eddie forward and promptly demanded if Cook had stuffed him in the duffel bag. Eddie replied: "Bag closed. Dark. I don't see nothing."

"The five officers on the board just rolled their heads and roared," Cook recalled. "That cinched it for me." Ignoring the obvious facts, the compassionate board found Cook not guilty of the charge of smuggling Eddie onboard, but radioed ahead to New York to have Immigration and Naturalization Service officers meet *Lejeune* at Pier 51 and take Eddie into custody for conveyance to Ellis Island. "Three months of red tape followed," Saunier wrote, during which bureaucrats investigated the case. In early April 1946 immigration officials informed Smiley that Eddie could move in with him and his family, but adoption would not be permitted until the authorities determined with certainty that

Eddie's parents were dead. That investigation took months; when it was finally completed, Eddie became Smiley's adopted son, and thereafter he called Donna May "mother," but always addressed Smiley simply as "Norman."

For eight months after Company E picked him up at Lippstadt, Eddie had stayed with the outfit "as a sort of field kitchen mascot," under the care of a kindly mess sergeant named Scipione. Another Company E 29er, PFC George Engeln, remarked that "Eddie learned English very quickly to supplement his knowledge of Russian, Polish, German, and Italian learned in the DP camps." The English learned from 29th Division dogfaces, however, was different than English learned in a proper school. His vocabulary came to feature so many obscenities, PFC Chuck Neighbor remembered, that Scipione "began cracking down when he used dirty language."

When Company E members chipped in to give Eddie some money the night before *Lejeune*'s arrival in New York, Eddie blurted, "I'll probably use this dough to buy a suit of clothes. Tomorrow I'll be a goddamn civilian." One day, after his adoption by Smiley, Eddie was playing baseball and the ball rolled into foul territory where the Boydton Elementary School principal was standing. "Hey, doc!" Eddie shouted. "Pick opp the ball!" Eddie enlisted in the U.S. Army when he reached adulthood, but he died at age forty-two in 1978.

The ferries and trains whisked the troops away to Camp Kilmer so speedily that the 29ers never got a moment to enjoy New York City. Too bad; despite the unfortunate labor problems, passing just a day in the city would have been a good way to readjust to stateside life and become acquainted with the many astonishing changes in American society over the past few years. Also, it would have been nice to witness the outpouring of appreciation that nearly three million New Yorkers displayed to the soldiery on January 12 when, as McCardell wrote in a front-page *Baltimore Sun* story, "every American soldier's dream came true." That afternoon, 13,000 men of the 82nd Airborne Division, led by Maj. Gen. James Gavin, paraded up Fifth Avenue from Washington Square all the way uptown to Central Park. "Every window on Fifth Avenue was a grandstand," McCardell noted. "A reviewing stand at 42nd Street had been filled since long before noon. . . . The curbs were packed solidly, ten and fifteen deep, with those in the back rows using periscopes distributed by a liquor concern." Sadly, the 29ers missed that memorable event.

Joe Ewing remembered that the 29ers' stay at Camp Kilmer was short, but hectic. "There was the steak dinner in the mess hall, with German PWs on the chow line," he wrote. "Formations, records, rosters, blank forms, examinations, movies, lying around your bunks in the barracks. . . . 'How the hell long are they going to keep us around here?' It wasn't long, however. Packets of troops formed for shipment to separation centers throughout the country [as near as possible to the 29ers' homes] left every day in a hubbub of handshaking, well-wishing and solemn promises to write. Troops marched in columns to the trains, shuffling along at route step, shouting and waving farewells to friends they spotted along the way."

No longer formed into coherent military units, but simply amassed in a jumbled group of men heading to the same separation center, the 29ers were at long last heading home. That final train ride could have lasted just an hour, to nearby Fort Dix, New Jersey; or it could have continued for days to a post as distant as Fort MacArthur, California. When they arrived at their separation centers, the men attended interviews with personnel officers and received their War Department "AGO Form 53-55," listing every bit of information about their military careers that could fit on one small sheet of paper, the most important of which was their "mustering out pay"—typically a few hundred dollars—and "travel pay" so they could reach home on the Army's dollar at five cents per mile. Treat the form like gold, the 29ers were told; it would be official proof of a U.S. Army Honorable Discharge—the form said as much on the reverse side. In the short term, it would be useful when looking for a job; much later, it would provide proof that an ex-soldier's family could bury him at government expense in a veterans' cemetery.

Assuming their forms had no errors, the 29ers provided a firm right-thumb fingerprint in the lower-left corner and, just below that, a signature. They were now officially discharged, although lacking civilian clothes—the Army would not provide any—they must wear their uniforms on the last leg of their homeward journey. In addition to the clothes they currently wore, regulations allowed the men to take home an extra Army shirt, hat, and pair of trousers; "all gloves, handkerchiefs, identification tags, neckties, socks, toilet articles, towels, underwear"; and one barracks bag to carry all those excess items home in addition to their personal possessions. Finally, enlisted men were issued an Honorable Discharge Emblem, known universally as the "Ruptured Duck," a diamond-shaped cloth patch to be sewn just above the right-breast jacket pocket, featuring an eagle encircled by a golden ring. Intended as "a badge of honor indicative of honest and faithful service while a member of the Armed Forces during World War II," the patch held the much more practical connotation that its wearer was no longer on active duty and therefore not subject to orders by NCOs, officers, or military policemen.

As the 29ers streamed out of Camp Kilmer throughout January 1946, the War Department initiated the steps required to deactivate the 29th Infantry Division. Ewing remarked: "The passing of the division from the ranks of the Army of the United States occurred prosaically, without benefit of ceremony. . . . There was no parade-ground formation to mark the inactivation of the division. No bands, no flapping standards and colors, no adjutant reading the last order, with restrained emotion." One by one, War Department general orders arrived at Camp Kilmer by telex, removing the great component units of the 29th Division from the U.S. Army's order of battle: the 116th Infantry, then the 175th, followed by the 115th and all the artillery units; then the 104th Medical Battalion, 121st Engineer Combat Battalion, and all the rest.

The 29th Infantry Division had ceased to exist.

FOR THE FREEDOM OF THE WORLD
Five years had passed since the 175th Infantry had assembled in the cavernous drill hall of the Fifth Regiment Armory on February 3, 1941, the day President Roosevelt had mobilized the 29th Division for one year of active service. Every one of the 950 men who reported for active duty that day at Baltimore's iconic armory, laid down in 1899 on Bolton Hill, was a member of the Maryland National Guard, accustomed to drilling one night per week for a dollar. Like it or not, a new army was forming, and plenty of changes loomed. Draftees would come later, when the regiment shifted to Fort Meade to link up with other 29th Division units and began to learn the rudiments of modern war. The first of those changes jolted old-time guardsmen, who learned upon reporting for duty that the historic regiment in which they had enlisted, the 5th Maryland Infantry—a title dating to 1792—would now be known by the unimaginative designation "175th Infantry Regiment." That would take some time to get used to.

Now, on the night of January 24, 1946, 500 men of the 175th gathered for a celebratory review in that same drill hall; the February 1941 mobilization seemed a part of a different epoch. Only a minute percentage of those 500 had been a part of the 1941 activation; the war had triggered profound changes in the lives of most of those present five years ago. Some had joined the Army Air Forces, others had become paratroopers or rangers, many had suffered debilitating wounds—and dozens were lying in American military cemeteries all over the world. "Let me assure you that every Marylander will always thrill with pride at the performance of the 175th in this greatest of all wars," Gov. Herbert O'Conor declared to the troops standing in formation on the drill floor. "When we have completed our welcome, let us all stand together, soldier and civilian, to make our state, our country, yes, our world itself, into a place fit for the heroes who have made it free."

Upon the bellowed command of Lt. Col. Tony Miller, who had enlisted as a private in this same armory in 1931, the men standing at attention in perfect ranks on the drill floor would pass in review before O'Conor and several other dignitaries, including Maj. Gen. Milton Reckord, the 29th Division's commanding general upon its 1941 mobilization and currently the Adjutant General of the

Maryland National Guard. The review, however, was one of the most curious in the storied history of the Fifth Regiment Armory. Months earlier nearly half the men in the ranks had been demobilized from the 175th and were now dressed in civilian clothes—one of those men had lost an arm in Brittany. Not a single man carried a weapon. The 175th's regimental color was conspicuously absent due to the War Department's recent decree that the 175th Infantry Regiment no longer existed: the flag had been unceremoniously furled at Camp Kilmer and shipped to Columbus, Ohio, for storage. Nevertheless, the troops—and civilians—marched as well as they ever had during wartime and gave perfect "eyes right" salutes to O'Conor as they passed the reviewing stand to the lively regimental march, "The Dandy Fifth of Maryland."

> Brooklyn Heights we stormed for Washington,
> Monmouth too, our valiant efforts won,
> Scott Key saw our colors flying,
> We took Monterrey half-trying . . .

"With the division battle cry, '29, Let's Go!' the men broke formation and headed for the lower floor [for a meal]," a *Sun* reporter wrote. "Over the bar rail in the Officers Club [on the second floor], former brass hats took time out to check up on peacetime jobs, then turned to the more entertaining memories of the seemingly endless hedgerow days, the battle of Hill 103 at Brest, the first leave in Paris, or perhaps the party in Joe Goebbels's castle."

Gerhardt always insisted the 29th Division was special, and he tried to prove it after the close of World War II by suggesting to his superiors in occupied Germany that the entire 29th Division deserved a highly coveted Distinguished Unit Citation—known today as the Presidential Unit Citation—in recognition of its achievements in the Rhineland offensive from November 16 to December 8, 1944. The odds against approval were overwhelming: Army guidelines indicated that a judging board of officers could grant a DUC only if they concluded that the unit in question had fought at the same extraordinary level required of an individual for a Medal of Honor or Distinguished Service Cross award, "with conspicuous gallantry and intrepidity above and beyond the call of duty." Typically regiments and battalions, sometimes even much smaller companies and platoons, were considered for DUC awards; only on a handful of occasions in World War II did the Army consider the action of an entire division worthy of such an exalted prize.

For anyone to claim that the 29th Division in its entirety deserved a DUC for the Rhineland offensive—a campaign that all participants agreed had failed—was asking for trouble. Nevertheless, sometime after V-E Day, Lt. Gen. Leonard

Gerow, head of the U.S. Fifteenth Army and Gerhardt's predecessor as 29th Division commander, submitted the recommendation for a DUC on the 29th's behalf to Maj. Gen. James Ulio, the Adjutant General of the U.S. Army. Gerow, however, had not been in Gerhardt's chain of command during the Rhineland offensive, so the Adjutant General's office eventually asked General Simpson, the Ninth Army commander under whom Gerhardt had served at that time, to comment on Gerow's recommendation. A tempest ensued when Simpson polled his former subordinates. "There is nothing in the history [of Ninth Army] to indicate that the activities of the 29th Infantry Division were of such a nature as to set it above any of the other divisions in the engagement," wrote Col. Clifford Kaiser. "I recommend disapproval." Simpson's former chief of staff, Brig. Gen. James Moore, was much more blunt. "There was nothing in the action that I remember which merited a Unit Citation," he remarked. "Just to the contrary. . . . I distinctly remember that as a result of this operation, General McLain took steps to relieve the division commander [Gerhardt]. That action was approved by everyone up to General Eisenhower, but was turned down by him."

A War Department board of officers ultimately rejected the DUC for the 29th Division, and even a special plea from Gerhardt to his West Point classmate, Ike Eisenhower, could not alter that judgment. "Although I am among the 29th Division's best rooters," Ike wrote back to Gerhardt on January 12, 1948, "I feel that I cannot reverse the decision of the Army Decorations Board."

The 29th Division received an honor at least equal to a Distinguished Unit Citation when the French Embassy in Washington announced on July 22, 1946, that the entire division had been awarded the exalted *Croix de Guerre avec Palme* by order of the President of France, Georges Bidault, for its participation in the Omaha Beach landing on D-Day. Of the *Croix de Guerre*'s many levels, this was one of the highest, indicating, as the inspiring citation noted, that the 29th Division was "a splendid unit, animated by the highest military virtues. . . . By seizing its objectives, the unit contributed greatly to the defeat of the enemy and the liberation of France." The embassy made arrangements to issue the award on January 10, 1947, to representatives of every outfit in the 29th Division in the Fifth Regiment Armory's vast drill hall, the only Maryland or Virginia armory big enough to hold so many men. The French military attaché in Washington, Gen. Maurice Mathenet—who had actually fought against the Americans for a few days in November 1942 as a Vichy general in Morocco—would do the honors by pinning the medal onto the colors or guidons of each of the twenty-two 29th Division units mentioned in the citation, including attached outfits such as the 747th Tank Battalion, which had loyally served the 29th in Operation *Overlord*. "It is with such baubles," Napoleon once remarked, "that men are led."

The Mayor of Baltimore, Theodore McKeldin, declared January 10 as "St. Lô Day" throughout the city and invited St. Lô's mayor, Georges Lavalley, to participate in the ceremonies. Upon Lavalley's arrival—a reporter noted he chewed gum like a GI—he and McKeldin proceeded to east Baltimore, where Lavalley cut the ribbon for a new road through Clifton Park named "St. Lô Drive." At the *Croix de Guerre* ceremony that night at the armory, Lavalley presented to the 29th Division a stone urn from Église Sainte-Croix, the wrecked St. Lô church upon whose rubble Maj. Tom Howie's body had lain under the Stars and Stripes after the 29ers' entry into the city on July 18, 1944. The urn was inscribed: "For the freedom of the world, American blood has flowed in France."

"What does it matter that we have lost our homes as long as our children do not live in slavery?" an emotional Lavalley asserted to the assemblage.

29, LET'S GO!

Col. Bill Witte knew the record of the 29th Infantry Division in the recent war better than anyone. The thirty-two-year-old Baltimorean, who had enlisted in the 5th Maryland as a private while pursuing a Johns Hopkins engineering degree, had been present at division headquarters as the 29th Division's chief operations officer throughout Gerhardt's tenure as commanding general. He had turned the general's fanciful whims into solid plans, soothed the bruised egos of those targeted by Gerhardt's wrath, and had a reputation as the 29th's number-one problem solver. Witte was so essential in the war room that Gerhardt referred to him as "my Napoleon."

For years Witte had fixated on the present; upon his return home to Baltimore, however, he began to fixate on the past. In his pivotal position at division headquarters in Europe, Witte had ensured that every piece of paper churned out by Gerhardt's war room since D-Day would be preserved. By the time the 29th Division moved into the Bremen Enclave in late May, that voluminous collection included transcripts of all telephone and radio conversations within the war room, monthly after-action reports, daily G-3 summaries, patrol reports, post-combat interviews, prisoner interrogations, photographs, a complete collection of mimeographed copies of the *29 Let's Go* newsletter, and every map and overlay used by the 29th Division from Omaha Beach to the Elbe River. Witte understood that time would dim the 29th Division's significant contributions to victory in World War II unless someone were selected to write the division's history straight away; whoever was named, the set of a dozen hefty wooden crates, stacked high in a storeroom at division headquarters in Grohn and filled to capacity with papers of all kinds, would be indispensable.

Witte had made an astute decision in the summer of 1945 when he selected the 175th Infantry's 1st Lt. Joseph Ewing as the prospective history book's author. Ewing had come to the attention of division headquarters when he created an unofficial Company G newsletter, titled *The Chin Strap*, in early 1945. Using nothing more than a captured German typewriter and a pencil, Ewing's light-hearted articles and accompanying caricatures poked fun at elements of front-line life. "Although I liked history in school," Ewing remembered, "I was not a historian—my academic major being journalism. But I believe my selection was because of *The Chin Strap*."

Ewing at first found the assignment an acute challenge, as he had not joined the 29th Division until after the fall of Brest in September 1944, but after spending the autumn of 1945 scrutinizing the division archives at the 29th Division's headquarters in Grohn, he knew he had more than enough information on hand to write the book. The real problem, Ewing noted, was "that the division had no idea of what the history should be. How long? How detailed? Was it to be a 'picture book' or a real history?" Not until Witte returned to the States in January 1946 did he reveal to Ewing that he wanted a "real history" book, not the simple yearbook-style collection of photos that many divisions were producing. Such an effort would take time, and Witte therefore had the thirty-six-year-old Ewing retained on active duty, first at Fort Meade and later at the War Department's Historical Division in Washington, D.C. For two years, under Witte's guidance, Ewing hammered out the 29th Division narrative on a typewriter, one chapter after another, using carbon paper to make a copy for Witte's perusal. "He would go over it word by word," Ewing recalled, "and return the chapter to me with an occasional change, a favorable or unfavorable comment, or a proposed addition." When Ewing completed the manuscript's first full draft, incorporating Witte's changes, he sent copies to "two generals and fourteen field grade officers" for their comments. Two of those recipients, John Purley Cooper and Glover Johns— both authors of future 29th Division histories—provided vital commentary that a grateful Ewing found invaluable.

Ewing understood his limits: although the book would not be an official governmental publication—it was to be issued, along with many other divisional histories, by the Infantry Journal Press in Washington—Ewing still wore the U.S. Army uniform, and any negativity or criticism of the 29th Division's leaders would have been promptly deleted by Witte, as Ewing recollected, "with a firm reprimand." Nevertheless, Ewing managed to boil down the vast trove of archival material at his disposal and produce a coherent, entertaining, and highly accurate story that stands nearly seven decades later as one of the finest U.S. Army divisional histories to emerge from World War II. He accomplished this while the war's proverbial dust still obscured the facts: before any combat veterans had penned their memoirs; before World War II 29ers had begun to attend reunions in large numbers; before any reliable information on the enemy had emerged; before official U.S. Army histories had been published—in fact, before any substantive book on World War II history could be found in a local library. He had neither computers nor copy machines nor tape recorders and had no budget for travel to interview fellow 29ers. Looking back on the project in 1996, when he was eighty-seven years old, Ewing regretted that for the most part former enlisted men had not contributed much to the book. "Were I to do it over again," he remarked, "I would urge broader distribution of the drafts."

Witte would consider no title other than *29 Let's Go*, the phrase contrived by Gerhardt as the division's motto in 1943. "Nothing reflected so much the temper of the 29th's commander," Ewing noted in the book's closing paragraph, "and nothing typified more the aggregate spirit of the Blue and Gray Division." In June 1947, Witte composed a letter to all former members of the 29th Division and mailed it to their last known addresses. "We have finally gotten the history of the 29th completed," he wrote. "The book will be mailed to subscribers early this fall. . . . This is the permanent record of your part in the war—a book which nudges a thousand old, half-forgotten memories of road marches, firefights, and occupation. It will remind you of men you marched with and fought with; raids, night patrols, counterattacks; cognac out of canteen cups; Thanksgiving dinner in K-ration boxes; dust and sweat in the hedgerows; the gray, muddy days on the Rhineland plain. . . . If you haven't already ordered, do it today—you can't afford to pass up a chance to get the history of the 29th—at this special pre-publication price, five dollars" [underlining in original].

One of Witte's letters, addressed to 1st Lt. Thomas Fernley of Flourtown Road, Plymouth Meeting, Pennsylvania, could not be opened by the addressee because he was dead, killed in action on April 24, 1945, near the Elbe River in Germany, while serving with the 29th Recon Troop. Instead, Fernley's father, George, opened the envelope. He promptly typed a single sentence on an index card—"I trust the history of the 29th Division is more accurate than your mailing list"—and mailed Witte's original letter back, enclosing not only the index card, but also the May 1945 condolence letter written to the senior Fernley by his son's commanding officer.

Witte received another letter that read: "In regard to the letter you sent to our foster son, Sgt. Charles Stenson [a member of Headquarters Battery, 224th Field Artillery Battalion], is it possible that you do not know he is supposed to be dead? At least that was the word we received in December 1944; that Charles was injured in Siersdorf, Germany, on November 18, 1944, and died in Holland the next day. His own mother in Winnipeg, Canada, is drawing his insurance. Charles came to us seven years before he went into the service, and we all dearly loved him. I want to know if you would let me have one of the histories of his 29th Division? I will send you five dollars."

Witte's promised early-fall 1947 publication date for *29 Let's Go* fell through due to unforeseen last-minute problems, causing a handful of impatient 29ers to write Witte and ask for their five dollars back. But with patience came rewards: when the Infantry Journal Press finally released the book in early 1948, it was an instant hit. After the first print run, "it was reprinted, and reprinted, and is being reprinted still again," a gratified Ewing noted in 1996. (It is about to be reprinted again in 2015.) "There must be some reason why 29ers and their families want to have and keep this book. And I think the reason is plain. Our personal wartime lives live on its pages." Ewing's poignant dedication page at the front of *29 Let's Go* touched the countless 29ers who had lost buddies in the war. Underneath the famous March 12, 1945, *LIFE* magazine photo by George Silk of a dead 29er—later identified as PFC Henry Slade Harrell—lying on a slender Roer River pontoon bridge, Ewing wrote: "To the soldiers of the 29th who fell in the battle."

Witte eventually deposited the complete set of the 29th Division's archival papers, photos, and maps in the Fifth Regiment Armory, the headquarters of the Maryland National Guard, and had the most important of the reports and transcripts bound into nearly fifty sturdy hardcover tomes. Ewing also collected all his notes, correspondence, and manuscript drafts and handed them over to Witte in a wooden box for safekeeping in the armory. Nearly five decades later Ewing opened that box for the first time since *29 Let's Go* was published and found his wartime diary, which long ago he had assumed was lost.

In the vast catalogue of 29th Division war trophies, the 175th Infantry assuredly had the most impressive collection. In addition to commonplace items such as Nazi flags, German Army small arms, helmets, and documents, the 175th also brought home a Cossack saber and a Russian submachine gun, gifts provided by the Red Army upon the regiment's first memorable encounter with the Soviets on May 2 and 3, 1945, near the Elbe River. All of those items would sooner or later end up in the Fifth Regiment Armory for display in the fledgling museum Col. William Purnell wished to set up. But the biggest trophies of all by far were the forty-four teakwood crates containing Crown Prince Wilhelm's silver collection, a vast set of early-twentieth-century tableware, statuettes, mirrors, decanters, and candlesticks captured by the 175th on May 2, 1945—and supposedly worth almost one million dollars. Purnell knew that War Department bureaucrats would start asking probing questions once they realized the set's immense value, so even before the 175th Infantry departed Bremerhaven for home, he composed a December 22, 1945, letter to Maj. Gen. James Ulio, the U.S. Army Adjutant General, "requesting authorization of a regimental war trophy." Purnell attached a thorough four-page inventory of the silver items for Ulio and concluded: "It is considered that the property listed in the enclosure should remain in the hands of the regiment as a suitable memorial of its participation in the late war, and as a valuable asset to the morale and spirit of the regiment when it resumes its National Guard status."

Purnell ordered the crates shipped home on one of the 29th Division's transports; they were unloaded in New York on January 4, 1946, packed into trucks, and delivered to the Fifth Regiment Armory. For nearly a year, while Purnell waited for a response from Ulio that never came, the 175th occasionally exhibited a few of the collection's most impressive pieces at private events within the armory. But a tempest erupted when a November 23 *Baltimore Sun* article reported that the 175th held custody of "an elaborate and valuable silver service

Some statuettes from Crown Prince Wilhelm's silver collection, captured by the 175th Infantry on May 2, 1945.

set" at the armory, taken from the enemy, as some 175th officers reported, as "legitimate booty." Despite Purnell's December 22, 1945, letter to Ulio—which the adjutant general's office never acknowledged receiving—the article reported that "records in Washington show no information about the silver service set."

The *Sun* article triggered an immediate response from Washington that Purnell had hoped to avoid: "The War Department has ordered the inspector general's [IG] office to investigate the silver service set now in the custody of the 175th Infantry Regiment," an official announcement declared on December 10, 1946. Two IG officers from the Pentagon arrived at the Fifth Regiment Armory a week later to resolve the affair. Purnell was not even a part of the 29th Division when the silver was captured, so he could merely pass the two investigators on to those men who had been present when the supposed "legitimate booty" fell into the 175th's hands. After a thorough study of the episode and examination of the teak boxes, the IG men hastily prepared a report that absolved the 175th of any wrongdoing, stating that the regiment's actions in May 1945 were "completely proper [and] in accordance with existing regulations." But Purnell's dream of an elegant armory museum, featuring the captured silver in a centerpiece exhibit, evaporated when the IG officers concluded that, according to the Seventy-Ninth Article of War, "All public property taken from the enemy is the property of the United States."

In early January 1947, a team from the provost marshal's office at Fort Meade transferred the entire silver collection from the armory to a U.S. Customs facility in Baltimore. It never came back. Several weeks later, the set was relocated once again to the National Gallery of Art in Washington "for safekeeping . . . pending a decision as to its ultimate disposition." That decision, when it was finally made in January 1949, disappointed a bitter Purnell. As related by a *Sun* reporter, "Although the collection was brought to this country in the belief it was a war trophy, the Army said it was finally decided that the silver set was not subject to capture as booty or as a war trophy under the provisions of the Hague Convention of 1907. One Army official explained that the collection was ruled out as booty because it was not the property of the German state but that of enemy individuals and not used in the prosecution of the war." With little fanfare, the silver was repacked in its original teak boxes and carried aboard a steamer in New York on January 11, 1949, for the voyage back to Germany. The crates would be stored at a Frankfurt bank, a War Department official said, "until proof of ownership can be established."

The Fifth Regiment Armory eventually took in an artifact that made a much better museum centerpiece than silver tableware: *Vixen Tor*, Gerhardt's 1942 Willys-Overland Motors MB jeep. What could be a better symbol of the 29th Division's gallant World War II service, Purnell surmised, than that iconic vehicle, with which thousands of wartime 29ers had become familiar due to the general's frequent visits to front-line command posts? Even before *Vixen Tor*'s arrival in New York aboard the transport *Lejeune*, reporter Lou Azrael of the *Baltimore News-Post* hinted at its destination in a January 5, 1946, story that declared the jeep might be headed to "a permanent exhibition at the Fifth Regiment Armory."

But neither Gerhardt nor the U.S. Army was willing to let *Vixen Tor* go just yet. The general had the curious notion that he would transfer the jeep "for safe-keeping" to his trusty driver, T/3 Bob Cuff, whom he held responsible for *Vixen Tor*'s "fine condition and upkeep during the war. There never was a commander who had a better vehicle." Gerhardt had to admit, however, that "I couldn't turn it over to you as your personal property because it still belongs to the government . . . [but] you would be at perfect liberty to use it in any way you saw fit." The general concluded: "You can use this letter as authority for having it in your possession, as I assume full responsibility for the jeep, its proper care and maintenance."

General Gerhardt seated in his jeep, *Vixen Tor*, which is now displayed in Baltimore's Fifth Regiment Armory. The driver is T/3 Robert Cuff of Ashton, Maryland.

In his role as chief of the Maryland National Guard, however, crusty sixty-seven-year-old Gen. Milton Reckord had authority over the jeep, and he turned down Gerhardt's request. *Vixen Tor* was thereupon assigned to an ordinary Fort Meade motor pool, and after a few years ended up in what one officer described as a post "junkyard." He remembered that "the jeep was a wreck. . . . No tires, dirty, and beat up." The Army assigned Gerhardt to a five-year stint as a Second Army staff officer at Fort Meade in late 1947, and when he learned of *Vixen Tor*'s deplorable condition, he designated an officer to restore it. In October 1951, 29th Division veterans convened in Newark, New Jersey, for their thirty-third annual reunion, and to the delight of the attendees, the jeep was turned on its side, squeezed through the front door of a hotel lobby, and kept on display throughout the weekend. (The young 29th Division World War II veterans were on their best behavior throughout the reunion. "There was none of the hilarity, none of the noise, none of the playboy activities usually associated with veterans' conventions," a reporter noted.) Eventually, Bill Purnell—who became the 29th Division's commander in 1957—got his wish, and *Vixen Tor* was retired to a place of honor in Baltimore's Fifth Regiment Armory, where it still sits today as the centerpiece in the "Blue and Gray Room" of the 29th Division Museum.

The 29th Division returned to the U.S. Army's order of battle in July 1946, just six months after its January inactivation at Camp Kilmer. According to the War Department's vast 1946 Army overhaul, the 29th would resume its prewar status as an all–National Guard division, one of twenty-seven division-size Guard units in the United States. The new 29th Division would be composed entirely of Maryland and Virginia National Guard units; divisional engineer and military police outfits that had been drawn from the District of Columbia National Guard before the war would now be raised in Maryland instead. Gerhardt's former artillery chief, the cantankerous fifty-four-year-old Brig. Gen. William Sands—a World War I veteran—was appointed the 29th's new commanding general and promoted to two-star rank. For a year or more, however, the 29th Division was little more than a shell as frazzled recruiters in towns and cities throughout Maryland and Virginia strove to enlist sufficient men so that local companies and batteries could gain official federal recognition as legitimate combat-ready military units.

On November 11, 1946, at the direction of President Truman, the U.S. Army symbolically acknowledged the reactivation of the National Guard by returning retired regimental and battalion colors to their rightful owners in Armistice Day ceremonies nationwide. "I was a National Guardsman myself in the First World War," Truman declared at one such observance at the Tomb of the Unknown Soldier in Arlington Cemetery. "I hope they will use [the colors] to train young men in the interests of peace and the welfare of the country. And I am sure they will do just that."

At simultaneous events in Baltimore and Richmond, the historic flags that had only recently been furled at Camp Kilmer were handed back to the Maryland and Virginia units comprising the new 29th Division. At Baltimore's War Memorial Plaza, across the street from City Hall, Sen. Millard Tydings—a World War I 29er—noted that "in this day of atom bombs, cosmic rays, supersonic planes, 15,000-mile bombers, and all the things that are still to come, another war would shake the very foundation of civilizations." As related by a *Sun* article, "The senator asked his listeners to make it their first duty to work for preparedness and not follow any futile disarmament movements until world affairs become settled," and concluded that "Hot-headed men who declare war on street corners are usually not the ones who give their lives on the field of battle."

In the U.S. Army's extensive postwar retrenchment, Gerhardt had to accept a reduction in rank from major general to brigadier general a few months after his return from Europe. He received a choice post, however, as chief of the Army section of the Joint Brazil–United States Military Commission in Rio de Janeiro. During his eighteen months in that role, the general noted, "The feeling by Brazilians for Americans was very warm, and I was tremendously impressed with this vast country." In late 1947, Gerhardt returned to the United States and was assigned as chief intelligence officer on the Second Army staff at Fort Meade. In July 1948, shocked 29th Division veterans learned that Brigadier General Gerhardt had automatically been reduced to the rank of colonel when his name did not appear on the list of officers recommended for permanent one-star rank in the U.S. Army. No official explanation was given for this omission, but those who knew the 29th Division's World War II history speculated that it had something to do with the many controversial episodes in which Gerhardt had been involved during the war: his six-day absence from the 29th Division in late September 1944, for example, when General Bradley had ordered the 29th shifted from Brittany to Holland with all possible speed; or Ninth Army's investigation of the 29th Division's illicit house of prostitution at Brest; or General McLain's exasperation with Gerhardt over the severe casualties suffered by the 29th in the November 1944 Rhineland offensive, during which Gerhardt would have been relieved had Eisenhower not intervened.

During their frequent visits to Fort Meade, Maryland and Virginia National Guard officers populating the new 29th Division now and then ran into the man under whom they had served in wartime; in some awkward encounters, Gerhardt had to salute former subordinates who now outranked him. That development so outraged loyal 29ers that when veterans gathered in Norfolk, Virginia, in September 1948 for the division's thirtieth annual convention, a scathing resolution passed, condemning the Army for its treatment of Gerhardt and charging that "politics was the reason" for the step. The Baltimore veterans' post sponsoring the resolution observed: "It is regrettable that their battle commander should be reduced and relegated below the rank of a general officer; it is a matter of shock, bitter resentment, and deep-seated disappointment to his men who served with and under General Gerhardt that he be so undeservedly, unconscionably, and unwarrantedly treated."

THE VANISHED ARMY

And so the men who fought the war came home, both the living and the dead, to a country that had little inclination to learn what they had endured. Those long-service 29th Division soldiers fortunate enough to return to the United States as living, breathing men desperately needed to release the jaded memories stored in their jumbled psyches, but found receptive audiences only among those men who had lived through similar experiences. When 1st Lt. Bob Easton of the 116th Infantry came home to California in November 1945 and held a joyful reunion with his parents, he noted with amazement: "They speak as if nothing has happened, as if everything will go on as before. Deep down inside I want to shout, 'No, no, it can't!'—to try and tell them all that has happened to me, to the world; but know that I cannot, that it is impossible and probably always will be. And deep down I know they're right. Nothing has changed. Life is made up of banalities and trivia. . . . Where are the words to express the horror, the glory, the destruction, the heroism, the suffering, the despair and hope, the miracle of survival and the new world we should be talking about?"

In October 1947, the first two ships transporting dead American servicemen home from their overseas burial sites arrived in the United States: first, the Army transport *Honda Knot*, with 3,027 dead from the Pacific Theater, docked in San Francisco on the tenth; little more than two weeks later, the *Joseph V. Connolly*, with 6,248 dead aboard from Europe, berthed in New York on the twenty-sixth. If anything could jolt Americans into sympathy for the scarred survivors who had experienced prolonged combat in World War II, it would be the unloading of the dead from those two vessels and the movement of the bodies to cemeteries throughout the United States for burial.

The solemn process had begun in 1946 with the distribution of the impersonal War Department OQMG (Office of the Quartermaster General) Form 345—"Request for Disposition of Remains"—to the next of kin of every American servicemember killed overseas in World War II. Form 345 required a widow, parent, or other close relative to choose one of four options by checking the appropriate box. "Having familiarized myself with the options which have been made available to me with respect to the final resting place of the deceased," the form stated, "I now do declare that it is my desire that the remains: 1. Be interred in a permanent American Military cemetery overseas; 2. Be returned to the United States or any possession or territory thereof for interment by next of kin in a private cemetery; 3. Be returned to a foreign country, the homeland of the deceased or next of kin, for interment by next of kin in a private cemetery; 4. Be returned to the United States for final interment in a national cemetery."

Postponed for months due to delays in the production of seamless steel caskets in the United States and their delivery to Europe, the laborious process of exhuming American World War II dead from temporary graves in Europe for reburial in permanent cemeteries overseas or in the States was initiated by the Office of the Quartermaster General in July 1947 and continued for over four years. "Civilians were largely employed to excavate the dead and work on the remains," wrote Lt. Col. Joseph Shomon of the Quartermaster Corps. "A temporary morgue building was set up to which the bodies were carried. Depending on the length of time a body lay in the temporary grave and the condition of the body at the time of burial, the corpses were either partially or fully decomposed, yet still pretty much intact. . . . Some bodies were still fleshy even after four years in the ground. [Bodies in temporary cemeteries had not been buried in caskets; simple cloth shrouds had been used.] All disinterred remains were taken to the morgue building where all clothing and flesh were removed, then burned, and the existing bones or full skeleton were washed, cleaned, sterilized, and then placed in identified and properly marked hermetically sealed [steel] caskets. . . . Caskets to be returned to America went into one section, those that were to be reburied in the permanent cemetery were carried to another section."

Twenty-niners whose next of kin had checked Form 345's Box 1—burial in a permanent American military cemetery overseas—would ultimately be spread among five European cemeteries: Colleville in Normandy, St. James in Brittany, Henri-Chapelle in Belgium, Margraten in the Netherlands, and Cambridge in Britain. Those whose next of kin had checked Boxes 2 or 4—burial in the United States—would be shipped home aboard U.S. Army transports, a process that commenced on July 28, 1947, when Belgian workers began to disinter thousands of bodies from the temporary Henri-Chapelle cemetery in Belgium. With a solemn dignity provided by ever-present U.S. Army escorts, the bodies were eventually floated on barges down the Maas River and various canals to the port of Antwerp. In the last week of September, Antwerp dock workers loaded them aboard the Army transport *Joseph V. Connolly*. Not all the Henri-Chapelle dead could fit into *Connolly*, however, so a second U.S. Army transport, *Robert F. Burns*, took on some 3,100 more in early November after a stop in Cherbourg, France, to embark 1,052 bodies from the temporary St. Laurent cemetery adjacent to Omaha Beach. *Connolly* departed Antwerp for the States on October 4, 1947; *Burns* set out for home on November 7.

A few days prior to *Connolly*'s departure, a somber ceremony was held on the Antwerp dockside, attended, as one historian noted, by "30,000 reverent

Belgian citizens." The governor-general of the U.S. occupation zone in Germany, Gen. Lucius Clay, stood next to a flag-draped casket before it was carried onto the ship and avowed: "We have not yet found the lasting peace for which these men died in their youth. We must determine that free men everywhere should stand together in solid front to ensure a world in which there is a lasting peace, in which the dignity of the individual is recognized and maintained."

Following a three-day stop in Newfoundland to pick up U.S. servicemen who had died at American bases there during the war, *Connolly* sailed into New York harbor on the morning of Sunday, October 26, 1947, escorted by the destroyers *Bristol* and *Beatty* and the Coast Guard cutter *Spencer*. The *New York Times* reporter Meyer Berger, a World War I veteran and writer of the hugely popular "About New York" column, watched *Connolly*'s approach from aboard *Bristol* and noted as *Connolly* sailed up the Hudson that the battleship *Missouri*'s twenty-one-gun salute from its massive 16-inch guns was like "echoing thunder . . . rumbling to the horizon." As the ship passed ferryboats plying the Upper Bay between Staten Island and Manhattan, Berger observed that the "crowds on their decks were bareheaded, and the passengers bowed as in prayer."

Connolly docked at Pier 61 at 21st Street at 11:25 A.M., and Berger overheard one sailor whisper to another: "They came in too late. The 'Welcome Home' signs and the signs with 'Well Done' are all painted out or have faded. There's something ironic in that." At that time of year, early-morning frosts usually permeated the city, but the day broke cloudless and warm, and that afternoon's 74-degree temperature would break a record. At 12:45 P.M., a party of soldiers carried a single flag-draped casket down the gangplank from the port side of *Connolly*'s boat deck and hoisted it onto a caisson flanked by eight men drawn from the Army, Navy, Marine Corps, Coast Guard, and the newly established Air Force—created exactly one month ago. Attached to a U.S. Army M8 Greyhound armored car, the caisson and its escorts moved off the dock onto Eleventh Avenue and took position behind a contingent of New York policemen mounted on horses. After proceeding two blocks north, the cortege swung east on 23rd Street as 6,000 men and women in uniform, veterans, and New York civic groups fell in behind.

New Yorkers thronged the sidewalks, but what struck Berger the most was their silence. "Nobody spoke, not even the children. Eyes were moist and lips moved in prayer as the flag-draped coffin passed," he wrote. "Far down the line came the music—the slow, soft tones of the dirges—and the slow, measured cadence of slow-marching boots. No other sounds broke in." A mile down 23rd Street the procession halted at Madison Square Park, where Gen. Courtney Hodges, under whom many of *Connolly*'s dead had served, laid a wreath at the base of the Eternal Light flagstaff, dedicated on Armistice Day, 1923, "to commemorate the first homecoming of the victorious Army and Navy of these United

States," as its plaque noted, "officially received by the City of New York on this site, Anno Domini MCMXVIII." Then, amid the pealing bells of the Metropolitan Life Tower—once the tallest building in the world—the cortege turned left and headed up Fifth Avenue as a band played "Onward, Christian Soldiers."

"The marchers were grim," Berger wrote in a front-page *Times* story the next day. "Behind the mounted police came the West Point cadets, then a battalion of middies. The boots of the 82nd Airborne beat out a steady step, and the sun struck lights from their helmets." Onward they marched, past the Empire State Building, past the slumbering lions of the New York Public Library, past Rockefeller Center and St. Patrick's Cathedral, past the Sherman statue and Pulitzer Fountain in Grand Army Plaza. Berger noted simply, "The crowds at the curb were moved." At 60th Street, he observed "a little street sweeper [who] held his broom stiffly with his left hand while his right hand rose in salute as the caisson rolled past him. No one smiled. Men and women stared at the street sweeper with grave understanding, and bowed their heads to their chests in silent salute."

The armored car pulled the casket into Central Park at 72nd Street and proceeded another third of a mile to the Sheep Meadow, a place "which in past Sundays," another *Times* reporter wrote, "has been the scene of youthful boisterousness and cavorting." Officials estimated 150,000 people waited in and around the meadow, all standing in reverential silence as the casket passed down a central path that police had roped off to hold back the multitude. Pallbearers then carried the casket up a ramp to a platform, eleven feet high, and set it upon a bier. After a two-minute silence, at exactly 3:10 P.M., a battery of artillery manned by West Point cadets boomed another twenty-one-gun salute, and Berger wrote that the sound "flattened against Central Park West's towering apartment facades"— the Dakota, the San Remo, the Langham, the Majestic—"and rolled back over the park. . . . Everywhere on the Meadow tears started and women stifled their weeping. In a front-row seat, a woman started up. She stretched out her arms and screamed the name 'Johnny.' The dirge lifted and fell. Then in a brief space of silence the woman screamed out again: 'There's my boy, there's my boy,' and other women, beside her, put comforting arms on her shoulders. She stifled her cries, but her shoulders shook with emotion."

After short speeches by Mayor William O'Dwyer and Gov. Thomas Dewey, a U.S. Navy chaplain spoke a somber benediction: "Almighty God, our Father, before thee is a chosen child of the American people, chosen in death to represent all our children." Three volleys fired by an honor guard then cracked over the meadow, followed forthwith by a bugler, whose version of "Taps," according to Berger, yielded a "choking sadness" over the crowd, "suspended in quivering, unseasonal heat." Returning to their charge, the pallbearers carried the casket back down the ramp to the caisson. "Emotional tension could almost be felt in

The October 26, 1947, ceremony in Central Park's Sheep Meadow, honoring the first dead American servicemen brought home from Europe.

waves," Berger reported. "Again the mother down front shrilled, 'Johnny, my Johnny,' and accents carried far, and they hurt. Men bit at their lips. The woman cried, 'Where is my boy?' but again kind arms enfolded her, and her cries were reduced to sobbing."

In keeping with the American military tradition that no ceremonial observance should end on a gloomy note, the caisson and its escorting troops proceeded out of the Sheep Meadow to the march "The Vanished Army," written in 1918 by the British Army composer Kenneth Alford in honor of Britons who had died in World War I. It was the perfect choice. Designated by Alford as a "Poetic March," the tune began with a stirring introduction by B-flat trumpets that shattered the solemn silence of the service. The first two-thirds of the march, described by Berger as "sweet melancholy," traded back and forth between dirge-like passages in a minor key and more upbeat major-key segments. But as the caisson with its casket pulled out of the Sheep Meadow toward one of Central Park's traverse roads, the tune closed with a triumphant finale that lived up to the march's uplifting subtitle: "They Never Die."

Life in the city would go on—must go on. "The camp-chairs were folded and stacked," a *Times* reporter noted, "and the Sheep Meadow was left to a few young boys and their football."

The escort returned the casket to *Connolly* at Pier 61 at 4:43 P.M. By that time, an observer remarked, "the pier was almost empty." On October 27 at 8:00 A.M., *Connolly* departed for the short trip to the Brooklyn Army Terminal in Bay Ridge to begin the laborious process of offloading all 6,248 caskets and dispatching them on their final journey home. *Connolly* docked at one of three enclosed piers, each a quarter-mile long, shortly before 11:00 A.M.; more than 2,000 people waited inside to witness a short memorial service. The only speaker, Brooklyn Borough president John Cashmore, concluded the observance with words no one could refute: "No matter what you think about the way things are going today, this would not have been so had the other side won." Upon the audience's departure, the longshoremen began the job at 1:25 P.M., using cranes to hoist pallets, each loaded with two flag-draped caskets, out of *Connolly*'s hold for transfer to a third-story loading dock on the adjacent pier shed. Meanwhile, fifty olive-drab mortuary train coaches—modified U.S. Army hospital cars with blackened windows—waited on two railroad tracks in an enclosed atrium of "Building B," a huge eight-story warehouse just a few hundred yards from the pier. From the moment workers hauled the pallets onto the loading dock from *Connolly*, the movement of the caskets to the train platform was performed entirely indoors by means of covered skybridges connecting the pier shed to Building B.

Watched intently by sentries dressed in spotless uniforms and white gloves, armed with M-1 rifles and standing at textbook "at ease" postures, the workers rolled the caskets onto the platform and up a small wooden ramp leading into the mortuary coach. Meanwhile a supervisor methodically checked his clipboard to ensure the voluminous paperwork was accurate: "Each shipping case [casket] required a Health Permit Marker," noted Edward Steere, the U.S. Army Quartermaster Corps historian, "certifying that all customs, municipal clearance, and New York Port of Embarkation interstate and intrastate transit requirements concerning the preparation, inspection, and transportation of remains had been met." As soon as each set of mortuary coaches was fully loaded with caskets, a locomotive pulled them to a harborside terminal just a few hundred yards distant, where they were shoved, six coaches at a time, onto barges known as "car floats." Tugboats then towed the barges three miles across the Upper Bay to Greenville, New Jersey; as soon as the barges tied up to the quay, yard workers hauled the coaches off into a huge railroad yard, where dispatchers assigned them to various sidings depending on their final destination. When sufficient coaches heading to the same place had been coupled together—some lengthy trains carried more than 500 caskets—a locomotive pulled the train out of the yard and began a journey to one of fourteen distribution centers across the United States, from San Francisco, California, to Schenectady, New York. That journey could take just a few hours or several days. From the distribution centers, local trains and motor vehicles would eventually transport the caskets to the grieving families' hometowns. (The Brooklyn Army Terminal, where *Connolly* had docked that morning, was itself also a distribution center, covering the New York City metropolitan area and southern New England.)

On November 25, 1947, *Robert F. Burns* docked at the Brooklyn Army Terminal with 4,212 more bodies from Europe. Although less than one month had passed since *Connolly*'s arrival, other news, particularly of the nascent Cold War, had shoved the repatriation of American war dead off the front pages of American newspapers. Had Americans already allowed the cost of World War II to sink into the depths of their psyches? The November 26 edition of the *New York Times* covered *Burns*'s homecoming with an eight-sentence article buried deep in the paper on page twenty-four. However, *Burns*'s cargo was of particular interest to 29th Division families, as 1,052 of its dead had been exhumed from the temporary cemetery at St. Laurent, France, and included many 29ers who had been killed on Omaha Beach and in the subsequent fighting in the Norman *bocage*. Several more 29th Division men were included among the other 3,160 remains aboard *Burns* disinterred from Henri-Chapelle cemetery in Belgium.

One of the dozens of 29ers onboard *Burns* was Capt. Maurice (pronounced "Morris") McGrath, killed in action on October 7, 1944, in Baesweiler, Germany, while in command of the 116th Infantry's Company L during his regiment's three-week attachment to the 2nd Armored and 30th Infantry Divisions in the ferocious battle for Aachen. A veteran of the Omaha Beach invasion, McGrath's dynamic D-Day leadership caused a U.S. Army lieutenant colonel to comment, "This captain's whole course of action on this day is unusually enterprising." Over the next four months, he gained a Silver Star, Bronze Star, and Purple Heart, leading a fellow officer to categorize him as "the most daring man I have ever met." But McGrath had a premonition his luck would soon run out. "He gave me a letter and asked me to mail it in case anything happened," a comrade recalled. "I insisted to him that he stop talking such nonsense, but he declared that he had a feeling and only hoped and prayed if and when [he was killed] that it would be in Germany."

It was. McGrath was buried at 1:00 P.M. on October 9, 1944, in a grave at Henri-Chapelle, Plot F, Row 7, Grave 131, with a 2nd Armored Division sergeant by the name of Fisher on his right and a 29th Division comrade from the 115th Infantry, PFC Vernard Murray, on his left. By checking Form 345's Box 2 sometime in 1946, McGrath's mother and father, Sarah and T. Edward McGrath—who

Capt. Maurice McGrath of the 116th Infantry in Britain in 1943. His body was disinterred from Henri-Chapelle Cemetery in Belgium and returned to the United States aboard *Robert F. Burns* in November 1947. He is buried at Westminster Cemetery in Philadelphia.

had been named by Captain McGrath as his beneficiaries—chose to have their son's body brought home for burial in Westminster Cemetery, situated on the banks of the Schuylkill River less than a mile from their modest brick duplex at 4436 Mitchell Street in the Roxborough section of northwest Philadelphia, where Maurice had grown up. Maurice's sister-in-law, Mary McGrath, recalled that in October 1944 Sarah had received the news of her son's death stoically. "There was no loud crying or uncontrollable grief," she wrote. "Sarah just sat with the cardboard box of Maurice's V-Mail letters, saying quietly and sadly, over and over, 'I won't have anymore letters from him.' Her courage was admirable. She had another son [Capt. Edward McGrath] at that very moment fighting with the 101st Airborne Division. In two months time, Ed would be living through the unbelievable Battle of the Bulge."

Capt. Maurice McGrath's body was disinterred from his Henri-Chapelle grave on September 22, 1947, and shipped down the Maas to Antwerp aboard the barge *Petrus* on October 3. On McGrath's official "Disinterment Directive," an embalmer named Harris Nelson noted: "body complete." *Burns* received McGrath's casket on November 6, departed Antwerp the next day with 4,211 other deceased American servicemen, and arrived in New York on the twenty-fifth. One week later, on December 2, longshoremen at the Brooklyn Army Terminal hoisted the casket from *Burns*'s hold, placed it aboard a mortuary coach, and speedily shipped it with dozens of others across New York's Upper Bay to New Jersey on a car float. The next day, a train bearing McGrath's casket departed the rail yard at Greenville, New Jersey, heading south for the Philadelphia Quartermaster Depot, just ninety miles to the south.

The War Department exerted prodigious effort to inform families of the imminent homecoming of their deceased servicemen. While *Burns* was still at sea, Edward and Sarah McGrath received a War Department message informing them to expect the arrival of their son's body in Philadelphia in the "near future," adding: "If you desire military honors at funeral, you should ask local patriotic or veterans organization of your choice to make arrangements." At noon on December 11, 1947, eight days after the arrival of McGrath's casket at the Philadelphia Quartermaster Depot, a driver and an immaculately dressed U.S. Army escort officer, Capt. Charles Tribbey, conveyed the body in a government hearse to the Emmett Fitzpatrick Funeral Home at 425 Lyceum Avenue, just around the corner from the McGraths' Mitchell Street house. That evening, the McGraths brought the casket into their living room and held a wake for close friends and family—including Maurice's two older brothers, Joe and Edward, and his younger sister, Katherine. The next day, December 12, a funeral mass was held just five blocks down the hill toward the Schuylkill River at St. John the Baptist Church on Rector Street—the same church at which Maurice had been baptized in 1918. Following the mass, the funeral procession crossed the Schuylkill and entered Westminster Cemetery, where Capt. Maurice McGrath of the 29th Infantry Division was finally laid to rest in the family plot, more than three years after his death at age twenty-six in a bleak German village amid the greatest cataclysm in world history.

Exactly one month later, the United States government fully reimbursed the McGraths for their funeral expenses, totaling $283.

LAST ROLL CALL

And so all that was left of Maury McGrath and the other 3,719 29ers who had answered the last roll call in the recent war was the jumbled remembrance of things past, fixed into the psyches of those parents, wives, sweethearts, siblings, and comrades who had known them in happier times: in infancy, in adolescence, in adulthood, and at that last overpowering moment when the throngs of soldiers had stepped aboard a troop train to begin a new life with prospects so hazy that no one dared to guess at the future. Perhaps the memory that stood out most was a kiss, a handshake, a hug, a simple touch; maybe it was an indelible image of a cheerful face, or a mournful one; possibly it was a poignant flashback of words spoken in love, anger, joy, even despair. Whatever memories stood out among the living, assuredly there were not enough to cling to, and over time they would fade; decades later, all that would be left would be photos, letters, and the muted remembrances of the elderly passed on to a younger generation who had never known the men who had fallen in battle. The future those civilians-turned-soldiers had tried to figure out before boarding that last troop train had turned out to be appallingly short. The lives they could have lived—the things that might have been—are now nothing but reveries held tightly by the dwindling few who knew them in the flesh. If only . . .

"At the going down of the sun and in the morning, we will remember them."

Notes

The following citations provide the bibliographic or archival sources from which the historical information in this book was derived. The following examples demonstrate how citations are read:

24   *"It was an unbelievable luxury"*: Ewing, *29 Let's Go*, 216.

Thus, on page 24, the source for the quote beginning with "It was an unbelievable luxury . . . " is Joseph Ewing's book *29 Let's Go*, page 216. For more details on the book *29 Let's Go*, consult the bibliography. Here is another example:

118   *"Nice going!"*: 29ID, *WRJ*, 1/17/45, 0747.

Thus, on page 118, when General Gerhardt states, "Nice going!" the source for that quote is the 29th Infantry Division Archives, specifically the division's *War Room Journal (WRJ)* for January 17, 1945, at 7:47 A.M. See the next page for a full list of abbreviations.

Most of the historical information provided in this book was derived from the 29th Infantry Division Archives, managed by the Maryland Military Department and housed in the Fifth Regiment Armory, 29th Division St., Baltimore, MD, 21201. The abbreviation "29ID" is used in citations to indicate historical details drawn from this source, followed by more specific information detailing the precise location in the archives where those details can be found. For example, the abbreviation "RCG" indicates that the information can be located in the archival boxes pertaining to the 29th Division's combat period in the Rhineland and Central Germany in the late winter and spring of 1945; "Personnel" means that the information can be found in the files on individual 29th Division soldiers.

For further information on the history of the 29th Infantry Division, please join our "29th Infantry Division Archives" page on Facebook or consult our websites at www.29div.com or www.angelfire.com/md/29division. To contact the author, email him at 29division@gmail.com.

The following abbreviations are used in the citations:

29ID: 29th Infantry Division Archives, Fifth Regiment Armory, Baltimore, MD; **29LG**: 29th Division newsletter *29 Let's Go*; **AAR**: After-action report; **BE**: "Bremen Enclave" archival box, 29th Infantry Division Archives; **CI**: Combat Interviews; **CIC**: Counter Intelligence Corps; **DEP**: Dwight Eisenhower Papers, Johns Hopkins University Press; **FM**: Field Manual; **GCM**: George C. Marshall Papers, Bland, ed., Johns Hopkins University Press; **G3J**: 29th Division G-3 Journal; **H/G**: "Holland/Germany" archival boxes, 29th Infantry Division Archives; **IDPF**: Individual Deceased Personnel File; **MHI**: Military History Institute, Carlisle Barracks, PA; **MR**: Morning Reports; **MS**: Manuscript; **NA**: U.S. National Archives and Records Administration, College Park, MD; **RCG**: "Rhineland-Central Germany" archival box, 29th Infantry Division Archives; **RG**: U.S. National Archives Record Group; **USMASC**: U.S. Military Academy Library Special Collections, West Point, NY; **VG**: *Volksgrenadier*; **WRJ**: 29th Division War Room Journal.

1. WE'VE COME A HELL OF A WAY
Bitter Delaying Actions

1   *"I am thoroughly convinced"*: 29ID, RCG, File 8, POW Interrogations, 12/17/44, Extracts of Psychological Warfare POW Interrogation reports.

2   *"surprised by the strength"*: Heiber and Glantz, *Hitler and His Generals: Military Conferences, 1942–1945*, 1045.

2   *"The offensive didn't succeed"*: Ibid., 557–58.

2   *"Offensive operations"*: Ibid., 557.

2   *"I am already preparing"*: Ibid., 558.

2   *"Stalingrad Number Two"*: Liddell Hart, *The German Generals Talk*, 292.

2   *"death blow"*: MacDonald, *A Time for Trumpets*, 608.

3   *"conduct operations with the objective of"*: GCM, vol. 4, 636.

3   *"Germany will go on fighting"*: USMASC, *Dickson Papers*, G-2 Estimates, 10/31/44.

3   *"It is entirely possible"*: Croswell, *Beetle*, 798.

4   *"You cannot have such a protracted struggle"*: George C. Marshall Library, Lexington, VA, microfilm reel 322, Marshall interview, 7/25/49, Part II, by Matthews, Smith, Lemson, and Hamilton, 7.

4   *"the year ended with a setback"*: The American Presidency Project, Franklin D. Roosevelt, State of the Union Address, 1/6/45, www.presidency .ucsb.edu/ws/index.php?pid=16595.

4   *"Hangover Raid"*: Craven and Cate, *The Army Air Forces in WWII: Europe, Argument to V-E Day*, 665.

5   *"I celebrated New Year's"*: 29ID, Personnel, Kenney, 1/1/45 letter.

6   *"all planes entered the area"*: 29ID, 554th AAR, Jan. 1945, 3.

6   *"just flew around aimlessly"*: Cooper, *History of the 110th Field Artillery*, 199.

6   *"a Focke-Wulf 190"*: 29ID, *WRJ*, 1/1/45, 1024.

6   *"This morning I saw three Jerry planes"*: 29ID, Personnel, Kenney, 1/1/45 letter.

6   *destroying nearly 200*: Davis, *Carl A. Spaatz and the Air War in Europe*, 535.

6   *"Again, the Luftwaffe had demonstrated"*: Craven and Cate, *Europe: Argument to V-E Day*, 665.

Learning Defensive Stuff

8   *"We've come a hell of a way"*: 29ID, *29LG*, 1/2/45.

9   *"General, what do you care"*: 29ID, Personnel, Gerhardt, Memoirs, 52.

9   *"While [Brady] was there"*: 29ID, *WRJ*, 1/2/45, 0010.

10   *"The officer in charge"*: 29ID, *WRJ*, 1/1/45, 2311.

10   *"was killed in action"*: 29ID, Personnel, Walker, 1945 McKenna letter to Ellen Walker.

11   *"The entire period was devoted"*: 29ID, 121st AAR, Jan. 1945, 3.

11   *"Each mine installation"*: 29ID, *29LG*, 1/6/45.

11   *"snowfall at times attained"*: "Weather and Visibility on the 2nd Canadian Division Front, Northwest Europe, July 1944 to May 1945," 1/8/45, www.calgaryhighlanders.com/history/weather.htm.

11   *"High winds and a blizzard"*: 29ID, *WRJ*, 1/19/45, 0815.

11   *"designed, constructed, and installed"*: 29ID, *29LG*, 1/6/45.

11   *"In the* Yank *[magazine]"*: 29ID, Personnel, Kenney, 1/17/45 letter.

13   *"a new twist"* and *"The New Hampshire 'looey'"*: 29ID, *29LG*, 2/12/45.

14   *"the most remarkable scientific achievement"*: Baxter, *Scientists Against Time*, 222.

14   *$20 per fuze*: Atkinson, *The Guns at Last Light*, 460.

14   *"When the 110th first fired shells"*: Cooper, *110th Field Artillery*, 199–200.

14   *millions of proximity fuzes*: Atkinson, *The Guns at Last Light*, 460.

14   *"The triumph of American research"*: Green, Thomson, and Roots, *The Ordnance Department: Planning Munitions for War*, 364.

14   *"The scarcity of artillery"*: NA RG319, *MS B-069*, "Report on Participation of 363VG Division in the Rhineland Campaign," 7.

15   *"As artillery shells fell short"*: Ewing, *29 Let's Go*, 217–18.

15   *fifty-seven in number*: *The 557th Field Artillery Battalion*, 45 (WWII 557th FAB History.pdf).

15   *sub-zero temperatures*: "Weather and Visibility on the 2nd Canadian Division Front, Northwest Europe, July 1944 to May 1945," 1/26/45, www.calgaryhighlanders.com/history/weather.htm.

16   *"the poor devils"*: 29ID, 175th AAR, Jan. 1945, "Enemy Forces Engaged," 1.

16   *"Who is going to launch"*: Ewing, *29 Let's Go*, 207.

16   *"The Daily Mail"*: 29ID, 175th AAR, Jan. 1945, "Enemy Forces Engaged," 1.

16   *"The effect of all this"*: Ibid., 210.

16   *"Propaganda shells landing in an area"*: Ibid., 207.

16   *"The Girl You Left Behind"*: Combined Arms Research Library, Fort Leavenworth, KS, *German Propaganda Leaflets*, http://cgsc.contentdm .oclc.org/cdm/ref/collection/p4013coll8/id/4016.

16   *"girl propagandist"* and *"And I just know"*: Ewing, *29 Let's Go*, 210.

16   *"In the meantime"*: U.S. Army Special Service Division, Army Service Forces, *Pocket Guide to Germany* (1944), 3.

17   *"unless otherwise permitted"*: Ibid., 2.

17   *Cooper and German girls*: 29ID, Personnel, 1985 Cooper interview with author.

18   *"We just aren't fighting humans"*: 29ID, Personnel, Kenney, 1/17/45 letter.

18   *"The people left behind"*: quoted in Ziemke, *The U.S. Army in the Occupation of Germany*, 139. From "Impressions of a Brief Tour of Occupied Germany," SHAEF, 11/4/44.

18   *"We work with the regiments"*: 29ID, *29LG*, 1/18/45.

18   *"to secure our forces"*: CIC School, *History and Mission of the Counter Intelligence Corps in World War II*, 48.

19   *"The lack of personnel"*: Ibid., 49.

19   *"agent"*: Ibid., 11.

19   *"investigated and appointed"*: 29ID, *29th Division CIC 1944 Unit History*, 5.

19   *"Without exception"* and *"Gerhardt eased the confusion"*: Walker, *With the Stonewallers*, 105.

20   *"The concept of non-fraternization"*: Ibid.

The Joes Appreciated It

20   *"tanks were too slow"*: Baltimore Sun, "New Armored Force Chief," 5/25/43, 13.

20   *"How's everything"*: 29ID, *WRJ*, 1/1/45, 1920.

21   *"General Gillem clearly desired"*: Cooper, *110th Field Artillery*, 202–3.

22   *"the whole happy crew"* and *"This is one detail"*: 29ID, *29LG*, 1/13/45.

22   *"soldiers [were] lying drunk"*: Pogue, *Pogue's War*, 229.

22   *"a sort of meatloaf"*: Ibid., 227.

23   *"Paris was OK"*: Hoffman, *I'll Be Home For The Christmas Rush*, 165.

23   *"it was so cold going there"*: 29ID, Personnel, Kenney, 1/25/45 and 1/29/45 letters.

23   *"Through these doors"*: 29ID, *29LG*, 1/7/45.

24   *"It was an unbelievable luxury"*: Ewing, *29 Let's Go*, 216.

24   *"Denying that the Army"*: NY Times, "Army Expanding Entertainment Program," 9/12/44, 7.

24   *"gaudy junk"*: NY Times, "The Screen," 11/22/45, 42.

24   *"In addition to these first-rate movies"*: Binkoski, *115th Infantry*, 269.

24   *"Garbed in a clinging"*: 29ID, *29LG*, 2/7/45.

25   *"was in a cold sweat"*: Ibid.

25   *"brash kid"* and *"Topeka typewriter-pounder"*: 29ID, *29LG*, 2/16/45.

25   *"frankly hostile"* and *"imitations, stories, and songs"* and *"Rooney was a regular Joe"*: Binkoski, *115th Infantry Regiment*, 276–77.

25   *"Troops overseas were beginning"*: NY Times, "Army Expanding Entertainment Program," 9/12/44, 7.

26   *"There are those who would"*: Time, "Great Katharine," 4/3/39.

26   *"We were afraid of the soldiers' reactions"*: 29ID, *29LG*, 1/31/45.

26   *"We thought they would go on"*: www.absoluteastronomy.com/topics/Katharine_Cornell.

26   *"Nothing but brass"* and *"gave a performance"* and *"Our only regret"*: 29ID, *29LG*, 1/31/45.

26   *"The rear echelon was always"*: Ewing, *29 Let's Go*, 216.

26   *"the dull, daily sameness"*: Ibid., 216–17.

Minutes Seemed Like Hours

27   *"Perhaps no single soldier impression"*: Ewing, *29 Let's Go*, 206.

27   *"No weapons were fired"*: 29ID, 224th AAR, Jan. 1945, 3.

28   *"In view of the dispersal"*: NA RG319, *MS B-069*, Dettling, "Report of the Participation of the 363rd VG Division in the Rhineland Campaign," 8/20/50, 6.

28   *"There would have been no surprise"*: 29ID, Personnel, Gerhardt, Memoirs, 51.

29   *"While it is comparatively simple"*: Binkoski, *115th Infantry*, 263.

29   *"The information gathered"*: 29ID, 175th AAR, Jan. 1945, 2.

29   *"A light snow had fallen"*: Ewing, *29 Let's Go*, 212.

30   *"We waded into the water"*: Ibid.

30   *"the element of surprise"*: *Baltimore Sun*, Bradley, "Patrol Skirmishes on Roer Line," 1/22/45, 4.

30   *"Then one of the men coughed"*: Ewing, *29 Let's Go*, 212.

31   *"I held up both arms"*: Arendt, *Midnight of the Soul*, 145.

31   *"My concern mainly involved"*: Ibid., 146.

31   *"If there ever was such a problem"*: Ibid., 151.

32   *"The men assigned"*: Binkoski, *115th Infantry*, 266.

33   *"Daniel Boone"*: 29ID, *29LG*, 1/19/45.

33   *"Sometimes the blackness is so thick"*: Easton, *Love and War*, 285.

33   *"walking on crackers"* and *"I'm accustomed to pistols"* and *"like an Eskimo igloo"*: 29ID, *29LG*, 1/19/45.

34   *"They went down on their bellies"*: Ibid.

34   *"Dempsey moved toward them"*: 29ID, *29th Division Daily Patrol Report File*, 116th Infantry, 1/17/45.

34   *"What he had thought"* and *"Boone Dempsey pulled one"*: 29ID, *29LG*, 1/19/45.

34   *"a rather pathetic-looking"*: Easton, *Love and War*, 286.

34   *"He was a sorry-looking sack"*: 29ID, *29LG*, 1/19/45.

34   *"He was in the 'rest' bunker"*: 29ID, *WRJ*, 1/17/45, 0203, 0255.

35   *"We caught one"*: Ibid., 0750.

35   *"Nice going!"*: Ibid., 0747.

35   *"the visibility gave no signs"*: Binkoski, *115th Infantry*, 266.

35   *T/Sgt. Aubin*: 29ID, Personnel, Aubin, 9/12/12 Aubin interview with author.

35   *"As one of the men covered him"*: Binkoski, *115th Infantry*, 267.

36   *"Believe Company F patrol"*: 29ID, 2/115 Journal, 1/29/45, 0330.

36   *"a great deal of small arms"* and *"When questioned later"*: Binkoski, *115th Infantry*, 267.

36   *"killed two enemy"*: 29ID, 2/115 Journal, 1/29/45, 0410.

36   *"Got the report"*: 29ID, *WRJ*, 1/29/45, 0742.

36   *"The plan of the raid"*: 29ID, 224th AAR, Jan. 1945, 2.

37   *"I'm going down"*: 29ID, *WRJ*, 1/13/45, 1915.

37   *"I just want to wish"*: Ibid., 2127.

37   *"About midnight"*: 29ID, 175th AAR, Jan. 1945, 4.

37   *"roads and paths"*: "Weather and Visibility on the 2nd Canadian Division Front, NW Europe, July 1944–May 1945," 1/13/45, www.calgary highlanders.com/history/weather.htm.

37 *"the principal obstacle"*: 29ID, 175th AAR, Jan. 1945, 4.

38 *Prasse*: 29ID, Personnel; also Univ. of Iowa 6/20/05 obituary, www
.hawkeyesports.com/sports/m-footbl/spec-rel/062005aaa.html.

38 *"reorganizing and preparing"*: 29ID, *WRJ*, 1/14/45, 0325.

38 *"Three whistle blasts were blown"*: 29ID, 175th AAR, Jan. 1945, 4.

38 *"that things were getting"*: 29ID, *WRJ*, 1/14/45, 0337. Later an unidentified 29er crossed out "out of control" and replaced that phrase with
"under control."

38 *"We thought we had covered"*: 29ID, *WRJ*, 1/14/45, 0748.

39 *"a large mansion"*: Ewing, *29 Let's Go*, 214.

39 *"the lone white house"*: Binkoski, *115th Infantry*, 285.

39 *"75 percent"*: 29ID, 116th AAR, Jan. 1945, "Battle Lessons Learned,"
viii.

39 *"Nothing happened"*: Ewing, *29 Let's Go*, 215.

40 *"I had wire cutters"*: Ibid.

40 *"It is [the raiders'] opinion"*: 29ID, *29th Division Daily Patrol Report
File*, 116th Infantry, "Raid on Broicherhaus," 1/22/45.

40 *"The withdrawal should have been"*: 29ID, 116th AAR, Jan. 1945,
"Battle Lessons Learned," viii.

40 *"that the [German] group"*: 29ID, *29th Division Daily Patrol Report
File*, 116th Infantry, "Raid on Broicherhaus," 1/22/45.

41 *Kussman*: 29ID, Personnel, Kussman, 9/21/12 Kussman email to author.

41 *"We got to the riverbank OK"*: Binkoski, *115th Infantry*, 275.

41 *"Webb and the sergeant stayed"*: 29ID, Personnel, Kussman, Memoirs,
42.

The First Parade

42 *pass in review*: 29ID, "Chin Strap" G/175 newsletter, 2/13/45.

42 *"the first parade"*: Ewing, *29 Let's Go*, 222.

43 *"replacement personnel"*: Brewer, *History of the 175th Infantry*, photo
caption following page 190.

2. HURRY UP AND WAIT
Localitis

45 *"My present estimate"*: DEP, *The War Years*, vol. 4, 2449.

45 *"My intention is to regain"*: Ibid., 2439.

46 *"meet this all-out German effort"*: Ibid., 2407.

46 *"will be pressed"*: Ibid., 2440.

46 *"Some regrouping will be necessary"*: Ibid., 2449.

46 *"As far as I am concerned"*: Crosswell, *Beetle*, 853.

47   *"Without exception"*: DEP, *The War Years*, vol. 4, 2415.

47   *"freak weather"*: MHI, Simpson papers, Ninth Army diary, 2/13/45.

47   *"tossed a bombshell"* and *"This would mean"*: Ibid., 1/15/45.

47   *"that this push was the main effort"* and *"as fast as God would let them"*: Ibid., 2/8/45.

48   *"on a narrow sector"* and *"progress is expected to be slow"*: Ibid., 2/7/45.

49   *"The field marshal is cocky"*: Ibid.

49   *"to tidy up"*: Wilmot, *The Struggle for Europe*, 610.

49   *"I employed the whole available power"*: Ibid., 611.

49   *"Montgomery was depicted"*: Bradley, *A Soldier's Story*, 483.

49   *"Any future moves"*: MHI, Simpson papers, Ninth Army diary, 1/19/45.

The Shoe Pinched Everywhere

49   *"A strategic withdrawal"*: *Strategy and Tactics*, Balkoski, "Operation Grenade," No. 84, Jan.–Feb. 1981, 8.

49   *"The enemy's capabilities grow fewer"*: NA RG407, Entry 427, Box 4406, XIX Corps Operations Reports, G-2 Periodic Report 266, Annex 2.

51   *"In the future"*: Speer, *Inside the Third Reich*, 423.

51   *"The German supreme command did not"*: *Strategy and Tactics*, Balkoski, "Operation Grenade," No. 84, Jan.–Feb. 1981, 15.

51   *"The shoe pinched everywhere"*: Ibid., 14.

52   *"The enemy is in a bad way"*: Parker, *Conquer*, 139.

52   *"meager strength"*: NA RG319, *MS B-069*, Dettling, "Report of the Participation of the 363rd VG Division in the Rhineland Campaign," 8/20/50, 6.

52   *"Our combat patrols"*: 29ID, 116th AAR, Nov. 1944, 2.

52   *"It is considered"*: *Strategy and Tactics*, Balkoski, "Operation Grenade," No. 84, Jan.–Feb. 1981, 10.

52   *"The corps operating on the Roer"*: Ibid., 10.

52   *"the sudden appearance"*: Ibid., 11.

52   *"counterthrusts require the best-trained"*: Ibid., 15.

52   *"had been split up"*: Ibid., 14–15.

52   *"the time of the enemy attack"*: Ibid., 11.

52   *"The population near the front lines"*: Ibid., 14.

53   *"It is recommended"*: Ibid., 9.

54   *"The water stored"*: Parker, *Conquer*, 162.

54   *"objected to the project"*: MacDonald, *The Siegfried Line Campaign*, 598.

54   *"dud"*: Sylvan, *Normandy to Victory*, 194.

54   *"at the earliest possible date"*: Parker, *Conquer*, 140.

54   *"until the [Schwammenauel] dam was in hand"*: MacDonald, *The Last Offensive*, 73.

55   *"The probability that the Roer River"*: Parker, *Conquer*, 151.

55   *"a muddy detour road"* and *"The sedan carrying"*: MHI, Simpson papers, Ninth Army diary, 2/6/45.

56   *nearly seven feet deep*: 29ID, *WRJ*, 2/9/45, 1508.

56   *"I understand there is 80–100 feet"* and *"It is not too favorable"*: MHI, Simpson papers, Ninth Army diary, conversation with Gillem, 1430, 2/9/45.

56   *"I think we ought to go"*: Ibid., conversation with McLain, 1600, 2/9/45.

56   *"You know, that [at] nine feet per second"*: Ibid., conversation with Gillem, 1430, 2/9/45.

56   *"We are right on the danger line"*: Ibid., 1725, 2/9/45.

56   *"We are going to postpone it"*: Ibid., 1600, 2/9/45.

56   *"was a hard one to make"*: Ibid., 1725, 2/9/45.

56   *"They expected at any moment"*: MacDonald, *Last Offensive*, 82.

56   *defiantly had disobeyed*: NA RG319, Entry 219, Box 3, Theater historian office files, MacDonald correspondence with von Manteuffel.

57   *"impossible"*: MHI, Simpson papers, Ninth Army diary, conversation with McLain, 1140, 2/10/45.

57   *"tremendous torrent"*: 29ID, *WRJ*, 2/10/45, 0003.

57   *"I ordered the 3rd Battalion"*: Ibid., 0026.

No Soap on the Party

58   *"No soap on the party"*: 29ID, *WRJ*, 2/9/45, 1650.

58   *two feet deeper*: 29ID, *WRJ*, 2/10/45, 0026.

58   *2,000 artillery pieces*: MacDonald, *Last Offensive*, 137.

58   *"the greatest barrage"*: Sylvan, *Normandy to Victory*, 305.

58   *for every ten yards of front*: MacDonald, *Last Offensive*, 137.

59   *"didn't devil his staff"*: MHI, Simpson papers, 1978 oral history interview, 268.

59   *"showed themselves thoroughly prepared"*: MHI, Simpson papers, Ninth Army diary, 2/8/45, 2.

60   *"I was impressed"*: MHI, Simpson papers, correspondence, 3/15/70 Simpson letter to Robert Hawk.

60   *"He hit it right"*: MHI, Simpson papers, 1972 oral history interview, 362.

60   *"Morale was at a high peak"*: Binkoski, *115th Infantry*, 274, 278.

61   *"to shoot only necessary registrations"*: Cooper, *110th Field Artillery*, 204.

61   *"For the first time"* and *"To insure spic and span condition"*: Ibid., 205.

61   *"have taken advantage of everything"*: Baltimore Sun, Bradley, "Forgotten Artillerymen Busy," 2/16/45, 3.

61   *"aggressive and genial"*: Baltimore Sun, Bradley, "Rubble of German Villages is Used," 2/19/45, 2.

62   *"maintenance of roads"*: 29ID, 121st AAR, Feb. 1945, 1.

62   *"All of this clearance"*: Ibid., 2.

62   *"We lost [Pisani]"*: 29ID, *WRJ*, 2/18/45, 1940.

62   *"Let's get some accurate daylight reconnaissance"*: 29ID, *WRJ*, 2/20/45, 0739.

63   *"A total of 750 yards"*: 29ID, 121st AAR, Feb. 1945, 1.

63   *"drenching downpour"*: 29ID, *29LG*, 2/13/45.

63   *"quagmire"*: MHI, Simpson papers, Ninth Army diary, 2/12/45.

63   *"attired in his familiar jaunty black beret"*: 29ID, *29LG*, 2/13/45.

63   *"a Georgia cracker"*: 29ID, *29LG*, 1/22/45.

64   *"a bitter slugging match"*: Ellis, *Victory in the West*, vol. 2, 264.

64   *"in the luxury"*: MHI, Simpson papers, Ninth Army diary, 2/12/45.

65   *"seriously threatened"*: 29ID, "Chin Strap" G/175 newsletter, 2/13/45.

65   *"It won't be long"*: 29ID, *WRJ*, 2/17/45, 1811.

65   *"was the key"*: MHI, Simpson papers, Moore oral history interview, 152–53.

65   *"Predictions look very promising"* and *"at 0330"*: MHI, Simpson papers, Ninth Army diary, 2/21/45.

65   *"We deliberately decided"*: MHI, Simpson papers, Moore oral history interview, 153.

65   *"The river banks themselves"*: MHI, Simpson papers, Ninth Army diary, 2/22/45.

Nervous Excitement

65   *six or seven*: 29ID, *WRJ*, 2/15/45, 0847.

66   *"Just as long as they keep on going"*: 29ID, *WRJ*, 2/15/45, 0845.

66   *"The City of Sudden Death"*: V-2 Rocket.com, www.v2rocket.com/start/chapters/antwerp.html.

66   *"Just one [German] round came in"*: 29ID, *WRJ*, 2/19/45, 1755.

67   *George, self-inflicted wound*: Gerhardt, Memoirs, 34.

67   *"There is a touch of spring"*: Baltimore Sun, Bradley, "Yanks on Flooded Roer Front Relax Under Touch of Spring," 2/18/45, 3.

68   *"the most intense"*: Ewing, *29 Let's Go*, 227.

69   *"At Jülich the Germans had an outpost line"*: NA RG407, 29CI, *Enemy*, Minor, Box 24036, 1.

69   *"The division was occupying a sector"*: NA RG319, *MS B-069*, Dettling, "Report of the Participation of the 363rd VG Division in the Rhineland Campaign," 8/20/50, 8.

70   *"was too restless to remain"* and *"A nightcap"*: MHI, Simpson papers, Ninth Army diary, 2/22/45.

70   *"carried combat packs"*: NA RG407, 29CI, *River Crossing at Jülich*, Belt, Box 24036, 1–2.

70   *"The soft tread and shuffle"*: Ewing, *29 Let's Go*, 227.

71   *"The large number of troops involved"*: 29ID, 29th Division AAR, Feb. 1945, 3.

71   *"The bridge trains started to roll"*: 29ID, *Roer River Crossing General Report*, HQ 1104th Engineer Combat Group report, 3/16/45, 7.

Sorry It Is So Messed Up

71   *"the mounting difficulties"*: Eisenhower, *Crusade in Europe*, 369.

71   *"clear with a bright moon"*: 29ID, 29th Division AAR, Feb. 1945, 3.

72   *"The whole riverbank"*: NA RG407, 29CI, *River Crossing at Jülich*, Hogan, Box 24036, 1–2.

72   *"with an average of nearly two and a half"*: Parker, *Conquer*, 169.

72   *"Against buildings and strongpoints"*: Cooper, *110th Field Artillery*, 209.

73   *"The fact that this [unplanned] dam existed"*: 29ID, *Roer River Crossing General Report*, HQ 1104th Engineer Combat Group report, 3/16/45, 5.

73   *"While the covering force was crossing"*: NA RG407, 29CI, *River Crossing at Jülich*, Geiglein and Bishop, Box 24036, 1–2.

75   *"The boats were crowded"*: NA RG407, 29CI, *River Crossing at Jülich*, Wolff, Dinerman, Hankinson, Box 24036, 3–4.

75   *"It was so pitch dark"* and *"One fellow near me"*: 29ID, Personnel, Panus, 1/12/89 Panus letter to Donald Miller.

76   *"When he saw Zhanel"*: Ibid.

76   *"he couldn't swim"*: Gutknecht, *We Were Foxhole Buddies*, 828, 7/16/45 Dickerson letter.

77   *"A fellow would do anything"* and *"I wasn't bleeding"*: USAREUR, TF Normandy Public Affairs, *A 29th Infantry Division Veteran Remembers*, 6/4/04, by Cpl. Murray Shugars.

78   *"in each attempt the swift current"* and *"This site was subjected to intense small arms"*: 29ID, *Roer River Crossing General Report*, HQ 1104th Engineer Combat Group report, 3/16/45, 9.

78   *"rifle, machine pistol, and machine gun fire"*: Ibid., 7.

78   *"The equipment in the boat"*: NA RG407, 29CI, *River Crossing at Jülich*, Geiglein and Bishop, Box 24036, 2.

78   *"The town was in utter ruin"*: Ibid., 2–3.

79   *"These German soldiers came out of an emplacement"*: 29ID, *Roer River Crossing General Report*, HQ 1104th Engineer Combat Group report, 3/16/45, 8.

79   *"We placed rifle and BAR fire"*: NA RG407, 29CI, *River Crossing at Jülich*, Brady and Ewing, Box 24036, 2–3.

79   *"The engineers were working busily"*: Ibid., 2.

79   *"until about H-plus-four hours"*: 29ID, *Roer River Crossing General Report*, HQ 1104th Engineer Combat Group report, 3/16/45, 8.

79   *"This bridge received long-range fire"*: NA RG407, 29CI, *River Crossing at Jülich*, Geiglein and Bishop, Box 24036, 4–5.

80   *"It was tough"*: 29ID, Personnel, Melnikoff, 1/16/13 Melnikoff interview with author.

80   *Harrell*: 29ID, Personnel, Harrell, 1/16/13 Suzanne Harrell interview with author.

80   *"cattle, hogs, and miles of fence"*: 29ID, Personnel, Harrell, 6/16/43 Congressman Frank Boykin letter.

81   *"I know everything you say"* and *"Please see all members"*: Ibid.

81   *"I am just fine"*: 29ID, Personnel, Harrell, 12/29/44 Harrell letter to aunt.

81   *"I hope that you"*: 29ID, Personnel, Harrell, 2/22/45 Harrell letter to Sidney Harrell.

82   *"I jumped over him"* and *"pulled [a] grenade"*: Loengard, *LIFE Photographers: What They Saw*, 177.

83   *"I made off to the nearest airport"*: Ibid.

83   *"To the soldiers of the 29th"*: Ewing, *29 Let's Go*, dedication.

84   *"You have done a fine job"*: 29ID, *WRJ*, 2/23/45, 1935.

85   *"We encountered no resistance"*: NA RG407, 29CI, *River Crossing at Jülich*, Geiglein and Bishop, Box 24036, 2–3.

86   *"Construction proceeded at an excellent rate"*: 29ID, *Roer River Crossing General Report*, HQ 1104th Engineer Combat Group report, 3/16/45, 8.

86   *"There were engineers lying everywhere"*: 29ID, Personnel, Aubin, 9/21/12 Aubin interview with author.

86   *"By nightfall"*: 29ID, 175th AAR, Feb. 1945, "Summary of Operations," 4–5.

86   *"By 6:00 P.M. we were across"*: 29ID, Personnel, Puntenney, Memoirs, 115–16.

87   *"a good kid"*: Balkoski, *Our Tortured Souls*, 175.

87   *"heavy automatic weapons fire"*: NA RG407, 29CI, *Fight for Jülich*, Brady, Box 24036, 1.

87   *"Private Radich ran to the wounded soldier"*: 29ID, *Ninth Army GO*, 117, 4/20/45.

Supermen, Hell

89   *"There are two possible ways"*: 29ID, 115th AAR, Feb. 1945, "Summary of Operations," 10, 13.

89   *"We'll have more firepower"*: Ibid., 10.

89   *"recession of flood waters"*: 29ID, *Roer River Crossing General Report*, HQ 1104th Engineer Combat Group report, 3/16/45, 6–7.

90   *"could only be done by blunt force"*: Ibid., 9.

90   *"were plastic and therefore not detected"*: 29ID, 747th AAR, Feb. 1945, "Statistical-Tactical Report of Tank Losses," 3/4/45.

90   *"not only immobilized one of the supporting tanks"*: 29ID, 115th AAR, Feb. 1945, "Summary of Operations," 26.

90   *"Moving halfway down the road"*: 29ID, *Roer River Crossing General Report*, HQ 234th Engineer Combat Battalion report, 6.

90   *"without too much trouble"* and *"The lead Alligator started forward"*: Ibid., 7.

91   *"that the road was impassable"*: Ibid.

91   *"The battle was on"*: 29ID, 115th AAR, Feb. 1945, "Summary of Operations," 26.

91   *"very dense and nauseating"*: NA RG407, 29CI, *River Crossing at Jülich*, Hogan, Box 24036, 1.

91   *"Company I is across river"*: 29ID, 3/115 Journal, 2/23/45, 0425.

91   *"The men of Company I found"*: Binkoski, *115th Infantry*, 283.

91   *"A nearby tree was felled"*: Ibid., 283–84.

92   *"considerable equipment"*: NA RG407, 29CI, *River Crossing at Jülich*, Hogan, Box 24036, 2.

92   *"We saw no dead Germans"*: Ibid., 3.

92   *"overheard the sound of voices"*: Binkoski, *115th Infantry*, 285.

93   *"unnerved"*: NA RG407, 29CI, *River Crossing at Jülich*, Hogan, Box 24036, 3.

93   *"I looked into one of the marmite food containers"*: 29ID, Personnel, Kussman, Memoirs, 43.

93   *"The engineers had three assault boats"*: Ibid., 44.

93   *"rather disorganized"*: 29ID, 3/115 Journal, 2/23/45, 0620.

93   *"[We] located a path"*: 29ID, *Roer River Crossing General Report*, HQ 234th Engineer Combat Battalion report, 7–8.

93   *"which completely overturned the vehicle"*: Ibid., 8.

94   *"command group"*: Binkoski, *115th Infantry*, 285.

95   *"tried to make a getaway"*: Ibid., 285–86.

95   *"There was some scattered opposition"*: 29ID, Personnel, Kussman, Memoirs, 44–45.

95   *"After trying to dissuade the medic"*: Binkoski, *115th Infantry*, 287.

96   *"Unfortunately the haze and smoke began to clear"*: Ibid., 288.

96   *"to abandon the plan of a frontal attack"*: 29ID, 115th AAR, Feb. 1945, "Summary of Operations," 27.

96   *"I saw two men hit by snipers"*: NA RG407, 29CI, *River Crossing at Jülich*, Belt, Box 24036, 2.

96   *"made a dash for the railroad embankment"*: Binkoski, *115th Infantry*, 289.

96   *"in the line of duty"*: 29ID, MR, Company G, 115th Infantry, 3/4/45.

96   *"Hand grenades were flying"*: Binkoski, *115th Infantry*, 290.

97   *"As the group moved up"*: Ibid.

97   *"Throughout the afternoon"*: Ibid., 290–91.

97   *"A German lieutenant waving a white towel"*: Ibid., 291.

97   *"On one of these trips"*: 29ID, *Roer River Crossing General Report*, HQ 234th Engineer Combat Battalion report, 9.

98   *"Whose side are those chemical warfare jerks on"*: Wellman, "Operation Grenade, Hill 109," *Twenty-Niner*, July 2001, 10.

98   *"You can expect to run into minefields"*: Ibid., 11.

98   *"Losses are painful"*: Ibid., 14.

98   *"Listen carefully"*: Ibid., 15.

98   *"Light opposition was met"*: Binkoski, *115th Infantry*, 290.

98   *"I got the report"*: 29ID, WRJ, 2/23/45, 1937.

98   *S/Sgt. Eyler*: 29ID, Personnel, Eyler.

99   *"Taking scissors from his aid pouch"*: Binkoski, *115th Infantry*, 290.

99   *"gave the medics one of their toughest days"*: Ibid., 286.

100   *310 German prisoners*: 29ID, WRJ, 2/24/45, 0739.

100   *"the infantry usually had"*: Gutknecht, *Foxhole Buddies*, 545, 2/25/45 Dickerson letter.

100   *"was one of the most physically miserable"*: Binkoski, *115th Infantry*, 292–93.

3. A FAST-MOVING WAR
The Big Push Begins

101   *"It had not been done easily"*: Parker, *Conquer*, 171.

101   *"went into battle"*: *NY Times*, "Massive Barrages Precede 1st and 9th Army Attacks," 2/24/45, 1–2.

101   *"If a year ago"*: Strategy and Tactics, Balkoski, "Operation Grenade," No. 84, Jan.–Feb. 1981, 12.

101   *"Eisenhower Opens Wide Roer Offensive"*: NY Times, headline, 2/24/45, 1.

102   *"The Big Push Toward Cologne"*: Ibid.

102   *"The great hammerblow of* Grenade": MacDonald, *Last Offensive*, 162–63.

102   *"Most of the German soldiers"* and *"The Nazi party is forcing the people"*: NY Times, "Germans Eager to Surrender," 2/24/45, 3.

102   *"the early crossing of the still-flooded Roer"*: MHI, Simpson papers, *Ninth Army's Operations in Germany*, 190.

102   *"twenty-eight battalions of infantry were across"*: MHI, Simpson papers, Ninth Army diary, 2/24/45.

102   *"I was delighted with the results"*: MHI, Simpson papers, Ninth Army diary, conversation with Maguire, 1030, 2/24/45.

102   *"ground conditions [that] could scarcely have been worse"*: Stacey, *The Victory Campaign*, 491.

102   *"was well pleased"*: MHI, Simpson papers, Ninth Army diary, 2/24/45.

103   *"is surrounded by a wall"*: NY Times, "Jülich Captured," 2/24/45, 1.

103   *"sore spot"*: 29ID, 29th Division AAR, Feb. 1945, 6.

103   *"the stout old walls have held up"* and *"complete reduction of this ancient stronghold"*: 29ID, RCG, File 2, Jülich Information.

104   *"We spent the night"*: Easton, *Love and War*, 10.

104   *"The leading troops were met"*: 29ID, 116th AAR, Feb. 1945, "The 3rd Battalion, 116th, Attached to the 175th Infantry in Operations Against Jülich," 2.

105   *"bullets—ours and Jerry's—whizzed everywhere"*: Easton, *Love and War*, 10.

105   *"The* coup de grâce *was administered"*: 29ID, 116th AAR, Feb. 1945, "The 3rd Battalion, 116th, Attached to the 175th Infantry in Operations Against Jülich," 2.

105   *"Almost as the fire ceased"*: Baltimore Sun, Bradley, "29th Takes Jülich Citadel," 2/25/45, 2.

105   *"yelling at the top of our lungs"*: Easton, *Love and War*, 10.

105   *"Ahead a Yank fired a tommy gun"*: Baltimore Sun, Bradley, "29th Takes Jülich Citadel," 2/25/45, 2.

105   *"a few dead bodies"*: Easton, *Love and War*, 11.

105   *"It was later found"*: 29ID, Personnel, Puntenney, Memoirs, 116.

106   *"I wish you would push to the east"*: 29ID, WRJ, 2/24/45, 1228.

107   *"The general feels that the whole thing is waiting"*: Ibid., 0616.

107   *"Positions were improved"*: Binkoski, *115th Infantry*, 295.

107   *"sporadic artillery and mortar fire"*: 29ID, 330th AAR, Feb. 1945, 3.

107   *"Unfortunately there had been some confusion"*: Binkoski, *115th Infantry*, 297.

108   *"a colossal mistake"*: 29ID, Personnel, Kussman, Memoirs, 45–46.

108   *"men from labor battalions"*: 29ID, 175th AAR, Feb. 1945, "Enemy Forces Engaged," 2.

109   *"On the east bank of the river"*: *Baltimore Sun*, Bradley, "29th Takes Jülich Citadel," 2/25/45, 2.

109   *"massive steel key of ancient design"* and *"Subject: Key to the City of Jülich"*: *Baltimore Sun*, Bradley, "Gerhardt Given Key to Jülich," 2/26/45, 2.

110   *"It was expected"* and *"The plan of attack"*: NA RG407, 29CI, *Stetternich*, Geiglein, Morris, Hold, Bishop, Box 24036, 1.

110   *"The tanks [and tank destroyers] were to give"*: Ibid., 2.

110   *"1st Platoon, led by 2nd Lt. Frank Holt"*: Ibid., 3.

111   *"were in foxholes under the gun"*: Ibid.

111   *"Company A advanced toward Stetternich"*: Ibid., 5–6.

111   *Sgt. Ackerman*: 29ID, 747th AAR, Feb. 1945, 2.

111   *"with instructions to fire green parachute flares"*: NA RG407, 29CI, Stetternich, Geiglein, Box 24036, 4.

111   *"took more than 150 prisoners"*: Ibid., 6–7.

Everyone Has Gone Away

112   *"Given a continuation of the conditions"*: *NY Times*, "Eisenhower Points New Push as Knockout Blow in West," 2/25/45, 1.

112   *"It was the most magnificent performance"*: Butcher, *My Three Years With Eisenhower*, 763.

112   *"Marshal von Rundstedt's armies"*: *NY Times*, "Eisenhower Points New Push as Knockout Blow in West," 2/25/45, 4.

112   *"final chapter"*: *NY Times*, "Final Chapter," 2/25/45, E1.

112   *"[I'll] head you to the north"*: 29ID, WRJ, 2/24/45, 2012.

113   *"Gentlemen, the division bridgehead"*: 29ID, audiovisual collection, 2/24/45 war room conference.

114   *"A concentration [of German artillery] fell"*: NA RG407, 29CI, *Welldorf-Güsten*, Meeks, Garcia, Box 24036, 1.

114   *"At one intersection"*: *Baltimore Sun*, Bradley, "29th Presses Past Stetternich," 2/26/45, 1–2.

114   *"proved to be no easy matter"*: 29ID, 116th AAR, Feb. 1945, "Phase III," 1.

114   *"pool-table flatlands"*: Ibid., 2.

114   *"a stubborn enemy"*: Ibid., 1.

115   *"a blanket of grazing fire"*: Ibid., 2.

116   *"Troops other than seasoned"*: 29ID, 116th AAR, Feb. 1945, "Phase III," 2.

116   *"The 30th [Division] on the right reports"*: 29ID, *WRJ*, 2/25/45, 1332.

116   *"At approximately 1500 hours"* and *"The 1st Battalion advanced steadily"*: 29ID, 116th AAR, Feb. 1945, "Phase III," 2.

116   *"machine-gun fire support"*: NA RG407, 29CI, *Welldorf-Güsten*, Garcia, Box 24036, 5.

116   *"a sheet of fire"*: Ibid., 2.

116   *"We placed a preparatory barrage on Güsten"* and *"The attack began at 1800"*: Ibid., 3.

117   *"The projectile went straight through the turret"* and *"We saw the flash"*: Ibid.

117   *"The tankers said it was too dark"*: Ibid., 4–5.

117   *"We have made the grade"*: 29ID, *WRJ*, 2/26/45, 0744.

117   *"We found tracks of a tank"*: NA RG407, 29CI, *Welldorf-Güsten*, Meeks, Box 24036, 4.

117   *"little glamor"*: *Baltimore Sun*, Bradley, "29th Presses Past Stetternich," 2/26/45, 2.

117   *"high morale of the troops"*: NA RG407, 29CI, *Welldorf-Güsten*, Garcia, Box 24036, 5.

118   *"Billeted in private homes"*: Anonymous, *History of Company M, 330th Infantry, 83rd Infantry Division*, 29ID, no publication data.

118   *"They were held up by fire"* and *"and by 0810 had occupied all of the town"* and *"Three light tanks [from Company D, 736th Tank Battalion]"*: 29ID, 330th AAR, Feb. 1945, 3.

118   *M24 light tanks*: 3/1/13 Steven Zaloga email to author.

118   *"Nice going"*: 29ID, *WRJ*, 2/25/45, 0843.

118   *"One company has taken three officers"*: Ibid., 0925.

118   *453rd Antiaircraft Artillery Battalion*: 29ID, 330th AAR, Feb. 1945, 3.

119   *"The 1st Battalion continued the attack"*: Ibid., 4.

119   *330th Infantry did not lose a single man killed*: MacDonald, *Last Offensive*, 168.

119   *"Pattern [and] Mersch . . . are some of the places"*: Anonymous, *The Story of the 330th Infantry Across Europe*, 29ID, no publication data.

119   *"Nothing emphasized the rapidity of the advance"*: Ewing, *29 Let's Go*, 235.

119   *"personnel and equipment . . . must be ready"*: War Dept., FM 10-35, "Quartermaster Truck Companies," (July 1945), 2.

119   *20,000 rounds*: 29ID, *G3J*, 2/25/45, 2.

119   *"Tired of the relative inactivity"*: Cooper, *110th Field Artillery*, 212.

120   *"It looks like things"*: MacDonald, *Last Offensive*, 167.

120   *"To the [XIX] Corps commander"*: Ibid., 168.

120   *"no longer [held] a coherent defensive front"*: NA RG319, *MS B-084*, First FS Army, 6–7.

120   *"The mobility of [German] units"*: NA RG319, *MS B-811*, Fifteenth Army Defense Battles at the Roer and Rhine, 103.

120   *"light"*: 29ID, 29th Recon Troop AAR, Feb. 1945, 2.

120   *"reconnoiter at once"*: 29ID, *WRJ*, 2/26/45, 1339.

121   *"I want you to put all you've got"*: Ibid., 1735.

121   *"patrols (on foot) continuing"*: Ibid., 1654.

121   *"Nice going!"*: Ibid., 1930.

122   *"It was good"* and *"It was an overcast morning"*: NA RG407, 29CI, *Ameln*, Johns, Slaughter, Box 24036, 1.

122   *"advanced at a fast walk"*: Ibid., 2.

122   *11th Panzer Division*: MacDonald, *Last Offensive*, 123–26, 167.

123   *"It was getting light"*: NA RG407, 29CI, *Ameln*, Johns, Box 24036, 3.

123   *killed four tankers and wounded several more*: 29ID, 747th AAR, Feb. 1945, 3.

123   *"the only man I have ever known"*: Balkoski, *Our Tortured Souls*, 179.

123   *"Germans ran out"*: NA RG407, 29CI, *Ameln*, Johns, Box 24036, 3.

123   *"told us he had hidden"*: Ibid., 3–4.

124   *"The Germans, however, weren't convinced"*: 29ID, 115th AAR, Feb. 1945, 26.

124   *"considerable German artillery"* and *"a brisk firefight"*: NA RG407, 29CI, *Ameln*, Slaughter, Box 24036, 5.

124   *"The German tanks and infantry started south"*: Ibid., 6.

124   *"two German tanks withdrew north"*: Ibid., 7.

125   *"What time do you think"*: 29ID, *WRJ*, 2/26/45, 1611.

125   *"The night sky was filled with the glare"*: Binkoski, *115th Infantry*, 301.

125   *"for my own enjoyment"* and *"I spent some time reasoning with him"* and *"sent up a large ball of fire"* and *"I climbed up on the track"*: 29ID, Personnel, Van Roosen, 3/14/13 Van Roosen email to author.

126   *"were happy to learn"* and *"the Germans [were] eager to surrender"* and *"running around the northeastern section"*: Binkoski, *115th Infantry*, 302.

126   *"threw a couple of flat-trajectory rounds"*: *Baltimore Sun*, Bradley, "29th Captures Big Road Hub Beyond Jülich," 2/28/45, 1.

126   *"He would have made a very fine officer"*: 29ID, Personnel, Van Roosen, 3/14/13 Van Roosen email to author.

127   *"It was difficult to distinguish any of our troops"*: Baltimore Sun, Bradley, "29th Captures Big Road Hub Beyond Jülich," 2/28/45, 2.

127   *"a collective grab for their bazooka"*: 29ID, *29LG*, 3/1/45.

127   *"I picked up the bazooka"*: Binkoski, *115th Infantry*, 304.

128   *"push it"*: 29ID, *WRJ*, 2/26/45, 2152.

128   *"The [American] artillery was already plastering"*: Baltimore Sun, Bradley, "29th Captures Big Road Hub Beyond Jülich," 2/28/45, 2.

128   *"a great soldier"*: 29ID, Personnel, Kussman, 3/19/13 Kussman email to author.

129   *"A short time later"*: 29ID, Personnel, Kussman, Memoirs, 47; also 11/5/14 Kussman email to author.

129   *"Off to the right, a haypile burned"*: Baltimore Sun, Bradley, "29th Captures Big Road Hub Beyond Jülich," 2/28/45, 2.

129   *"having a hell of a fight"*: 29ID, *WRJ*, 2/27/45, 0542.

129   *"We got it [Opherten]"*: Ibid., 0655.

129   *"buildings over to the left of us blazed up"*: Baltimore Sun, Bradley, "29th Captures Big Road Hub Beyond Jülich," 2/28/45, 2.

130   *"AA [code for Opherten] is officially cleared"*: 29ID, *WRJ*, 2/27/45, 0938.

130   *"The [German] troops we encountered"*: Binkoski, *115th Infantry*, 309.

130   *"The Germans were showing signs of disorganization"*: NA RG407, 29CI, *Ameln*, Johns, Stoen, Hecker, Blalock, Box 24036, Annex 13, 1.

130   *"broken overcast with scattered clouds"*: 29ID, *G3J*, 2/27/45, 1.

130   *"a fine company commander"*: Johns, *Clay Pigeons of St. Lô*, 154.

130   *"The tanks formed behind a hill"*: NA RG407, 29CI, *Ameln*, Johns, Stoen, Hecker, Blalock, Box 24036, Annex 13, 2.

130   *"German morale was crumbling"*: Ibid., 3.

131   *"There were trenches in the orchard"*: Ibid., 2–3.

131   *"All finished with BB [Jackerath]"*: 29ID, *WRJ*, 2/27/45, 1112.

131   *"sent [the POWs] south along the road"*: NA RG407, 29CI, *Ameln*, Johns, Stoen, Hecker, Blalock, Box 24036, Annex 13, 3.

131   *"German civilians milled about"*: 29ID, RCG, File 21, 1946 Johns letter to Ewing.

131   *"lasted only a few minutes"*: NA RG407, 29CI, *Ameln*, Johns, Stoen, Hecker, Blalock, Box 24036, Annex 13, 5.

131   *"allowed the tanks to get in close"*: 29ID, *29LG*, 3/17/45.

131   *Hobbs actually had only one bazooka*: 29ID, Personnel, Hobbs, 3/20/13 Hobbs phone call to author.

131   *"The grenades did not penetrate"*: NA RG407, 29CI, *Ameln*, Johns, Stoen, Hecker, Blalock, Box 24036, Annex 13, 4–5.

131   *The next day, Johns inspected the shattered enemy vehicle*: 29ID, Personnel, Hobbs, 3/20/13 Hobbs phone call to author.

131   *"One followed the street"*: NA RG407, 29CI, *Ameln*, Johns, Stoen, Hecker, Blalock, Box 24036, Annex 13, 4.

132   *"Realizing that if he remained in the town"*: Binkoski, *115th Infantry*, 306.

132   *"When the crews of the crippled tanks"*: 29ID, *29LG*, 3/17/45.

132   *"The 29th had knocked off another town"*: *Baltimore Sun*, Bradley, "29th Captures Big Road Hub Beyond Jülich," 2/28/45, 2.

132   *"was successful because of carefully made plans"*: NA RG407, 29CI, *Ameln*, Johns, Slaughter, Box 24036, cover page, also Annex 13, 6.

132   *"Make [the Germans] understand"*: NA RG407, 29CI, *Ameln*, Johns, Stoen, Hecker, Blalock, Box 24036, Annex 13, 7.

133   *"What time did your column get underway?"*: 29ID, *WRJ*, 2/27/45, 0902.

133   *"There was to be no rest for the weary"*: 29ID, 116th AAR, Feb. 1945, "Phase III," 3.

134   *wounding of S/Sgt. George and PFC Davis*: Cox, *Twenty-ninth Infantry*, 173–74.

135   *"added the town of Immerath"* and *"Following a quick and skillful reorganization"*: 29ID, 116th AAR, Feb. 1945, "Phase III," 3.

135   *"Men troubled with sore feet"*: 29ID, MR, Company K, 116th Infantry, 2/27/45.

135   *"Congratulations! Well done, all the way through"*: 29ID, *WRJ*, 2/27/45, 2043.

135   *"As usual there were hastily improvised white flags"*: Easton, *Love and War*, 18–19.

137   *"Paths had been cleared by engineers"*: 29ID, 747th AAR, Feb. 1945, "Report of Tank Losses for Month of February 1945."

137   *"In assaulting enemy positions"*: 29ID, 175th AAR, Feb. 1945, "Battle Lessons and Conclusions," 1.

137   *"never had a chance to organize"*: Ewing, *29 Let's Go*, 239–40.

Some Pretty Fast Company

138   *"Elements of three armored divisions"*: Parker, *Conquer*, 180.

138   *"proceeded in a steady, unrelenting march"*: Ewing, *29 Let's Go*, 241.

139   *"the first rich industrial prize"* and *90 percent of the 200,000-plus citizens*: Cairns *(Australia) Post*, "Capture of München-Gladbach," 3/3/45, 1.

139   *"The field marshal doesn't think there is anything"*: 29ID, *WRJ*, 2/28/45, 0746.

139   *"I was in some pretty fast company"*: 29ID, Personnel, Puntenney, Memoirs, 117.

139   *"We are not making the speed"*: 29ID, *WRJ*, 2/28/45, 1328.

139   *"They got a lot of direct fire"*: Ibid., 1113.

140   *"the leading battalion [2nd] attacked Wanlo"*: 29ID, 175th AAR, Feb. 1945, 10.

140   *five tanks and 100 troops*: 29ID, *WRJ*, 2/28/45, 1105.

141   *"it was too weak for any mission"*: NA RG319, *MS B-812*, von Zangen, "Fifteenth Army Defensive Battles on the Roer and Rhine," 8/20/50, 19.

141   *"175th is moving up"*: 29ID, *WRJ*, 2/28/45, 1416.

141   *"resistance crumbled rapidly"*: 29ID, 116th AAR, Feb. 1945, "Phase III," 4.

141   *"We took about 450 POWs"*: 29ID, *WRJ*, 2/28/45, 1950.

141   *"In an attic, Lt. Col. Roger Whiteford, of Ruxton"*: *Baltimore Sun*, Bradley, "Bradley Sees Rheydt Attack," 3/2/45, 2.

141   *"This has the characteristics of a breakthrough"*: 29ID, 116th AAR, Feb. 1945, cover.

142   *"The word spread like the wind"*: Ewing, *29 Let's Go*, 243.

142   *"one of the cities which the Germans were expected"*: Austin, *Sydney (Australia) Morning Herald*, "München-Gladbach Falls Without Fight," 3/3/45, 1.

142   *"Employing the village of Waat"* and *"Village after village fell"*: 29ID, 116th AAR, Mar. 1945, "Phase I," 2.

143   *"[Bingham] couldn't believe it"*: 29ID, Personnel, Puntenney, Memoirs, 118.

143   *"the Joe of the hour"*: 29ID, *29LG*, 3/10/45.

143   *"I sent a runner"*: 29ID, Personnel, Puntenney, Memoirs, 118.

143   *"carried a trio of Brigham Young University tacklers"*: AZ Central website, "No. 20: Back Walter Nielsen, 1936–1938," www.azcentral.com/sports/ua/articles/20130813top-50-ua-football-players-of-all-time-walter-nielsen.html.

143   *"We had a brief visit"*: 29ID, Personnel, Puntenney, Memoirs, 118.

143   *"became very wealthy"*: Slaughter, *Omaha Beach and Beyond*, 177–78.

144   *"Fire burned here and there"*: *NY Times Sunday Magazine*, "Notes From Goebbels' Home Town," 3/18/45, 9.

144   "Es lebe Adolf Hitler": Ewing, *29 Let's Go*, 242.

144   "Was hast du heute für das Vaterland": *NY Times*, "Reich City Spurned Nazi Plea to Fight," 3/2/45, 1–2.

144   *"There were many signs"*: Ibid., 2.

144   *"The comparatively few enemy troops remaining"*: 29ID, 29th Division AAR, Mar. 1945, G-2 Narrative, 1.

144   *"Our losses have been very light"*: NY Times, "Reich City Spurned Nazi Plea to Fight," 3/2/45, 2.

144   *"Colonel Melancon was singed"*: Baton Rouge Advocate, "First U.S.," 3/3/45, 2.

145   *"I had a feeling"*: Baton Rouge Advocate, "With the Services," 6/30/45, 3.

145   *"Even as the troops were moving up"*: Ewing, *29 Let's Go*, 243.

145   *"Masses of people lined the streets"*: Cooper, *110th Field Artillery*, 213.

145   *"The people must be taught"*: Hoffman, *I'll Be Home*, 180.

145   *"meek German civilian"*: 29ID, *29LG*, 4/3/45.

145   *"they were drunk and disorderly"*: Wilkes, *APO 230*, 168.

146   *"the greatest day for Allied arms"*: NY Times, Daniel, "Neuss is Captured," 3/3/45, 1.

146   *"the battle itself was won"*: Parker, *Conquer*, 183.

146   *"Move the people out"*: 29ID, *WRJ*, 3/3/45, 0920.

146   *"Let's have no looting"*: 29ID, *WRJ*, 3/2/45, 1935.

146   *"The 29th Infantry Division, with attached 821st"*: 29ID, *WRJ*, 3/4/45, 2105, 2325.

4. HITLER—*KAPUT*
A Study in Contrasts
147   *"Adolf Hitler, I love you"*: Kershaw, *Hitler: 1889–1936, Hubris*, 277.

147   *"The news that the town of Rheydt"*: Goebbels, *Final Entries 1945: The Diary of Joseph Goebbels*, 49.

147   *"Leaders of the [Nazi] party came around"*: NY Times Sunday Magazine, "Notes From Goebbels' Home Town," 3/18/45, 9.

149   *"a sprawling country house"*: Ibid., 37.

149   *"ornate lamps which belonged"*: Ibid., 9.

149   *"After seeing your establishment"*: 29ID, *WRJ*, 3/2/45, 1935.

149   *Hitler portrait and cardboard cutout*: 29ID, RCG, 1/14/47 Cooper letter to Ewing.

149   *"proposed a series of salutes"*: Baltimore Sun, Bradley, "29th Drinks Goebbels' Wine," 3/6/45, 1–2.

149   *"What time did the last [guest] leave"*: 29ID, *WRJ*, 3/4/45, 0745.

150   *"German propaganda minister Joseph Goebbels should have a new headache"*: *Baltimore Sun*, Bradley, "Goebbels's Castle Turns Synagogue," 3/7/45, 2.

150   *"The Jews are to blame"*: Das eherne Herz, *Die Juden sind schuld!* Munich: Zentralverlag der NSDAP, 1943, pp. 85–91; from 11/16/41 Goebbels essay.

150   *"I'd much prefer holding a service"*: 29ID, *29LG*, 3/8/45.

150   *"They wanted services then and there"*: Poliakoff, *Twenty-Niner*, July 1991, 8.

151   *"A log fire crackled"*: 29ID, *29LG*, 3/8/45.

151   *"Marty was in a foxhole"*: *Baltimore Sun*, Kelly, Willen obituary, 4/29/11.

152   *into which they promptly urinated*: 29ID, Personnel, Poliakoff, 3/7/06 Poliakoff interview with author.

152   *"He never came here"*: *NY Times Sunday Magazine*, "Notes From Goebbels' Home Town," 3/18/45, 37.

152   *"Joseph Goebbels was never any good"*: Ibid., 9, 36.

153   *"I lived in fear every moment"*: Jewish Federation of Greater Santa Barbara website, "Gela Baser Percal," http://jewishsantabarbara.org/portraits-of-survival/survivor-stories/gela-percal.

153   *"I need a good, cold drink"*: 29ID, Personnel, Poliakoff, 3/7/06 Poliakoff interview with author.

153   *"When a German who lived through that time"*: Jewish Federation of Greater Santa Barbara website, "Gela Baser Percal."

153   *"riding bicycles, pulling wagons"*: Ewing, *29 Let's Go*, 243, 245.

153   *"was a study in contrasts"*: Ziemke, *Occupation of Germany*, 185–86.

154   *"In Rheydt, Battery A notified"*: Cooper, *110th Field Artillery*, 213.

154   *"The children stare, smile, wave"*: Easton, *Love and War*, 14.

154   *"Seems they had been peering out"*: 29ID, *29LG*, 3/2/45.

154   *"All we had to do"*: 29ID, Personnel, Puntenney, Memoirs, 118–19.

154   *"To the victors belong . . . "*: 29ID, 116th AAR, Mar. 1945, cover.

155   *"Courtesy of"*: 29ID, 224th AAR, Mar. 1945, cover.

155   *"They came in very high"*: 29ID, Personnel, Puntenney, Memoirs, 116.

Something to Think About

155   *"No other single habit of hygiene"*: War Dept., Pamphlet 21-13, "Army Life" (Aug. 1944), 67.

155   *"brush on both the inside and outside"*: Ibid., 69.

155   *"long hair is often unsanitary"*: Ibid., 68.

155   *"Very minor details of maintenance"*: Ibid., 108.

156   *"As [Gerhardt] was going down the line"*: 29ID, Personnel, Kussman, Memoirs, 49.

156   *howitzer calibration*: 29ID, 110th, 224th, 227th AARs, Mar. 1945.

156   *"The howitzers were regrouped"*: Cooper, *110th Field Artillery*, 215.

156   *Lt. Col. and Pvt. White*: 29ID, *29LG*, 3/8/45.

157   *"those perennial favorites"*: Binkoski, *115th Infantry*, 310.

157   *"The main thing is to get comfortable"*: 29ID, WRJ, 3/2/45, 1947; 3/4/45, 1941.

157   *"We're bearing down"*: 29ID, WRJ, 3/2/45, 1947.

157   *"helped to add sparkle"*: Ewing, *29 Let's Go*, 246.

157   *"For every man who got drunk"*: 29ID, RCG, 1/26/47 Cooper letter to Ewing.

157   *"We're advancing as fast as the looting will permit"* and *"This remark was quoted"*: Walker, *Stonewallers*, 111.

158   *"In a message to all batteries"*: Cooper, *110th Field Artillery*, 214.

158   *War room visit by three generals*: 29ID, WRJ, 3/2/45, 1146.

158   *"For the only time in the war"*: Eisenhower, *Crusade in Europe*, 377.

159   *"narrow escape"* and *"Jülich will be something"*: *NY Times*, "Eisenhower Tours Ninth Army Front," 3/3/45, 3.

159   *"The Allied armies have broken through"*: *NY Times*, "Eisenhower Sees Massacre in Reich," 3/4/45, 6.

159   *"There is a security blackout"*: 29ID, *29LG*, 3/9/45.

The Hell with This Morale

160   *U.S. Army table of organization*: Hogan, *A Command Post at War*, 298–99.

160   *"cow-towns"* and *"not unlike those [we] had come to know"*: Binkoski, *115th Infantry*, 313.

161   *"a judicious mixture of activities"*: 29ID, 116th AAR, Mar. 1945, "Phase II," 1.

161   *"It was hard to absorb"*: 29ID, Personnel, Holberton, *Touched by Fire*, 89.

162   *"I met a gorgeous French girl"*: Walker, *Stonewallers*, E7–E10.

162   *Heerlen attractions*: 29ID, H/G, Box 2, File 49, Information on Dutch Towns.

162   *"immaculate"* and *"evening of beer"*: Easton, *Love and War*, 25.

162   *"The Dutch are the most up-and-coming people"*: Ibid., 25–26.

163   *"They [soldiers] are my favorite"* and *"backed by one of the finest all-soldier orchestras"*: 29ID, *29LG*, 3/20/45.

163   *Millholland*: 29ID, 3/115 Journal, 3/12/45.

164   *Slaughter's death*: 416th Bombardment Group website, "Mission No. 246, 3/31/45, Vreden, Germany," http://416th.com/missions/mission 246.html.

164   *Melancon*: *Baton Rouge Advocate*, "With the Services," 6/30/45, 3.

165   *"an appropriate streamer"*: Executive Order 9075, 2/26/42, http://en .wikisource.org/wiki/Executive_ Order_9075.

166   *"It won't be long now"*: 29ID, *29LG*, 3/14/45.

167   *"For each of the parades"*: Cooper, *110th Field Artillery*, 216.

167   *"We looked good"*: 29ID, *29LG*, 4/23/45.

167   *"The hell with this morale"*: War Dept., Pamphlet 21-13, "Army Life" (Aug. 1944), 4.

I Could Think of Tomorrow

168   *"assault the Rhine on a broad front"*: Ellis, *Victory in the West*, vol. 2, 275.

168   *"It was a great opportunity"*: MHI, Simpson papers, 1972 oral history interview, 371, 376.

168   *65,200 rounds*: Parker, *Conquer*, 243.

168   *"could only pretend to resist"*: MacDonald, *Last Offensive*, 301.

168   *"There was no real fight to it"*: Hewitt, *Workhorse of the Western Front*, 239.

168   *"The operation, as expected"*: Parker, *Conquer*, 245.

169   *"We blew our stacks"*: 29ID, *29LG*, 4/9/45.

169   *"Main Occupation"*: War Dept., Manual TM 12-223, "Reception Center Operations" (Dec. 1944), 28.

169   *"scoot up and down"*: 29ID, *29LG*, 4/9/45.

169   *"cross the Rhine River north of the Ruhr"*: Parker, *Conquer*, 228.

169   *"a sooty ellipse"*: Atkinson, *The Guns at Last Light*, 223.

169   *"that extraordinary region"*: Butcher, *My Three Years With Eisenhower*, 782.

169   *"While there are many indications"*: Parker, *Conquer*, 227.

169   *Gerhardt as corps commander*: 29ID, *WRJ*, 3/26/45, 1655.

170   *"Swede"*: West Point 1914 yearbook, *The Howitzer*, 40.

170   *Rhine bridges*: Parker, *Conquer*, 244, 253, 256, 259.

170   *"I was bottled up there"*: MHI, Simpson papers, 1972 oral history interview, 376–77.

171   *"orderly"*: 29ID, 116th AAR, Mar. 1945, "Phase III."

171   *Company I injuries, PFC Meeg*: 29ID, MR, Company I, 116th Infantry, 4/1/45.

171   *"After a month of inactivity"* and *"The scene of construction"*: Binkoski, *115th Infantry*, 319.

172   *"We felt a great elation"*: Barnes, *Fragments of My Life*, 126.

5. THE GREAT MIGRATION
The Past Was the Past

173   *"We may want to use the 116th Infantry"*: 29ID, WRJ, 3/31/45, 1227.

174   *"There will be a little confusion"*: Ibid., 2010.

174   *"largest double envelopment"*: Pogue, *The Supreme Command*, 438.

174   *two million souls*: Parker, *Conquer*, 273.

175   *"Pittsburgh of Germany"*: *The Story of the 75th Infantry Division* booklet, Paris: Stars and Stripes, 1945.

175   *"veritable fortresses"*: Samson Abelow, *History of XVI Corps*, 59.

175   *"a pretty German girl came toward us"*: Easton, *Love and War*, 28.

175   *"The Dortmund–Ems Canal"*: 29ID, 116th AAR, Apr. 1945, "Phase I," 2.

175   *"a bit of a confused start"*: Barnes, *Fragments of My Life*, 126.

176   *"Scaling ladders"*: 29ID, 116th AAR, Apr. 1945, "Phase I," 2.

176   *"enemy resistance was found"*: 29ID, 116th AAR, Apr. 1945, "Phase I," Intelligence.

176   *"each time we found an obstacle"*: Barnes, *Fragments of My Life*, 126.

176   *"James rushed forward"*: *Florence (SC) Morning News*, "Lt. Dudley James Wins Silver Star," 8/19/45, 1.

176   *"one platoon as a point"*: 29ID, 116th AAR, Apr. 1945, "Lessons Learned," 1–2.

176   *Company A prisoners*: 29ID, MR, Company A, 116th Infantry, 4/4/45.

178   *seventy-one different German units*: 29ID, 116th AAR, Apr. 1945, "Phase I," Intelligence.

178   *"definitely a bottom-of-the-barrel organization"*: U.S. Army Intelligence Bulletin, Feb. 1945, website, "The German Volkssturm," www.lonesentry.com/articles/volkssturm.

178   *"The* Volkssturm *troops proved ineffective"*: 29ID, 116th AAR, Apr. 1945, "Phase I," Intelligence.

178   *"Since it was my job"*: Barnes, *Fragments of My Life*, 127.

178   *"This landing permitted him"*: Ewing, *29 Let's Go*, 247.

179   *"tank and tank destroyer units"*: 29ID, 116th AAR, Apr. 1945, "Phase I," 3.

179   *"light [with] moderate mortar"*: 29ID, MR, Company C, 116th Infantry, 4/5/45.

179   *PFC Galloway*: Barnes, *Fragments of My Life*, 128.

180   *"At 0515 hours the work was completed"*: 29ID, 121st AAR, Apr. 1945, 2.

180   *"It was a little like attacking New York City"*: Easton, *Love and War*, 323.

180   *"The enemy seized the opportunity"*: 29ID, 116th AAR, Apr. 1945, "Phase I," 3–4.

180   *"The German FOs were up"*: Easton, *Love and War*, 323.

180   *"overpowered with a violent barrage"*: 29ID, 116th AAR, Apr. 1945, "Phase I," 3–4.

180   *"ceased as soon as the tanks closed in"*: 29ID, 747th AAR, Apr. 1945, 1.

180   *"We advanced rather grandly"*: Easton, *Love and War*, 323.

180   *thirteen casualties*: 29ID, MR, 3/116th Infantry, 4/6/45.

181   *"saw him lying in a plowed field"*: Easton, *Love and War*, 314.

181   *"Already he looked like a man"*: *Collier's*, Robert Easton, "The Man Who Went Back," 5/8/48, 18.

182   *"I'd talked to [him] heart-to-heart"*: Easton, *Love and War*, 323.

182   *"character . . . Nothing he didn't know"*: *Collier's*, Robert Easton, "The Man Who Went Back," 5/8/48, 54.

182   *"He'd made good"*: Easton, *Love and War*, 323.

182   *"a good friend"* and *"Captain Hawks was on the second floor"*: 29ID, Personnel, Puntenney, Memoirs, 121.

182   *124 casualties*: 29ID, 116th AAR, Apr. 1945, "Casualties."

182   *"an efficient officer, respected by his men"* and *"His death under those circumstances"*: Wilkes, *APO 230*, 176.

183   *"the unit that relieves us"*: 29ID, *WRJ*, 4/6/45, 1712.

183   *"quite a haul, and we have lots of stuff"*: Ibid., 1413.

183   *twenty-four trucks*: Ibid., 2131.

183   *"still in the line"*: 29ID, *WRJ*, 4/7/45, 0842.

183   *"Some of their people"*: Ibid., 0642.

183   *"it was with some relief"*: 29ID, 116th AAR, Apr. 1945, "Phase I," 5.

Just Like a Movie

184   *"The great chase to the east was on"*: Cooper, *110th Field Artillery*, 218.

184   *Duisburg, half a million people*: Parker, *Conquer*, 272.

184   *"It was just like a movie"*: *NY Times*, "Germans Back Down on Surrender Offer," 4/4/45, 10.

184   *"This was like fighting in industrial areas"*: 29ID, RCG, 2/2/47 Cooper letter to Ewing.

184 *"experienced strange feelings"* and *"established headquarters in an office building"*: Cooper, *110th Field Artillery*, 218.

186 *"was extremely bad"*: 29ID, 29th Division Artillery AAR, Apr. 1945, "Report of Air OP," 1.

187 *"In the Ruhr area alone"*: Parker, *Conquer*, 322.

187 *"Many liberated slave workers came streaming toward us"*: Easton, *Love and War*, 27–28.

187 *"to be prepared to mount guard"*: 29ID, *WRJ*, 4/1/45, 2125.

187 *"It is OK to use that platoon"*: Ibid., 2011.

187 *"a mission to take over a security job"*: 29ID, *WRJ*, 4/7/45, 2210, 2207.

189 *"the great migration"*: Ziemke, *Occupation of Germany*, 225.

189 *"the designation DP turned out to be"*: Ibid., 205.

189 *"Most established camps were in a horrible state of filth"*: 29ID, 29th Division AAR, Apr. 1945, "Rear Area Protection," Appendix A, 1.

189 *"The first step taken"*: Ibid., 1–2.

189 *200,000 rations per day*: Ziemke, *Occupation of Germany*, 239.

189 *"staffed by two Belgian physicians"*: Cooper, *110th Field Artillery*, 221–22.

189 *"the ingenuity and patience of every soldier"*: 29ID, 110th AAR, Apr. 1945, 2.

190 *"What appeared to be"*: 29ID, 29th Division AAR, Apr. 1945, "Rear Area Protection," Appendix A, 4.

190 *"Once the people understood"*: 29ID, Personnel, Holberton, *Touched By Fire*, 94.

190 *"The truth is"*: quoted in Ziemke, *Occupation of Germany*, 240. From "Up the Weser River," NA SHAEF G-5 papers.

190 *"Notice was given"*: Binkoski, *115th Infantry*, 324–25.

191 *"Little did [we] realize"*: 29ID, 110th AAR, Apr. 1945, 1.

191 *13,917 people*: 29ID, RCG, 2/2/47 Cooper letter to Ewing.

191 *"The sanitary conditions in Wesel"* and *"immediately reduced"*: Cooper, *110th Field Artillery*, 221.

191 *"Most of the displaced workers"*: 29ID, Personnel, Holberton, *Touched by Fire*, 94.

192 *"the motley traffic"*: 29ID, 116th AAR, Apr. 1945, "Phase II," Enforcing Military Government Policies.

192 *"They are Red Army PWs"*: quoted in Ziemke, *Occupation of Germany*, 240. From "Up the Weser River," NA SHAEF G-5 papers.

192 *10,789 Red Army members*: 29ID, 116th AAR, Apr. 1945, "Phase II," Enforcing Military Government Policies.

192   *"Normally the officer or non-commissioned officer of highest rank"*:
        29ID, 29th Division AAR, Apr. 1945, "Rear Area Protection," Annex 4,
        2.

192   *"a tall, husky, soft-spoken lad"*: 29ID, *29LG*, 4/15/45.

193   *"stood their first formation"* and *"These German people will tell you"*:
        Ibid.

193   *"They were suffering so much"*: Cooper, *110th Field Artillery*, 224.

193   *"They realized the tables had been turned"*: 29ID, Personnel,
        Holberton, *Touched by Fire*, 94.

193   *five officers, eleven enlisted men*: 29ID, *29LG*, 5/17/45.

193   *T/Sgt. Curtiss*: The Remington Site website, "Donald H. Gabor,"
        www.soundfountain.org/rem/remgabor.html.

193   *"For the initial phase, we go slow"*: 29ID, *29LG*, 5/17/45.

194   *"German farmers say"*: quoted in Ziemke, *Occupation of Germany*,
        240. From "Up the Weser River," NA SHAEF G-5 papers.

194   *"In one such case the investigators found"*: Cooper, *110th Field
        Artillery*, 223.

194   *"an aristocratic young man"*: Slaughter, *Omaha Beach and Beyond*,
        181–82.

194   *"people who killed German people"*: Easton, *Love and War*, 28–29.

195   *"to the last man"* and *"With such men I cannot fight"* and *"The irate
        burgomeister"* and *"When the 'Hitler boy' threatened"*: 29ID, *29LG*,
        4/11/45.

195   *"Menkel explained to his buddies"*: 29ID, *29LG*, 4/12/45.

195   *"I was greatly impressed"*: Ewing, *29 Let's Go*, 251–52.

195   *"I never saw him when he was low"*: MHI, Simpson papers, 1972 oral
        history interview, 453.

196   *"President Roosevelt Dies Suddenly"*: 29ID, *29LG*, 4/13/45.

196   *"went to bed depressed"*: Eisenhower, *Crusade in Europe*, 409.

196   *"I bitterly regret"*: DEP, *The War Years*, vol. 4, 2603.

196   *"I congratulate you"*: Toland, *Last 100 Days*, 377.

196   *"Wearing of mourning badges"*: Atkinson, *The Guns at Last Light*, 595.

6. SOMETHING TO WRITE HOME ABOUT
Giving the Woods a Haircut

197   *"President Roosevelt is Dead"*: *NY Times*, 4/13/45, 1.

197   *"It was incredible to us"*: Barnes, *Fragments of My Life*, 128.

198   *"Many members of the 110th"*: Cooper, *110th Field Artillery*, 219.

198   *"So far as I am concerned"*: Ellis, *Victory in the West*, vol. 2, 299.

199   *"Upon closing in assembly area"*: 29ID, *WRJ*, 4/17/45, 1514.

199   *"like an old war horse"*: 29ID, 116th AAR, Apr. 1945, "Phase III," 1.

199   *"just as it had developed"*: 29ID, 116th AAR, Apr. 1945, "Phase II," Enforcing Military Government Policies, 6.

199   *"The [military government] experience had been a new one"*: Binkoski, *115th Infantry*, 327.

200   *"Half in jest, half in earnest"* and *"a force estimated at a thousand men"*: MacDonald, *Last Offensive*, 400.

200   *"At night small parties would come out"*: Ewing, *29 Let's Go*, 254.

200   *"to give Klötze Forest a real haircut"*: MacDonald, *Last Offensive*, 400.

201   *"The air was full of conflicting stories"*: 29ID, RCG, File 26.

201   *"a wild-game hunt"* and *"For men who had seen fighting at its roughest"*: Baltimore Sun, Bradley, "Klötze Forest Pocket Eliminated," 4/23/45, 1.

201   *"nearly 400 prisoners"*: 29ID, 175th AAR, Apr. 1945, "Operations Narrative," 5.

201   *"[We] thought how tough Jerry could have made it"*: Baltimore Sun, Bradley, "Klötze Forest Pocket Eliminated," 4/23/45, 1.

201   *"Company K [1st Lt. Clyde Reed, CO] held the center"*: 29ID, 175th AAR, Apr. 1945, "Operations Narrative," 5.

202   *"the easy-going atmosphere"*: Ewing, *29 Let's Go*, 254.

202   *forty-three Germans were killed*: 29ID, 175th AAR, Apr. 1945, "Operations Narrative," 6.

203   *"The density of the woods"*: Ibid., 6–7.

Old Enough to Kill

203   *"Living conditions in the area"*: Cooper, *110th Field Artillery*, 226.

203   *"The situation was none too clear"*: 29ID, 116th AAR, Apr. 1945, "Phase III," 1.

204   *"This type of warfare was something entirely new"*: Binkoski, *115th Infantry*, 329.

204   *"thrust forward into the unknown"*: 29ID, 116th AAR, Apr. 1945, "Phase III," 1.

205   *"The probing and clearing operations"*: Ibid., 2.

205   *"absolutely flat and quite densely wooded"*: Easton, *Love and War*, 307.

205   *"All was still ordered"*: Cawthon, *Other Clay*, 167.

206   *"Houses invariably had bed sheets"*: Ibid., 168.

206   *"greatly facilitated the advance"*: 29ID, 29th Cavalry Recon Troop AAR, Apr. 1945.

207   *"When the five minutes passed"*: Ewing, *29 Let's Go*, 253.

207   *"We found ourselves"*: Binkoski, *115th Infantry*, 331–32.

207 *"The men who observed the incident"*: Ibid., 332.

207 *"that they had wanted to surrender"*: Ewing, *29 Let's Go*, 253.

207 *"an almost empty town"*: 29ID, RCG, File 22, 1946 Johns letter to Ewing.

208 *"The men looked around"*: Ibid.

209 *"0700—Companies began moving out"*: 29ID, 2/115 Journal, 4/21/45, 0700–0910.

209 *"Reports from higher headquarters"*: Binkoski, *115th Infantry*, 333–34.

210 *"communication between the two"* and *"The Company E outposts didn't know"*: Ibid., 334.

210 *"a [German] mustard gas dump"*: 29ID, 3/115 Journal, 4/21/45, 1020.

210 *"almost always unopposed"*: 29ID, Personnel, Kussman, Memoirs, 51–52.

210 *"The war is lost!"*: Toland, *Adolf Hitler*, 868.

210 *"Russians getting close"*: 29ID, 115 Journal, 4/22/45.

211 *"No mines had previously been encountered"*: 29ID, RCG, File 22, 1946 Johns letter to Ewing.

211 *"The jeep passed"*: Binkoski, *115th Infantry*, 335.

212 *"We are going so fast"*: 29ID, WRJ, 4/22/45, 1434.

212 *"Would like to know"*: 29ID, 115 Journal, 4/21/45, 2200.

212 *"a total of 850 miles of road"*: 29ID, 121st AAR, Apr. 1945, 5.

212 *"about two feet square"*: Ewing, *29 Let's Go*, 254.

212 *"You better do something"*: 29ID, WRJ, 4/25/45, 1412.

213 *"They say they're not magnetic"*: 29ID, WRJ, 5/2/45, 0744.

213 *"last seen examining"*: 29ID, RCG, File 22, 1946 Johns letter to Ewing.

213 *"there were three or four Teller mines"*: 29ID, WRJ, 4/24/45, 1725.

213 *"fooled with the new type"*: Gutknecht, *Foxhole Buddies*, 701, 5/21/45 Dickerson letter.

213 *"to keep out"*: 29ID, 121st AAR, Apr. 1945, 5.

213 *"Well, you are it"*: 29ID, WRJ, 4/24/45, 1725.

213 *"Further investigation of the charge"*: 29ID, 121st AAR, Apr. 1945, 4–5.

213 *"Even in this war"*: Binkoski, *115th Infantry*, 337.

214 *"left a hollow, aching feeling"*: Ibid., 336.

214 *"The first thing we started to do"*: 29ID, Personnel, Holberton, *Touched by Fire*, 97.

214 *"It is impossible to clear mines"*: 29ID, 115th AAR, Apr. 1945, "Battle Lessons," 18.

214 *"The reconnaissance [platoon] is at Phase Line Jane"*: 29ID, WRJ, 4/23/45, 1025.

215 *"authority to go up to 'Lottie'"*: 29ID, WRJ, 4/23/45, 1145.

215 *"Be prepared to make a reconnaissance"*: 29ID, 115 Journal, 4/23/45, 1150.

215 *two hours to clear Pudripp*: Binkoski, *115th Infantry*, 339.

215 *"As we got deep into the woods"*: 29ID, Personnel, Kussman, Memoirs, 51.

215 *"all the workers we saw"* and *"I contacted Captain Armstrong"*: 29ID, Personnel, Kussman, 4/26/14 Kussman email to author.

215 *"I quickly lost control of my platoon"*: 29ID, Personnel, Kussman, Memoirs, 51; 4/26/14 Kussman email to author.

216 *"Had it been a real combat situation"*: 29ID, Personnel, Kussman, 5/24/14 Kussman email to author.

216 *"a possibility exists"*: 29ID, *WRJ*, 4/23/45, 2059.

216 *"found and deactivated"*: Binkoski, *115th Infantry*, 340.

216 *"The German captain led Captain Armstrong"*: Ibid., 339.

217 *"making their way westward"*: 29ID, Personnel, Holberton, *Touched by Fire*, 97–98.

217 *"There were more than enough grisly sights"*: Binkoski, *115th Infantry*, 342.

217 *"reported hearing sounds"* and *"Coming out on one side"*: Ibid., 337.

217 *"a beautiful spring day"*: 29ID, Personnel, Kussman, Memoirs, 52.

217 *"was hardly started"*: Cawthon, *Other Clay*, 170.

217 *"an international boundary"*: 29ID, 2/115 Journal, 4/24/45, 2100.

217 *"sandy ridges and rounded bluffs"*: Cooper, *110th Field Artillery*, 229.

218 *"We can smell the Baltic Sea"*: Easton, *Love and War*, 307.

218 *"seemed quite unreal"*: Binkoski, *115th Infantry*, 341–42.

218 *"the ease, calmness, and thoroughness"*: 29ID, Personnel, Fernley, 5/19/45 Jones letter to George Fernley.

218 *"resistance was heavy"*: 29ID, *G3J*, 4/24/45.

219 *"cold, cloudy weather"* and *"There was the familiar roar"*: *Baltimore Sun*, Bradley, "9th Clears Area to West of Elbe," 4/29/45, 1.

220 *"one fat, perspiring Kraut"* and *"There was nothing any of us could do"* and *"we were in the edge of town"*: Ibid.

221 *"German riflemen, well dug in"*: 29ID, MR, Company K, 116th Infantry, 4/24/45.

221 *"The boys really sat up"*: 29ID, *29LG*, 5/2/45.

221 *"I rounded the corner"*: Easton, *Love and War*, 308.

221 *"mere youth—just sixteen"* and *"Not yet old enough to vote"* and *"returned to wherever major generals are supposed to stay"*: 29ID, *29LG*, 5/2/45.

221 *"one of those rare humans"*: Easton, *Love and War*, 309–10.

221   *"wide, muddy, and rushing"*: Cawthon, *Other Clay*, 170.

222   *"was very well handled"*: 29ID, *WRJ*, 4/26/45, 2058.

222   *"Must have small people"*: Cooper, *110th Field Artillery*, 228.

222   *"We [Company K members] were quartered"*: 29ID, Personnel, Kussman, Memoirs, 52–53.

223   *"been warned we would rape"*: Easton, *Love and War*, 308.

223   *"Krautland"*: Gutknecht, *Foxhole Buddies*, 642–43, 4/26/45 Dickerson letter.

Venty-noin, Let's Goot

224   *"it was hard merely to sit"*: Cooper, *110th Field Artillery*, 210.

224   *"that a round from a sniper's rifle"*: 29ID, Personnel, Holberton, *Touched by Fire*, 98.

224   *"The distinction of being the last casualty"*: Cawthon, *Other Clay*, 171.

225   *"he knows the only solution"*: Leinbaugh, *The Men of Company K*, 275.

225   *"A considerable number of war crimes were investigated"*: 29ID, 29th Division AAR, Apr. 1945, "G-2 Narrative, Counterintelligence," 3.

225   *"got the devil shelled out of it"*: 29ID, RCG, File 25, 2/2/47 Cooper letter to Ewing.

225   *"At night, lone Luftwaffe planes"*: Cooper, *110th Field Artillery*, 210.

226   *"no harassing or interdiction missions"*: 29ID, *WRJ*, 4/26/45, 1515.

226   *21 missions, 411 rounds; 151 fire missions, 2,988 shells*: 29ID, *G3J*, Apr. 1945 and 2/23/45.

226   *"that the entire outpost had been confidently asleep"*: Cawthon, *Other Clay*, 171.

226   *"when [the Germans] were challenged"*: 29ID, *WRJ*, 4/30/45, 0910.

226   *"I didn't expect the Germans"*: Ibid., 0843.

226   *"It was obvious"*: 29ID, 116th AAR, Apr. 1945, "Intelligence and Military Government," 1.

226   *"We don't want to go across"*: 29ID, *WRJ*, 4/26/45, 1002.

227   *"A regular ferry system was set up"*: Barnes, *Fragments of My Life*, 129.

227   *"walked about freely"*: Ewing, *29 Let's Go*, 256.

227   *"Remembering the tremendous transportation problems"*: Cooper, *110th Field Artillery*, 229.

228   *"Now it has gone so far"*: Ryan, *The Last Battle*, 497.

228   *"Hitler Reported Dead"*: 29ID, *29LG*, 5/2/45.

228   *"[Hitler] had been killed in action"*: 29ID, *29LG*, 5/3/45.

228   *"A brain stroke killed Hitler"*: *Pittsburgh Press*, 5/2/45, 1.

228   *"to give the German people"*: Butcher, *My Three Years With Eisenhower*, 819.

228   *"two strapping Krauts"*: 29ID, *29LG*, 5/3/45.

All Fear Was Gone

229   *"the commanding officer"*: Ewing, *29 Let's Go*, 256.

229   *"It seems that there is a lieutenant colonel"*: 29ID, *WRJ*, 4/30/45, 2110.

229   *"We don't want to get involved"*: Ibid., 2240.

229   *"We will tell McDaniel that it is OK"*: Ibid., 2246.

229   Division z.V. *details*: 29ID, RCG, File 20, German V-2 Rocket Division.

231   *"have the order and the right"*: 29ID, 29th Division Museum, V-2 Rocket Division Surrender Document.

231   *"The two senior [German] officers"*: 29ID, *WRJ*, 5/1/45, 0150.

232   *"All troops should immediately disengage"*: 29ID, RCG, File 20, German V-2 Rocket Division.

232   *"They are all interested"*: 29ID, *WRJ*, 5/2/45, 0926.

232   *"The Krauts have put the white flags up"*: Ibid., 0714.

232   *"Hundreds of German vehicles lined the road"*: 29ID, 175th AAR, May 1945, 1.

233   *"arrogant beyond belief"*: 29ID, Personnel, Robertson, 12/4/09 Robertson interview with author.

233   *"were about thirty German shepherd dogs"*: Ewing, *29 Let's Go*, 259.

233   *"puts a different outlook on the thing"* and *"I think we should do what we can"*: 29ID, *WRJ*, 5/2/45, 0805.

233   *10,367 POWs*: 29ID, 175th AAR, May 1945, 2.

234   *"Lord, what a sight!"*: Gordon, *One Man's War*, 124.

234   *"went over [the Elbe], without permission"*: Gutknecht, *Foxhole Buddies*, 649, 6/6/45 Dickerson letter.

234   *"The impending surrender"*: Ewing, *29 Let's Go*, 257, 259.

234   *"While assisting in the ferrying operations"*: *Baltimore Sun*, "Royal Silver Trophy Lost," 2/18/47, 28.

235   *"Capt. Hirschmann advised the civilian"*: Ibid.

236   *"All public property taken from the enemy"*: Articles of War, Sept. 1920, Preliminary Provisions, 22.

236   *500 people; one million dollars*: *Baltimore Sun*, "Elaborate German Silver Set," 11/23/46, 22.

We Are Friends!

237   *"the staple of discussion"*: Ewing, *29 Let's Go*, 259.

237   *"There is a lot of firing"*: 29ID, *WRJ*, 5/2/45, 1903.

237   *"something very unusual is going on"*: 29ID, *WRJ*, 5/2/45, 1921.

237   *"The Russians are here!"*: Ibid., 2054.

237   *"go out and find the Russians"*: 29ID, *29 Let's Go* booklet, Stars and Stripes, 1945.

238   *"long gray coats"*: Ewing, *29 Let's Go*, 259.

239   *"There will be more [cavalry] in tomorrow"*: 29ID, *WRJ*, 5/3/45, 0033.

239   *"Blue and Grayers were crossing"*: 29ID, *29LG*, 5/6/45.

240   *"a very good man"*: 29ID, *WRJ*, 5/3/45, 1955.

240   *"like equal rank"*: Ibid., 0742.

240   *"Inevitable toasts to the president"*: Ewing, *29 Let's Go*, 259.

241   *"lavish fashion"*: Ibid.

241   *"The Red Joes were feeding their horses"*: 29ID, *29LG*, 5/6/45.

7. THE LAST ACT
Victory in Europe

243   *"assigned the southwestern zone"*: Foreign Relations of the U.S., *Conference at Quebec, 1944*, 365.

244   *"It would be desirable"*: Ibid., 373.

244   *"suggested that the American area"*: Ibid., 375.

244   *"They have changed our mission"* and *"a lot of specialists"*: 29ID, *WRJ*, 5/3/45, 1621.

244   *"Task Force Bremen"*: 29ID, 29th Division AAR, May 1945, 2.

244   *"overcast with occasional rain"*: 29ID, *G3J*, 5/4/45.

244   *"via Luchow, Uelzen"*: Cooper, *110th Field Artillery*, 234.

244   *"we overloaded some trucks"*: 29ID, *WRJ*, 5/4/45, 1545.

245   *"The situation was becoming too complicated"*: Cooper, *110th Field Artillery*, 235.

245   *"were forced to refuse"*: Ibid., 234.

245   *"the tributes were for German soldiers"*: Ibid., 235.

245   *"This is a great moment"*: Atkinson, *The Guns at Last Light*, 622.

247   *"mine clearance"*: 29ID, 121st AAR, May 1945, 2.

247   *"The bridge situation"* and *"It slows things up"*: 29ID, *WRJ*, 5/6/45, 0929.

247   *"a Class 40 steel treadway"* and *"a definite traffic circulation plan"*: 29ID, 121st AAR, May 1945, 3.

247   *"considerable confusion"*: 29ID, *WRJ*, 5/7/45, 0315.

247   *"What they need up there is you"*: 29ID, *WRJ*, 5/6/45, 0929.

248   *"The people down below"*: 29ID, *WRJ*, 5/7/45, 0747.

248   *"A representative of the German high command"*: Ibid., 0805.

248   *"The mission of this Allied force"*: DEP, *The War Years*, vol. 4, 2696.

248   *"The war room as such"*: 29ID, *WRJ*, 5/7/45, 2130.

It's Been a Long Way

248   *"Omaha Beach to the Elbe River"*: 29ID, *29LG*, 5/8/45.

249   *"keeping with the mood"*: Cawthon, *Other Clay*, 172.

249   *"somehow the entire event"*: Binkoski, *115th Infantry*, 347–48.

249   *"I suggest we mount"*: 29ID, *WRJ*, 5/7/45, 0900.

249   *"It is those superficial things"*: Balkoski, *From Brittany to the Reich*, 16.

250   *"I never liked parading"*: Easton, *Love and War*, 313.

250   *"It was, after all, a great day"*: 29ID, 116th AAR, May 1945, 1.

250   *"a brilliantly sunny day"*: Cooper, *110th Field Artillery*, 236.

250   *"was a dramatic and fitting end"*: Ibid., 237.

250   *"On February 3, 1941, this battalion"*: Ibid., 286.

251   *"created a memory"* and *"with schnapps from a nearby plant"*: Ibid., 237.

251   *"This battalion, with the 116th and 115th"*: 29ID, 121st AAR, May 1945, 5–6.

251   *"3,000 men standing with bowed heads"* and *"by columns of compa-nies"*: Easton, *Love and War*, 312.

252   *"I saw them sharing the same frozen foxhole"*: Ibid., 313.

252   *"It's been a long way"*: Ibid., 314.

How Many Points Do *You* Have?

252   *"You have completed your mission"*: GCM, vol. 5, 168.

252   *"a vital stimulus to morale"*: DEP, *The War Years*, vol. 4, 2308.

252   *"otherwise we shall have"*: GCM, vol. 4, 614.

252   *"The showing of this film"*: DEP, *The War Years*, vol. 4, 2308.

253   *"The Army said that the first men"*: Stars and Stripes (London), 5/11/45, 1.

254   *"Trip Ticket Home"*: Ibid.

255   *"satisfactory record"*: Stars and Stripes (London), 5/11/45, "Tomor-row" Supplement.

255   *"tougher than the plan"*: Stars and Stripes (London), 5/11/45, 1.

255   *"The return of officers to the United States"*: Stars and Stripes (London), 5/11/45, "Tomorrow" Supplement.

255   *forty-one Military Occupational Specialties*: Sparrow, *History of Per-sonnel Demobilization*, 174, 324.

255   *"[The plan] seems to satisfy"*: Ibid., 114. From *Boston Post*, 5/12/45 editorial, 4.

255   *"will apply equally to soldiers"*: *Stars and Stripes (London)*, 5/11/45, "Tomorrow" Supplement.

255   *"A small and perhaps irreducible minority"*: Sparrow, *History of Personnel Demobilization*, 317.

255   *"a long ways from being fair"*: Ibid., 127.

257   *"What gripes me"* and *"Twelve points for a no-good brat"*: Gutknecht, *Foxhole Buddies*, 691, 5/17/45 Dickerson letter.

258   *Four categories*: Sparrow, *History of Personnel Demobilization*, 173.

258   *"Whenever two or more men"*: 29ID, 116th AAR, May 1945, "Phase 1," 2.

Illusions Make Me Impregnable

259   *"We had not practiced"*: 29ID, Personnel, Earll, 10/18/14 Earll interview with author.

259   *"understand the art of ceremonial marching"*: Patton, *War As I Knew It*, 44–45.

259   *"Task Force Bremen"*: 29ID, 29th Division AAR, May 1945, 3.

260   *"nothing better than Bremerhaven"* and *"surpassed anything"* and *"world's largest floating cranes"* and *"the endless wrangling"*: *Baltimore Sun*, Whitcomb, "Bremen Joy to Port Officers," 5/31/45, 10.

260   *"as level as a table top"*: Cooper, *110th Field Artillery*, 241.

260   *"a flat country of small towns"*: Ewing, *29 Let's Go*, 261.

260   *"the water level"*: *Baltimore Sun*, Norton, "Bremen Air Cargo Terminus," 6/3/45, 10.

260   *"the section from Bremen to Hamburg"*: *Baltimore Sun*, Whitcomb, "Attitudes in Occupied Germany," 5/24/45, 14.

261   *twenty-five supplementary units*: 29ID, 29th Division AAR, May 1945, 4.

261   *1,400-square-mile zone*: 29ID, *Operation Tally Ho*, 1.

261   *"Germany has created"*: Foreign Relations of the U.S., *The Conference at Berlin (Potsdam Conference)*, vol. 2, 755–56.

262   *"to defeat German efforts"*: 29ID, BE, File 2, Demond items.

262   *"engaged in friendly contact"*: Ziemke, *Occupation of Germany*, 322.

262   *"a non-fraternization policy anywhere"*: Ibid., 283, 321.

263   *"it is believed desirable"*: Ibid., 325.

263   *"the Germans regard American MPs"*: 29ID, Personnel, Giannini.

263   *"The dereliction here is ghastly"*: Easton, *Love and War*, 344.

263   *"there were a lot more Germans"* and *"were too preoccupied"*: *NY Times*, Hill, "Few Fraternize as Ban is Lifted," 7/16/45, 3.

263   *"You can't organize Americanism"*: Easton, *Love and War*, 355.

263 *"The first organized, officially sanctioned dance"*: 29ID, BE, File 1, 1/115 in Bremen Enclave.

264 *"the most famous, or infamous, meeting place"*: Binkoski, *115th Infantry*, 352.

264 *"to German girls"*: 29ID, BE, File 3.

265 *Hellmut Schnackenburg*: *Washington Post*, "Maestro Who Defied Gestapo," 7/25/45, 5.

265 *"has moved me as no other"*: Avins, *Johannes Brahms: Life and Letters*, 355.

265 *"marked a watershed"*: Ibid., 357.

266 *"The part of my World War II military career"*: 29ID, Personnel, Walker, 10/10/08 Walker interview with author.

266 *"The rumors passed quickly"*: Ewing, *29 Let's Go*, 272.

266 *"stuttering and shit-scared"*: 29ID, Personnel, Henne, Henne interview with author.

266 *"Search parties unearthed"*: Cooper, *110th Field Artillery*, 245.

267 *"groups of idle German youths"*: *Baltimore Sun*, "Ike Uneasy on Germany," 11/1/45, 2.

267 *"Two walls facing the building's inner courtyard"*: *Baltimore Sun*, "Two Mysterious Blasts," 6/5/45, 1.

267 *"a slow gas leak"*: *NY Times*, "Bremen Blast From Gas," 6/18/45, 5.

267 *"moulded in the Nazi philosophy"*: Ewing, *29 Let's Go*, 269.

268 *"was taught in the* Hitler Jugend" and *"several possible suspects"* and *"German civil officials"*: 29ID, 29th Division AAR, May 1945, "G-2 Narrative," 5.

268 *"Sgt. [Warren] Rifenbark"*: 29ID, Personnel, Holberton, *Touched by Fire*, 102.

268 *"was promptly shot"*: 29ID, Personnel, Henne, Henne interview with author.

268 *"automatic arrest"*: U.S. European Command, *First Year of the Occupation*, Pt. V, Vol. 2, 137.

268 *"denied with vigor"*: Ewing, *29 Let's Go*, 268–69.

269 *"A total of 387 arrests"*: 29ID, 29th Division AAR, June 1945, "G-2 Activities," 1.

269 *"the most modern and elaborate headquarters"*: Ewing, *29 Let's Go*, 262.

269 *"the most comfortable place"*: Hoffman, *I'll Be Home*, 207.

269 *"most active and visible member"*: Walker, *Stonewallers*, E4–5.

270 *"What happened to the rug?"*: Ibid., E5–6.

270 *"designed as a security check"*: 29ID, 29th Division AAR, July 1945.

271 *"the populace was extremely cooperative"*: Ibid.

271 *"was taken into custody"*: 29ID, *Operation Tally Ho*, 3–4.

271 *"The behavior of the troops"*: 29ID, 29th Division AAR, July 1945.

271 *"cases of murder and organized looting"* and *"The German populace has become increasingly bitter"*: *Baltimore Sun*, "Ike Uneasy on Germany," 11/1/45, 2.

271 *"after dark, maulings and knifings occurred"*: Ewing, *29 Let's Go*, 272.

271 *"serious proportions"*: *NY Times*, "Bremen Crime Wave Ends," 8/26/45, 16.

272 *"In an effort to curb"*: Ewing, *29 Let's Go*, 272.

272 *"a short but furious battle"*: 29ID, BE, File 1, 1/115 in Bremen Enclave.

272 *"with bottles and buckets"*: Ewing, *29 Let's Go*, 272.

272 *"Our latest report from Bremen"*: *NY Times*, "Bremen Crime Wave Ends," 8/26/45, 16.

Disarmed Enemy Forces

272 *"would be responsible"*: 29ID, DEF Staging Area AAR, Nov. 1945, 1.

273 *"At the docks in Bremerhaven"* and *"with screened latrines"*: Ibid., 5.

274 *"periodic stops were made"* and *187,355 disarmed troops*: Ibid., 6.

274 *128,788 men and women*: Ibid., map.

Thanks for the Memory

275 *"We were all just marking time"*: Walker, *Stonewallers*, E13.

275 *"of military significance"*: 29ID, 116th AAR, May 1945.

275 *"I slept in the same room"*: 29ID, Personnel, Holberton, *Touched by Fire*, 103.

275 *"gave me a memorable chance"*: Walker, *Stonewallers*, E14–15.

276 *"Beck's is my brewery!"*: 29ID, Personnel, Walker, 10/10/08 Walker interview with author.

276 *"the authorities declared"*: Walker, *Stonewallers*, E15.

276 *"The 121st Engineer Battalion"*: *Baltimore Sun*, Norton, "Blue and Gray Turns to Sport," 6/7/45, 17.

277 *"very competitive"*: Walker, *Stonewallers*, E11.

277 *"huge [Nazi] party demonstrations"* and *"This first Thanksgiving"*: 29ID, BE, File 2, 11/22/45 football program.

278 *"The New York and London Dramatic Hit"*: 29ID, BE, File 2.

278 *"actually he's from Brooklyn"*: *Blood and Fire 63rd Division News*, "Night Must Fall Thrills and Chills," 8/15/45, 1.

278   *"their first radio appearance"*: Washington Post, "Bob Hope to Broadcast from Plane Tonight," 7/16/45, 3.

279   *"with the compliments"* and *"The first performance"*: 29ID, *29LG*, 7/18/45.

279   *"ninety percent wore the Purple Heart"*: Hope, *So This is Peace*, 117.

279   *"[It] was witnessed by practically 100%"*: 29ID, 116th AAR, July 1945.

279   *"were a great audience"*: Hope, *So This is Peace*, 117–18.

279   *"Through your loudspeakers"*: 29ID, BE, File 2, 11/22/45 football program.

279   *"Date with Duke Ellington"*: 29ID, *29LG*, 9/3/45.

280   *"When the smoke cleared away"*: Hoffman, *I'll Be Home*, 226.

280   *"one of the most basically sound programs"*: Binkoski, *115th Infantry*, 356.

280   *"doesn't mean much"*: Hoffman, *I'll Be Home*, 211.

280   *"a thousand other matters"*: Ibid., 213.

280   *"We have nearly 500 men"*: Ibid., 238.

280   *"One Jewish chaplain"*: Ibid., 238–39.

280   *"the men who'd seen our shows"*: Hope, *So This is Peace*, 118.

Touching Hearts and Souls

281   *"20,688 casualties"*: Baltimore Sun, "29th Division's Losses," 5/30/45, 1.

281   *3,653 of those men*: Ewing, *29 Let's Go*, 305–6.

281   *10,328 Americans*: Steere, *The Graves Registration Service in WWII*, 116.

281   *950 were unidentified*: Shomon, *Crosses in the Wind*, 190.

281   *"Our main problem"*: Ibid., 119.

282   *"two hundred deep in places"* and *"filled with deep emotion"*: Ibid., 120.

283   *"touched the heart"* and *"When mass started"*: Ibid., 121.

283   *"These women are, for the most part, very young"*: Eleanor Roosevelt, *My Day*, 9/17/45, www.gwu.edu/~erpapers/myday/displaydoc.cfm?_y=1945&_f=md000132.

284   *"amounted to $55 per month"*: U.S. Dept. of Defense, "Gold Star Wives Founder Remains Active," 4/21/05, www.defense.gov/news/newsarticle.aspx?id=31373.

284   *"the cemetery was in excellent condition"*: Shomon, *Crosses in the Wind*, 129.

284   *"But for the grace of God"*: Ibid., Foreword.

284   *"to save succeeding generations"*: United Nations, *Charter—Preamble*, www.un.org/en/documents/charter/preamble.shtml.

A Bed Was a Bed

285 *500 GIs departing*: *Baltimore Sun*, Norton, "150 Marylanders Among 500 Men of 29th on Way Home," 5/29/45, 22.

286 *"a bed was a bed"*: 29ID, Personnel, Cooper, 1984 Cooper interview with author.

286 *"erect and soldierly"*: *NY Times*, "High U.S. Officers and 10,000 Troops Here From Europe," 6/4/45, 1.

287 *"small band of conquerors"*: *NY Times*, "Philadelphia Hails Bradley," 6/5/45, 7.

287 *"along a twenty-mile lane of humanity"*: *NY Times*, Blair, "1,000,000 Welcome Gen. Patton Home," 6/8/45, 6.

287 *more than a million Angelenos*: *NY Times*, "Patton, Doolittle Get Coast Ovation," 6/10/45, 20.

288 *"at a given signal"*: 29ID, Personnel, Gerhardt, Memoirs, 54.

289 *"Red Cross girls were on hand"*: 29ID, *29LG*, "Fighting 69th Sentinel," 6/30/45.

289 *"it will likely be at least several weeks"*: *Baltimore Sun*, Norton, "3,557 in 29th Move in Step Toward Home," 6/29/45, 24.

289 *"Troops newly arrived"*: Ewing, *29 Let's Go*, 264.

290 *"The men who came in"*: Binkoski, *115th Infantry*, 355.

290 *"It wasn't very difficult"*: Ibid., 358–59.

290 *"The division dropped down"*: Ibid., 359.

291 *"No one minded"*: Ibid., 360.

291 *"Clothing and Equipment Adjustment Form"*: 29ID, BE, File 2, Demond items.

291 *"Tentative sailing dates"*: Ewing, *29 Let's Go*, 274.

291 *"Men who had transferred"*: Binkoski, *115th Infantry*, 360.

291 *"Letter of Instruction"*: 29ID, BE, File 2, Demond items.

292 *"This was [Lejeune's] roughest trip"*: Ibid.

292 *"biggest complaint was boredom"*: *Baltimore Sun*, Bradley, "29th Division GIs Arrive in US," 1/12/46, 7.

292 *"mountainous seas"*: *Baltimore Sun*, Bradley, "29th Troops Late But Home," 1/16/46, 7.

293 *Gerhardt decided it was his time to come home*: 29ID, Personnel, Gerhardt, Memoirs, 54.

8. THEY NEVER DIE
Tomorrow I'll Be a Goddamn Civilian

296 *"Yeah! Uncle Charlie!"* and *"Hi, babe!"* and *"An Army tug, with a band"*: *Baltimore Evening Sun*, McCardell, "First Combat Team," 1/6/46, 4, 14.

297 *"Welcoming committees are a thing of the past"*: 29ID, *29LG*, Final edition.

297 *"All the windows of the skyscrapers"* and *"yelped when he saw them"*: *Baltimore Evening Sun*, McCardell, "First Combat Team," 1/6/46, 4, 14.

297 *"was disloyal"*: 29ID, Personnel, Gerhardt, Memoirs, 54.

298 *"They didn't offer the liquor"*: 29ID, Personnel, Earll, 10/18/14 Earll interview with author.

298 *"Down the gangplank"*: *Baltimore Evening Sun*, McCardell, "First Combat Team," 1/6/46, 4, 14.

298 *"welcome to Camp Kilmer"*: Camp Kilmer "Welcome Home" pamphlet, www.skylighters.org/places/ckpamph.html.

299 *"joined by Representative Vito Marcantonio"*: *NY Times*, "Wire Strike Stops Messages," 1/11/46, 1.

299 *"This is certainly a fine way"*: *Baltimore Sun*, Bradley, "First 175th Yanks," 1/11/46, 26.

299 *"He ignored anyone"*: Walker, *Stonewallers*, E21.

300 *"is not made like a boy"* and *"Three years of beating"*: *Richmond Times-Dispatch*, Saunier, "Stowaway Russian Boy," 4/28/46, 4B.

300 *"Bag closed"* and *"The five officers on the board"*: Mulligan, "29th Back in Action for its Kid," *Twenty-Niner*, Nov. 1992, 13.

300 *"Three months of red tape"*: Saunier, *Richmond Times-Dispatch*, "Stowaway Russian Boy," 4/28/46, 4B.

301 *"as a sort of field kitchen mascot"*: Ibid.

301 *"Eddie learned English"*: *Twenty-Niner*, Mar. 1990, 20.

301 *"began cracking down"*: Neighbor, *One Man's War Story*, 275.

301 *"I'll probably use this dough"*: Mulligan, "29th Back in Action," *Twenty-Niner*, Nov. 1992, 13.

301 *"Hey, doc!"*: *Richmond Times-Dispatch*, Saunier, "Stowaway Russian Boy," 4/28/46, 4B.

301 *"every American soldier's dream"*: *Baltimore Sun*, McCardell, "Dream Comes True for GIs," 1/13/46, 1.

301 *"There was the steak dinner"*: Ewing, *29 Let's Go*, 274.

302 *"as a badge of honor"*: U.S. Army, The Institute of Heraldry, "Honorable Discharge Emblem," www.skylighters.org/places/ckpamph.html.

302 *"The passing of the division"*: Ewing, *29 Let's Go*, 274.

For the Freedom of the World

303 *"Let me assure you"*: *Baltimore Sun*, "Dandy Fifth Heroes Hailed," 1/25/46, 24.

304   *"With the division battle cry"*: Ibid.

305   *"There is nothing in the history"*: 29ID, H/G, Box 2, Folder 32, 4/22/47 Kaiser letter, 4/30/47 Moore letter.

305   *"Although I am among"*: Ibid., 1/12/48 Eisenhower letter.

305   *"a splendid unit"*: Baltimore Sun, "Croix de Guerre Awarded to 29th Division," 11/24/46, 32.

306   *"St. Lô Day"* and *"For the freedom of the world"* and *"What does it matter"*: Baltimore Sun, Day, "France Gives War Cross to 29th Division," 1/11/47, 22.

29, Let's Go!

307   *"Although I liked history"* and *"that the division had no idea"* and *"He would go over it"* and *"two generals"*: Ewing, "The Writing of the Book," *Twenty-Niner*, Mar. 1996, 4.

307   *"with a firm reprimand"*: 29ID, Personnel, Ewing, 1989 Ewing letter to author.

308   *"Were I to do it over"*: Ewing, "The Writing of the Book," *Twenty-Niner*, Mar. 1996, 4.

308   *"Nothing reflected so much"*: Ewing, *29 Let's Go*, 289.

308   *"We have finally gotten the history"*: 29ID, Personnel, Fernley.

308   *"I trust the history"*: 29ID, Personnel, Fernley, 1947 George Fernley letter to Witte.

308   *"In regard to the letter"*: 29ID, Personnel, Stenson, 7/5/47 Hawley letter to Witte.

309   *"it was reprinted"*: Ewing, "The Writing of the Book," *Twenty-Niner*, Mar. 1996, 4.

309   *"requesting authorization"*: Brewer, *History of the 175th Infantry*, 231.

309   *"It is considered that the property"*: Ibid., 232.

310   *"an elaborate and valuable silver service set"*: Baltimore Sun, "Elaborate German Silver Set," 11/23/46, 22.

311   *"The War Department has ordered"*: Baltimore Sun, "Order Probes Silver Set," 12/11/46, 28.

311   *"completely proper"* and *"All public property"* and *"for safekeeping"*: Baltimore Sun, "Royal Silver Trophy Lost," 2/18/47, 28.

311   *"Although the collection was brought"* and *"until proof of ownership"*: Baltimore Sun, Ruth, "175th's Hohenzollern Silver," 1/18/49, 11.

312   *"a permanent exhibition"*: Baltimore News-Post, Azrael, "Vets of 29th to Land in NY," 1/5/46.

312   *"fine condition and upkeep"*: 29ID, Personnel, Cuff, 11/19/46 and 1/22/47 Gerhardt letters to Cuff.

313   *"the jeep was a wreck"*: Sherman, "My Days with Gen. Gerhardt," *Twenty-Niner*, Nov. 2003, 28–29; also Nov. 1994 Sherman letter to editor, 44.

313   *"There was none of the hilarity"*: Baltimore Sun, Dorsch, "29th Division Unit Elects Officers," 10/15/51, 26.

313   *"I was a National Guardsman"*: Doubler, *I Am The Guard*, 197.

314   *"in this day of atom bombs"*: Baltimore Sun, "Tydings in Peace Plea," 11/12/46, 30.

314   *"The feelings by Brazilians"*: 29ID, Personnel, Gerhardt, Memoirs, 55.

314   *"politics was the reason"*: Baltimore Sun, "29th Division Files Protest," 9/8/48, 4.

315   *"It is regrettable"*: Baltimore Sun, "Rank is Cut," 8/25/48, 7.

The Vanished Army

315   *"They speak as if nothing has happened"*: Easton, *Love and War*, 370.

315   *"Having familiarized myself"*: 29ID, Personnel, Harrell.

316   *"A temporary morgue"*: Shomon, *Crosses in the Wind*, 147–48.

316   *"30,000 reverent Belgian citizens"*: Steere, *Final Disposition of WWII Dead*, 353.

317   *"We have not yet found"*: Ibid.

317   *"echoing thunder"* and *"They came in too late"*: NY Times, Berger, "400,000 in Silent Tribute," 10/27/47, 1.

317   *"Nobody spoke"* and *"The marchers were grim"*: Ibid.

318   *"which in past Sundays"*: NY Times, "Thousands Attend Rites," 10/27/47, 3.

318   *"flattened against Central Park"* and *"Almighty God"* and *"choking sadness"*: NY Times, Berger, "400,000 in Silent Tribute," 10/27/47, 1.

319   *"sweet melancholy"*: Ibid.

320   *"The camp-chairs were folded"*: NY Times, "Thousands Attend Rites," 10/27/47, 3.

320   *"the pier was almost empty"*: NY Times, "Transport Docks With 6,248 Coffins," 10/27/47, 2.

320   *"No matter what you think"*: NY Times, "Workmen Remove War Dead," 10/28/47, 2.

320   *"Each shipping case"*: Steere, *Final Disposition of WWII Dead*, 669.

321   Burns's *homecoming*: NY Times, "City to Honor War Dead," 11/26/47, 24.

321   *"This captain's whole course of action"* and *"the most daring man"* and *"He gave me a letter"*: Balkoski, *From Brittany to the Reich*, 185.

322   *"There was no loud crying"*: 29ID, Personnel, McGrath, family history provided by Peter McGrath in 10/21/14 email to author.

322   *"body complete"*: 29ID, Personnel, McGrath, IDPF, "Disinterment Directive."

323   *"near future"*: Ibid., 11/21/47 "Message Form."

323   *McGrath wake and funeral*: 29ID, Personnel, McGrath, 11/19/14 interview with Katherine McGrath Cranney.

323   *$283 funeral expense*: 29ID, Personnel, McGrath, IDPF, "Certificate of Interment Expenses."

Last Roll Call

323   *"At the going down of the sun"*: Robert Laurence Binyon, *For the Fallen*, as quoted in James Persoon and Robert Watson, *Encyclopedia of British Poetry: 1900 to the Present*, Second Edition, New York: Facts on File, 2013.

Bibliography

Abelow, Samson. *History of XVI Corps*. Washington: Infantry Journal Press, 1947.

Arendt, William. *Midnight of the Soul*. Omaha: PRA, Inc., 2000.

Atkinson, Rick. *The Guns at Last Light*. New York: Henry Holt, 2013.

Avins, Styra. *Johannes Brahms: Life and Letters*. New York: Oxford University Press, 1997.

Balkoski, Joseph. *Beyond the Beachhead: The 29th Infantry Division in Normandy*. Harrisburg: Stackpole Books, 1989.

———. *From Beachhead to Brittany: The 29th Infantry Division at Brest*. Mechanicsburg, PA: Stackpole Books, 2008.

———. *From Brittany to the Reich: The 29th Infantry Division in Germany*. Mechanicsburg, PA: Stackpole Books, 2012.

———. *The Maryland National Guard: A History of Maryland's Military Forces*. Baltimore: Maryland Military Dept., 1991.

———. *Omaha Beach: D-Day June 6, 1944*. Mechanicsburg, PA: Stackpole Books, 2004.

———. *Our Tortured Souls: The 29th Infantry Division in the Rhineland*. Mechanicsburg, PA: Stackpole Books, 2013.

Barnes, John. *Fragments of My Life with Company A, 116th Infantry*. New York: JAM, 2000.

Baxter, James Phinney. *Scientists Against Time*. Cambridge: MIT Press, 1968.

Binkoski, Joseph, and Arthur Plaut. *The 115th Infantry Regiment in World War II*. Nashville: Battery Press, 1988.

Bland, Larry, ed. *The Papers of George Catlett Marshall*, vols. 3, 4, 5. Baltimore: Johns Hopkins.

Bradley, Holbrook. *War Correspondent*. Lincoln: iUniverse, 2007.

Bradley, Omar. *A Soldier's Story*. New York: Henry Holt, 1951.

Bradley, Omar, and Clay Blair. *A General's Life*. New York: Simon and Schuster, 1983.

Brewer, James. *History of the 175th Infantry (Fifth Maryland)*. Baltimore: Maryland Historical Society, 1955.

Butcher, Harry. *My Three Years with Eisenhower*. New York: Simon and Schuster, 1946.

Cawthon, Charles. *Other Clay*. Niwot: University Press of Colorado, 1990.

Chandler, Alfred, ed. *The Papers of Dwight David Eisenhower: The War Years*. Baltimore: Johns Hopkins, 1970.

Cooper, John. *History of the 110th Field Artillery*. Baltimore: Maryland Historical Society, 1953.

Cox, Eugene and Joyce. *Twenty-Ninth Infantry*. Washington County, TN: self-published, 2011.

Craven, Wesley, and James Cate. *The Army Air Forces in WWII*, vol. 3: *Europe: Argument to V-E Day*. Chicago: University of Chicago, 1951.

Crosswell, D. K. R. *Beetle: The Life of Gen. Walter Bedell Smith*. Lexington: University Press of Kentucky, 2010.

Davis, Richard. *Carl A. Spaatz and the Air War in Europe*. Washington: GPO, 1993.

Doubler, Michael. *I Am the Guard*. Washington: Department of the Army, 2001.

Easton, Robert. *Love and War*. Norman: University of Oklahoma Press, 1991.

Eisenhower, Dwight. *Crusade in Europe*. New York: Doubleday, 1948.

Ellis, L. F. *Victory in the West*, vol. 2. Nashville: Battery Press, 1994.

Ewing, Joseph. *29 Let's Go!* Washington: Infantry Journal Press, 1948.

———. *The 29th: A Short History of a Fighting Division*. Paducah, KY: Turner, 1992.

Goebbels, Joseph. *Final Entries, 1945*. New York: G. P. Putnam, 1978.

Gordon, Harold. *One Man's War: A Memoir of World War II*. New York: Apex Press, 1999.

Green, Constance. *The Ordnance Department: Planning Munitions for War*. Washington: Office of the Chief of Military History, 1955.

Gutknecht, Kay. *We Were Foxhole Buddies*. San Jose: private, 2006.

Heiber, Helmut, and David Glantz, eds. *Hitler and His Generals: Military Conferences, 1942–1945*. New York: Enigma Books, 2004.

Hewitt, Robert. *Work Horse of the Western Front: The Story of the 30th Infantry Division*. Washington: Infantry Journal Press, 1946.

Hoffman, David, ed. *I'll Be Home For The Christmas Rush*. Bennington: Merriam, 2009.

Hogan, David. *A Command Post at War*. Washington: Center of Military History, 2000.

Holberton, William. *Touched By Fire*. Bethlehem, PA: private, 1995.

Hope, Bob. *So This is Peace*. New York: Hope Corp., 1946.

Johns, Glover. *The Clay Pigeons of St. Lô*. Harrisburg: Military Service Publishing Co., 1958.

Kershaw, Ian. *Hitler: 1889–1938, Hubris*. New York: Norton, 1998.

Leinbaugh, Harold. *The Men of Company K*. New York: Bantam, 1987.

Liddell Hart, Sir Basil. *The German Generals Talk*. New York: Morrow, 1948.

Loengard, John. *LIFE Photographers: What They Saw*. Boston: Little, Brown, 1998.

MacDonald, Charles. *The Last Offensive*. Washington: Office of the Chief of Military History, 1973.

———. *The Siegfried Line Campaign*. Washington: Office of the Chief of Military History, 1963.

———. *A Time for Trumpets*. New York: William Morrow, 1985.

Maryland National Guard. *Historical and Pictorial Review of the National Guard and Naval Militia of the U.S., State of Maryland, 1940*. Baton Rouge: Army and Navy, 1940.

Mitcham, Samuel. *German Order of Battle*, vols. 1–3. Mechanicsburg, PA: Stackpole Books, 2007.

Neighbor, Charles. *One Man's War Story*. Reading, PA: Aperture, 2013.

Parker, Theodore, and William Thompson. *Conquer: The Story of Ninth Army*. Nashville: Battery Press, 1993.

Patton, George. *War As I Knew It*. New York: Pyramid, 1966.

Pogue, Forrest. *George C. Marshall: Organizer of Victory, 1943–1945*. New York: Penguin, 1993.

———. *Pogue's War*. Lexington: University Press of Kentucky, 2001.

———. *The Supreme Command*. Washington: Office of the Chief of Military History, 1954.

Ruppenthal, Roland. *Logistical Support of the Armies*, vol. II. Washington: Office of the Chief of Military History, 1959.

Ryan, Cornelius. *The Last Battle*. New York: Simon and Schuster, 1966.

Shomon, Joseph. *Crosses in the Wind*. New York: Stratford House, 1947.

Slaughter, John R. *Omaha Beach and Beyond*. St. Paul: Zenith, 2007.

Sparrow, John. *History of Personnel Demobilization in the U.S. Army*. Washington: GPO, 1952.

Speer, Albert. *Inside the Third Reich*. New York: Scribner, 1970.

Stanton, Shelby. *WWII Order of Battle*. New York: Galahad, 1984.

Steere, Edward. *Final Disposition of WWII Dead*. Washington: Office of the Quartermaster General, 1957.

———. *The Graves Registration Service in WWII*, Quartermaster Historical Study 21. Washington: GPO, 1951.

Stone, Thomas. "1630 Comes Early on the Roer River," *Military Review*, October 1973.

———. "Gen. William Hood Simpson: Unsung Commander of U.S. Ninth Army," *Parameters*, vol. XI, no. 2, 1981.

Sylvan, William. *Normandy to Victory: The War Diary of Gen. Courtney Hodges and the First U.S. Army*. Lexington: University Press of Kentucky, 2008.

Tessin, Georg. *Verbände und Truppen der deutschen Wehrmacht und Waffen-SS im Zweiten Weltkrieg, 1939–1945*. Osnabrück, Germany: Biblio-Verlag, 1973.

Toland, John. *Adolf Hitler*. Garden City: Doubleday, 1976.

———. *The Last 100 Days*. New York: Bantam, 1970.

Twelfth U.S. Army Group. *Effect of Air Power on Military Operations in Western Europe*. Germany: Twelfth Army Group, 1945.

U.S. Army. *Counter Intelligence Corps History and Mission in World War II*. Baltimore: Counter Intelligence Corps School, n.d.

———. *Normandy to the Elbe: XIX Corps*. Germany: XIX Corps, 1945.

———. *Pocket Guide to Germany*. Washington: Army Information Branch, 1944.

———. *U.S. Army Order of Battle: ETO, 1943–1945*. Germany: ETOUSA, 1945.

U.S. Dept. of the Army. *Führer Directives, 1942–1945*. Washington: GPO, 1948.

U.S. Dept. of State. *Foreign Relations of the U.S.: The Conference at Berlin (Potsdam Conference)*, vol. 2. Washington: GPO, 1960.

U.S. Dept. of State. *Foreign Relations of the U.S.: The Conference of Quebec, 1944*. Washington: GPO, 1972.

U.S. European Command. *First Year of the Occupation: Occupation Forces in Europe*, Part V, vol. 2. Frankfurt-am-Main: Office of the Chief Historian, U.S. European Command, 1947.

U.S. Military Academy. *Roster of Graduates and Former Cadets, 1982*. West Point: Association of Graduates, 1982.

U.S. War Dept. *Pamphlet 21-13, Army Life*. Washington: GPO, August 1944.

———. *FM 100-5, Field Service Regulations: Operations*. Washington: GPO, June 1944.

———. *FM 27-5, Military Government and Civil Affairs*. Washington: GPO, December 1943.

———. *FM 101-10, Staff Officers' Field Manual.* Washington: GPO, October 1944.

———. *Handbook on German Military Forces.* Washington: GPO, 1945.

———. *Official National Guard Register 1939.* Washington: GPO, 1940.

Virginia National Guard. *Historical and Pictorial Review of the National Guard of the Commonwealth of Virginia, 1940.* Baton Rouge: Army and Navy, 1940.

Walker, Robert. *From Vierville to Victory: With the Stonewallers of the 116th Infantry.* Los Angeles: private, 1998.

Weigley, Russell. *Eisenhower's Lieutenants.* Bloomington: Indiana University Press, 1981.

Wilkes, Homer. *APO 230: The 747th Tank Battalion.* Scottsdale: private, 1982.

Wilmot, Chester. *The Struggle for Europe.* London: Collins, 1952.

Zaloga, Steven. *US Flamethrower Tanks of WWII.* Oxford: Osprey, 2013.

Ziemke, Earl. *The U.S. Army in the Occupation of Germany, 1944–1946.* Washington: Center of Military History, 1975.

Acknowledgments

This book, like the four that came before it, was greatly enhanced by the input of 29th Division veterans. Indeed, over thirty-one years I have never met a 29er at a reunion, post meeting, or any other veterans' event—including the funerals of their comrades—who failed to respond in some meaningful way to my inquiries. Many responded so devotedly that they became friends for life.

Researching and writing *The Last Roll Call* was an acute challenge, as not many wartime 29ers survive; those who do are in their nineties. (I know at least one who is a centenarian.) Nevertheless, several 29ers contributed mightily to this book, and for their input I am deeply grateful. From the 115th Infantry: Bob Aubin, Bob Henne, Mills Hobbs, Bill Holberton, Jack Kussman, Don Van Roosen, and Mal Walker. From the 116th: John Barnes, Arden Earll, Glenwood Hankins, Chuck Neighbor, and Bob Walker. From the 175th: Nelson Horan and Steve Melnikoff.

Kay Gutknecht, the daughter of 29er Marvin Gutknecht of the 121st Engineers, volunteered dozens of hours to the effort by reading the manuscript and offering suggestions that materially benefitted the final product, and for that she will always have my appreciation.

The following children or other descendants and relatives of 29ers also kindly contributed to the book: James Cranney, David Hoffman, Katherine McGrath Cranney, Fran Sherr-Davino, Linda Englert, Molly Harrell, Susanne Harrell, Peter McGrath, Cathy Harrell Pennington, Steve Rickeard, Georgiana Silk (daughter of *LIFE* photographer George Silk), Denise Slaughter, and John Wilkinson III.

I am privileged to call many historians and archivists of the World War II period my friends, and many of them graciously offered to me their vast knowledge of the period: Rick Atkinson, author of the *Liberation Trilogy*;

Joost Claassens; Antonin Dehays; Jonathan Gawne; Timothy Nenninger of the National Archives; Brian Siddall; Dr. Richard Sommers of the Military History Institute; and Steve Zaloga.

Finally, during the editing and production process at Stackpole Books, Dave Reisch and Brittany Stoner offered many beneficial suggestions that contributed essentially to the final product.

Index